Big Ideas in Collaborative Public Management

Big Ideas in Collaborative Public Management

Editors

Lisa Blomgren Bingham and **Rosemary O'Leary**

M.E.Sharpe
Armonk, New York
London, England

Library of Congress Cataloging-in-Publication Data

Big ideas in collaborative public management / edited by Lisa Blomgren Bingham
and Rosemary O'Leary.
    p. cm.
 Includes bibliographical references and index.
  ISBN 978-0-7656-2118-4 (cloth : alk. paper) — 978-0-7656-2119-1 (pbk. : alk. paper)
  1. Public administration—United States. 2. Intergovernmental cooperation—United States.
3. Public-private sector cooperation—United States. 4. Political participation—United
States. I. Bingham, Lisa (Lisa B.), 1955- II. O'Leary, Rosemary, 1955–

JF1351.B525 2008
351.7301'1—dc22   2007050477

Printed in the United States of America

The paper used in this publication meets the minimum requirements of
American National Standard for Information Sciences
Permanence of Paper for Printed Library Materials,
ANSI Z 39.48-1984.

∞

BM (c) 10   9   8   7   6   5   4   3   2   1
BM (p) 10   9   8   7   6   5   4   3   2   1

We dedicate this book
to our fathers
Arthur Charles Blomgren, Jr.
and
Franklin Hayes O'Leary

CONTENTS

ACKNOWLEDGMENTS

This volume is a product of collaboration among all the participants at the September 2006 Greenberg House Conference on Collaborative Public Management organized by the Program on the Analysis and Resolution of Conflicts (PARC) and the Maxwell School of Syracuse University. We owe a deep debt to Catherine Gerard, co-director of PARC, for her part in organizing the conference. We are also grateful to Lisa Mignacci, Chris Praino, Rob Alexander, and Rachel Fleishman for great work on logistics, and the staff of Greenberg House for providing a wonderful environment for rich conversation. We wish to thank all our participants for their willingness to participate in the conference and to share ideas generously with each other to advance this field of inquiry. Our participants, authors, speakers, and presenters included Robert Agranoff, Alejandro Amerzcua, Terry Amsler, Alison Anker, Stu Bretschneider, Jeffrey L. Brudney, Thomas A. Bryer, John M. Bryson, Christine Carlson, Bin Chen, Chung-Lae Cho, Terry L. Cooper, Barbara Crosby, Kirk Emerson, Sue R. Faerman, Richard C. Feiock, George Frederickson, Archon Fung, Beth Gazley, Heather Getha-Taylor, Catherine Gerard, Elizabeth Graddy, Alisa Hicklin, Maja Husar Holmes, Patricia Wallace Ingraham, Soon Hee Kim, Hyun Joon Kim, Malka Kopell, W. Harry Lambright, Jooho Lee, David D.T. Matkin, Michael McGuire, Jack W. Meek, Ken Meier, Theodore K. Miller, H. Brinton Milward, Larry O'Toole, Stephen Page, James L. Perry, Carla Pizzarella, Paul Posner, Bill Potapchuk, Keith G. Provan, Hal Rainey, Scott Robinson, Jay Eungha Ryu, Jodi Sandfort, Melissa Middleton Stone, Ann Marie Thomson, Mary Tschirhart, David Van Slyke, Bill Waugh, and Deil Wright. We are grateful to Eugene B. McGregor and John Stephens for many helpful discussions. We are also indebted to Stacey Johnstone and Kimberly J. Evans for their wonderful editorial assistance.

We gratefully acknowledge financial support from Dean Mitchel Wallerstein and Senior Associate Dean Mike Wasylenko of the Maxwell School. Lisa would also like to acknowledge the generous support of the late Eloise Beardsley to Indiana University through the Keller-Runden Chair. In addition, as co-editors, we gratefully acknowledge a grant of general support from the William and Flora Hewlett Foundation to the Indiana Conflict Resolution Institute of Indiana University, through which we have been able to collaborate on many rewarding research efforts over the past eight years.

Big Ideas in Collaborative Public Management

CHAPTER 1

Frameshifting
Lateral Thinking for
Collaborative Public Management

LISA BLOMGREN BINGHAM,
ROSEMARY O'LEARY, AND CHRISTINE CARLSON

We titled this book *Big Ideas in Collaborative Public Management* because we wanted to encourage our contributors and our readers to think outside their usual frame. The phrase "lateral thinking" is used to describe creativity that stems from taking knowledge from one substantive context or discipline and seeing how useful it is in an entirely different one. For example, Da Vinci's genius stems from his mastery of lateral thinking; he moved fluidly from art to science, engineering, mathematics, medicine, architecture, and beyond, finding universal rules of nature manifest in widely varying contexts (Riding 2006). He dissected the human arm and a bird's wing, and then tried to engineer a machine to enable people to fly; in this way, he applied what he learned from human physiology and natural science to engineering.

"Collaborative public management" has become a catchphrase for an increasingly rich body of knowledge. We adapted the following definition from the work of Agranoff and McGuire (2003):

> Collaborative public management is a concept that describes the process of facilitating and operating in multiorganizational arrangements to solve problems that cannot be solved or easily solved by single organizations. Collaborative means to co-labor, to achieve common goals, often working across boundaries and in multisector and multiactor relationships. Collaboration is based on the value of reciprocity.

In our view, collaborative public management must encompass not only collaboration between and among organizations but also the role of the public and citizens in governance. Henton and others (2005) review emerging forms of collaboration in governance, specifically forms in which government engages not only with other organizational partners and stakeholders but also with citizens. They describe participatory governance as the active involvement of citizens in government decision making. The term governance is generally viewed as steering the process that influences decisions and actions within the private, public, and civic sectors (O'Leary, Gerard, and Bingham 2006a).

In order to take what we have learned about collaborative public management and governance to the next level, we need to apply lateral thinking. We need to view collaboration in a broader frame and examine what we can learn from other literatures. This book resulted from a conference sponsored by the Maxwell School of Syracuse University and held at its facility in Washington, DC, known as Greenberg House. Approximately forty leading scholars and practitioners attended. We intentionally combined scholars and practitioners of public management with those of participatory democracy and conflict resolution. As a result of this exercise in lateral thinking, we concluded that

- We need better conceptualizations of collaboration;
- We need a more comprehensive vision of antecedents, processes, and outcomes from collaboration;
- We need to do a better job in making connections for practice such as design of collaborative structures; and
- We need to make new and broader connections with other disciplines for theory.

In this book, our authors review the evolving literature on collaboration in management and governance and contribute new theoretical and empirical frames for future research. In this chapter, we introduce collaboration and leadership and provide an overview of some of the connections our authors make.

COLLABORATION AND PUBLIC LEADERSHIP

There is a growing role for collaboration in public leadership. According to Van Wart (2003), scholars' thinking about leadership has evolved radically over the years. Prior to 1900, the literature focused on "great man" theories of leadership. As Van Wart summarized, from 1900 to 1948, theories moved to discussing individual physical, personal, motivational, and aptitude traits. From 1948 to the 1980s, contingency theories abounded, largely emphasizing situation variables with which leaders must deal.

From 1978 to the present, both transformational and servant theories have been popular. Transformational theories emphasize the need to create deep change in organization structures, processes, and culture. Servant theories emphasize service to followers, citizens, and democracy.

Transformational and servant theories, while still popular today, have been joined by theories that Van Wart labels "multifaceted." Multifaceted approaches integrate the major ideas and approaches concerning leadership and acknowledge what some call situational leadership. Situational leadership says that one's leadership strategy and style will change as determined by the situation. There is a time to lead and a time to follow. At some times there is a need for top-down authority, at other times there is a need to enable others to achieve what needs to be done; and at still other times there is a need for both approaches simultaneously. There are times leaders need to be directive, and there are times leaders need to be collaborative.

Gerzon likens old leadership theories to a carpenter's toolbox filled with only hammers and nothing else. In his presentations on leadership, Gerzon shows up with a toolbox and pulls out one hammer after the other, asking workshop participants, " How would you feel if a handyman came to your house to do home repairs with a toolbox containing nothing but hammers?" (2006, 5). Here are the answers he typically receives:

"Our house would be a wreck. . . ."
"He'd never finish the job. . . ."
"I would lose confidence in him right away. . . ."
"Unless he promised to invest in new tools and learned how to use them . . . I would fire him." (ibid.)

Gerzon then goes on to overview some new approaches to leadership—including collaboration.

It is interesting to note that while this example powerfully "hammers home" (pun intended) the need for a wide variety of leadership tools and approaches that include collaboration, there is only *one handyman* who is expected to fix the house. Even Van Wart's depiction of a "contemporary" model of leadership seems to overemphasizes the actions of a *single* leader. First, the leader assesses organization, environment, and constraints, Van Wart explains, then the leader sets personal and organizational goals. Next, the leader uses his or her traits and skills within a varied style range. Following this the leader acts in three areas relating to task, people, and organization. Finally the leader evaluates personal and organizational effectiveness (Van Wart 2003, 216).

Yet public managers now find themselves not as unitary leaders of unitary organizations. The prevalence of network management, contracting out, and greater collaboration with citizens has altered the dynamics of public administration, public management, and what it means to be a leader. There is a growing interest in "integrative leadership": working across boundaries, diverse individuals, organization functions, levels, geography, sectors, and borders. Managers find themselves convening, facilitating, negotiating, mediating, and collaborating with a multitude of partners. Connelly, Zhang, and Faerman (chapter 2) conclude that in today's "shared power world" (Crosby and Bryson 2005), good leadership demands collaboration.

CHANGING VIEWS OF MANAGEMENT

Similarly, twentieth-century approaches to government grew out of the experience of the industrial age and were based on command and control structures and mechanisms. The scope of the problems and the means for addressing them used to be within the capacity of a particular government's authority and jurisdiction. Powerful forces have altered the conventional approaches to addressing public issues. Increasing demands on public and private resources contribute to the complexity of today's problems and require new approaches if we, as a society, are to meet our challenges. These factors are compounded by the fact that there is no longer a constituency for expanding the role of government to address current problems.

This is not a matter of governmental reform, but of finding better governance mechanisms that combine the efforts of leaders, public and private institutions, and citizens to solve problems with innovation, fairness, and integrity. Particularly at the local level, people are demanding a greater role in the decision-making process.

Beginning in the 1970s in response to these challenges, there has been an increasing array of experiments and demonstrations, many of them ad hoc, with cross-sector collaborations, public–private partnerships, and more direct forms of public engagement in policy setting. From these efforts, ongoing networks for service delivery and other kinds of more or less permanent institutional arrangements have evolved. A variety of descriptors have emerged for these phenomena, including collaborative public management, collaborative governance, privatization, devolution, decentralized governance, the new governance, and participatory governance. However, central to all of them is government's effort to collaborate with others in accomplishing its work, rather than exercise authority in a top-down hierarchy.

A driving force behind this increased use of collaboration has been the dramatic evolution of information technology. The advent of inexpensive instant means of communication has reduced the transaction costs of collaborating. Moreover, this web of communication has contributed to the accelerated integration of collaborative structures across national boundaries known as globalization. Hierarchy continues to be the most common way to organize the public's work. Moreover, there has always been some collaboration across sectors to achieve policy goals. The significant and accelerating change is in the extent of collaboration in public management.

WE NEED BETTER CONCEPTUALIZATIONS AND DEFINITIONS OF COLLABORATION

Our contributors concluded that we need better conceptualizations and definitions of collaboration. They offer a variety of definitions. Bryson and Crosby (chapter 4) distinguish among cooperation, coordination, and collaboration. Cooperation is the absence of conflict; it is less formal, involves sharing information, may be short term, and presents little risk (Winer and Ray 1994, 22). Coordination is the orchestration of people toward a particular goal; it involves more formal and longer-term interaction, increased risk, and shared rewards (ibid.). Collaboration, however, suggests a closer relationship; we use "co-labor" to signal this difference. It entails a new structure, shared resources, defined relationships, and communication (ibid.). One of our participants observed that collaboration involves creating, enhancing, and building on social and organizational capital in pursuit of shared purposes. Other participants suggested a variety of ways to classify collaboration, and many provided more useful typologies for these evolving manifestations. These distinctions can foster better and more completely specified research models. A list of possible dimensions for examining collaboration includes the following:

- *Collaboration occurs within and across organizations.* A single organization may have multiple districts, units, or offices that need to collaborate (e.g., various extension offices of a university with multiple campuses). Our contributors ask: Does this differ from collaboration across organizations (e.g., the extension services of different universities)?

- *Collaboration occurs within and across sectors.* There are networks of agencies, for example, federal agencies coordinating on environmental conflict resolution or the Interagency Alternative Dispute Resolution Working Group (www.adr.gov). Our contributors ask: How do these compare with networks of public, private, and nonprofit organizations, such as watershed management networks with local, regional, state, federal, nonprofit, and other members?

- *Collaboration occurs with like-minded or homogeneous and diverse partners.* Environmental groups may form a coalition; yet in a collaborative effort, they may work with putative private sector polluters, conflicting local, regional, state, and federal government agencies, and concerned citizen groups.

- *Collaboration occurs among those with shared and different goals.* Our contributors analyze the fact that collaboration does not nullify competition and paradoxically may yield conflict. For example, higher education may band together to develop an alternative to the U.S. News ranking formula. However, each institution may seek to best the other in the quest for top applicants, and schools will still compete against each other for advances in reputation.

- *Collaboration occurs when it is mandatory and also when it is emergent or voluntary.* Page (chapter 8) documents how states vary in mandating collaboration regarding community efforts to serve children and families. Some states mandate which agencies have to participate, while other states set goals with proportions of members representing certain categories. Still other states used an open-ended approach, allowing the networks to self-organize.

- *Collaboration has been occurring in planning and environmental settings.* In land use, for example, fifty-nine different municipal authorities collaborated in Hamilton County, Ohio, to develop a plan for growth and development (www.americaspeaks. org); they reached unanimous agreement on its outlines. In the Florida Everglades, stakeholders collaborated to resolve a conflict over the science of restoring the watershed and how to foster and measure progress (www.usiecr.gov).

- *Collaboration occurs with and without broader public participation.* Emergency management planning in New Orleans prior to Hurricane Katrina involved representatives of local, state, and federal government and was largely limited to professionals (Kiefer and Montjoy 2006). This has engendered substantial criticism. Planning for the recovery now involves collaboration of local, state, and federal agencies and a series of large-scale, high-profile citizen forums and participation by elected officials (www.unifiedneworleansplan.com).

- *Collaboration occurs on highly contentious issues as well as on less controversial ones.* The field of environmental conflict resolution is a testament to the use of collaboration on highly contentious issues such as natural resource allocation and development, cleanup of water, land, or air, and land use development (O'Leary and Bingham 2003). In lower conflict settings, Feiock (chapter 10) documents the emergence of regional, voluntary service coordination and collaboration among local governments. Cooper,

Bryer, and Meek (chapter 11) document how local neighborhood councils collaborate with city service agencies to enhance communication and responsiveness.

- *Collaboration occurs with professional facilitators or mediators and without.* Facilitated or mediated collaboration has occurred at highly polluted sites involving local, regional, state, and federal government, Native American tribes, nonprofit organizations, environmental advocacy groups, and groups of local residents since the 1970s (www.resolv.org and www.usiecr.gov). It has also occurred in food safety, HIV/AIDS treatment, urban air quality, and dam decommissioning (see the gallery of successes at www.resolv.org, for a number of case studies). In watershed management (Leach and Sabatier 2003), some groups use professionals and others have not.
- *Collaboration occurs with large and small numbers of actors.* RESOLVE, a mediation services nonprofit, documents mediated collaboration on a variety of policy issues with dozens of participants (www.resolv.org). The Policy Consensus Initiative documents how the state of Maryland collaborated with Wicomico County to develop better ways to coordinate the delivery of human services (www.policyconsensus.org, a Web site with numerous case studies).

These are just a few examples of the wide variation of collaborative networks in practice. Better typologies would provide a means to distinguish theory and skills in the myriad different contexts that collaboration, collaborative public management, and collaborative governance are now observed to exist.

WE NEED A MORE COMPREHENSIVE VISION OF ANTECEDENTS, PROCESSES, AND OUTCOMES OF COLLABORATIVE PUBLIC MANAGEMENT

Our authors point to the need for systematic research on the antecedents of collaboration, the processes through which it occurs, and the outcomes it produces. Their research suggests promising directions for the future.

Antecedents

Our contributors suggest that antecedents may include the nature of resources and number of actors. Provan, Kenis, and Human (chapter 7) suggest that a key factor may be to establish the legitimacy of a collaborative public management network as a means to handle the problem, the legitimacy of its membership, and of its processes for interaction. Bryson and Crosby (chapter 4) suggest that collaboration emerges and succeeds after the failure of a sector acting alone. Antecedents may include a typology of roles based on competition and capacity.

Feiock (chapter 10) examines the development of voluntary coordination mechanisms in collaborative networks for the provision of public services, and particularly those in metropolitan areas where local governments coordinate to solve regional problems without a single superior coordinating agency. Based on a review of ongoing research, he suggests that voluntary collaborative governance will emerge when circumstances reduce transaction costs of cooperation; once coordination exists, the level of collaboration is related to a history of reciprocal dyadic relationships. In economic development, more direct neighbors and economic homogeneity reduce problems with division, agency, and information costs.

Processes

We need to explore variables related to the collaborative process. Thomson, Perry, and Miller (chapter 6) propose that key factors include network governance, its administration, the presence or absence of mutuality among the members, behavioral norms in collaboration, and the degree to which each member of the network has organizational autonomy. Lambright and Pizzarella (chapter 12) suggest that the quality of leadership for each member and the network as a whole is critical, particularly in the form of a champion of collaboration.

Our authors speculate that this exploration of variables related to the collaboration process may yield us points on a continuum. Agranoff (chapter 9) observes that life is a mix of interactive and solitary activities; collaboration is natural human activity, like organizing. He suggests that we may resist collaboration due to boundaries, and asks that we examine what boundaries mean in public action and how they affect collaboration. A question for future research is whether it matters if the boundaries are mutable.

Outcomes

We also need to explore the outcomes of collaboration, not simply in terms of completing a task, goal, or project, but building legitimacy and social or organizational capital. In other words, how might collaborative public management generate internal and external legitimacy in landscapes of distrust and cynicism? How do we evaluate outcomes? Some suggest that collaborative public management at best yields small wins, and at worst, inevitable failure. As mentioned previously, there have been efforts to evaluate collaborative public management in environmental governance and conflict resolution in land use planning that may prove instructive in the broader frame of collaborative public management.

Page (chapter 8) examines the intersection between interagency collaboration and managing for results (strategic planning around outcomes, measuring progress, analyzing data, and using findings). He discusses the tension between administrators sharing discretion and wielding authority across organizational lines and the absence of formal controls or mandates that are the traditional mechanisms for accountability. Managers may be reluctant to collaborate when they are accountable for outcomes over which they have less direct control. While managing for results is a promising approach for ensuring that collaboration produces measurable outcomes and public value, he suggests aligning data around key network activities (activating the network, framing purposes, mobilizing commitment and support, and synthesizing the network dynamics) to foster collaboration.

Our contributor Robert Agranoff examines the characteristics of collaboration for knowledge and its management and finds that outcomes include networks collaborating on problem-oriented working-level knowledge creation by building databases, using communities of practice, and creating knowledge maps.

Cooper, Bryer, and Meek (chapter 11) document how neighborhood councils in Los Angeles have produced a variety of positive outcomes through citizen-centered collaborative public management. These include building trust and mutual understanding between public administrators and their stakeholders, enhanced departmental responsiveness of bureaucrats to neighborhoods and their councils, in some instances sustainable agreements and continuing relationships, and draft memoranda of understanding that have opened communication channels, provided education about services, allowed stakeholder participation, and/or provided for service updates.

We Need to Make Connections for Practice and Designing Structures for Collaboration

Collaboration yields different organizational structures and designs. The intentional design of structures for collaboration includes networks and network governance. Design also includes network decision rules or ground rules such as consensus, aggregation of votes for majority or super-majority rule, and behavioral norms such as principled or interest-based negotiation and conflict. It includes systems for resolving conflict within the network. It includes systematic incorporation of the public's voice through civic engagement. It includes design of means for transparency in communicating the work of collaboration. It also includes mechanisms for accountability (O'Leary and Bingham 2007).

The field of public administration has been describing, documenting, and analyzing collaboration and network governance. However, we need to apply the emerging research literature to the intentional design of structures and collaborative practices. Salamon (2002) uses the term "new governance" framed in terms of tools such as tax incentives and partnership agreements. These tools create some structures for collaboration. However, there are also broader conceptions of the new governance that include the practices and processes through which citizens and stakeholders participate in the work of government (Bingham, Nabatchi, and O'Leary 2005). These practices and processes too are part of design and structure. Public administration literature does not always connect collaborative public management with collaborative governance, which is the involvement of citizens in policy decisions through civic engagement, dialogue, and deliberation. However, collaborative public management needs democratic accountability, and the literature on collaborative governance is instructive. Leach (2006) suggests that we should think about the democratic merits of collaboration in terms of seven normative ideals: inclusiveness, representativeness, impartiality, transparency, deliberativeness, lawfulness, and empowerment.

In practice, networks are not always called by that name, nor do these networks label themselves as being engaged in collaborative public management. The phenomenon is widespread and has many names. Government is already funding organizational structures to convene collaborative working groups in certain policy areas. For example, Congress created agencies such as the U.S. Institute for Environmental Conflict Resolution (www.ecr.gov). Civil society's philanthropic institutions are funding experiments in collaborative governance. The Hewlett Foundation (www.hewlett.org) identifies the breadth of activities that fall within the term "collaborative governance" (Henton et al. 2005):

- Forums for Public Deliberation—These forums are used to educate the public, build stronger relationships, and promote cooperation and conflict resolution, as well as provide advice for policy and action to public officials.
- Community Problem Solving—These activities involve collaborations among community, government, and private groups who work to address problems together over an extended period of time.
- Multistakeholder Dispute Resolution—These processes typically bring together stakeholder groups representing different interests and points of view, such as environmentalists, businesspeople, and government officials, to negotiate in an attempt to settle their dispute.

Collaboration is happening under the auspices of nonprofit organizations such as America Speaks, which has assembled a collaborative public management network of dozens of municipal government entities, regional and state jurisdictions, and a number of philanthropies to conduct a massive civic engagement effort focused on economic development in northeastern Ohio; through "Voices and Choices," 39,000 people will participate in one form and forum or another (www.cleveland.com/voices).

To illustrate how these issues are already being addressed in practice, consider the Policy Consensus Initiative's model for collaboration in the public sphere, Public Solutions. For the past nine years, the Policy Consensus Initiative (PCI), a national, bipartisan, nonprofit organization, has worked at the state level with governors, legislators, agency leaders, programs, and universities throughout the United States to build leadership and capacity to support the use of collaborative practices to achieve more effective governance. This emphasis on collaborative governance, rather than government, has come about because traditional government institutions, acting alone, are no longer able to address many of the complex challenges of modern society. Its particular focus is on the role collaborative governance can play in problem solving. PCI believes that the elements of an infrastructure for collaborative governance include new forums or "public spaces," new roles and capacities on the part of leaders and citizens, new rules or systems of engagement, and new institutional mechanisms. Table 1.1 shows PCI's model.

These examples all illustrate the need for systematic thinking on the design of collaborative public management. While PCI frames the following list of questions in terms of collaborative governance, defined by participation by citizens and stakeholders, they apply equally to collaborative public management, even though it has been defined somewhat more narrowly in some academic literature as focusing primarily on collaboration at the organizational level. PCI asks:

- How do those with authority under the traditional governance system authorize the use of collaborative governance mechanisms?
- What procedures ensure the legitimacy of collaborative governance mechanisms?
- Is it necessary to ensure that, when set up by governments, collaborative structures conform to established democratic principles so that they are credible and legitimate?

Table 1.1

Public Solutions System: A New Form of Leadership and Governance

The best public solutions come when people work together on issues. The Public Solutions collaborative governance system is one where leaders convene all sectors—public, private, and civic—to develop effective, lasting solutions to public problems that go beyond what any sector could achieve on its own.

Public Solutions System for Collaborative Governance

Issues	Principles	A System	A Network	Solutions
Issues are good candidates for the Public Solutions System when:	The System is based on a set of principles:	The System integrates the principles and networks to assure the effective application of collaborative governance:	The System relies on a network that provides the essential linkages:	Solutions reached through a collaborative governance approaches are:
• Fragmentation of government organizations and programs stands in the way of solutions	• Transparency and accountability	• Sponsors identify and raise an issue	*Sponsor*—An agency, foundation, civic organization, public-private coalition, etc. to initiate and provide support	*Lasting*—Solutions developed in this way won't simply be undone in the next year or legislative session
• There is a need to integrate policies, programs, and resources to address the problem or issue	• Equity and inclusiveness	• Assessment is made to determine the feasibility for collaboration, the process to be used, and who needs to be involved	*Convener*—A governor, legislator, local official, respected civic leader, etc. with power to bring diverse people together to work on common problems	*Effective*—Broad participation and joint responsibility for the process and product ensure that results are benefited by the collective wisdom and resources
• Many levels of government along with other sectors need to be involved	• Effectiveness and efficiency	• Leader(s) convene all needed participants	*Neutral forum*—An impartial organization or venue, etc. to provide and ensure skilled process management	*Have more buy-in and commitment*—From the outset, all with a stake are involved in authentic ways; all have a role in the final agreement and ultimately its implementation
• Opportunities emerge and people are ready to work together on a common issue	• Responsiveness	• Neutral forum/facilitator designs and manages the process	*Participants*—All sectors (public, private, civic) and levels of government are involved to ensure representation of all interests and points of view	
	• Forum neutrality	• Participants adopt the process framework for deliberation		
	• Consensus-based decision making	• A written agreement establishes a framework for implementation and accountability for meeting jointly established objectives		

Source: Copyright © 2006 Policy Consensus Initiative. Used by permission.

- Some of the questions that need to be examined include:
  - Who gets to participate? How are collaborative groups chosen? Do there need to be specifications about how representative or inclusive they are?
  - What authorities do these groups have? Are they advisory or decision-making? Who has rights to be involved, to influence, to be heard, and to challenge the exercise of power?
  - What access do these groups have to resources—time, space, information, data, and skills? Do they have access to funds?
  - What procedures, if any, guide how they operate?
  - To whom or what are they accountable: the state, community, or other entities? How and when do they need to be linked to traditional democratic mechanisms?

Our contributors begin to address issues of design. These issues include creating incentives to collaborate for individuals, programs, and organizations, for example, opportunities to build social capital. Ingraham and Getha-Taylor (chapter 5) suggest that significant organizational and individual barriers to effective collaboration exist in public organizations, including: communication problems, turf issues, trust deficiencies, lack of commitment, and ill-matched system reform initiatives. They argue against focusing on pay reform as the only way to incentivize performance (and collaborative performance specifically). Rewarding collaboration requires a new set of objectives, they maintain.

Feiock (chapter 10) suggests that structuring opportunities for officials to interact can help build the networks and social capital. Formal and informal institutional arrangements that increase information flow and reduce obstacles to bargaining can also lead to cooperation. Gazley (chapter 3) discusses what a public or nonprofit executive needs to know that might have an influence on improved attitudes about collaboration.

Framing the issue for collaboration is also a design choice; it will have an impact on the willingness to collaborate. Lambright and Pizzarella (chapter 12) illustrate this in their case study of the international space station.

Design issues include the relationship of collaboration to accountability structures. Networks need to identify the new contribution, product, or output expected from collaboration; they need to align accountability structures accordingly. They need to build data collection on direct measures of collaborative behaviors and actions. Regarding networks managing for results, contributor Page (chapter 8) discusses how some states created governance structures in terms of formal organizational requirements, while others allowed collaboratives to develop their own organizational form. States added self-assessment tools and process standards and created incentives. All of these were conscious design choices to help structure and foster accountable collaboration.

Cooper, Bryer, and Meek (chapter 11) point to obstacles to collaboration success, including turnover and lack of continuity of membership. They ask what structures and incentives might help create and maintain institutional memory in the face of this turnover.

These authors begin to address an area that needs substantially more attention from scholars and practitioners in public administration. There is a gap in our knowledge of institutional design; we need to identify the most useful design features and practices for effective collaboration. The fields of conflict resolution and consensus building in public policy can help inform the design of collaborative decision processes. There are established practice skills including conflict assessment, convening stakeholder groups, developing governance structures for these groups through ground rules, facilitating network meetings, and using consensus-building processes to help groups reach a decision or outcome (Susskind, McKearnan, and Larmer 1999).

The field of conflict resolution has also developed a literature on dispute system design that may provide a useful model for the practice of collaborative public management. This literature grew out of innovations in labor relations, specifically, efforts to build more collaborative practice into labor-management conflict (Ury, Brett, and Goldberg 1989). It provided a useful frame for federal agencies developing conflict management systems following amendments to the Administrative Procedure Act authorizing dispute resolution and negotiated rulemaking (Bingham, chapter 13; Costantino and Merchant 1996). These federal agency programs built collaborative practice into procurement, employment, regulatory enforcement, and environmental regulation (see gateway Web site of the Federal Interagency Alternative Dispute Resolution Working Group, www.adr.gov). Agencies also began creating networks for the purpose of drafting proposed regulations. The field of public administration needs to assist managers in the intentional, thoughtful, participative design of systems for collaboration and can build on the work of other fields in that effort.

We Need to Make Connections with Other Disciplines to Build Theory

As a field, public management and administration is developing a substantial knowledge base on collaborative public management (in addition to reviews of the literature in our contributors' chapters, see Agranoff and McGuire 2003; O'Leary, Gerard, and Bingham 2006b; O'Leary and Bingham 2008, forthcoming) and network governance. However, there is relevant theoretical work on collaboration in a variety of substantive and disciplinary contexts. Our contributors have concluded that we need to make connections with other literatures and disciplines.

For example, in the field of business, in addition to scholarship on networks (see Provan, Kenis, and Human, chapter 7), there is relevant negotiation theory and research at the organizational level (e.g., Lewicki, Barry, and Saunders 2005), examining the tension between collaboration and competition in economic markets. Collaboration and negotiation skills are relevant in a variety of contexts, from the interpersonal level between and among people representing organizations in a network, to the organizational level in which network members approve policy choices. There is a growing body of negotiation theory that can help inform analyses of the dynamics among network partners, not only at the micro level of human communications but also at the larger level of institutional interests (e.g., Lewicki, Barry, and Saunders 2005; Lewicki et al. 2006; Schneider and Honeyman 2006). The related fields of conflict management (e.g., Deutsch and Coleman 2000) and dispute resolution (for more discussion, see Bingham and O'Leary 2006) provide a variety of structural approaches for governance and resolving disagreements within the network. Literature on trust in negotiation and conflict management (Lewicki, Barry, and Saunders 2005) distinguishes between identity-based trust (an antecedent to collaboration in that people trust those who are more like themselves) and interaction-based trust (an outcome of collaboration in that people learn to trust others based on experiences of their behavior).

In political science, scholars have examined the emergence of collaborative governance structures in common pool resources (e.g., Ostrom 1990). The field of planning has confronted the need for collaboration in land use, where no one jurisdiction necessarily has complete authority not only to adopt a plan but also effectively to implement it (e.g., Innes and Booher 2004). In environmental governance, public managers have confronted the need for collaboration inherent in multijurisdictional, multisectoral policy issues (e.g., Durant, Fiorino, and O'Leary 2004). The fields of planning and environmental governance have contributed theory and practice on consensus building in public and environmental policy to foster more constructive and productive collaboration (e.g., Susskind, McKearnan, and Larmer 1999).

Political science has also contributed to our understanding of the role of the public in collaborative public management. It addresses questions of the democracy deficit and citizenship deficit inherent in decentralized governance (e.g. Putnam 2000). These may necessitate new forms of civic engagement and public participation. This body of theory raises relevant research issues for collaborative public management. For example, how does participation in a network as part of an organization change an individual's experience from participation as a citizen? New thinking on deliberative democracy suggests that one answer is to structure a process for true citizen dialogue and deliberation that is tied meaningfully to policymaking. This has been called empowered deliberation. Scholars are attempting to assess the quality of deliberation. Collaboration is itself a deliberative process. Work on the quality of deliberation may inform research on the quality of collaboration.

It is true that these disciplines present wide variation in methods used to investigate processes and outcomes, differing units of analysis, and different frames based on the substantive context in which collaboration occurs. However, lateral thinking may foster creativity. We can transplant ideas and approaches from these contexts to public management and learn something entirely new.

CONCLUSION

Collaborative public management is neither top down nor bottom up; it is lateral public management. Contributors to this volume present cutting-edge research, provocative questions, and stimulating inquiries designed to shift the frame. After presenting the latest research, we close this volume by grappling with the implications of these recent developments in collaborative public management thinking for the way we educate and train current and future public managers.

REFERENCES

Agranoff, Robert, and Michael McGuire. 2003. *Collaborative Public Management.* Washington DC: Georgetown University Press.

Bingham, Lisa B., and Rosemary O'Leary. 2006. "Conclusion: Parallel Play, Not Collaboration: Missing Questions, Missing Connections." *Public Administration Review* 66, no. S1: 161–67.

Bingham, Lisa B.; Tina Nabatchi; and Rosemary O'Leary. 2005. "The New Governance: Practices and Processes for Stakeholder and Citizen Participation in the Work of Government." *Public Administration Review* 65, no. 5: 547–58.

Costantino, Cathy A., and Christina Sickles Merchant. 1996. *Designing Conflict Management Systems: A Guide to Creating Productive and Healthy Organizations.* San Francisco: Jossey-Bass.

Crosby, Barbara C., and John M. Bryson. 2005. *Leadership for the Common Good.* San Francisco: Jossey-Bass.

Deutsch, Morton, and Peter T. Coleman, eds. 2000. *The Handbook of Conflict Resolution: Theory and Practice.* San Francisco: Jossey-Bass.

Durant, Robert; Daniel Fiorino; and Rosemary O'Leary, eds. 2004. *Environmental Governance Reconsidered: Challenges, Choices, and Opportunities.* Cambridge, MA: MIT Press.

Gerzon, Mark. 2006. *Leading Through Conflict: How Successful Leaders Transform Differences into Opportunities.* Cambridge, MA: Harvard Business School Press.

Henton, Doug; John Melville; Terry Amsler; and Malka Kopell. 2005. *Collaborative Governance: A Guide for Grantmakers.* Menlo Park, CA: William and Flora Hewlett Foundation.

Innes, Judith, and David Booher. 2004. "Reframing Public Participation: Strategies for the 21st Century." *Planning Theory and Practice* 5, no. 4: 419–36.

Kiefer, John J., and Robert S. Montjoy. 2006. "Incrementalism Before the Storm: Network Performance for the Evacuation of New Orleans." *Public Administration Review* 66, no. S1: 122–30.

Leach, William D. 2006. "Collaborative Public Management and Democracy: Evidence from Western Watershed Partnerships." *Public Administration Review* 66, no. S1: 100–110.

Leach, William, and Paul Sabatier. 2003. "Facilitators, Coordinators, and Outcomes." In *The Promise and Performance of Environmental Conflict Resolution,* ed. Rosemary O'Leary and Lisa B. Bingham, 148–71. Washington, DC: Resources for the Future Press.

Lewicki, Roy J.; Bruce Barry; and David M. Saunders. 2005. *Negotiation.* 5th ed. New York: McGraw-Hill.

Lewicki, Roy J.; D. Saunders; B. Barry; and J. Minton. 2006. *Negotiation: Readings, Exercises and Cases.* 5th ed. New York: McGraw-Hill/Irwin.

O'Leary, Rosemary, and Lisa Blomgren Bingham, eds. Forthcoming 2008. *The Collaborative Public Manager.* Washington, DC: Georgetown University Press.

O'Leary, Rosemary, and Lisa B. Bingham, eds. 2003. *The Promise and Performance of Environmental Conflict Resolution.* Washington, DC: Resources for the Future Press.

O'Leary, Rosemary and Lisa Blomgren Bingham. 2007. *A Manager's Guide to Resolving Conflicts in Collaborative Networks.* Arlington, VA: IBM Center for the Business of Government.

O'Leary, Rosemary; Catherine Gerard; and Lisa B. Bingham, eds. 2006a. "Introduction to the Symposium on Collaborative Public Management." *Public Administration Review* 66, no. S1: 6–9.

O'Leary, Rosemary; Catherine Gerard; and Lisa B. Bingham, eds. 2006b. "Symposium on Collaborative Public Management." *Public Administration Review* 66, no. S1.

Ostrom, Elinor. 1990. *Governing the Commons: The Evolution of Institutions for Collective Action.* New York: Cambridge University Press.

Putnam, Robert D. 2000. *Bowling Alone: The Collapse and Revival of American Community.* New York: Simon & Schuster.

Riding, Alan. 2006. "Glimpses of a Genius Who Blazed His Paper Trail." *New York Times,* September 26, Section E, 1.

Salamon, Lester, ed. 2002. *The Tools of Government: A Guide to the New Governance.* New York: Oxford University Press.

Schneider, Andrea Kupfer, and Christopher Honeyman, eds. 2006. *The Negotiator's Fieldbook: The Desk Reference for the Experienced Negotiator.* Washington, DC: American Bar Association.

Susskind, Lawrence; Sarah McKearnan; Jennifer Thomas Larmer, eds. 1999. *The Consensus-Building Handbook: A Comprehensive Guide to Reaching Agreement.* Thousand Oaks, CA: Sage.

Ury, William; Jeanne M. Brett; and Stephen B. Goldberg. 1989. *Getting Disputes Resolved: Designing Systems to Cut the Cost of Conflict.* San Francisco: Jossey-Bass.

Van Wart, Montgomery. 2003. "Public-Sector Leadership Theory: An Assessment." *Public Administration Review* 63, no. 2: 214–28.

Winer, Michael, and Karen Ray. 1994. *Collaboration Handbook: Creating, Sustaining, and Enjoying the Journey.* Saint Paul: Amherst H. Wilder Foundation.

CHAPTER 2

The Paradoxical Nature of Collaboration

DAVID R. CONNELLY,
JING ZHANG, AND SUE R. FAERMAN

In the past two decades, there has been an increasing use of intra- and interorganizational collaborations across organizations in the public, for-profit, and nonprofit sectors. In the public and nonprofit sectors, in particular, agencies have begun to recognize that many policy problems are not neatly bounded by the organizational lines of particular government agencies, and there are numerous case examples of agencies working with other agencies across levels of government; across agencies at the federal, state, and local levels; and across sectors, as state and local agencies work more collaboratively with nonprofit agencies and for-profit organizations (Bardach 1998; Linden 2002; Milward and Provan 2006). Perhaps one of the most dramatic examples of the creation of collaborative systems can be seen in the events following September 11, 2001, where, in the aftermath of this tragedy, a call was made to coordinate federal, state, and local initiatives aimed at securing the United States from further domestic and international attack and, in fact, a new cabinet-level agency—the Department of Homeland Security—was created to coordinate the efforts of more than forty federal agencies along with state and local counterparts in defending the homeland. Of course, many less-dramatic examples of collaboration exist, as agencies recognize the value of sharing information and resources with other agencies working toward similar, if not the same, goals.

While much of the literature tends to focus on the benefits of sharing information and resources across agencies, there is also a growing recognition of the inherent difficulties of collaboration (Connelly 2005; McCaffrey, Faerman, and Hart 1995; Milward and Provan 2006; Mizrahi and Rosenthal 2001; Ospina and Saz-Carranza 2005; Vangen and Huxham 2003). This simultaneous attention to the benefits and difficulties of collaboration suggests a basic paradox, that collaborations are both inherently appealing (as a result of the potential benefits) and unappealing (as a result of the potential costs) to organizations that are either mandated or voluntarily seeking to engage in such collaborations. While the notion that collaborative systems are both appealing and unappealing might create great dissonance for many individuals, this chapter argues that such paradoxes are unavoidable in organizational life and that leaders would do well to embrace, rather than deny the existence of, such paradoxes. Moreover, consistent with Handy's (1994) view, we take the position that, rather than seeing organizational paradoxes as evidence that we live in an "imperfect world" (12), we should see paradoxes as "inevitable, endemic and perpetual" (ibid.), recognize that "we cannot make them disappear, or solve them completely or escape from them" (ibid.), and consider the notion that "(p)aradoxes are like the weather, something to be lived with, not solved, the worst aspects mitigated, the best enjoyed and used as clues to the way forward (12–13)." In line with the title of this volume, *Big Ideas in Collaborative Public Management,* we argue that collaborative leaders need to see the world in this new way and learn to take paradoxical actions that embrace, rather than deny or avoid, the paradoxical nature of collaborative systems.

Drawing on the literature and prior research carried out by the authors (Connelly 2005; Faerman, McCaffrey, and Van Slyke 2001; Zhang 2003), the goal of this chapter is to explore the complexity of collaborative systems, emphasizing several paradoxes that are pervasive in public management collaborations and the delicate balancing act that collaborative leaders must perform in bringing together individuals and organizations with both similar and different goals. Beginning with a general discussion of collaboration that describes the various ways that this phenomenon has been approached in the literature, the chapter then provides a brief overview of paradox within organizations, and collaboration as a paradoxical phenomenon. Finally, using the framework of collaboration developed by Faerman and colleagues (Faerman, McCaffrey, and Van Slyke 2001; McCaffrey, Faerman, and Hart 1995), the chapter presents several key paradoxes of collaboration that raise issues that leaders engaged in collaborative efforts must consider. This leads to several suggestions for how leaders in the public and nonprofit sectors might develop more effective collaborative systems.

COLLABORATION

Much current literature focuses on the phenomenon of individuals and organizations coming together to accomplish tasks that could not (or should not) be accomplished alone. This phenomenon has been given a variety of names—including alliances, coalitions, community-based collaboratives, networks, and partnerships—and includes a variety of different ways to collaborate. Particularly in the public sector, researchers focus on how the "devolution revolution" (Nathan 1996) and other efforts to increase public agency effectiveness and accountability have resulted in an increase in collaborative relationships between public and nonprofit organizations.

Milward and Provan (2006), for example, differentiate among four different types of *networks* of public, nonprofit, and for-profit organizations—service implementation networks, information diffusion networks, problem-solving networks, and community capacity-building networks—noting that "[t]he network logic is that collaboration is needed to deal with problems that don't fit neatly within the boundaries of a single organization" (8). Service implementation networks, for example, are funded by government to provide direct services to vulnerable populations, such as the elderly and the mentally ill. In these networks, government provides the funding for the services, but its primary role in the collaboration is to ensure the effectiveness of service delivery by for-profit and nonprofit organizations. Information diffusion networks, on the other hand, generally involve only government agencies and focus on the sharing of information across government boundaries, a task that is both enabled by and potentially made riskier by new information technologies (Connelly 2005). Problem-solving networks, like service implementation networks, cut across sectors and may involve public, for-profit, and nonprofit agencies that previously have provided services or collaborated but are used to solve immediate problems, and likely disperse when the immediate problem is resolved. Finally, community capacity-building networks focus on current and future needs of communities and attempt to build social capital to address these needs. Milward and Provan argue that although these networks have different purposes, similar tasks are involved in managing these four types of networks. Moreover, because networks "do not have a hierarchical chain of command but . . . rely on trust and reciprocity as the levers of collaboration . . . the tasks of managers [are] much different from those in organizations" (2006, 6).

Others have used the term *partnerships* to describe collaborative systems that cut across agencies and are voluntary in nature. Researchers examining partnerships may focus on a particular setting, such as health care delivery (Alexander et al. 2001), or examine a wide variety of settings (Vangen and Huxham 2003). Interestingly, Vangen and Huxham use the term *partnership manager* to describe those individuals with responsibility for organizing and serving as a resource for the partnerships, although they may not themselves be members of the partnership, and describe a wide variety of such arrangements, including "urban and rural regeneration initiatives, a social inclusion network, health promotion partnerships, poverty alleviation and family support alliances, a collaboration of universities, local health co-operatives, a special education partnership, a learning disability initiative, and a public leadership programme" (2003, S63). As with the discussion of networks, research focusing on partnerships stresses the fact that partnerships have no inherent hierarchical structure or controls that generally accompany hierarchical organizations.

Research on mandated collaborations has noted that government and private funding for service implementation increasingly comes with the requirement that community-based agencies engage in interorganizational collaboration and/or involve members of the community in the decision-making processes (Bailey and Koney 1996; Mizrahi and Rosenthal 2001; Slater 2005). Such mandated collaborations are based on the assumption that developing programs that appropriately meet the needs of the community demands the involvement of those individuals and family members who will directly benefit from the actions of the collaboratives. These collaboratives, however, may pose special problems, particularly with respect to questions of agency autonomy.

In other cases, collaborations are not mandated, but are seen as creating a competitive advantage for nonprofit agencies attempting to secure funds from government and for-profit organizations, as well as foundations. In an increasingly competitive funding environment, voluntary *coalitions* (Bailey and Koney 1996; Mizrahi and Rosenthal 2001; Ospina and Saz-Carranza 2005) have formed to increase chances of survival. Mizrahi and Rosenthal (2001) describe coalitions as "organizations of organizations whose members commit to an agreed-upon purpose and shared decision making to influence an external institution or target, while these member organizations maintain their own autonomy" (64), and note that "[t]his type of coalition is part of the social change tradition" (ibid.). Similarly, Ospina and Saz-Carranza explain that "[b]ecause the coalition is created to change or influence a target in the larger environment, collaborative efforts may also develop between the coalition as an organizational entity and external organizations or other stakeholder groups that are part of its environment, including the target organization" (2005, 5). Coalitions can thus be characterized as having a political as well as a social agenda.

Regardless of what they are called, each of these organizational entities follows the basic definition provided by Bardach (1998), who defines collaboration "as any joint activity by two or more agencies that is intended to increase public value by their working together rather than separately" (8). Moreover, all of these entities face similar challenges as they struggle with the primary paradox of collaboration, wanting to reap the benefits afforded by being part of the larger entity while trying to avoid the losses that are felt when others must be involved in key decisions. Thus, the potential benefits create centripetal forces that work to keep the collaboration together, while subtle differences in long-term goals, belief systems about appropriate strategies for accomplishing goals, resources, and organizational cultures and norms among the various constituent members create centrifugal forces that sometimes threaten to pull the groups apart. Given the central role that this paradox plays in the ability of collaboratives to survive, much less thrive, it is important to examine the nature of paradox and how it drives organizational action. The next section presents a brief review of the literature on organizational paradox and sets the stage for a more in-depth examination of the paradoxical nature of collaboration.

PARADOX

As noted in the introduction to this chapter, paradox has become a topic of increasing interest in organizational studies, as researchers and practitioners alike recognize that organizations are driven by seemingly contradictory forces. For example, organizations are expected to be both flexible and stable, providing employees with a sense of continuity while adapting to changing environments. Similarly, we regularly decry the bureaucratic nature of government organizations and call for greater efficiency, while also emphasizing the importance of accountability to the public and the need to develop systems that monitor the actions of public employees, even if these systems create inefficiencies. Organizations are also expected to treat individuals (both employees and consumers) fairly, which sometimes means that all persons are treated alike and that no one receives "special favors" and at other times means that each person is treated as an individual, with consideration given to individual circumstances. And organizations are expected to bring different voices to the decision-making table and to value the diversity of perspectives that result from differences in individuals' race/ethnicity, sex, age, educational background, and other personal characteristics, as well as their functional areas, but they are also expected to align employees to work more effectively as a team within and across units so that they are able to present a single voice to the community.

Cameron and Quinn (1988) note that there is no consensus regarding the definition of paradox, but that it generally "involves contradictory, mutually exclusive elements that are present and operate equally at the same time" (2). They, like others (Handy 1994; Lewis 2000; Price Waterhouse Change Integration Team 1996), emphasize that paradox is an inevitable characteristic of organizations (and life) and cannot be resolved. Thus, rather than try to resolve paradoxes, Cameron and Quinn (1988) argue we should accept or transcend the paradox and move from an "either-or" perspective to a "both-and" perspective.

Much of what is written today about collaborative systems recognizes, implicitly or explicitly, that one of the inherent paradoxes of collaboration involves the need for individuals and/or organizations to work to meet their own needs and simultaneously work to meet the needs of others. This view of collaboration was presented by Thomas (1976, 1977) in his conceptualization of conflict and conflict management along two juxtaposed dimensions (see Figure 2.1), each representing how individuals think and act in approaching situations in which there is conflict. The first dimension represents cooperativeness, or the extent to which one is willing to work in order to meet the other party's needs and concerns. The second dimension represents assertiveness, or the extent to which one is willing to work in order to meet one's own needs and concerns. These two dimensions define five conflict management approaches: avoidance, accommodation, competition, compromise, and collaboration. While Thomas argued that all of these approaches can be useful under some circumstances, the first four approaches carry a win-lose (or lose-lose) assumption, which is consistent with most activities in our daily lives. For example, in political elections, only one candidate can win; in sports, only one team can win; and in organizations, only one person is hired for or promoted to the manager's job. Even compromising approaches, where individuals are concerned with both their own interests and goals and those of the other party, carry an assumption that there is a fixed resource or sum to be divided among the interested parties and that each must give up (i.e., lose) something in order to gain something else. Thus, although neither party will end up the loser, neither party ends up the winner, and people often remember what they had to give up in order to get what they wanted.

Collaborating approaches, on the other hand, assume that individuals can be concerned both with their own interests and goals *and* with those of the other party. The difference is that there is no underlying assumption of a fixed resource that will force one or more parties to give up something in order to gain something else. Rather, the assumption is that by creatively engaging the problem, a solution can be generated that makes everyone a winner and everyone better off. Thus, collaborations are built on a basic paradox, the notion that everyone can "win" simultaneously, that is, that if one individual, group, or organization wins, it is not necessary that another individual, group, or organization loses something.

A second paradox associated with collaborative systems concerns the notion of collaborative leadership. As noted above, collaborative systems generally do not have a defined leader. As a result, while there may be a convener who is not necessarily a member of the group (Huxham and Beech 2003), collaborative systems are more likely to have many leaders who emerge depending on the task at hand. While this is increasingly true for so-called hierarchical organizations as well (Cleveland 2002; Fletcher and Kaüfer 2003),

Figure 2.1   **Approaches to Conflict Management**

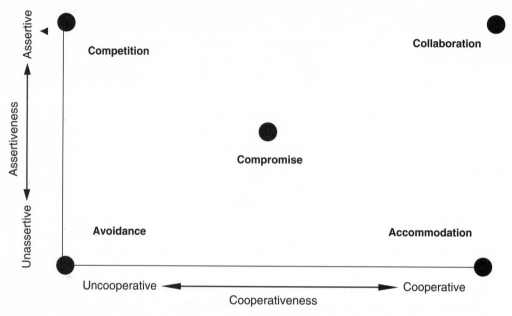

Source: K. Thomas, "Conflict and Conflict Management" in *Handbook of Industrial and Organizational Psychology,* ed. M.D. Dunnette (Chicago: Rand McNally College Publishers, 1976), 900. Copyright © 1976 Rand McNally. Reprinted by permission of the estate of Marvin D. Dunnette.

it is an underlying assumption for collaborative systems, which are in fact established so that they can take advantage of the different abilities and resources collaboration members bring to the collaboration. Indeed, in presenting a leadership framework for cross-sector collaboration, Crosby and Bryson (2005) argue that "an important meta-skill for a leader seems to be knowing when he or she is best suited to provide a type of leadership and when to turn that work over to someone else" (183). Thus, in collaborative systems, one must accept the paradoxical notions that (1) there will be situations where a leader may lead best by allowing or encouraging others to lead, and (2) effective leadership involves knowing when and how to follow.

These two basic paradoxes of collaboration—everyone can win and leaders must learn to be effective followers—provide a preview for the remainder of this chapter. In the next section, we present a framework that was originally developed from a review of the literature of participative systems (McCaffrey, Faerman, and Hart 1995), and then elaborated based on an empirical investigation into a collaborative system (Faerman, McCaffrey, and Van Slyke 2001). The framework describes four factors—initial dispositions toward cooperation/collaboration,[1] issues and incentives, number and variety of groups, and leadership—which have been identified consistently across the literatures examining cooperation and collaboration as both explaining the success of collaborative systems and also why collaborative systems are so difficult to develop and maintain. The framework also recognizes the importance of the interactions across the factors (see Figure 2.2).

Figure 2.2   **Factors Influencing Collaboration**

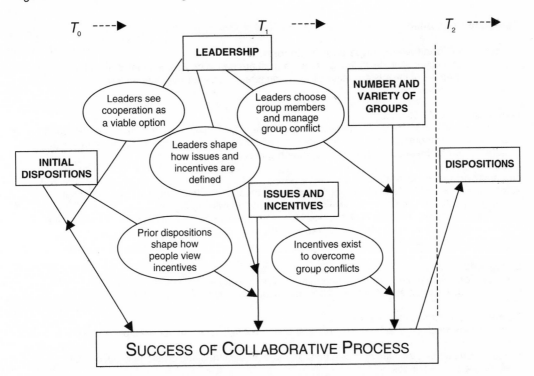

Source: From Sue R. Faerman, David P. McCaffrey, and David M. Van Slyke, "Understanding Interorganizational Cooperation: Public-Private Collaboration in Regulating Financial Market Regulation," *Organization Science* 12, no. 3 (2001): 383. Copyright © 2001 by the Institute for Operations Research and the Management Sciences, 7240 Parkway Drive, Suite 310, Hanover, MD 21076 USA. Reprinted by permission.

INHERENT PARADOXES OF COLLABORATIONS

As argued above, collaborative systems hold great potential for increasing public value, but are difficult to develop and maintain, making them both appealing and unappealing mechanisms for organizations to accomplish together what no single organization can accomplish on its own. Here we examine the four factors presented in this framework and explore how each of the factors can be characterized in terms of paradoxes that lead to various challenges for leaders of such systems. Table 2.1 summarizes the paradoxes associated with the four factors and their interactions.

Initial Dispositions Toward Cooperation/Collaboration

Initial dispositions toward the value of collaboration, shaped by personal experience and institutions, can favor or inhibit initial efforts to form a new collaborative system. People are more likely to cooperate when they expect their own "nice" behavior to be rewarded

---

Table 2.1

Paradoxes of Collaboration

Initial dispositions toward cooperation/collaboration
- Institutional mechanisms designed to enhance trust are based on assumptions of mistrust.
- The effectiveness of the system requires attention to autonomy and interdependencies of collaborating units.

Issues and incentives
- Collaborative leaders must recognize the importance of both diversity and unity in the collaboration.
- Successful collaborations allow participants to maintain separate, diverse goals, while developing and working toward the accomplishment of common goals.

Number and variety of groups
- Increasing the number and diversity of voices increases the likelihood of identifying potential solutions, but also decreases the likelihood that everyone will agree.
- In the long run, collaborative systems need to match the diversity of constituents affected by the collaboration, but may require a more homogeneous group during initial stages to make enough progress to legitimize the collaboration.

Leadership
- Collaborative leaders need to be authoritative, without being authoritarian.
- Collaborative leaders sometimes lead best by encouraging followers to lead.

Relationships among the factors
- Interactions among the factors can lead to success, as well as failure; for example, leaders can frame issues and incentives to stress benefits of collaboration or costs of collaboration.
- Interactions among the factors in one time period both constrain and create new options for subsequent time periods.

---

with nice behavior by others (Axelrod 1984). If there is no history, at least for a time, people may regard setbacks as temporary aberrations not threatening the relationship. Alternatively, when parties have prior information or experiences that lead them not to trust each other initially, they are more likely to worry about making early gestures necessary to increase trust; thus, individuals favoring cooperation will have a hard time selling it as an approach, and fragile successes can be undermined easily by "I told you they can't be trusted" reactions (Ariño and de la Torre 1998; Gulati 1995; McAllister 1995). Similarly, when organizations have historically battled for turf, institutionalized practices can inhibit cooperation.

A paradox emerges, however, when institutionalized practices of mistrust dominate over any personal dispositions to trust. For example, interorganizational collaborations, such as those involving public agencies working with nonprofit agencies, often develop legal safeguards and/or establish mechanisms to monitor behavior, thus increasing faith in the process by reducing the risks of being cheated (Ostrom 1990, 1998; Williamson 1996; Zucker 1986). Legal safeguards and the monitoring of behaviors, however, are not indicators of trust. Thus, paradoxically, the mechanisms that have been used historically to enhance trust by limiting the possibility that an individual or group will behave inappropriately, are, at their core, statements of mistrust.

Another paradox that emerges with respect to initial dispositions toward collaboration is the degree to which these dispositions are influenced by levels of autonomy and interdependence, two factors that are generally seen as contradictory forces. That is, it is generally assumed that the more interdependencies that exist among individuals or groups, the less autonomy each will have. Recognizing this paradox of organizing, Kets de Vries (1999) argues that high-performance teams—and by extension, organizations in general—can learn some lessons from pygmy society, where both values are consistently demonstrated in interpersonal interactions. He explains that "[g]iven the potential hardships of the forest, [pygmies'] survival depends on interdependence" (69), but also notes that pygmies have a "deeply anchored sense of independence and autonomy" (68). Kets de Vries argues that this simultaneous sense of independence and interdependence develops in childhood, where children are taught "the art of survival in the rainforest" (72), which requires that they learn subsistence skills, as well as to recognize that survival depends on respecting and trusting each other, and acting upon mutually agreed-upon common goals.

Connelly (2005) found a similar phenomenon in the development of shared information systems for use across criminal justice agencies. While the organizational and institutional structures of criminal justice agencies differ greatly among states and localities (autonomy), developing such systems requires all participating agencies to agree to certain uniform standards and practices (interdependence). Connelly notes that creating such information-sharing systems generally involves five types of agencies/organizations: (1) law enforcement, (2) court operations and administration, (3) prosecution and legal administration (prosecuting/district attorneys, states' attorneys, attorneys general), (4) defense (public and private), and (5) incarceration (including parole). Of the five, three typically fall under the executive branch of government (law enforcement, prosecution and legal administration, and incarceration). In a number of states, however, the executive branch at each level can include constitutionally independent executives (e.g., separately elected attorneys general, district attorneys, etc.). In all cases, the courts are a separate branch of government, but often dependent on the executive and legislature for funding. The legislature is, of course, involved directly through funding and oversight of these other branches, as well as through legislation on crime and criminal procedures. Most important, these different components of government seldom share the same objectives or views of criminal justice information integration (autonomy). The courts tend to see criminal justice as only part, and, in terms of caseload, the minority part, of their business. Improved court information integration, however, can mean improved management, better input for decisions, and better justification of budget and workload. In the law enforcement area, the primary concerns are public safety, reduced risk to officers, and less chance of making major mistakes, as well as reducing paperwork. Ultimately, all parties recognize that smooth and effective information sharing throughout all of these diverse branches, functions, and levels of government can result in increased public safety, enhanced justice in society, and more efficient government operations (interdependence). Connelly (2005) found that the ability to develop information systems that were usable across organizational boundaries depended on a simultaneous awareness of the autonomy and interdependence of these agencies.

Issues and Incentives

Initial dispositions establish a presumption in favor of or against cooperation, but those leanings can change depending on the extant issues and incentives. Using Anthony Giddens's (1984) terms, initial dispositions are an important part of a "structure," while the issues and incentives present occasions for the ongoing "structuring" of relationships. People who favor more extensive collaboration emphasize its "pragmatic necessity" in dealing with the tighter economic, technological, and social connections that accompany collaborative systems (Daft and Lewin 1993; Gray 1989). They argue that collaborations provide benefits that result when parties pool knowledge and complementary strengths; deal with their interdependencies more effectively; combine similar operations and thus take advantage of economies of scale; manage geographically dispersed operations and diverse laws, cultures, and politics; and handle crises more effectively (Gulati and Singh 1999; Powell, Koput, and Smith-Doerr 1996). Of course, conflicts over values, ambitions, and interests may give people incentives *not* to collaborate, and even long-standing collaborative relationships can decay when the forces pulling people together—such as a compelling task or a charismatic leader—no longer offset such tensions and differences (Bennis and Biederman 1997).

Rather than view these forces as either-or propositions, several researchers have begun to recognize that, by definition, collaborative systems comprise individuals and organizations with both common and diverse goals (Huxham and Beech 2003; Mizrahi and Rosenthal 2001; Ospina and Saz-Carranza 2005). Indeed, Ospina and Saz-Carranza (2005) argue that the most successful leaders of coalitions were characterized as "honoring the competing demands for unity and diversity," and note, paradoxically, that "[t]oo much unity among coalition members weakens the essence of the coalition to create synergy from the organizations' diversity" (25). They thus argue that differences in goals may be one of the strengths of the collaboration.

Zhang (2003) similarly found that differences in goals and incentives led collaboration leaders to try a new approach, which ultimately led to great success. In the development and implementation of a knowledge management (KM) system, the two initial groups of stakeholders—the central and regional offices of one division of a state agency—had both shared and differing objectives. Both offices wanted to reduce paperwork and improve communication. In addition, because the system was the first enterprise-wide application within this agency, people wanted to be associated with a task that was innovative and had a high potential to succeed. On the other hand, the central office was the leading force for the KM system because it had the pressing need to gain access to information and knowledge held by the regional offices. The regional offices, however, had little motivation to share this information, and assumed that this system would shift existing relationships, as well as add additional workload to them with no substantial benefits resulting from the system. Nonetheless, the regional offices also knew that the central office had the authority to mandate the adoption of the system if it wanted to. Given that the central office did not want to approach this project in an authoritarian fashion, the office intentionally refrained from using its authority and adopted a participative (collaborative) approach, soliciting the concerns and needs from the regional staff. In addition, the central office expanded the collaboration to include other divisions within the agency with similar information needs. Ultimately, as other divisions were included, there was a change in the course of implementation, which also added new incentives to collaborate. These new incentives led to a solution to which all the parties could commit.

In this case, the KM system had several components and the original plan had called for implementation of one of the more controversial components, in terms of divergent interests between the central and regional offices. To accomplish this, the agency would have had to ensure that both central and regional offices were aligned around the details of implementing this component. As other divisions of this agency were included, it appeared that another, less controversial component that carried more common interests would better clarify the agency-wide incentives for developing an agency-wide KM system and thus gain a higher level of support in the agency. Zhang found that, after successful implementation of this and some other components, the benefits of the KM system became much more concrete to the stakeholders and the more controversial components became more attractive. Thus, by focusing on a different component, where incentives were more obvious, the agency was able to move to a more successful implementation strategy.

Number and Variety of Groups

The number and variety of groups involved in a task make collaboration more or less likely by affecting group dynamics and the costs of arriving at agreements. Parties are often more willing to enter into collaborative relationships with other parties that are similar and/or with which they have personal ties. In addition, collaborative decisions are most easily reached when the number of parties is small enough that agreements can be reached at a reasonable cost; and it is generally assumed that collaborations become more difficult when group size and diversity increase and introduce so many different perspectives and needs that disagreements can overwhelm potential agreements (Kumar and Nti 1998; Parkhe 1993; Zaheer, McEvily, and Perrone 1998). Yet, as seen in the example above, increasing the number and diversity of participants can also paradoxically *facilitate* agreements by creating possibilities for bargains among people with different but compatible preferences. Moreover, the essential value of collaborations is generally seen in the differing perspectives that collaboration members can bring to the table. Diversity helps all groups, not just collaborative groups, to avoid the phenomenon of groupthink (Janis 1972), which has been associated with small homogeneous groups. Similarly, Wenger, McDermott, and Snyder (2002) argue that communities of practice—"groups of people who share a concern, a set of problems, or a passion about a topic, and who deepen their knowledge and expertise in this area by interacting on an ongoing basis" (4)—lose their effectiveness if they "are there dominated by a powerful core group that acts as an imperious gatekeeper" (145) and there is not a continual flow of new members with new ideas into the community.

In their study of top management teams, Pitcher and Smith (2001) hypothesized that cognitive diversity among team members would be vital to their success, noting that "there are strong theoretical reasons to believe that heterogeneous top management teams will be more successful because they permit a more comprehensive search and analysis of strategic alternatives and exhibit greater creativity due to the exchange of diverse ideas originating in different cognitive perspectives" (2). Although Pitcher and Smith found that personality and power can moderate the effect of heterogeneity on strategic outcomes, they concluded that top team heterogeneity is critical to innovation and that, with better measurement, future research may be in a position to demonstrate that leaders of top management teams need to "be prepared to experience and even encourage the conflict that it may engender" (16).

Studies by both Zhang (2003) and Faerman, McCaffrey, and Van Slyke (2001) found that while it may be necessary to start with a small homogeneous group, in the long run, collaborative systems need to build the diversity of the collaboration to match the diversity of the constituents who are affected by the collaboration. In particular, Zhang (2003) found that collaboration members consistently expressed that a critical factor for the success of building a KM system, as well as for knowledge sharing itself, is the involvement of diverse groups. Group diversity was particularly important to the development of the KM system because the system had to reflect the differing needs of the staff from across the organization, and so the collaboration needed to include management and central staff as well as field staff. While leadership recognized that the growing diversity of collaboration members could potentially complicate the processes of communication, consensus building, and resources sharing, which could further create problems for the implementation of the system, specific actions were taken to ensure that the collaborative benefited from the different voices.

First, in its early development, the project included only a relatively small number of groups, and the number and diversity of those groups were considered to be "manageable." Indeed, a stakeholder analysis was conducted to reduce the number and heterogeneity of the participating groups, allowing the early discussion to focus primarily on the needs of facilitating communication among central and regional offices of the original division, without being distracted by cross-agency issues. Although the geographic locations presented a certain level of diversity among the initial groups, the fact that all the offices were performing similar functions, consisted of similar types of personnel, and reported to a single authority made the divergence less of a problem to reconcile. Then, after the idea grew to be a mature proposal and concrete prototype, the involvement of a larger number of, and more heterogeneous groups became less problematic. Thus, when the KM system was introduced as a possible solution for addressing cross-agency information needs, the possible variations were automatically limited and could only occur within a certain frame. As a result, overall diversity of the cross-agency collaborative was found to enhance creativity and synergies, but, as was also found by Ospina and Saz-Carranza (2005), the value of diversity in the collaborative system was best realized when accompanied by a conscious unity of purpose.

Leadership

Leadership, at all levels of organizations, can play an important role in defining the situation for the individuals involved, by getting people to think about the issues and incentives, and even their initial dispositions, in particular ways. Leaders with strong reputations can legitimize certain ways to deal with a problem, and prod or persuade people to act in ways favoring or inhibiting cooperation/collaboration (Crosby and Bryson 2005; Gray 1989, 1996). Case studies of successful collaboration show leaders actively managing the process, particularly in its early stages and during trying moments. Studies also show failures of collaborative systems that occurred when leaders acted in narrowly self-interested ways or relished political battles (Browning, Beyer, and Shetler 1995; Huxham 1996; Weber 1998; Westley and Vredenburg 1997).

Whether managing a collaborative system or a unit that is part of a hierarchical system, leaders today are faced with the paradox of needing to be both directive and participative. That is, they are being expected to have a vision while encouraging others to modify the vision, and to behave sometimes as a leader and sometimes as a follower. Huxham and Beech (2003) differentiate between romantic and heroic styles of leadership, where the former is associated with leaders who encourage participation in decision making by members and the latter is associated with leaders who believe that they should provide direction and clear role expectations. In a similar vein, Bailey and Koney (1996) talk about the need for collaboration leaders to be "both assertive (guiding and directing) and responsive," arguing that "[u]nlike autocratic leadership, good leadership is good follower-ship" (606). Vangen and Huxham (2003) refer to this issue as a dilemma of ideology and pragmatism and argue that the findings of their study indicate that leaders of collaborative systems should "operate constantly from both perspectives and that both are essential to making progress" (S73).

This paradox was similarly seen in Connelly's (2005) research, where study participants would, in the course of a single interview, criticize leaders who made decisions without consulting others, arguing that they are "doomed to failure" (103), and then argue that leaders needed to provide direction and push organizational members to make things happen. Connelly consistently found that interview comments seemed to show a "conflict" in the minds of the participants concerning leaders. On the one hand, individuals recognized that leadership can be a role shared by many in a single organization or even interorganizational setting, one that does not demand top-down hierarchical single-person control; yet, at the same time, they seemed to recognize a need for control, someone or a group of individuals who is "high up" and who can push and make things happen. Study participants spoke regularly about leaders who could make phone calls and talk with decision makers and obtain commitments for needed resources, as well as get around normal or formal channels of operation. Indeed, some study participants argued that collaboration projects may have failed without individual leaders' focused efforts.

In one of the cases from Connelly's study, participants described one individual who in fact had the ability to call the governor without notice and solicit whatever was needed. Yet, this individual always seemed to seek the input of the group prior to any external contact and was remarkably restrained in using his influence, according to some observations, even though it might have made things run more smoothly in terms of overall project activity if he had. This leader clearly saw the value of allowing those around him to work things out and allowing the project to evolve in a manner that best suited the participants as opposed to short-circuiting processes and accomplishing things in what could be described as unnatural time frames. Interorganizational collaborations require buy-in, and this person allowed the time to get that buy-in without resorting to behaviors that might have achieved short-term results but not developed the overall strength of the collaborative. Thus, in one sense, it was clear to the participants in Connelly's study that single-leader models fail to capture the essence of leadership but it also seemed equally clear to those participants that individuals and formal positions do matter. This duality parallels Kets de Vries's (1999) notion that leaders can be authoritative, that is, offering guidance and structure while encouraging dialogue and interaction, without being authoritarian, demanding complete control over organizational decisions.

Relationships Among the Factors

Figure 2.2 on page 23 indicates that the four factors do not act independently in influencing the likelihood of successful collaboration, and proposes specific interactions between and among the four key factors discussed above. In addition, it suggests that one needs to understand collaboration as a process in which outcomes at one period set the stage for the next (Gray 1989; Gray and Wood 1991; Larsson et al. 1998; Ring and Van de Ven 1994). While Figure 2.2 does not try to capture all potential relationships among the four factors, it does identify relationships that we believe are pivotal, based on our reading of the literature and our own empirical work. It also recognizes that a key paradox of collaborative systems involves time, and the degree to which short-term actions are not always clearly tied to specific long-term effects.

Initial dispositions at time T_0 favor or inhibit the development of collaborative systems. In the ensuing time T_1, how leaders frame and handle choices, and the extant issues and incentives, interact with these initial dispositions. It should also be noted that leadership may influence the *perceptions* of issues and incentives as well as the actual underlying conditions giving rise to the issues and incentives themselves. Leadership and the issues and incentives also interact with the effects of the number and variety of groups on cooperation. For example, as noted above, leaders can strategically shape the nature of the discussions of incentives and issues in ways that allow diverse mixes of groups to coalesce. Thus, the initial dispositions toward cooperation, and the number and variety of groups involved, influence the possibilities of collaboration, but we have to consider carefully how leadership and extant issues and incentives expand or contract these possibilities. How these relationships develop in one period sets the stage for the next phase of action in T_2. Cooperative success in T_1 helps build a foundation for cooperation in T_2, but so can failure. Indeed, Connelly (2005) found that individuals were often willing to learn from past mistakes and try again with new leadership or with new resources. Thus, successful collaborations can lay the foundation for future success, but so too can initial failures; and success in one time period can also lead to complacency, which can ultimately lead to failure (Wenger, McDermott, and Snyder 2002).

CONCLUSION

This chapter has focused on ways that collaborative systems are characterized by inherent paradoxes. As noted above, researchers who have studied paradox (Cameron and Quinn 1988; Handy 1994; Huxham and Beech 2003; Lewis 2000; Ospina and Saz-Carranza 2005; Vangen and Huxham 2003) have emphasized that effective leaders do not attempt to resolve paradoxes, but rather that they manage paradox by accepting, indeed embracing, the existence of simultaneous opposites, in some cases transcending the paradox to develop alternative approaches. In presenting the framework and the four factors that facilitate and inhibit successful collaboration, this chapter has contributed to the literature by providing a new way of thinking about why collaborative systems are simultaneously appealing and unappealing, and why researchers (and many practitioners) assert the many benefits of collaborative systems, while practitioners find these systems so difficult to implement. It has also contributed to practice by suggesting several actions for collaborative leaders that will enable them to accept and embrace, rather than attempt to resolve, the paradox. For example, in discussing initial dispositions, we argued that leaders need to allow for collaborators to maintain their autonomy, while ensuring the development of healthy interdependence among the collaborators. Similarly, in discussing both issues and incentives and the number and variety of groups, it was suggested that it is important to bring as many diverse groups to the table as can "fit," but it was also suggested that leaders need to consider the timing and may want to begin with a smaller, more focused group and then, over time, move to a more diverse group with broader goals and greater resources. In addition, it was argued that collaboration leaders need to be as comfortable with following as with leading, and to know when to give direction and when to allow the collaboration members to take charge of the situation.

Based on the literature and our own research, we would also like to suggest one additional paradoxical action and return to one paradox discussed above. First, leaders need to work at seeing both the forest and the trees, that is, they need to understand the big picture but they must also be aware of important details. While much writing on leadership urges leaders to take a systems view (Alexander et al. 2001; Senge 2006), the paradoxical nature of collaborations would suggest that leaders should also simultaneously understand the details. While it is important for collaboration leaders not to get caught up in the minutiae, awareness of and attention to some of the details could make collaboration leaders more effective at identifying alternative solutions. Mareschal (2003), for example, in studying skills of federal mediators, found that the most effective mediators had what she termed "bifocal vision," which involves being able to take both a broad and narrow view of mediation, being able to see things on the horizon as well as the more immediate pressing events.

Second, leaders need to develop their skills at balancing advocacy and inquiry (Senge 2006), recognizing that advocacy is not merely arguing for one's side but also involves making one's "thinking explicit and subject to public examination" (Senge 2006, 184). This recommendation follows directly from Thomas's (1976, 1977) notion of collaboration as a conflict management strategy that simultaneously involves caring about one's own interests and goals (assertiveness) *and* caring about other parties' interests and goals (cooperativeness). It also builds on the need not only to bring diverse views to the table but also to be willing to understand and value the differences that these diverse voices bring. Moreover, it suggests that collaborative leaders need to encourage people to go beyond caring about their own and others' interests and values to the point where they question the basis for these ideas, think critically about what assumptions support each set of ideas, and then think creatively about how the commonalities can support new solutions that continue to support the diversity of voices. Thus, collaborative leaders need to actively approach collaborative situations with an assumption that, by using divergent thinking, it may be possible to have everyone's needs fully met, but that this is more likely to happen if the reasoning behind each party's views is made explicit.

While the recommendations for paradoxical actions by collaborative leaders presented in this chapter are based on existing literature and our own empirical work, there is still much research to be done to understand more fully the paradoxical nature of collaboration and the implications of these paradoxes for leadership action. Particularly in the public sector, where the policy problems reach across agency boundaries, it is imperative that we gain a better understanding of the obstacles to effective collaboration. As Bardach (1998) notes, "Political and institutional pressures on public sector agencies in general push for differentiation rather than integration, and the basis for differentiation is typically political rather than technical" (11). Moreover, he argues that "even if the basis for differentiation is technically optimal at the time agencies and their missions are created, changes in the nature of problems and the availability of solutions—or perhaps changes in our understanding if not necessarily in the realities—make the older pattern of differentiation obsolete" (ibid.). We are thus living in a world where collaborative systems are likely to simultaneously become increasingly more important and increasingly more difficult to develop and maintain, unless we make use of the wide variety of policy issues that provide laboratories for studying collaborative processes and take action to gain a deeper understanding of how the inherent paradoxes of collaboration influence the likelihood of success. To do this, we must also learn how to help collaborative leaders diminish their tendencies to try to resolve, avoid, and deny the inherent paradoxes of collaboration, and instead learn to embrace them.

NOTE

1. While the literature on cooperation, which relies heavily on game theory to study how parties with divergent interests either develop or fail to develop cooperative relationships (e.g., Axelrod 1984; Heide and Miner 1992), and the literature on collaboration, which uses intensive study of individual cases, often with organization development techniques, to examine how conflicting parties may manage to settle disputes in less confrontational ways (e.g., Bryson and Crosby 1992; Gray 1989), have developed independently—that is, there is virtually no citation across them—the two theoretical approaches identify similar, reinforcing themes. The terms are thus used interchangeably here.

REFERENCES

Alexander, Jeffrey A.; Maureen E. Comfort; Bryan J. Weiner; and Richard Bogue. 2001. "Leadership in Collaborative Community Health Partnerships." *Nonprofit Management & Leadership* 12: 159–75.

Ariño, Africa, and Jose de la Torre. 1998. "Learning from Failure: Towards an Evolutionary Model of Collaborative Ventures." *Organization Science* 9, no. 3: 306–25.

Axelrod, Robert. 1984. *The Evolution of Cooperation.* New York: Basic Books.

Bailey, Darlyne, and Kelly M. Koney. 1996. "Interorganizational Community-Based Collaboratives: A Strategic Response to the Social Work Agenda." *Social Work* 41: 602–11.

Bardach, Eugene. 1998. *Getting Agencies to Work Together.* Washington, DC: Brookings Institution.

Bennis, Warren, and Patricia Biederman. 1997. *Organizing Genius: The Secrets of Creative Collaboration.* Reading, MA: Addison-Wesley.

Browning, Larry D.; Janice M. Beyer; and Judy C. Shetler. 1995. "Building Cooperation in a Competitive Industry: Sematech and the Semiconductor Industry." *Academy of Management Journal* 38: 113–51.

Bryson, John, and Barbara Crosby. 1992. *Leadership for the Common Good.* San Francisco: Jossey-Bass.

Cameron, Kim S., and Robert E. Quinn. 1988. "Organizational Paradox and Transformation." In *Paradox and Transformation: Toward a Theory of Change in Organization and Management,* ed. Robert E. Quinn and Kim S. Cameron, 1–18. Cambridge, MA: Ballinger.

Cleveland, Harlan. 2002. *Nobody in Charge: Essays on the Future of Leadership.* San Francisco: Jossey-Bass.

Connelly, David R. 2005. "Leadership in the Collaborative Interorganizational Domain: A Qualitative Analysis of Three Intergovernmental Initiatives." Ph.D. diss. State University of New York at Albany.

Crosby, Barbara C., and John M. Bryson. 2005. "A Leadership Framework for Cross-Sector Collaboration." *Public Management Review* 7: 177–201.

Daft, Richard, and Arie Lewin. 1993. "Where Are the Theories for the 'New' Organizational Forms? An Editorial Essay." *Organization Science* 4: i–vi.

Faerman, Sue R.; David P. McCaffrey; and David M. Van Slyke. 2001. "Understanding Interorganizational Cooperation: Public-Private Collaboration in Regulating Financial Market Regulation." *Organization Science* 12: 372–88.

Fletcher, Joyce K., and Katrin Kaüfer. 2003. "Shared Leadership: Paradox and Possibility." In *Shared Leadership: Reframing the Hows and Whys of Leadership,* ed. Craig L. Pearce and Jay A. Conger, 21–47. Thousand Oaks, CA: Sage.

Giddens, Anthony. 1984. *The Constitution of Society.* Princeton, NJ: Princeton University Press.

Gray, Barbara. 1989. *Collaborating: Finding Common Ground for Multiparty Problems.* San Francisco: Jossey-Bass.

———. 1996. "Cross-Sectoral Partners: Collaborative Alliances among Business, Government and Communities." In *Creating Collaborative Advantage,* ed. Chris Huxham, 57–79. Thousand Oaks, CA: Sage.

Gray, Barbara, and Donna Wood. 1991. "Collaborative Alliances: Moving from Practice to Theory." *Journal of Applied Behavioral Science* 27: 3–22.

Gulati, Ranjay. 1995. "Does Familiarity Breed Trust? The Implications of Repeated Ties for Contractual Choices in Alliances." *Academy of Management Journal* 38: 85–112.

Gulati, Ranjay, and Harbir Singh. 1999. "The Architecture of Cooperation: Managing Coordination Costs and Appropriation Concerns in Strategic Alliances." *Administrative Science Quarterly* 43: 781–814.

Handy, Charles. 1994. *The Age of Paradox.* Boston: Harvard Business School Press.

Heide, Jan, and Anne Miner. 1992. "The Shadow of the Future: Effects of Anticipated Interaction and Frequency of Contact on Buyer-Seller Cooperation." *Academy of Management Journal* 35: 265–91.

Huxham, Chris. 1996. *Creating Collaborative Advantage.* Thousand Oaks, CA: Sage.

Huxham, Chris, and Nic Beech. 2003. "Contrary Prescriptions: Recognizing Good Practice Tensions in Management." *Organization Studies* 24: 69–93.

Janis, Irving. 1972. *Victims of Groupthink.* Boston: Houghton Mifflin.

Kets de Vries, Manfred F.R. 1999. "High-Performance Teams: Lessons from the Pygmies." *Organizational Dynamics* 27, no. 3: 66–77.

Kumar, Rajesh, and Kofi O. Nti. 1998. "Differential Learning and Interaction in Alliance Dynamics: A Process and Outcome Discrepancy Model." *Organization Science* 9: 356–67.

Larsson, Rikard; Lars Bengtsson; Kristina Henriksson; and Judith Sparks. 1998. "The Interorganizational Learning Dilemma: Collective Knowledge Development in Strategic Alliances." *Organization Science* 9: 285–305.

Lewis, Marianne W. 2000. "Exploring Paradox: Toward a More Comprehensive Guide." *Academy of Management Review* 25: 760–76.

Linden, Russell M. 2002. *Working across Boundaries: Making Collaboration Work in Government and Nonprofit Organizations.* San Francisco: Jossey-Bass.

Mareschal, Patricia. 2003. "Solving Problems and Transforming Relationships: The Bifocal Approach to Mediation." *American Review of Public Administration* 33: 423–48.

McAllister, Daniel J. 1995. "Affect- and Cognition-Based Trust as Foundations for Interpersonal Cooperation in Organizations." *Academy of Management Journal* 38, no. 1: 24–59.

McCaffrey, David. P.; Sue R. Faerman; and David W. Hart. 1995. "The Appeal and Difficulties of Participative Systems." *Organization Science* 6: 603–27.

Milward, Brinton H., and Keith G. Provan. 2006. *A Manager's Guide to Choosing and Using Collaborative Networks.* Washington, DC: IBM Center for the Business of Government.

Mizrahi, Terry, and Beth B. Rosenthal. 2001. "Complexities of Coalition Building: Leaders' Successes, Strategies, Struggles, and Solutions." *Social Work* 46: 63–78.

Nathan, Richard P. 1996. "The "Devolution Revolution": An Overview." In *Rockefeller Institute Bulletin: Symposium on Federalism,* 5–13. Albany: Nelson A. Rockefeller Institute of Government, State University of New York.

Ospina, Sonia, and Angel Saz-Carranza. 2005. "Paradox and Collaboration in Coalition Work." Paper presented at the annual meeting of the Academy of Management, Honolulu, HI (August 8–10, 2005).

Ostrom, Elinor. 1990. *Governing the Commons: The Evolution of Institutions for Collective Action.* Cambridge: Cambridge University Press.

———. 1998. "A Behavioral Approach to the Rational Choice Theory of Collective Action." *American Political Science Review* 92: 1–22.

Parkhe, Arvind. 1993. "Strategic Alliance Structuring: A Game Theoretic and Transaction Cost Examination of Interfirm Cooperation." *Academy of Management Journal* 36: 794–829.

Pitcher, Patricia, and Anne D. Smith. 2001. "Top Management Team Heterogeneity: Personality, Power and Proxies." *Organization Science* 12: 1–18.

Powell, Walter W.; Kenneth W. Koput; and Laurel Smith-Doerr. 1996. "Interorganizational Collaboration and the Locus of Innovation: Networks of Learning in Biotechnology." *Administrative Science Quarterly* 41: 116–45.

Price Waterhouse Change Integration Team. 1996. *The Paradox Principles: How High-Performance Companies Manage Chaos, Complexity, and Contradiction to Achieve Superior Results.* Chicago: Irwin Professional Publishing.

Ring, Peter, and Andrew Van de Ven. 1994. "Developmental Processes of Cooperative Interorganizational Relationships." *Academy of Management Review* 19: 90–118.

Senge, Peter M. 2006. *The Fifth Discipline: The Art and Practice of the Learning Organization* (rev'd). New York: Doubleday Currency.

Slater, Lorraine. 2005. "Leadership for Collaboration: An Affective Process." *International Journal of Leadership in Education* 8: 321–33.

Thomas, Kenneth W. 1976. "Conflict and Conflict Management." In *Handbook of Industrial and Organizational Psychology,* ed. Marvin D. Dunnette, 889–935. Chicago: Rand McNally.

———. 1977. "Toward Multidimensional Values in Teaching: The Example of Conflict Management." *Academy of Management Review* 2: 484–90.

Vangen, Siv, and Chris Huxham. 2003. "Enacting Leadership for Collaborative Advantage: Dilemmas of Ideology and Pragmatism in the Activities of Partnership Managers." *British Journal of Management* 14: S61–S76.

Weber, Edward P. 1998. *Pluralism by the Rules: Conflict and Cooperation in Environmental Regulation.* Washington, DC: Georgetown University Press.

Wenger, Etienne; Richard A. McDermott; and William M. Snyder. 2002. *Cultivating Communities of Practice: A Guide to Managing Knowledge.* Boston: Harvard Business School Press.

Westley, F., and H. Vredenburg. 1997. "Interorganizational Collaboration and the Preservation of Global Biodiversity." *Organization Science* 8: 381–403.

Williamson, Oliver. 1996. *The Mechanisms of Governance.* New York: Oxford University Press.

Zaheer, Akbar; Bill McEvily; and Vincenzo Perrone. 1998. "Does Trust Matter? Exploring the Effects of Interorganizational and Interpersonal Trust on Performance." *Organization Science* 9, no. 2: 141–59.

Zhang, Jing. 2003. "Cross-Boundary Knowledge Sharing: A Case Study of Building the Multi-Purpose Access for Customer Relations and Operational Support." Ph.D. diss. State University of New York at Albany.

Zucker, Lynne G. 1986. "Production of Trust: Institutional Sources of Economic Structure, 1840–1920." *Research in Organizational Behavior* 8: 53–111.

CHAPTER 3

Intersectoral Collaboration and the Motivation to Collaborate
Toward an Integrated Theory

BETH GAZLEY

In order to understand the increasingly complex nature of public service delivery at the local level, many scholars have recognized the value in employing inclusive theoretical frameworks. Such frameworks "allow us to develop insights [about organizational relationships] at different layers of visibility and interpretability" (Daellenbach, Davies, and Ashill 2006, 74). Thus, we have seen virtually every aspect of social science theory brought to bear on key public management questions such as the rationale behind privatization efforts, the management of interorganizational networks, and the nature of effective leadership.

Not all theoretical frameworks comfortably coexist, and some by nature or design contrast with others. Nonetheless, in the study of intersectoral dynamics, particularly the scope of government–nonprofit relations, we tend to see among scholars an increasing receptivity to a more integrated framework, and often a greater effort at incorporating multiple units of analysis in their empirical work (Agranoff and McGuire 2003; Berry et al. 2004; Brown, Potoski, and Van Slyke 2006; DeHoog 1984; Guo and Acar 2005; Rethemeyer and Hatmaker 2006; Smith and Grønbjerg 2006; Thomson and Perry 2006; Van Slyke 2007; Vigoda-Gadot 2003).

In my contribution to this volume on "big ideas" in collaborative public management, I suggest that this larger interdisciplinary framework can help to explain an important question for local government service delivery: How can public managers foster partnerships with nonprofit organizations? This is not a simple question, as the decision on whether or not to commit organizational time and resources to pursuing joint action with private nonprofit agencies can rest on a number of factors, both within and without the control of the public manager. Figure 3.1 illustrates the potential variety in the source and nature of these influential factors. The circumstances of each

Figure 3.1 **Influences on Collaborative Tendencies**

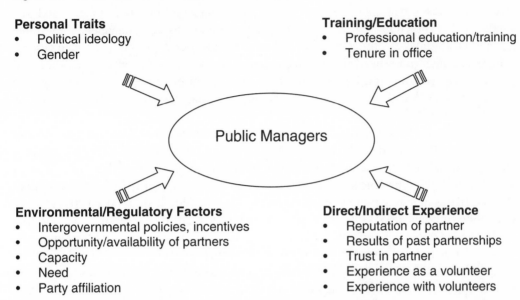

Personal Traits
- Political ideology
- Gender

Training/Education
- Professional education/training
- Tenure in office

Public Managers

Environmental/Regulatory Factors
- Intergovernmental policies, incentives
- Opportunity/availability of partners
- Capacity
- Need
- Party affiliation

Direct/Indirect Experience
- Reputation of partner
- Results of past partnerships
- Trust in partner
- Experience as a volunteer
- Experience with volunteers

particular partnership opportunity will dictate the degree to which each of these four areas of influence—personal traits, training and education, environmental or regulatory factors, and experience—determine choices and outcomes. However, there will be no disagreement on the point that the nature and quality of each partnership, and possibly the outcomes as well, will be determined by a combination of personal, institutional, and environmental factors. For example, while a public manager may be compelled to collaborate through legislative mandate, the quality of that partnership is likely to be determined by more than the scope of the statute: The manager's level of bureaucratic discretion, institutional capacities, the nature of the joint effort, and past institutional relationships with a potential partner will all contribute as well. In addition, training, political ideology, recognition of institutional norms, or a response to other intergovernmental incentives or constraints will also determine the extent to which a manager supports or resists these potential joint efforts. A nonprofit manager also brings a closely related set of experiences, incentives, and constraints to bear on collaborative or partnership decisions.

Collaborative and partnership activity can also be limited in numerous ways, such as by limitations on the mutuality of goals and aims, by restraints on budget or staff time, or by the unwillingness of potential partners to share resources and information. Public policymakers and private donors frequently encourage organizations to collaborate for normative reasons or under an expectation that cooperative activity will achieve economic efficiencies. However, those who have experience with collaboration quickly come to realize that a successful outcome requires more than statutory authority and depends on more than passive compliance.

The recent research of Kumar, Kant, and Amburgey (2007) offers an example of how to incorporate the motivational characteristics of public managers in a multidimensional way similar to that shown in Figure 3.1. In their study of Indian forest managers, they frame managerial attitudes as a function of socialization factors, personality traits, organizational culture and other job-related factors, and external environmental events such as political pressure. Their distinction between the first and second of these dimensions suggests the need to understand endogenous and exogenous influences on the public manager as separate elements.

These various internal and external influences on collaborative behavior demonstrate that research frameworks addressing how and where collaborative activity originates are likely to work best when they incorporate more than one perspective, unit, or level of analysis. Although some scholars have pointed out the danger in ignoring individual characteristics in public management research, this literature is thin (Allen 2001; Crawford 1999; Kelman 2005; O'Toole 1989). Most empirical efforts addressing collaborative public management to date have focused on institutional and network levels of analysis. Table 3.1 illustrates the potential ways in which other levels of analysis, including the perspectives and behaviors of individuals, groups, or networks, communities, and even sectors can provide a richer understanding of internal and external influences on behavior related to collaborative activity. As this table illustrates, the theoretical frameworks that can help to explain collaborative behavior are at least as broad as the field of public management.

The opportunities offered by a broader conceptual framework for understanding collaborative behavior in intersectoral settings require similarly comprehensive empirical and conceptual approaches. The goal of this chapter is not to offer a meta-theory of government–nonprofit collaboration, although this may be achievable once we have accumulated a greater body of research. Rather, I outline a research path that can guide us toward a fuller and more comprehensive understanding of collaborative behavior in the public management setting, drawing on a broader range of the theoretical tools at our disposal. I believe there are opportunities both for multidisciplinary and interdisciplinary approaches to this question: Some of the key theoretical fields, including collaborative theory, are interdisciplinary by nature.

This chapter begins by briefly summarizing the ways in which collaboration has been defined and measured. I then use the framework offered by Table 3.1 to describe the status of current scholarly efforts to explain collaborative activity at the sectoral level, group level, and individual level. Where possible, I offer additional research questions that can help to build an emerging field loosely defined at present as "collaborative theory."

The reader should also note that this chapter limits itself to a discussion of relationships between governments and nonprofit organizations, especially at the local levels of government, rather than government–business partnerships. This focus allows an exploration of issues related to the nonprofit sector in the context of managerial discretion at the local level. It is not intended to address all possible forms of government–private sector partnership.

Table 3.1

An Integrated Framework of Explanations for the Motivation to Collaborate

	Unit of analysis	Theoretical/experiential framework	Potential variables and the hypothesized influence of these related characteristics on receptivity to intersectoral collaboration	
Sectoral-level approaches	Sector	Agency theory Public choice/political theories Classical economics	Formal/informal structures Political constraints/incentives Independence of sectors	↔→ ↔←→ →
Group-level approaches	Group/social network/ partnership	Isomorphism Social network, relational and trust theories; group theory	Professional experience Professional training/education Volunteerism Collaborative experience	←← ←← ↔→
	Institution/community	Resource dependence Transaction costs Institutional theories Life cycle	Size/capacity Poverty or rural rate Amount of shared funding Efficiency incentives Environmental uncertainty Regulatory constraints/incentives Organizational age	←←←←←← ↔→ ↔→
	Service sector/policy network	Policy networks	Differences in constraints, incentives, norms, and patterns of behavior according to network or service sector	↔→
Individual-level approaches	Individual	Gender theory Political orientation Game theory; cognitive theories	Female Ideology Advantage/disadvantage	←→ ↔→ ←→

THE SCOPE AND MEANING OF
GOVERNMENT–NONPROFIT COLLABORATION

Collaboration describes a set of evolving relationships between stakeholders (organizations or individuals) who share some mutual goal (Bardach 1998; Gazley 2008; Gray 1989; Thomson and Perry 2006). Some consider shared risk and resources to be optional partnership ingredients; others view them as essential (Fosler 2002; Peters 1998). In the practical context of local government management and public service provision, collaboration involves active, formal or informal partnerships and exchanges of resources between service providers to implement a policy, jointly recruit or manage staff and clients, or jointly plan and deliver services (Gazley and Brudney 2007).

Huxham (1996) and Hall and others (1977) address some of the nuances in the definition of this term. These authors note, in particular, the need to distinguish between "voluntary" and "mandated" collaborative relationships. Many public–private partnerships occur through mandated relationships involving the implementation of public laws, regulations, and financial programs. Examples include juvenile justice programs, welfare to work and other poverty reduction programs, economic development initiatives, and so on (Hall et al. 1977). Gazley and Brudney (2007) observe that fewer than one-quarter of local government partnerships with nonprofit organizations in the state of Georgia are legally mandated, and fewer than half involve public funding. Nevertheless, enough information has been accumulated about mandated partnerships to suggest that they behave differently and require separate study.

Since much of the research on collaboration has associations either with network or privatization research, it is also important to emphasize that collaboration between the sectors is neither driven nor defined by networks or purchase-of-service contracts. Collaborative activity is, in fact, broader than either of these phenomena since some collaborative partnerships are dyadic and much collaboration occurs informally. In addition, although we owe a great deal of the literature on public sector collaboration to network theorists, public managers collaborate both within and outside of networks. Intersectoral collaboration is best viewed as an area of government interaction with the private sector that overlaps with relationships that occur within policy networks and those dependent on contracts and formal agreements. These relationships can involve a broad and sometimes informal exchange of resources, including staff, information, grants, equipment, skills, and expertise (Gazley 2008).

Collaboration both within the public sector and between sectors is often thought to exist on a continuum alongside similar kinds of relationships (e.g., mergers, alliances, cooperation, cooptation, contracting, and competition) (Becker 2001; Coston 1998; Grønbjerg 1993; Najam 2000; Thomson and Perry 2006). Although there is little consistency in the scholarship as to the qualities that distinguish these various relationships from one another, there is general agreement that collaboration has a contingent and multidimensional nature based on the mutuality of goals, the level of resources, its political and administrative leadership, and various other internal and external qualities.

Very little data have been collected that describe the actual scope or extent of intersectoral collaboration at the local government level. In large part, this gap is due to the wide variation in the modes and level of skill with which collaboration has been defined and empirically measured. Many scholars have looked at collaboration through studies of networks, contracts, and privatization activities. Because they are measuring many kinds of relationships, the resulting datasets are difficult to compare with one another to form a coherent picture of intersectoral collaboration. Only recently have scholars tackled the widespread use of informal, noncontractual relationships to understand the nature of collaborative activity that does not depend on formal agreements or policy directives (Gazley 2008; Grønbjerg and Child 2004).

AN INTEGRATED FRAMEWORK FOR EXAMINING THE MOTIVATION TO COLLABORATE

The remainder of this chapter explores the ways in which the motivation to collaborate can be understood. Rationales for joint action have often been generated from economic and institutional theories of resource dependence, exchange, and transaction cost economics. In past empirical studies, often in combination with political theories, these frameworks have performed well in explaining how internal and external factors combine to influence collaborative decisions, and how these decisions are often motivated by a desire to increase resources or reduce financial or political uncertainties (Grønbjerg 1993, 2006; Pfeffer and Salancik 1978; Saidel 1994; Williamson 1985, 1996; Williamson and Masten 1995). Efforts have also been made to combine these economic theories with theories of human behavior, including those that define social networks. These theories offer a role for an individual level of behavior and new levels of analysis that explain "the . . . social mechanisms that allow network governance to emerge and thrive" (Jones, Hesterly, and Borgatti 1997, 923). In such frameworks, the public manager and his attitudes about collaboration become a new and important unit of analysis. Figure 3.2 illustrates the potential way in which theories from a number of disciplines might combine to explain collaborative motivations from both a human and an organizational or policy perspective.

The overarching premise here is that partnerships are supported or thwarted by a combination of individual, institutional, and other factors. And while each of the four major disciplinary fields (economics, organizational behavior, political science and policy studies, and sociology and human behavior) described in Figure 3.2 will help to explain the nature and quality of these relationships, the most comprehensive understanding of these partnerships, of how and why they form, and how they are structured or controlled, will emerge from cross-disciplinary approaches using integrated or multiple theoretical frameworks. The current state of some of these literatures and some suggested areas for future inquiry are described in the remainder of this chapter. Using the framework described in Table 3.1, I note in particular the distinction between theories that address sectoral characteristics, those that address group-level (e.g., institutional- or jurisdictional-level) characteristics, and those that focus on the individual manager. The hypothesized influence of these related characteristics on receptivity to intersectoral collaboration is discussed, and where research is scarce, I suggest additional avenues of exploration.

Figure 3.2   **Theoretical Frameworks Addressing Public–Private Collaboration**

Economics
- Agency theory
- Incomplete contracts
- Relational contracting
- Transaction costs

Organizational Behavior
- Institutional and neoinstitutional
- New governance
- Privatization, public management
- Resource dependence
- Organizational life cycles

Collaboration and
Public–Private
Partnership Research

Political Science and Policy Studies
- Pluralism, interest group politics
- Public choice theory
- Policy networks

Sociology and Human Behavior
- Social networks
- Game theory
- Gender theory

The Motivation to Collaborate at the Sectoral Level

When public and nonprofit managers collaborate to address mutual goals, do they work under the same or under different motives and incentives? This question is worth asking, since theories of collaboration have been built largely on single-field studies. As a result, they have rarely tested their propositions on institutions or actors from other sectors, whether public, commercial, or nonprofit. This section of the chapter is largely speculative, and many more comparative and cross-sectoral studies are needed to point out the most useful directions for further research. I offer three propositions as starting points.

New Governance and Collaboration

When we examine the evolving nature of governmental institutions and policies, collaboration between the sectors can be viewed as a product of the blurring of the sectors. Many trends account for the increased interest in collaboration within the public sector as it embraces New Governance and New Public Management models of public service delivery. As governments outsource their services, it could become easier to collaborate because public and nonprofit institutions are already accustomed to working together. The "hollow state" often becomes the "collaborative state," albeit with the same concerns about capacity and control (Agranoff 2005; Milward and Provan 2000).

As social problems outstrip the ability of public agencies to respond, it also becomes more necessary to collaborate. Virtually no contemporary "wicked problem" has been addressed without reference to intersectoral collaboration, including homeland security, avian flu, and emergency planning (McGuire 2006; Rittel and Webber 1973). One recent outcome of this trend is an increased interest in "collaborative performance" as a distinct area of study alongside network performance (Agranoff 2005, 18). To demonstrate how collaborative performance management can be measured, Comfort (2006) has mapped the joint efforts organized around Gulf Coast hurricane relief to understand how well public and private activities were jointly coordinated. Others observe that since public agencies can be required to collaborate by statute or under unofficial pressure from elected officials, the performance of "mandated" (and potentially unfunded) collaboration may be different than that of "voluntary" collaboration (Huxham and Vangen 2005).

Internally, many public agencies have embraced new models of organizational development (OD) or models of participatory governance that emphasize the benefits of collaboration (Rainey 1997). Legislative mandates and incentives often support these OD efforts, and directly or indirectly build the public sector's capacity to collaborate with the private sector. Nonetheless, the research efforts that can explain intersectoral collaboration as an intergovernmental phenomenon are fairly new. We must continue the exploration of how federal and state-level mandates and incentives influence the nature and outcomes of local collaborations and government–nonprofit partnerships both within and outside the contracting arena (Agranoff and McGuire 2003; Choi et al. 2005).

Resource Dependence and Collaboration

There is a particularly strong potential for resource-related matters to dominate partnership decisions. As a theory of organizational behavior, resource dependence has consistently demonstrated its value. However, we still need to develop our understanding of how sectoral status will influence resource-based decisions. A good working hypothesis is that the motivation to partner will be driven by a desire to secure whatever resources are most scarce for the respective sector, but that the goals of one sector are not necessarily the same as those of the other. Gazley and Brudney (2007) find support for this hypothesis when they discover that nonprofit managers are motivated by financial resources to a much greater extent than public managers, who in turn are more interested in accessing private sector skills and expertise.

Further, an assumption is often made that collaboration between the sectors generates positive outcomes for all partners. A body of comparative research is only just emerging, but suggests that this is not necessarily so. Rather than a "win-win" proposition, intersectoral collaboration appears to elicit greater satisfaction from public managers than from private sector managers (Gazley and Brudney 2007; Vigoda-Gadot 2003). The potential for a power imbalance between government–nonprofit partners is a recurring theme in the literature, but tends to be addressed largely as a problem for conflict resolution (Bryson, Crosby, and Stone 2006; Huxham and Vangen 2005). Further, although resource-related issues are explored quite often, the impact that other kinds of power imbalances might have on collaborative outcomes is still largely untested empirically (for exceptions, see Casciaro and Piskorski [2005] and Hall et al. [1977]).

Public Accountability and Collaboration

For public managers, any discussion of intersectoral collaboration will be particularly concerned with how joint activities might support or undermine perceptions of public accountability. Two opposing perspectives are found in the literature. The traditional perspective argues that public services are more difficult to supervise when they are indirectly provided and, therefore, undermine public accountability (Kettl 1988). A counterposing argument suggests that intersectoral alliances can actually promote greater public accountability, which is achieved by the potentially greater ability of government agencies involved in strategic alliances to meet goals and public expectations for results (Linden 2002). Gazley (2008) observes that the trade-off that is assumed to occur between level of collaboration and the amount of governmental control over a partnership may actually happen infrequently if funding and decision-making authority still rest in the hands of public managers. New research should continue to move beyond purchase-of-service agreements to explore other means by which public managers manage accountability expectations (e.g., norms, relationships, and reputational information) and should attempt to understand the circumstances under which managerial discretion helps or hinders effective partnerships.

The Motivation to Collaborate at the Organizational Level

The literature is replete with "factors that compel and factors that restrain the impetus to cooperate" (Gazley and Brudney 2007, 392). The potential gains of intersectoral collaboration include economy efficiencies, more effective responses to shared problems and public needs, improvements in both the quality and scope of public or private services, risk diffusion, and increased access to funding or other resources, including volunteers and equipment. Collaboration can be fostered by closely aligned missions, and may offer individual agencies increased institutional legitimacy, financial stability, and opportunities for organizational learning (Bamford, Gomes-Casseres, and Robinson 2003; Bardach 1998; Connor, Taras-Kadel, and Vinokur-Kaplan 1999; Foster and Meinhard 2002; Gazley and Brudney 2007; Gray 1989; Grønbjerg 1993, 2006; Huxham 1996; Linden 2002; Mattessich and Monsey 1992; Mulroy and Shay 1997; Oliver 1990; Provan and Milward 1995; Rapp and Whitfield 1999; Snavely and Tracy 2000).

Much of the literature on interorganizational collaboration tends to be oriented toward its potential benefits for participants and to overlook the problems that may arise. In a scan of the public and nonprofit literature, Gazley and Brudney (2007) cite a variety of sources to note the danger in such a normative approach (Ferris 1993; Gray 2003; Grønbjerg 1993; Huxham 1996; Shaw 2003). They observe that possible drawbacks of joint efforts include the potential for "mission drift, loss of institutional autonomy or public accountability, cooptation of actors, greater financial instability, greater difficulty in evaluating results, and the expenditure of considerable institutional time and resources in supporting collaborative activities" (392).

Organizational Capacity to Collaborate

It is almost too self-evident to observe that partnerships take time and resources to manage. What we still need to understand is the extent to which a manager's attitudes about the potential value of collaborative activity are influenced by his assessment of how actively and effectively his institution can participate. We also do not yet understand the forms of exchange within these partnerships—although network scholars are making progress—so that we can assess which resources are most useful in supporting partnerships.

Capacity is defined here as the ability of an institution to secure the human, technological, political, or other necessary resources that allow it to participate in collaborative activities. Capacity has both internal and external dimensions. Capacity is often associated with organizational size or fiscal health, but other capacity-related elements might also apply, such as organizational age or access to larger resource networks. Nonprofit scholars speculate that larger organizations will be more receptive to collaborative opportunities because they have a greater capacity to take advantage of them, but the empirical evidence is mixed (Mulford and Mulford 1977). With local governments, Greene (2002) and O'Toole and Meier (2004) have found that fiscally stronger communities or institutions engage in more privatization activities. Such findings are consistent with the more general arguments in the public management literature regarding the importance of strong managerial capacity when implementing indirect government (Kettl 1988; Rainey 1997).

A moderate association has been found between nonprofit size, technological resources, and the number of affiliations and partnerships (both public and private) (Grønbjerg and Child 2004). Little or no association has been found between organizational age and either collaborative frequency or collaborative motivation (Foster and Meinhard 2002; Grønbjerg and Child 2004). The limited collaborative activity of smaller organizations is not well understood but could result from weaker perceptions of need or the lack of a developed network—that is, capacity considerations of a different kind (Foster and Meinhard 2002).

Gazley and Brudney (2007) find that a manager's previous collaborative experience may increase partnership activity but only slightly reduce his concern about having the capacity to partner with the other sector. Such findings suggest that public managers who are already engaged in partnerships may still find the collaborative experience difficult to manage alongside other organizational priorities. A useful area of future research would be to investigate the specific kinds of resources that public or nonprofit managers find most helpful in managing collaborative relationships. For example, while information is touted in the practitioner literature as one of the most valuable commodities of partnership activity, it would be useful to understand how nonprofit and public managers might rank information alongside other tangible benefits of collaboration.

The Motivation to Collaborate at the Individual Level

Shared Experience and Relationships

Many scholars have noted the extraordinary amount of career interpenetration between the government and nonprofit sectors and the "increasing seamlessness" of the professions (Doig and Hargrove 1990; Hall 1987; Light 1999; Saidel 1989, 340). Brewer (2003) also finds a high level of civic engagement among public managers. A public manager's previous work or volunteer experience with a nonprofit organization—in addition to direct collaborative experience—can build familiarity with the nonprofit sector. The quality of the experience is likely to contribute to a city's or county's pursuit of other nonprofit alliances. Similarly, a nonprofit executive's attitudes are likely to be shaped by his familiarity with government functions and the nature of past encounters.

Trust often becomes the most valuable ingredient generated by these shared experiences and professional norms. Trust is a slippery notion to build into research models, but scholars are making the attempt nonetheless, in areas as far-flung as social network analysis, game theory, and contract theory. Agranoff and McGuire (2003) and McGuire (2006) write about the value of trust-based relationships in collaborative public management, while in the contracting arena, trust built on previous relationships is thought to encourage new alliances and improve outcomes (Brown, Potoski, and Van Slyke 2006; Williamson 1985). Yang (2006) also finds associations between a public administrator's trust in citizens and other characteristics such as gender; this research might also be useful to collaborative theory if focused more directly on trust-related characteristics in public–private partnerships. Kumar, Kant, and Amburgey's (2007) study of community-based forestry management in India is also instructive: They find that a public manager reports less resistance toward these more inclusive, participatory approaches to local forest management following a successful collaborative experience with nongovernmental organizations.

Even when alliances exist, a public or nonprofit manager's level of trust in or familiarity with the other sector should not be assumed. A small study of active public–private partnerships in North Carolina found a deep lack of understanding between the sectors. The authors suggest that a relationship exists between an understanding of the other sector and a willingness to work with it (Altman-Sauer, Henderson, and Whitaker 2001). In related community-level research, studies that associate direct collaborative experience with a more favorable attitude toward collaboration find that the outcomes are contingent on factors and characteristics associated with each partnership (e.g., the level of shared purpose, presence/absence of political support, resources, leadership, and expertise) (Foster and Meinhard 2002; Gazley and Brudney 2007; Grønbjerg 2006). Similar conclusions have been made about networked forms of service delivery (Milward and Provan 1998). Such findings suggest caution in hypothesizing that experience builds receptivity toward collaboration given the complex dynamics of each partnership.

In addition to the research explored above, this chapter suggests some additional questions worth investigating. First, are public managers more resistant to collaborating when they, themselves, have no direct nonprofit volunteer or employment experience? And are nonprofit executives more resistant when they have no government employment experience? Finally, how do current or past collaborative experiences shape the attitudes of either public or nonprofit managers about the advantages and disadvantages of intersectoral collaboration?

We might also consider the influence on collaborative tendencies of less direct managerial characteristics: similarities in training and education. Some previous research has linked managerial forms of local government (e.g., council-manager and commission-manager forms) with greater contracting frequency (Brudney et al. 2005; Morgan, Hirlinger, and

England 1988). The connection is thought to depend on the kind of professionalization a public manager receives, with the assumption that professional education fosters shared norms, builds familiarity with other sectors, and encourages managers to adopt new ideas such as privatization (Saidel 1989). Other local research focused more directly on public contracts with nonprofit organizations has found no statistically significant connection between council-manager forms of government and the frequency of complete contracts (Brown and Potoski 2003).

The lack of consistent findings could result from variations in research models, but could also result from the inapplicability of an institutional framework for testing this question of training and education on managerial attitudes. Researchers might more successfully develop qualitative and mixed-methods studies that address directly the influence of training, education, and professionalism on collaborative attitudes and tendencies, using public managers rather than jurisdictions as the units of analysis (Kelman 2005). Scholars could also examine how a common education influences these attitudes, by linking research on academic programs to explore whether or how public affairs degree programs that graduate both nonprofit and public managers build collaborative tendencies.

Volunteer Involvement

Scholars have speculated that volunteers can offer a tool for bridging intersectoral differences, although volunteers themselves may not always benefit from closer government–nonprofit ties (DeLaat 1987; Lenkowsky 2003; Smith and Lipsky 1993). The potential association of volunteerism with intersectoral cooperation introduces an intriguing "chicken and egg" dimension to this area of scholarship. Namely, does a certain level of civic engagement in a community help to promote intersectoral relations, or are volunteers a product rather than a cause of collaboration? This question warrants greater scholarly attention because volunteers represent a potentially overlooked and undervalued resource for local governments. If volunteers help to foster intersectoral engagement, they represent an important ingredient in the mix of supportive relational networks commonly referred to as social capital.

The potential contribution of volunteers to intersectoral cooperation offers a counterposing argument to theories that the government–nonprofit relationship is fundamentally competitive because it offers a means of bridging the gap between sectors. Volunteers, as individuals who pass freely between the public and private sectors, are most likely to perceive commonalities of interest between sectors and thus to support intersector alliances. Volunteers bring information and help to spread common values and interests (Puffer and Meindl 1995). Volunteers may even enter their role with the explicit assignment to promote collaboration among service agencies, a common task assigned to AmeriCorps volunteers (Lenkowsky 2003). This argument suggests two things: first, that the lines between the public and private sectors may become softened when volunteers are involved, and second, that volunteers can serve less as a resource over which sectors must compete, and more as a means of decreasing intersector competition and building collaborative tendencies (DeLaat 1987).

Politics and Ideology

Previous studies have observed the importance of a favorable political or social climate in the community when intersectoral alliances are attempted (Mattessich and Monsey 1992). However, outside of the contracting literature, few studies address political factors that might influence the scope or nature of other, noncontractual kinds of government–nonprofit partnerships. And the privatization research itself does not consistently support a connection between political ideology and privatization frequency (Fernandez and Smith 2006). Controlled studies find no association between the frequency of state contracting and the ideology of state leadership, or the electorate's party preferences (Brudney et al. 2005; Warner and Hebdon 2001). The most likely explanation for these findings is that privatization decisions based solely on party politics are no longer easy to predict. Both liberals and conservatives have reasons to support privatization, especially when it is based on anticipated cost savings and other resource considerations. Privatization has become widespread enough to have lost much of its ideological association.

Notwithstanding the growth in these more pragmatic forms of privatization, there are still good reasons to continue research in this area. When we examine the wider range of potential partnerships beyond the purchase-of-service contract, we do not yet understand how politics will shape the decision to collaborate or not, especially on an informal level and without an external mandate. The question is this: When the choice is the manager's, to what extent are attitudes about working with the nonprofit sector shaped by ideological beliefs? The "free market" public official who views intersectoral alliances as inherently unnatural, and intersectoral competition as economically healthy, is likely to behave differently than his more pragmatic colleague, who might care less about intersectoral divisions if it means securing additional external resources to support public service delivery in his jurisdiction. One approach to identifying ideological distinctions in collaborative tendencies would be to gather and then tease out attitudinal data, to compare the more or less ideological rationales for partnering (Fernandez and Smith 2006).

Gender

While it has long been established that women can bring a different set of interpersonal skills to group dynamics than men, the impact this difference has on interorganizational or intersectoral dynamics is not at all clear. Surprisingly, very little gender-related research has occurred in either the public or nonprofit sectors that attempts to link gender to organizational outcomes with a high degree of methodological rigor. Fernandez and Smith (2006) find no association between gender and attitudes about privatization among public employees, but Wilkins (2007) has observed a relationship between gender and attitudes about casework, and both Pratchett and Wingfield (1996) and Fox and Schuhmann (1999) have identified differences in attitudes about public service motivations that may be based on gender. In the nonprofit sector, Goldman and Kahnweiler (2000) found that men were more likely than women to fit a collaborator "profile," but were hesitant to generalize given the potential for sampling bias (i.e., their subjects might not fit traditional role models).

Foster and Meinhard (2002) have found that Canadian feminist organizations are less likely to have a competitive outlook regarding collaboration and more likely to collaborate with other nonprofits. However, their study did not capture the gender of the respondent directly or test the same association on government–nonprofit partnerships.

Scholars who wish to investigate the association between gender and collaborative tendencies might consider several questions, including how the gender of public and nonprofit executives influences both their rate of entry into partnerships and the attitudes about the advantages or disadvantages of collaboration that precede or follow these joint efforts. However, any attempts to perform research in this area must be well informed by theories of diversity and representative bureaucracy. In particular, scholars observe that attempts to find direct associations between many kinds of demographic characteristics and organizational outcomes are unlikely to bear fruit without consideration of the institutional and social contexts in which managerial decisions are made (Keiser et al. 2002; Pitts 2006; Saidel and Loscocco 2005; Selden 1997; Wise and Tschirhart 2000).

CONCLUSION

In studies of public sector contracting and outsourcing, economists tend to describe the "make or buy" decision in terms of a set of organizational and environmental character-istics that influence managerial choices. This perspective emphasizes the role that public managers play as individual decision makers in privatization activities (Van Slyke and Hammonds 2003). From a much broader outlook, this chapter asks a simple question: What causes a public manager to "make or buy" when it comes to his or her participation in a wide array of intersectoral opportunities, particularly collaborative opportunities? And how do we frame such human attitudes and behaviors within the larger context of inter-organizational and intersectoral behavior? While this chapter has emphasized the human element in collaborative behavior, we should not lose sight of the fact that "collaboration is not an end in itself" (McGuire 2006, 40). Ultimately, our goal becomes an understand-ing of how collaborative behavior achieves better organizational performance and public policy outcomes.

To help answer such questions, this framework offers a role for traditional economic, political, organizational, and institutional theories of management, but also calls on schol-ars to pay greater attention to theories that can explain how personality and experience will influence the actions of public managers, and how sectoral status will influence these behaviors. This chapter also suggests that the unique circumstances of public governance will influence collaborative motivations, particularly with regard to the specific account-ability goals of the public sector. As a result, theoretical frameworks drawn from the private sector and management sciences must be adjusted to accommodate the context of intersectoral collaboration.

In exploring the research questions I have proposed in this chapter, some of the ap-proaches that might bear fruit are outside the traditional disciplinary constraints of public management; the most venturesome scholars will incorporate the realms of cognitive, behavioral, and social network theory. The disciplines of psychology and sociology are likely to offer very useful frameworks for explaining how managerial attitudes about collaboration are defined both by personality and by direct or indirect experience. Vigoda-Gadot (2003, 19) suggests that this larger theoretical framework could explain the "philosophy of collaboration" in terms of three constructs: how common political views and shared policy targets are created; how common social norms and views are developed; and how common managerial strategies and organizational views are encouraged. There is also a potential connection between research on leadership and research on collaborative behavior; I note, for example, the rise of new terms to describe managerial behavior in collaborative environments, such as Connelly's (2007, 1231) conceptual discussion of "collaborative leadership."

In a large sense, such an effort is a return to the roots of a large portion of public management theory, where administrative leadership, bureaucratic discretion, and the "human and social side of public organizations" have long been topics of interest (Bardach 1998; McGuire 2006; Vigoda-Gadot 2003, 9). Notwithstanding the long literature on administrative decision making, current scholars will still observe that a collaborative public manager is different from a responsive bureaucrat, since collaboration requires a different set (some would say a higher order) of skills and traits (Vigoda 2002). I suggest in this chapter that the spirit of collaboration is in large part rooted in the experiences of local government managers. These individuals are especially likely to recognize the value in citizen involvement. They are also likely to be accustomed to working side by side with their nonprofit counterparts (as contractors, consultants, volunteers), and to have experience serving together on boards. In these local partnerships, public managers could most readily recognize that "the critical element depend[s] more on having the right kinds of people involved . . . than relying on traditional policy management approaches [and] institutional arrangements" (Abramson, Breul, and Kamensky 2006, 24). The extent to which we can deepen our understanding of these effective qualities and learn how to capture them at more widespread levels of governance is likely to remain one of the most intriguing questions of this generation of scholarship.

REFERENCES

Abramson, Mark A.; Jonathan D. Breul; and John M. Kamensky. 2006. *Six Trends Transforming Government.* Washington, DC: IBM Center for the Business of Government.

Agranoff, Robert. 2005. "Managing Collaborative Performance." *Public Performance and Management Review* 29, no. 1: 18–45.

Agranoff, Robert, and Michael McGuire. 2003. *Collaborative Public Management: New Strategies for Local Governments.* Washington, DC: Georgetown University Press.

Allen, Chris. 2001. "'They Don't Just Live and Breathe the Policy Like We Do . . .': Policy Intentions and Practice Dilemmas in Modern Social Policy and Implementation Networks." *Policy Studies* 22, no. 3/4: 149–66.

Altman-Sauer, Lydian; Margaret Henderson; and Gordon P. Whitaker. 2001. "Strengthening Relationships between Local Governments and Nonprofits." *Popular Government* (Winter): 33–39.

Bamford, James D.; Benjamin Gomes-Casseres; and Michael S. Robinson. 2003. *Mastering Alliance Strategy: A Comprehensive Guide to Design, Management, and Organization.* 1st ed. San Francisco: Jossey-Bass.

Bardach, Eugene. 1998. *Getting Agencies to Work Together: The Practice and Theory of Managerial Craftsmanship.* Washington, DC: Brookings Institution Press.

Becker, Fred W. 2001. *Problems in Privatization Theory and Practice in State and Local Governments.* Lewiston, NY: Edward Mellen Press.

Berry, Frances S.; Ralph S. Brower; Sang Ok Choi; Wendy Zinfang Goa; HeeSoun Jang; Myungjung Kwon; and Jessica Word. 2004. "Three Traditions of Network Research: What the Public Management Research Agenda Can Learn from Other Research Communities." *Public Administration Review* 64, no. 5: 539–52.

Brewer, Gene A. 2003. "Building Social Capital: Civic Attitudes and Behavior of Public Servants." *Journal of Public Administration Research and Theory* 13, no. 1: 5–26.

Brown, Trevor L., and Matthew Potoski. 2003. "Transaction Costs and Institutional Explanations for Government Service Production Decisions." *Journal of Public Administration Research and Theory* 13, no. 4: 441–68.

Brown, Trevor L.; Matthew Potoski; and David M. Van Slyke. 2006. "Managing Public Service Contracts: Aligning Values, Institutions, and Markets." *Public Administration Review* 66, no. 3: 323–31.

Brudney, Jeffrey L.; Sergio Fernandez; Jae E. Ryu; and Deil S. Wright. 2005. "Exploring and Explaining Contracting Out: Patterns of Relationships among the American States." *Journal of Public Administration Research and Theory* 15, no. 3: 393–419.

Bryson, John M.; Barbara C. Crosby; and Melissa Middleton Stone. 2006. "The Design and Implementation of Cross-Sector Collaborations: Propositions from the Literature." *Public Administration Review* 66, no. 6 (Supplement): 44–55.

Casciaro, Tiziana, and Mikolaj Jan Piskorski. 2005. "Power Imbalance, Mutual Dependence, and Constraint Absorption: A Closer Look at Resource Dependence Theory." *Administrative Science Quarterly* 50: 167–99.

Choi, Yoo-Sung; Chung-Lae Cho; Deil S. Wright; and Jeffrey L. Brudney. 2005. "Dimensions of Contracting for Service Delivery by American State Administrative Agencies." *Public Performance and Management Review* 29, no. 1: 46–66.

Comfort, Louise. 2006. "The Dynamics of Policy Learning: Catastrophic Events in Real Time." Paper presented at the annual meeting of the National Association of Schools of Public Affairs and Administration, Minneapolis, MN, October 19–21.

Connelly, David R. 2007. "Leadership in the Collaborative Interorganizational Domain." *International Journal of Public Administration* 30: 1231–62.

Connor, Joseph A.; Stephanie Taras-Kadel; and Diane Vinokur-Kaplan. 1999. "The Role of Nonprofit Management Support Organizations in Sustaining Community Collaborations." *Nonprofit Management & Leadership* 10, no. 2: 127–36.

Coston, Jennifer M. 1998. "A Model and Typology of Government-NGO Relationships." *Nonprofit and Voluntary Sector Quarterly* 27, no. 3: 358–82.

Crawford, Adam. 1999. *The Local Governance of Crime: Appeals to Community and Partnerships.* Oxford: Oxford University Press.

Daellenbach, Kate; John Davies; and Nicholas J. Ashill. 2006. "Understanding Sponsorship and Sponsorship Relationships—Multiple Frames and Multiple Perspectives." *International Journal of Nonprofit and Voluntary Sector Marketing* 11 (February): 73–87.

DeHoog, Ruth H. 1984. *Contracting Out for Human Services: Economic, Political, and Organizational Perspectives.* Albany: State University of New York Press.

DeLaat, Jacqueline. 1987. "Volunteering as Linkage in the Three Sectors." In *Shifting the Debate: Public-Private Sector Relations in the Modern Welfare State,* ed. S. Ostrander and S. Langton, 97–111. New Brunswick, NJ: Transaction Books.

Doig, Jameson W., and Erwin C. Hargrove, eds. 1990. *Leadership and Innovation: Entrepreneurs in Government.* Abridged ed. Baltimore: Johns Hopkins University Press.

Fernandez, Sergio, and Craig C. Smith. 2006. "Looking for Evidence of Public Employee Opposition to Privatization: An Empirical Study with Implications for Practice." *Review of Public Personnel Administration* 26, no. 4: 356–81.

Ferris, James M. 1993. "The Double-Edged Sword of Social Service Contracting: Public Accountability Versus Nonprofit Autonomy." *Nonprofit Management & Leadership* 3, no. 4: 363–76.

Fosler, R. Scott. 2002. *Working Better Together: How Government, Business, and Nonprofit Organizations Can Achieve Public Purposes Through Cross-Sector Collaboration, Alliances, and Partnerships.* Washington, DC: Independent Sector.

Foster, Mary K., and Agnes G. Meinhard. 2002. "A Regression Model Explaining Predisposition to Collaborate." *Nonprofit and Voluntary Sector Quarterly* 31, no. 4: 549–64.

Fox, Richard L., and Robert A. Schuhmann. 1999. "Gender and Local Government: A Comparison of Women and Men City Managers." *Public Administration Review* 59, no. 3: 231–42.

Gazley, Beth. 2008. "Beyond the Contract: The Scope and Nature of Informal Government-Nonprofit Partnerships." *Public Administration Review* 68, no. 1: 141–54.

Gazley, Beth, and Jeffrey L. Brudney. 2007. "The Purpose (and Perils) of Government-Nonprofit Partnership." *Nonprofit and Voluntary Sector Quarterly* 36, no. 3: 389–415.

Goldman, Samuel M., and William N. Kahnweiler. 2000. "A Collaborator Profile for Executives of Nonprofit Organizations." *Nonprofit Management & Leadership* 10, no. 4: 435–50.

Gray, Andrew. 2003. *Collaboration in Public Services: The Challenge for Evaluation.* New Brunswick, NJ: Transaction.

Gray, Barbara. 1989. *Collaborating: Finding Common Ground for Multiparty Problems.* 1st ed. San Francisco: Jossey-Bass.

Greene, Jeffrey D. 2002. *Cities and Privatization: Prospects for the New Century.* Upper Saddle River, NJ: Prentice Hall.

Grønbjerg, Kirsten A. 1993. *Understanding Nonprofit Funding: Managing Revenues in Social Services and Community Development Organizations.* 1st ed. San Francisco: Jossey-Bass.

———. 2006. "Researching Collaborative Structures and Their Outcomes: Challenges of Measurement and Methodology." Paper presented at the annual meeting of the Academy of Management, Atlanta, GA, August 14–16.

Grønbjerg, Kirsten A., and Curtis Child. 2004. *Indiana Nonprofits: Affiliations, Collaborations and Competition. Report #5 in the Nonprofit Survey Series.* Bloomington: Indiana University.

Guo, Chao, and Muhittin Acar. 2005. "Understanding Collaboration among Nonprofit Organizations: Combining Resource Dependency, Institutional, and Network Perspectives." *Nonprofit and Voluntary Sector Quarterly* 34, no. 3: 340–61.

Hall, Peter Dobkin. 1987. "Abandoning the Rhetoric of Independence: Reflections on the Nonprofit Sector in the Post-Liberal Era." In *Shifting the Debate: Public/Private Sector Relations in the Modern Welfare State,* ed. S. Ostrander and S. Langton, 11–28. New Brunswick, NJ: Transaction Books.

Hall, Richard H.; John P. Clark; Peggy C. Giordano; Paul V. Johnson; and Martha Van Roekel. 1977. "Patterns of Interorganizational Relationships." *Administrative Science Quarterly* 22, no. 3: 457–74.

Huxham, Chris. 1996. "Collaboration and Collaborative Advantage." In *Creating Collaborative Advantage,* ed. Huxham, 1–18. Thousand Oaks, CA: Sage.

Huxham, Chris, and Siv Vangen. 2005. *Managing to Collaborate: The Theory and Practice of Collaborative Advantage.* New York: Routledge.

Jones, Candace; William S. Hesterly; and Stephen P. Borgatti. 1997. "A General Theory of Network Governance: Exchange Conditions and Social Mechanisms." *Academy of Management Review* 22, no. 4: 911–45.

Keiser, Lael R.; Vicky M. Wilkins; Kenneth J. Meier; and Catherine A. Holland. 2002. "Lipstick and Logarithms: Gender, Institutional Context, and Representative Bureaucracy." *American Political Science Review* 96, no. 3: 553–64.

Kelman, Steven. 2005. *Unleashing Change: A Study of Organizational Renewal in Government.* Washington, DC: Brookings Institution.

Kettl, Donald F. 1988. *Government by Proxy.* Washington, DC: CQ Press.

Kumar, Sushil; Shashi Kant; and Terry L. Amburgey. 2007. "Public Agencies and Collaborative Management Approaches: Examining Resistance among Administrative Professionals." *Administration & Society* 39, no. 5: 569–611.

Lenkowsky, Leslie. 2003. "Can Government Build Community? Lessons from the National Service Program." Paper presented at the symposium Gifts of Time to America's Communities. Syracuse University, Campbell Public Affairs Institute, Program in Nonprofit Studies, Syracuse, NY, October 24.

Light, Paul C. 1999. *The New Public Service.* Washington, DC: Brookings Institution Press.

Linden, Russell M. 2002. *Working Across Boundaries: Making Collaboration Work in Government and Nonprofit Organizations.* San Francisco: Jossey-Bass.

Mattessich, Paul, and Barbara Monsey. 1992. *Collaboration: What Makes It Work?* St. Paul, MN: Amherst H. Wilder Foundation.

McGuire, Michael. 2006. "Collaborative Public Management: Assessing What We Know and How We Know It." *Public Administration Review* 66, no. 6 (Supplement): 33–43.

Milward, H. Brinton, and Keith G. Provan. 2000. "Governing the Hollow State." *Journal of Public Administration Research and Theory* 10, no. 2: 359–79.

———. 1998. "Principles for Controlling Agents: The Political Economy of Network Structure." *Journal of Public Administration Research and Theory* 8, no. 2: 203–21.

Morgan, David R.; Michael W. Hirlinger; and Robert E. England. 1988. "The Decision to Contract Out City Services: A Further Explanation." *Western Political Quarterly* 41, no. 2: 363–72.

Mulford, Charles L., and Mary A. Mulford. 1977. "Community and Interorganizational Perspectives on Cooperation and Conflict." *Rural Sociology* 42, no. 4: 569–90.

Mulroy, Elizabeth A., and Sharon Shay. 1997. "Nonprofit Organizations and Innovation: A Model of Neighborhood-based Collaboration to Prevent Child Mistreatment." *Social Work* 42, no. 5: 515–25.

Najam, Adil. 2000. "The Four-C's of Third Sector-Government Relations: Cooperation, Confrontation, Complementarity, and Co-optation." *Nonprofit Management & Leadership* 10, no. 4: 375–96.

Oliver, Christine. 1990. "Determinants of Interorganizational Relationships: Integration and Future Directions." *Academy of Management Review* 15, no. 2: 241–65.

O'Toole, Laurence J., Jr. 1989. "Alternative Mechanisms for Multiorganizational Implementation: The Case of Wastewater Management." *Administration & Society* 21, no. 3: 313–39.

O'Toole, Laurence J., Jr., and Kenneth J. Meier. 2004. "Parkinson's Law and the New Public Management? Contracting Determinants and Service Quality Consequences in Public Education." *Public Administration Review* 64, no. 3: 342–52.

Peters, B. Guy. 1998. "'With a Little Help from Our Friends': Public-Private Partnerships as Institutions and Instruments." In *Partnerships in Urban Governance,* ed. J. Pierre, 11–33. New York: St. Martin's Press.

Pfeffer, Jeffrey, and Gerald Salancik. 1978. *The External Control of Organizations: A Resource Dependence Perspective.* New York: Harper & Row.

Pitts, David W. 2006. "Modeling the Impact of Diversity Management." *Review of Public Personnel Administration* 26, no. 3: 245–68.

Pratchett, Lawrence, and Melvin Wingfield. 1996. "Petty Bureaucracy and Woolly-Minded Liberalism? The Changing Ethos of Local Government Officers." *Public Administration* 74 (Winter): 639–56.

Provan, Keith J., and H. Brinton Milward. 1995. "A Preliminary Theory of Network Effectiveness: A Comparative Study of Four Mental Health Systems." *Administrative Science Quarterly* 40, no. 1: 1–33.

Puffer, Sheila M., and James R. Meindl. 1995. "Volunteers from Corporations: Work Cultures Reflect Values Similar to the Voluntary Organization's." *Nonprofit Management & Leadership* 5, no. 4: 359–75.

Rainey, Hal G. 1997. *Understanding and Managing Public Organizations.* 2d ed. San Francisco: Jossey-Bass.

Rapp, Cynthia A., and Carolyn M. Whitfield. 1999. "Neighborhood-Based Services: Organizational Change and Integration Prospects." *Nonprofit Management & Leadership* 9, no. 3: 261–76.

Rethemeyer, R. Karl, and Deneen M. Hatmaker. 2006. "Network Management Reconsidered: An Inquiry into Management of Network Structures in Public Sector Service Provision." Paper presented at the Academy of Management Annual Meeting, Atlanta, GA, August 11–16.

Rittel, Horst W.J., and Melvin M. Webber. 1973. "Dilemmas in a General Theory of Planning." *Policy Sciences* 4, no. 2: 155–69.

Saidel, Judith R. 1989. "Dimensions of Interdependence: The State and Voluntary-Sector Relationship." *Nonprofit and Voluntary Sector Quarterly* 18, no. 4: 335–47.

———. 1994. "The Dynamics of Interdependence between Public Agencies and Nonprofit Organizations." *Research in Public Administration* 3: 210–29.

Saidel, Judith R., and Karyn Loscocco. 2005. "Agency Leaders, Gendered Institutions, and Representative Bureaucracy." *Public Administration Review* 65, no. 2: 158–70.

Selden, Sally Coleman. 1997. *The Promise of Representative Bureaucracy: Diversity and Responsiveness in a Government Agency.* Armonk, NY: M.E. Sharpe.

Shaw, Mary M. 2003. "Successful Collaboration between the Nonprofit and Public Sectors." *Nonprofit Management & Leadership* 14, no. 1: 107–20.

Smith, Stephen Rathgeb, and Kirsten A. Grønbjerg. 2006. "Government-Nonprofit Relations." In *The Nonprofit Sector: A Research Handbook.* 2d ed., ed. Walter W. Powell and Richard Steinberg, 221–42. New Haven, CT: Yale University Press.

Smith, Stephen Rathgeb, and Michael Lipsky. 1993. *Nonprofits for Hire: The Welfare State in the Age of Contracting.* Cambridge, MA: Harvard University Press.

Snavely, Keith, and Martin B. Tracy. 2000. "Collaboration Among Rural Nonprofit Organizations." *Nonprofit Management & Leadership* 11, no. 2: 145–65.

Thomson, Ann Marie, and James L. Perry. 2006. "Collaboration Processes: Inside the Black Box." *Public Administration Review* 66, no. 6 (Supplement): 20–32.

Van Slyke, David M. 2007. "Agents or Stewards: Using Theory to Understand the Government–Nonprofit Social Services Contracting Relationship." *Journal of Public Administration Research and Theory* 17, no. 2: 157–87.

Van Slyke, David M., and Charles A. Hammonds. 2003. "The Privatization Decision: Do Public Managers Make a Difference?" *American Review of Public Administration* 33, no. 2: 146–63.

Vigoda, Eran. 2002. "From Responsiveness to Collaboration: Governance, Citizens, and the Next Generation of Public Administration." *Public Administration Review* 62, no. 5: 527–40.

Vigoda-Gadot, Eran. 2003. *Managing Collaboration in Public Administration: The Promise of Alliance among Governance, Citizens and Businesses.* Westport, CT: Praeger.

Warner, Mildred E., and Robert Hebdon. 2001. "Local Government Restructuring: Privatization and Its Alternatives." *Journal of Policy Analysis and Management* 20, no. 2: 315–36.

Wilkins, Vicky M. 2007. "Exploring the Causal Story: Gender, Active Representation, and Bureaucratic Priorities." *Journal of Public Administration Research and Theory* 17: 7–94.

Williamson, Oliver E. 1985. *The Economic Institutions of Capitalism: Firms, Markets, Relational Contracting.* New York: Free Press.

———. 1996. *The Mechanisms of Governance.* New York: Oxford University Press.

Williamson, Oliver E., and Scott E. Masten. 1995. *Transaction Cost Economics.* Brookfield, VT: Edward Elgar.

Wise, Lois R., and Mary M. Tschirhart. 2000. "Examining Empirical Evidence on Diversity Effects: How Useful is Diversity Research for Public Sector Managers?" *Public Administration Review* 60, no. 5: 386–94.

Yang, Kaifeng. 2006. "Trust and Citizen Involvement Decisions." *Administration & Society* 38, no. 5: 573–95.

CHAPTER 4

Failing into Cross-Sector Collaboration Successfully

JOHN M. BRYSON AND BARBARA C. CROSBY

In the United States and elsewhere, collaboration among government agencies, businesses, and nonprofits to handle community or societal needs has become commonplace. Unfortunately, at the present time the use of cross-sector collaborations is proceeding at a faster pace than our research ability to understand what contributes to the formation of cross-sector collaboration and to its effective or ineffective operation. While there is considerable research on antecedents to interorganizational relationships more generally (e.g., Oliver 1990) and the dynamics of specific collaborations (e.g., Huxham and Vangen 2005), an overarching theory has yet to emerge.[1]

This chapter lays the groundwork for such a theory by arguing that *successful cross-sector collaboration arises from failure.* The argument goes as follows: Each sector has characteristic strengths and weaknesses for the work of solving or remedying community and societal problems (and thus creating public value). Yet, U.S. communities often rely, at least initially, on a single sector to take responsibility for dealing with a public need. Only when single-sector solutions fail or prove inadequate (or are anticipated to do so) do leaders, policymakers, and activists turn to cross-sector collaboration. The cross-sector collaboration will succeed only if it draws appropriately on the separate sectors' strengths, while minimizing or overcoming their weaknesses.

At a broader level, our sectors failure argument raises questions about the adequacies of the design of current institutions—the market, government, and voluntary associations—and their ability to work independently to solve complex public problems. To the extent that certain institutional logics (Friedland and Alford 1991) guide the assumptions and behaviors of sector actors, they are apt to frame problems and solutions only partially. For example, Keast and colleagues (2004) argue that these complex public problems resist solution by government's typical single public agency or silo approach to problem-solving. They quote Clarke and Stewart (1997): "Wicked problems . . . challenge existing patterns of organization and management" (2).

This chapter goes on to explore the question: How is the ability of cross-sector collaborations to achieve public value affected by their having stemmed from the failure or

Figure 4.1   **Continuum of Organizational Sharing**

What Is Shared	Mechanism for Sharing			
Authority				Merger
Power or capabilities			Collaboration	
Activities and resources		Coordination		
Information, good will, and good intentions (i.e., the absence of conflict)	Cooperation			
Nothing	None			

Source: Adapted from Crosby and Bryson (2005).

inadequacy of single-sector solutions? We offer several propositions derived from our study of the literature and a number of cases that could guide further research into this question. Finally, the chapter explores implications of our view of cross-sector collaboration for research, teaching, and practice.

By cross-sector collaborations, we mean those involving government, business, non-profits, and/or communities and the public or citizenry as a whole. Often media of various sorts, philanthropies, and higher education are involved as well, and represent specialized versions of the broader sector categories, such as business or nonprofits. More specifically, we define *cross-sector collaboration* as *the linking or sharing of information, goodwill, and good intentions; resources; activities;* and *power or capabilities by organizations in two or more sectors to achieve jointly what could not be achieved by organizations in one sector separately* (see Himmelman 1996; Hubbard 1995). (See Figure 4.1.)

Cross-sector collaborations are hardly recent phenomena and, in fact, have been central to some of this country's greatest public affairs successes. For example, if one examines Light's (2002) list of achievements by the U.S. federal government during the last half of the twentieth century, one is struck by how many of these achievements were accomplished not by the federal government alone but by the combined efforts of local government, business, and nonprofit organizations. At the same time, cross-sector collaborations do not solve all of the problems they tackle; they are no panacea. This is in part because of the interconnectedness of things, such that changes anywhere reverber-ate unexpectedly and sometimes even dangerously throughout the system (Luke 1998). Complex feedback effects abound (Senge 1994). And issues previously thought about in fairly narrow terms, such as health care, are now being redefined as issues of economic competitiveness, industrial policy, education policy, tax and expenditure policy, immi-gration policy, and more. It is no surprise then that collaborations often fall far short of achieving their goals, becoming victims of "collaborative inertia" in which their actual output fails to exceed inputs, or the time, energy, and resources expended to meet goals (Huxham 1996; Huxham and Vangen 2000).

Despite the difficulties with collaboration, government and foundations in the United States and Europe have increasingly required or expected funding recipients to engage in cross-sector collaboration. The popular labels over the past few decades are varied—public–private partnerships, joint working, collaboratives—but the assumption is that communities can be better served and that innovative and sustainable solutions to public problems can be crafted more effectively by such arrangements than by a single sector operating alone (Barringer and Harrison 2000; Keast et al. 2004; Ostrower 2005). On their part, organizational leaders typically decide to partner across sectoral boundaries because they cannot get what they want without collaborating (Hudson et al. 1999; Roberts 2000). Perhaps they have tried and failed to accomplish their mission alone (or realize they are likely to fail without a partner). Or they may be pushed into cross-sector collaboration because funders think that no sector has adequate expertise or other resources for solving public problems. Either way, we can say that, typically, organizational participants in effective cross-sector collaborations have had to *fail* into their role in the collaboration. (Note that we have encountered considerable resistance and defensiveness among academics and practitioners to the use of the "failure" language; they prefer to talk about sector "inadequacy." We stick with the term "failure" and the notion of "failing into cross-sector collaboration" in order to parallel and complement the long-established tradition in the literature and practice of discussing and acting on market failures.)

The case for the "failure" argument and our first proposition are presented in the next section of this chapter. Next, we examine additional propositions related to the effects of antecedent failure on the structure, process, and outcomes of cross-sector collaboration.

FAILING INTO CROSS-SECTOR COLLABORATION

This section begins with an elaboration of the characteristic contributions and failings of each sector, which include markets and business, nonprofit and voluntary sector organizations, and governments. We also consider "community" as an informal sector capable of collective action to solve public problems (Hall 2006), and give special attention to the media, which may be based in any of the sectors. We illustrate these contributions and failures with examples involving affordable housing.

Note that some may object to the notion of the community being a "sector," but we argue that it is and rely in part on Hall (2006), who points out that historically "community" as a category preceded the idea of sectors and only as we developed more formal legal structures in the United States did fairly clear definitions of a public sector, business sector, and, much later, a nonprofit sector emerge. We think it is useful to at least maintain attention to community as an informal sector. We also discuss the characteristic contributions and failures of the media, which span all the sectors, but have an extremely important and distinctive role to play in creating public value. (We might also have pulled out for special attention additional institutions that span sectors, such as philanthropy and higher education, but because of space limitations have chosen not to do so.)

This section concludes with a researchable framework for thinking about policy inter-vention in light of sector contributions and failures. At least on its face, the framework helps account for the oft-observed situation of *failing* into cross-sector collaboration—by which we mean that single-sector efforts are typically tried first and found wanting before cross-sector efforts are attempted. Alternatively, the framework may be used to account for the failure to collaborate across sectors at all.

Sector Contributions and Weaknesses or Failures

As a society, we rely on the different sectors both to contribute to the creation of public value and public values *and* to help overcome the weaknesses or failures of the other sectors. We use "creating public value" (Moore 1995, 2000) to mean the design and implementation of policies, programs, and practices that benefit a community as a whole at reasonable cost.

Markets and Business

When the conditions underlying perfect markets are met, they can be counted on to provide optimum amounts of goods and services in the most efficient way.[2] Many goods and services are offered in competitive or nearly competitive markets, and U.S. citizens have grown used to the choice, productivity, innovativeness, service, and quality that markets can provide. Public value can be created by businesses operating in competi-tive markets in several ways, including through efficiently managing a large fraction of the economy, providing employment, paying taxes, and in general creating financial wealth. Businesses also can act as good corporate citizens, and are often relied upon to provide leadership and funding around public issues and causes. Unfortunately, markets are rarely perfect and can fail to create public value for a variety of well-known reasons (Weimer and Vining 2004). For example, markets are predicated on self-interested in-teractions and do not assume long-term commitments or relationships between buyers and sellers. While markets have important coordinating effects, they do not, by design, have integrating effects (Powell 1990). The institutional logic of the market includes the practices of accumulation, ownership, buying and selling, and commodification of human behavior. Various instruments of exchange, competition, and efficiency are part of its symbolic system (Friedland and Alford 1991). Solving public problems, however, often requires long time horizons and entails "inefficiencies" associated with long-term relationships through which trust is developed (Huxham and Vangen 2005; Ring and Van de Ven 1994).

The housing industry provides an example. People in the housing construction business respond to demand for affordable housing by offering starter homes or condos for sale; developers build and operate barebones rental units; and homeowners offer their existing homes for resale. Unfortunately, there is a mismatch between what many people (includ-ing many elderly and disabled persons) need and what they are able to pay. As a result, there is a gap in supply as not enough "affordable" housing is available for starter homes or barebones apartments and the market for housing has partially failed.

Governments

Democratic governments have a different role to play, including providing much of the framework necessary for markets, businesses, and nonprofit organizations to operate effectively, correcting or coping with market and philanthropic failures, and even guarding against their own possible failures through elections, checks and balances, and the rule of law. Democratic governments can create public value through a number of overlapping activities, some of which are more appropriate to one level or type of government than another (Bozeman 2002; Moore 1995; Weimer and Vining 2004), and some of which might be thought of as activities for the polity as a whole.

Like markets, government operating agencies—as opposed to government direction-setting, oversight, support (or overhead), and regulatory units—are prone to characteristic failures (Brandl 1998; Osborne and Plastrik 1997; Weimer and Vining 2004). Brandl (1998, 64) argues that government operating agencies can fail when they lack an external orientation to accomplish public purposes (as a result of monopoly practices, lack of an appropriate pricing mechanism, or distracted monitoring); because they are not organized internally to achieve public purposes (resulting in or from bounded rationality or imperfect information); or because they are systematically indifferent to the fairness of the distributions of income or wealth. Note that these failures parallel the failures of markets.

Government direction-setting, oversight, support, and regulatory agencies also can fail to do their job. When direction setting fails (due to legislative or bureaucratic gridlock, a lack of visionary leadership, or faulty understanding of a problem or need), government's responsibility to steer policy systems has been reduced (Osborne and Hutchinson 2004; Osborne and Plastrik 1997). When oversight bodies fail (due to poor organizational design, insufficient resources, perverse incentives, inadequate authority, or poor information), accountability has been compromised (Romzek 1996). When support agencies fail (due to poor organizational design, insufficient resources, or perverse incentives), the government itself does not get the service it deserves (Barzelay 1992). And when regulatory agencies fail (due to poor organizational design, insufficient resources, perverse incentives, inadequate authority, capture by the regulated, poor information, or corruption), the public is not adequately served or protected (Weimer and Vining 2004).

More generally, the bureaucratic organizational form often associated with government agencies is especially well suited to stable environments and predictable routines of problem definition and problem solution. The logic of the bureaucratic state concerns practices that regulate human activity and include legal and bureaucratic hierarchies, rules, regulations, and standard operating procedures (Friedland and Alford 1991). However, as Keast and colleagues (2004) state, complex public problems present significant challenges to government bureaucracies because they resist traditions, rules, and routines.

In terms of the affordable housing example, if decent housing is considered essential (or even a right) for all citizens regardless of income, government can supply housing itself, ensure that markets are operating efficiently and fairly (e.g., no price gouging, warranties enforced, no speculation), or can subsidize poor buyers or renters, among other options.

Nonprofit Organizations

Nonprofit organizations in the United States can create public value, provided they pass some basic requirements about their purpose, asset distribution, and nonpartisanship.[3] The array of types of nonprofit organizations and their specific purposes is extraordinary (Bryce 2000, 684–95), encompassing nearly thirty tax code sections. The vast majority, however, include "charities," covered by Section 501(c)(3) and (4) of the Internal Revenue Code; and social welfare or mutual aid organizations covered by Section 501(c)(4) of the IRS Code. These organizations are self-governing, private entities created to fulfill a public purpose (Boris and Steuerle 2006). They are granted tax exemption because they are presumed to create public value when they: (1) express the First Amendment right of assembly; (2) promote public rather than individual welfare; (3) promote public welfare in a manner that goes beyond what government does or at a cost less than government would incur; or (4) serve public purposes in a charitable way (Bryce 2000, 32, 40).

Dominant economic theories suggest that nonprofit organizations arise in market economies because of market failure (Hansmann 1981), government failure (Weisbrod 1986), or failure by agents other than nonprofits to satisfy the needs of principals in contracting relationships (Bryce 2005). In other words, nonprofits are derivative, forming only when markets or the state cannot or will not provide goods and services demanded by particular groups or individuals. Salamon (1987) presents an alternative view, arguing that government intervention occurs only after the philanthropic sector has failed because its resources are insufficient or its response too narrow, paternalistic, or unprofessional to meet public needs.

Nonprofit organizations (if we emphasize the charities and the social welfare/mutual aid entities) can be thought to operate under the logic of democracy, emphasizing voluntary association and popular control over human activity (Friedland and Alford 1991). However, Alford (1992) argues that while many advocates and scholars of the nonprofit sector use the logic of democracy to paint a picture of the sector as "voluntary" and "independent" and hence distinct from either the state or the capitalist market, in fact many nonprofit organizations express the logic of the bureaucratic state and/or the logic of capitalism.

Nonprofit organizations may provide affordable housing because of their concern for a particular group, such as elderly members of a religious congregation, or low-income families. They may be able to operate more cheaply because they are not required to make profits. They also may advocate government action, put pressure on business, and compete with business. Nonprofits may also be well situated to develop or oversee cross-sector collaboratives to provide affordable housing.

Communities, or the Public in General

Communities can create public value by promoting a sense of individual and collective identity, belonging, recognition, and security; by providing people a place to live, work, learn, enjoy, express themselves, and build families; by building and maintaining physical, human, intellectual, social, and cultural capital of various sorts; and by fostering a civically engaged, egalitarian, trusting, and tolerant democratic society (Boyte and Kari 1996; Chrislip 2002). Social capital in particular has been shown to have a broad range of positive effects on health, education, welfare, safety, and civic activism (Brandl 1998; Putnam 2000). Communities are necessary for our existence as human beings, and serving communities provides a justification for our existence as humans (see, for example, Becker 1973; Friedmann 1979; Grayling 2003). Communities provide rich local knowledge and relationships that are crucial to sustainable public policy improvements (Scott 1998). Communities fail when they exclude or isolate some groups, accept unthinkingly the domination of traditional elites, neglect collective identity, become parochial, ignore harm to individuals and the environment, and offer few opportunities for civic engagement.

Communities have an important role to play in providing affordable housing. For example, families take in relatives who cannot afford their own homes; neighbors assist a family whose home has burned; and a group of stay-at-home parents band together to force city officials to crack down on landlords who allow their rental properties to deteriorate. Communities can fail when, for example, neighbors do not band together to challenge irresponsible landlords because they do not have time or organizing skills, when families are too poor themselves to take in others, and when homeowners and renters do not see renters as belonging to the community.

The Media

The news media might be thought of as a hybrid sector, since they may be based in businesses, nonprofits, or community action. (The media therefore are not highlighted separately in Figure 4.2, p. 63) In democratic societies they make a unique contribution to public value. Specifically, the news media create public value by performing a watchdog role; that is, by holding public servants and governments to high standards of ethical practice, legality, and transparent, fair decision making; and by holding individuals and organizations in other sectors to relevant standards as well. They also inform and educate the citizenry about public issues, and they gather and articulate public opinion. In the United States, the special role of the media is enshrined in the Constitution. The news media fail in these roles for several reasons: Journalists may become too close to political or other elites and even become elites themselves; journalists may allow personal bias to strongly affect their reporting; and they may wear professional blinders that keep them from seeing nonsensational, less-visible events as newsworthy. Additionally, the financial interests of news media owners can influence what is covered and how it is treated. Finally, alternative media and news departments of big media enterprises may not have the resources needed to hire highly skilled staff or investigate stories.

In terms of affordable housing, the media can act as a watchdog. For example, they may investigate unfair market practices like redlining, or inefficient or corrupt government programs that spend lots of public funds yet fail to adequately help people in need of decent shelter. The media may inform those people about affordable housing or housing assistance offered by business, government, or nonprofits. They may educate the public about the need for public subsidy of mortgages or rents for low-income people. The media also may fail, by, for example, waiting until a crisis emerges as exemplified by lots of visible homeless people or when the plight of a special group, such as children, becomes apparent. Reporters and editors may simply ignore the problem of affordable housing. Or the media may not publicize developers' shoddy construction practices because they are big advertisers.

Policy Intervention in Light of Sector Strengths and Weaknesses

We argue that the *implicit* current dominant theory of policy intervention in the United States builds on the idea that sectors have differential strengths and weaknesses and is summarized in Figure 4.2.

In the United States, one place public policy intervention typically begins is with what Schultze (1977, 44) calls the "rebuttable presumption." The presumption is that we will let markets work until they fail, and only if they fail will we seek an intervention. (In other words, the presumption that markets will succeed must be rebutted before we move toward public policy intervention.) Schultze and others argue that if markets fail, attention should first be directed toward fixing the market failures through whatever mechanism is appropriate, given the nature of the failures and the public purposes to be served. Taxes, subsidies, regulations, information provision, and various other tools might adequately address the failure. Government action typically is needed to fix the failures, but the action does not involve direct product or service provision that substitutes for what the market or businesses could provide themselves once failures were fixed.

If the market failures cannot be fixed, then the case is compelling for direct government provision of products or services. For example, the rise of public schools in the United States was tied to a belief that a compelling public interest in universal, professional, non–church-based education could not be satisfied by markets; thus tax-financed public schools were thought to be the only viable alternative. Similarly, the creation of the Social Security system was a response to a widely perceived failure of the market to provide adequate pensions for ordinary workers, their spouses, and surviving dependents. In the current school-choice movement, advocates believe that the public schools—as government-owned and -operated monopolies—are failing and that markets or market-like mechanisms would produce better outcomes. They advocate offering parents more choices of schools, particularly through the use of vouchers and fostering the creation of charter schools (perhaps even by allowing vouchers to be used in church-owned schools to provide yet more choice) and through allowing home schooling (Brandl 1998). Fixing the government failure may be seen in part as a move to market-based solutions, but also as a move to voluntary action, since parochial schools and charter schools are nonprofit organizations. Home schooling also represents a kind of voluntary action.

Governments also make extensive use of the voluntary sector to carry out a number of government services, especially in social services, health, employment and training, and the arts (Salamon 2002). Policymakers rely on nonprofits for a variety of reasons, but especially because they believe nonprofits are cheaper, more flexible, more innovative, more

Figure 4.2 **Multisector Failures Leading to Cross-Sector Solutions**

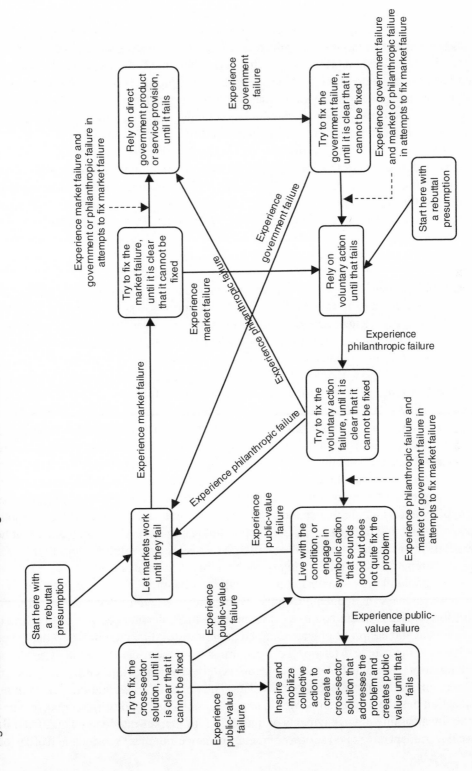

trustworthy, and more easily terminated than government units (Bryce 2005; Smith and Lipsky 1993). In others words, government often relies on nonprofits because policymakers see the sector as having strengths that the government itself does not have (Salamon 1987). Indeed, Salamon (1995) argues that historically the United States has relied *first* on voluntary action (with or without the existence of nonprofit organizations) before moving to government service provision. In other words, government service provision historically has been a product of *either* market failure *or* voluntary action failure. Thus, *two* rebuttable presumptions are presented as starting points in Figure 4.2.

If the public problems are unsolvable by any sector, then they are more accurately called *conditions* rather than problems, and will remain conditions until they are turned into problems that can be solved (Wildavsky 1979). Sometimes the condition may be addressed through symbolic action that claims the problem is fixed when it is not, or does not exist when it does (Edelman 1988, 2001; Stone 2002). If the condition remains serious, and no effective action is undertaken by any sector to alleviate it, we might speak of a *public-value* failure. Bozeman (2002, 150) says that a "public failure occurs when neither the market nor the public sector provides goods and services required to achieve core public values." We would extend his argument to say that a public-value failure occurs when neither the market, government, nonprofits, news media, nor community provides whatever is needed (policies, goods, services, revenues, and/or accountability) to create desirable public value or achieve core public values. Clearly broad-based leadership for the common good is necessary in such situations in order to create cross-sector collaborative solutions that advance the common good.

To summarize, the implicit theory of policy intervention in the United States seems to be as follows: We will let a market or the voluntary sector work until it fails. If either fails, we will first try to fix the failures, without recourse to direct government product or service provision. This might mean relying on voluntary action to fix a market failure, or vice versa. If the failures cannot be fixed, we will consider relying on government product or service delivery. If all three sectors fail and the failures cannot be fixed, we have a public value failure that we address in one of several ways. We can live with it; engage in some form of symbolic action that sounds good, but does not actually address the problem; or seek to inspire and mobilize collective action to fashion a cross-sector solution that holds the promise of creating public value. Effective cross-sector solutions will build on each sector's strengths while minimizing or overcoming its weaknesses.

An example of cross-sector failure leading to collaboration is the recent campaign to end homelessness in Hennepin County, Minnesota (the county that contains Minneapolis). Homelessness in the county is at an all-time high, despite decades of investment in government and nonprofit programs aimed at building and maintaining affordable homes for low-income people. Many of those programs were themselves a result of cross-sector collaboration—among for-profit developers, government, community and corporate foundations, and nonprofit service providers. The previous collaborations grew out of the realization that the market alone would not produce adequate housing for people who had difficulty affording down payments or qualifying for market-rate loans. Thus, federal and state government developed an array of rental and home-purchase subsidies and often joined with developers in building apartments and single-family homes. Meanwhile, government and nonprofits often collaborated on programs that helped low-income people navigate the process of acquiring housing loans and rental vouchers. Governments and nonprofits also established community shelters as a stopgap solution for people who were in transition between homes or who were hardcore "street people."

Increasingly, though, the assistance programs and the shelter system are overwhelmed. More and more families have lost their homes, bringing a growing new clientele to shelters designed for single men. People with mental health problems are unable to acquire supportive housing and wind up on the streets after being discharged from treatment programs. Teenagers exit foster care with no provisions for permanent housing. People who have completed jail terms have trouble finding landlords who will rent to them.

In March 2006, seventy city and county elected officials, religious leaders, nonprofit and business executives, foundation presidents, school and police officials, and academics agreed to serve on a commission charged with developing a blueprint for ending homelessness in Minneapolis and Hennepin County in ten years. The commission's draft plan details the high cost to homeless people and taxpayers of the current system, marked by failure both to adequately coordinate the existing services and to further develop collaborative efforts that could prevent homelessness rather than serving it (Hennepin County and City of Minneapolis Commission to End Homelessness 2006). News media have announced and publicized the campaign. Hennepin County commissioners and the Minneapolis city council approved the draft plan. Congregations are mobilizing, as are a number of other organizations in many sectors.

Our analysis of the theoretical literature and numerous cases like the Hennepin County homelessness example leads to our first proposition:

P1: Public policymakers are most likely to try cross-sector collaboration if they believe that separate efforts by different sectors to address a public problem have failed, or are likely to fail, and that the actual or potential failures cannot be fixed by the sectors acting alone.

In the next section we offer a number of additional propositions that are directly occasioned by the actual or anticipated failures of one or more sectors and the consequent need to collaborate across sectors in order to effectively address the public problem at issue.

ADDITIONAL RELATED PROPOSITIONS

A number of additional propositions follow from this argument. Below we present propositions related to environmental factors, building leadership, building legitimacy, building trust, structure and design, competing institutional logics, planning, power imbalances, public value, and the general difficulty of creating successful cross-sector collaborations.

Environmental Factors

Work on interorganizational relationships has directly linked certain environmental conditions to the necessity for single organizations to join with others. Most notably, Emery and Trist (1965) argued more than forty years ago that increased environmental complexity, such that the "ground is in motion" (21), necessitated linkages among organizations to decrease uncertainty and increase organizational stability. Fundamental needs of organizations to reduce resource dependencies in their environments (Pfeffer and Salancik 1978) or decrease transaction costs (Williamson 1975) also propel organizations toward various types of interorganizational relationships. In the example of persistent homelessness, the new Hennepin County collaboration stems in large part from obvious market failures and recent fluctuations in federal and state funding for social services. Additionally, the organizers highlighted the significant transaction costs for families trying to access uncoordinated housing assistance programs and for the organizations trying to help them.

Collaborations also are subject to both competitive and institutional pressures that significantly affect their formation as well as long-term sustainability (Oliver 1990; Sharfman, Gray, and Yin 1991). The institutional environment includes normative, legal, and regulatory elements with which organizations must conform if they are to achieve the legitimacy necessary for survival (DiMaggio and Powell 1983, 1991). For partnerships focused on public policy or public problem solving, the institutional environment is especially important because it includes broad systems of relationships across public jurisdictional areas (Scott and Meyer 1991) that can directly affect collaborative purpose, structure, and outcomes. For example, in their study of a public–private partnership in the garment industry, Sharfman, Gray, and Yin (1991) found that driving forces in both the competitive and institutional environments helped stimulate the partnership's formation but quickly shifted to restraining forces that hindered its sustainability. Institutional forces appeared to be more intractable than competitive forces; for example, a decrease in public funds and changes in welfare payment policies created strong disincentives for the partnership to continue.

P2: Similar to all interorganizational relationships, cross-sector collaborations are more likely to form in turbulent environments. In particular, the formation and sustainability of cross-sector collaborations will be affected by driving and constraining forces in their competitive and institutional environments.

Building Leadership

Collaborations provide multiple roles for formal and informal leaders (e.g., Agranoff and McGuire 2003; Crosby and Bryson 2005b). Examples of formal leadership positions are: co-chairs of a steering committee, coordinator of a collaborative, and project director. To be effective, these people need formal and informal authority, vision and long-term commitment to the collaboration, integrity, and relational and political skills (Crosby and Bryson 2005a; Gray 1989; Waddock 1986). Two key leadership roles are "sponsors" and "champions" (Crosby and Bryson 2005a), who are crucial for fueling the collaboration with hope and the other resources needed and for managing conflicts and crises. Sponsors are individuals who have considerable prestige, authority, and access to resources they can use on behalf of the collaboration, even if they are not closely involved in the day-to-day collaborative work. In the Hennepin County case, the Minneapolis mayor and a city council member, a county commissioner, state legislator, and a chamber of commerce official are examples of powerful sponsors. The participation of the mayor, city council member, and a county commissioner were especially important, since the collaboration would be asking the Minneapolis City Council and Hennepin County Board of Commissioners to approve its proposals. Champions are people who focus intently on keeping the collaboration going and use process skills to help the collaboration to accomplish its goals. The most visible champions are Cathy ten Broeke, commission coordinator and former shelter director, and James Gertmenian, the senior pastor of a downtown Minneapolis church.

The parceling out of formal leadership positions has implications for the level of buy-in by collaborating partners; if more powerful partners receive "plum" positions, less powerful partners may require other assurances that their interests will be taken into account (Alexander et al. 2001). If one sector seems dominant in the leadership of the collaboration, representatives of the other sectors may worry that their sector's strengths will be overlooked. In the Hennepin County case, the most prominent sponsors come from the government sector, but champions come from elsewhere. Ten Broeke brings credibility in nonprofit and community sectors as a long-term activist on behalf of homeless people and Gertmenian brings a high profile among downtown religious congregations.

The development of informal leadership throughout a collaboration is likely to be especially important, since participants often cannot rely on a lot of clear-cut, easily enforced, centralized direction. (For example, "lead organizations" may not be powerful enough to lead in a traditional sense; or an individual participant may be a formal leader in a partner organization, but not play a formal leadership role in the collaboration.) Since turnover of leaders is to be expected in collaborations that continue for years, collaborating partners have an incentive to prepare successors and build in ways to sustain the collaboration during changes in leadership (Alexander et al. 2001; Merrill-Sands and Sheridan 1996).

P3: Cross-sector collaborations are more likely to succeed if they have committed sponsors and effective champions at many levels and from different sectors who provide formal and informal leadership.

Building Legitimacy

As institutional theory contends, an organization seeking to acquire the resources necessary to survive must build legitimacy through making use of structures, processes, and strategies that are deemed appropriate within its institutional environment (Suchman 1995). However, when a newly organized entity is a network of organizations, not a single organization, how does the network gain legitimacy to begin with? A network or collaboration is not automatically regarded by others, either insiders or outsiders, as a legitimate organizational entity, because it is less understandable and recognizable than more traditional forms, such as bureaucratic structures. In their research, Human and Provan (2000) found three neces-sary and distinct dimensions to be critical for networks: (1) the legitimacy of *network as form* in order to attract internal and external support and resources; (2) the legitimacy of the *network as entity* that is recognizable to both insiders and outsiders; and (3) the legitimacy of *network as interaction,* building trust among members to freely communicate within the network. In the Hennepin County case, the new collaboration has considerable legitimacy because it builds on existing networks of service providers and funders and includes widely recognized leaders from multiple sectors. The drafters of the collaboration's report have been careful to bolster the trust within the collaboration by not blaming a particular sector for the failures of existing antihomelessness efforts and highlighting previous successes achieved by cross-sector collaboration.

P4: Cross-sector collaborations are more likely to succeed if they establish with both internal and external stakeholders the legitimacy of collaboration as a form of organizing, as a separate entity, and as a source of trusted interaction among members.

Building Trust

Trusting relationships are often depicted as the essence of collaboration. Paradoxically, they are both lubricant and glue—that is, they facilitate the work of collaboration and they hold the collaboration together. Trust can comprise interpersonal behavior, confidence in organizational competence and expected performance, and a common bond and sense of goodwill (Chen and Graddy 2005). Many researchers realize that collaborations begin with varying degrees of trust, but emphasize that trust building is an ongoing requirement for successful collaborations (Huxham and Vangen 2005; Ring and Van de Ven 1994). This may be especially important when collaborations follow a history of single-sector failure, and partners can too easily blame another sector for being too heartless, ideological, or incompetent.

   Collaboration partners build trust by sharing information and knowledge and demon-strating competency, good intentions, and follow-through; conversely, failure to follow through and unilateral action undermine trust (Ariño and de la Torre 1998; Merrill-Sands and Sheridan 1996). For example, Huxham and Vangen (2005) emphasize the effectiveness of achieving "small wins" together. In the Hennepin case, the publicity surrounding the announcement of the campaign to end homelessness and the publication of its draft report help build a record of small wins.

P5: Cross-sector collaborations are more likely to succeed if trust-building activities (in-cluding nurturing of cross-sectoral and cross-cultural understanding) are continuous.

Structure and Design

Sectoral differences may show up in differing views of how to organize work. Government representatives are likely to emphasize accountability mechanisms; business representatives are likely to emphasize results, reporting relationships, and CEO approval (and possibly involvement); nonprofit representatives are more comfortable with informality than either business or government; media are unlikely to want formal involvement; and community members may be distrustful of most institutions and large organizations.

P6: In general, collaboration across sectors will produce particular tensions around formality and informality of structure and processual arrangements.

Competing Institutional Logics

Building legitimacy, leadership, and trust, along with managing conflict, all become more complex for multisector collaborations because of the likelihood that members represent and enact competing institutional logics. Institutional logics are macro-level, historical patterns, both symbolic and material, that establish formal and informal rules of the game and provide interpretations of action (Friedland and Alford 1991; Thornton and Ocasio 1999). For example, the *logic of the market* includes the material practices of accumulation and ownership, where competition and efficiency are part of its symbolic system. The *logic of the bureaucratic state* concerns the regulation of human activity and includes legal and bureaucratic hierarchies, rules, and standard operating procedures. The *logic of democracy* emphasizes popular control over human activity and citizen participation with symbolic supporting systems such as voluntary association (Friedland and Alford 1991). Logics influence organization-level behavior by focusing the attention of decision makers on certain issues, outcomes, and sources of power consistent with the dominant logic, and away from those inconsistent with the logic (Thornton and Ocasio 1999). In the Hennepin County case, police officers have become de facto the main outreach workers to homeless people. They are likely to "go by the book"—enforcing rules against loitering, public intoxication, drunk and disorderly conduct, and panhandling. The commission report emphasizes that Philadelphia has established a 24/7 hotline system that citizens can call if they spot a person in need, so that other types of workers can be deployed to help. The result has been a 50 percent drop in "street homelessness" (Hennepin County and City of Minneapolis Commission to End Homelessness 2006, 79).

Logics compete because actions, processes, norms, and structures that are seen as legitimate from the vantage point of one institutional logic may be seen as less legitimate or even illegitimate from the perspective of another logic. For example, contradictions embedded in a cross-sector collaboration might include the extent to which efficiency (the market), adherence to bureaucratic rules (the state), or inclusive participation (democracy) is regarded by collaboration members as essential to the design of a collaboration's structure, process, and set of outcomes.

P7: Competing institutional logics are likely within cross-sector collaborations and may significantly influence the extent to which collaborations can agree on essential elements of process and structure as well as outcomes.

Planning

Careful attention to stakeholders clearly is crucial for successful planning regardless of whether emergent or deliberate planning approaches are used (Bryson 2004a, 2004b; Dobel and Day 2005; Sandfort and Stone 2006; Stone and Sandfort 2006). The process also should be used to build trust and the capacity to manage conflict effectively (Bryson 2004a). Planning is more likely to be successful to the extent that it builds on the competencies and distinctive competencies of the collaborators, including those arising from the distinctive sectors in which they operate (Bryson, Ackermann, and Eden 2007). The plan to end homelessness in Hennepin County and Minneapolis was developed in a fast-track 100-day process that included six full meetings of the multistakeholder commission and included input from homeless and formerly homeless people. The implementation plan calls for organizing a Cultural Competency/Consumer Feedback Team that will continue to elicit input from homeless people and culturally savvy community experts as the project goes forward.

P8: Cross-sector collaborations are more likely to succeed if their planning makes use of stakeholder analyses, emphasizes responsiveness to key stakeholders, uses the process to build trust and the capacity to manage conflict (including through understanding competing logics), and builds on the competencies and distinctive competencies of the collaborators and their respective sectors.

Power Imbalances

Huxham and Vangen (2005) identify power imbalances among collaborating partners as a source of mistrust and therefore a threat to effective collaboration. Power imbalances become most significant when partners have difficulty agreeing on a shared purpose. In addition, over time a collaboration is likely to experience exogenous (and endogenous) shocks that affect relations among partners, resources, and even the purpose of the collaboration. Once-reliable funding streams may dry up and others may flow as political trends reshape government priorities, corporate donors respond to market conditions, and foundations pursue new causes. Collaborating partners must assume that funding allocations are likely to change. In the Hennepin County plan to end homelessness, the implementation strategy includes appointment of a finance committee to marshal and monitor the multiple funding sources identified by the plan.

Besides fluctuating funding streams, the demographics of the collaboration's clientele may change—for example, immigrants and political refugees have become an increasing proportion of the homeless population in Hennepin County. The collaboration may be caught up in scandals involving one or more members or in partisan political shifts. Some members may drop out and new ones join. Tactics like strategic planning and scenario development can help collaborations anticipate and shape future developments and manage shifts in power effectively (Bryson 2004a).

P9: Cross-sector collaborations are more likely to succeed if they build in resources and tactics for dealing with power imbalances and shocks.

Public Value

We argue that the point of creating and sustaining cross-sector collaboratives ought to be the production of "public value" (Moore 1995) that could not be created by single sectors alone (Bozeman 2007). Public value in cross-sector collaborations seems most likely to be created through making use of each sector's characteristic strengths while also finding ways to minimize, overcome, or compensate for each sector's characteristic weaknesses. Playing to the strengths of the different sectors seems logically linked to managing costs effectively and attending to diverse human needs and aspirations.

Especially valuable is the creation of a "regime of mutual gain" that produces widespread, lasting public benefits at reasonable cost and that taps people's deepest interest in, and desires for, a better world (Crosby and Bryson 2005a, 23). By regime we mean "sets of implicit or explicit principles, rules, norms, and decision-making procedures around which actors' expectations converge in a given area" (Krasner 1983, 2). We suspect that to be lasting, such regimes must effectively link individuals' and organizations' self-interests and sector capabilities with the common good. The plan to end homelessness in Hennepin County sets the price tag for the first two years of implementation at an additional $45,000 beyond the existing and projected resources for combating homelessness. The plan, however, emphasizes that keeping homeless people out of emergency rooms, detox units, and jails, for example, is far less costly than continuing the current system. It proposes a number of preventive strategies that would require more affordable and supportive housing and coordinated outreach. "Homelessness," it declares, "is more costly than housing" (Hennepin County and City of Minneapolis Commission to End Homelessness 2006, 2). The report stirs a sense of communal responsibility for diverse groups of people experiencing homelessness, such as schoolchildren, adults with mental illness, former inmates, refugees, and single mothers. Moreover, it applauds previous efforts of the community to assist homeless people. The detailed recommendations assign roles and tasks to partners from all the sectors except media, which probably is an unfortunate oversight.

P10: Cross-sector collaborations are most likely to create public value if they build on individuals' and organizations' self-interests along with each sector's characteristic strengths, while finding ways to minimize, overcome, or compensate for each sector's characteristic weaknesses.

As the propositions indicate, cross-sector collaborations are difficult to create and even more difficult to sustain because so much has to be in place or work well for them to succeed. The challenge of designing and implementing effective cross-sector collaboration is daunting—a conclusion that leads to a possibly unwelcome summary proposition:

P11: The normal expectation ought to be that success will be very difficult to achieve for cross-sector collaborations.

IMPLICATIONS FOR RESEARCH, EDUCATION, AND PRACTICE

A number of implications for research, teaching, and practice flow from the idea that organizations in single sectors typically must *fail* into cross-sector collaboration and that creating successful cross-sector collaborations will be very difficult.

Research

Given their current institutional configurations, neither markets, government bureaucracies, nor nonprofits are up to the complex task of solving public problems that transcend sector boundaries. Markets, government bureaucracies, and nonprofits fail—or only partially succeed—when relied on to address public problems that are beyond their sector-specific abilities to do so. For example, government bureaucracies tend to break public problems down into manageable parts that often coincide with the way legislatures and funding streams are organized. Public problems are typically "organized" quite differently. Markets try to make public problems something that can be solved by transactions between buyers and sellers. But often the public problem involves public goods aspects or externalities that cannot be handled effectively by ordinary market transactions. Nonprofits typically have insufficient funds, talent, and legitimacy to solve the problems, and they find it difficult to challenge governments and businesses and their institutional legitimacy and supports. There is therefore an increasing need to experiment with cross-sector, hybrid forms of organizations and networks that in effect bring inside—that is, make endogenous—the failures that would remain exogenous when looking only at a single sector or organization within the sector. Once failures are viewed as endogenous, efforts can be made to make use of differential sector strengths to minimize or overcome particular sector failures. Said differently, the real power and potential of cross-sector collaboration lie in its capacity to make sector failures endogenous—meaning, *you fail into cross-sector collaboration successfully by bringing the single-sector failures inside the collaboration (at least conceptually) so that there is a chance they and the public problem at issue can be addressed successfully.* The research challenge of exploring the effectiveness of cross-sector collaboration is therefore to reformulate questions of overall effectiveness at a higher, more systemic level—the level of the public problem that is at issue—so that sector failure is made endogenous (Schön 1971; Senge 1994).

Another major challenge affecting research on cross-sector collaboration is that practice currently outstrips theory—and in particular, outstrips disciplinary boundaries. Given its current state of development, cross-sector collaboration research should not be the captive of any single discipline or theory. Instead, our view is that research is mostly likely to advance through relying on teams that bring diverse disciplines, knowledge, and skill sets together so that the team is not blind to the complexity of what they are observing, and also has multidisciplinary theories, skills, and tools to bring to bear on the research enterprise. In other words, the team should attempt to mirror in wise ways the complexity of what they are investigating. We think it is particularly important that the training of investigators include building understanding of the differential logics (e.g., dominant schemas, accounting methods, regulatory regimes) of the sectors.

Research should also emphasize more sophisticated modeling of sector interactions to take account of dynamics and feedback relationships over time. This will help explain counterintuitive outcomes or how feedback relations undermine good intentions and policy prescriptions (Senge 1994).

Teaching and Practice

The first implication for teaching and practice is that students and practitioners need to have a well-developed conception of the differential strengths of the sectors and the various ways in which they can fail. They also need a conception of how regimes of mutual gain might be constructed by building on the strengths of the different sectors while minimizing or overcoming their weaknesses. As an important first step, exercises should be developed to help students understand the characteristic strengths and weaknesses of each sector and how public value might be created by playing to the strengths.

Additionally, more attention needs to be devoted to the context for collaborative public problem solving. For example, the law applies differently to the different sectors (e.g., commercial law is different from laws governing governments and nonprofit organizations). Practical ways of "mapping" the context would help, so that students and practitioners have assistance with understanding situational complexity and leverage points (Bryson 2004b; Dobel and Day 2005; Sandfort and Stone 2006; Stone and Sandfort 2006).

In addition, more cases illustrating successful and unsuccessful cross-sector collaboration should be developed and made available for teaching purposes. The cases should facilitate a systematic investigation of the various factors that seem to affect whether successful outcomes are achieved. The mapping tools mentioned in the previous paragraph could be applied to the cases.

In order to build even deeper comprehension, opportunities should be created to help students and practitioners experience and understand the competing logics of the different sectors and think through how they can be reconciled or complemented in cross-sector collaborations. For example, internships, role-playing exercises, and simulations might be developed to facilitate such an exploration. Thorough discussion and debriefing of the learning experiences should be emphasized. Client-based and community-based work-shops provide a useful vehicle, giving student teams direct experience with cross-sector collaborations.

Another way to facilitate understanding of the competing logics would be to have courses team taught by faculty from public affairs schools, business schools, and law schools. The varying logics of business, government, and the nonprofit world could be explored in depth over the course of a quarter or semester. A step farther down this path would be the creation of joint master's degree programs between public affairs schools, business schools, and law schools.

Finally, we note again the resistance to the "failure" language among practitioners. It would be useful to explore the sources of this resistance, since embedded in it are likely to be clues about why cross-sector collaboration is so challenging. Perhaps the resistance comes from people's psychological attachment to their sector, to the point that their identity gets wrapped up in sector identification. The failure language may be perceived as an identity threat, threat to feelings of self-efficacy, or more practically, a job threat. To us the term failure is somewhat neutral. We are generalizing or extrapolating from well-established literature on market and government failure and newer literature on nonprofit failure. In an endogenous world, failures and inadequacies are normal. But to practitioners this discussion may have more of a life-and-death flavor. Indeed, for government, "failure" isn't really an option.

SUMMARY

This chapter explores how cross-sector collaborations typically result from single-sector failures, and how public value may be created by building on the differential strengths of each sector while minimizing or overcoming sector weaknesses. Creating successful cross-sector collaborations is hardly easy, as the cumulative difficulties highlighted by the series of propositions presented in the chapter point out. Purpose and action, trust and legitimacy, and a host of other factors are difficult to create when doing so depends on understanding the interests and logics of actors in multiple sectors. On the other hand, a major fraction of the difficulties confronting the nation and world will not be addressed effectively unless successful cross-sector collaborations are forged. Building a deeper understanding of how to do so based on solid research and new educational initiatives clearly is needed if the potential for successful cross-sector collaboration in practice is to be realized.

NOTES

This chapter draws extensively on Bryson, Crosby, and Stone (2006); and Crosby and Bryson (2007). The authors gratefully acknowledge the extremely important contributions of Melissa Middleton Stone to this chapter as well as the research assistance of Michael Barringer-Mills and the helpful comments of an anonymous reviewer.

1. As Huxham and Vangen (2005) note, scholars have used four main approaches to the study of collaboration. These are: focusing on phases or steps in collaboration (e.g., Gray 1989), factors affecting success and failure (e.g., Hudson et al. 1999; Mattessich, Murray-Close, and Monsey 2001), themes in collaboration. (e.g., Huxham and Vangen 2005), and tools and techniques to assist collaboration (e.g., Bryant 2003). We draw on all four approaches.

2. Perfectly competitive markets result when there are many buyers, many sellers, perfect information, easy entry into and exit from the market, a framework of contract law that allows contracts to be enforced and fraud avoided, and so on (Weimer and Vining 2004, 58–73).

3. There are three tests that an organization must pass to be granted 501(c)(3) status (Bryce 2000, 40–41, 49–50). The *organizational* test requires that the nonprofit be organized to improve public welfare, rather than to benefit individuals or owners, by pursuing one or more of eight specific purposes: education, religion, charity, science, literary interests, testing that promotes public safety, fostering certain national or international sports competitions, or preventing cruelty to children or to animals. The *political* test requires the nonprofit organization to have a charter that forbids it from participating in any political campaign on behalf of a candidate. And the *asset* test requires that the charter must prohibit any distribution of assets or income to benefit individuals as owners or managers, except for fair compensation for services rendered, and must forbid the use of the organization for the personal benefit of founders, supporters, managers, their relatives, or associates.

REFERENCES

Agranoff, Robert, and Michael McGuire. 2003. *Collaborative Public Management: New Strategies for Local Governments.* Washington, DC: Georgetown University Press.

Alexander, Jeffrey A.; Maureen B. Comfort; Bryan J. Weiner; and Richard Bogue. 2001. "Leadership in Collaborative Community Health Partnerships." *Nonprofit Management and Leadership* 12, no. 2: 159–75.

Alford, Robert R. 1992. "The Political Language of the Nonprofit Sector." In *Language, Symbolism, and Politics,* ed. Richard M. Merelman, 17–50, Boulder, CO: Westview Press.

Ariño, Africa, and Jose de la Torre. 1998. "Learning from Failure: Towards an Evolutionary Model of Collaborative Ventures." *Organization Science* 9, no. 3: 306–25.

Barringer, Bruce, and Jeffrey Harrison. 2000. "Walking a Tightrope: Creating Value Through Interorganizational Relationships." *Journal of Management* 26, no. 3: 367–403.

Barzelay, Michael. 1992. *Breaking Through Bureaucracy: A New Vision for Managing in Government.* Berkeley: University of California Press.

Becker, Ernest. 1973. *The Denial of Death.* New York: Free Press.

Boris, Elizabeth, and C. Eugene Steuerle. 2006. *Nonprofits and Government: Collaboration and Conflict.* 2d ed. Washington, DC: Urban Institute Press.

Boyte, Harry C., and Nancy N. Kari. 1996. *Building America: The Democratic Promise of Public Work.* Philadelphia, PA: Temple.

Bozeman, Barry. 2002. "Public-Value Failure: When Efficient Markets May Not Do." *Public Administration Review* 62, no. 2: 145–61.

———. 2007. *Public Value and Public Interest: Counterbalancing Economic Individualism.* Washington, DC: Georgetown University Press.

Brandl, J. 1998. *Money and Good Intentions Are Not Enough.* Washington, DC: Brookings Institution.

Bryant, John. 2003. *The Six Dilemmas of Collaboration: Inter-organizational Relationships as Drama.* New York: Wiley.

Bryce, Herrington J. 2000. *Financial and Strategic Management for Nonprofit Organizations.* San Francisco: Jossey-Bass.

———. 2005. *Players in the Policy Process: Nonprofits as Social Capital and Agents.* New York: Palgrave Macmillan.

Bryson, John M. 2004a. "Strategic Planning and Action Planning for Nonprofit Organizations." In *The Jossey-Bass Handbook of Nonprofit Leadership and Management,* ed. R. Herman, 154–183. San Francisco: Jossey-Bass.

———. 2004b. "What To Do When Stakeholders Matter: Stakeholder Identification and Analysis Techniques." *Public Management Review* 6, no. 1: 21–53.

Bryson, John M.; Fran Ackermann; and Colin Eden. 2007. "Putting the Resource-Based View of Strategy and Distinctive Competencies to Work in Public Organizations." *Public Administration Review* 67, no. 4: 702–17.

Bryson, John M.; Barbara C. Crosby; and Melissa Middleton Stone. 2006. "The Design and Implementation of Cross-Sector Collaborations: Propositions from the Literature." *Public Administration Review* 66 (Special Issue): 44–55.

Chen, Bin, and Elizabeth A. Graddy. 2005. "Inter-Organizational Collaborations for Public Service Delivery: A Framework of Preconditions, Processes and Perceived Outcomes." Unpublished manuscript.

Chrislip, David D. 2002. *The Collaborative Leadership Fieldbook: A Guide for Citizens and Civic Leaders.* San Francisco: Jossey-Bass.

Clarke, Michael, and John Stewart. 1997. *Handling the Wicked Issues: A Challenge for Government.* Birmingham, AL: University of Birmingham, Institute of Local Government Studies.

Crosby, Barbara C., and John M. Bryson. 2005a. *Leadership for the Common Good: Tackling Public Problems in a Shared-Power World.* San Francisco: Jossey-Bass.

———. 2005b. "A Leadership Framework for Cross-Sector Collaboration." *Public Management Review* 7, no. 2: 177–201.

———. 2007. "Leadership for the Common Good: Creating Regimes of Mutual Gain." In *Transforming Public Leadership for the 21st Century,* ed. Ricardo S. Morse and Terry F. Buss, 185–202. Armonk, NY: M.E. Sharpe.

DiMaggio, Paul J., and Walter W. Powell. 1983. "The Iron Cage Revisited: Institutional Isomorphism and Collective Rationality." *American Sociological Review* 48 (April): 147–60.

———. 1991. *The New Institutionalism in Organizational Life.* Chicago: The University of Chicago Press.

Dobel, J. Patrick, and Angela Day. 2005. "A Note on Mapping: Understanding Who Can Influence Your Success." Seattle, WA: Daniel J. Evans School of Public Affairs, Electronic Hallway. Available at www.hallway.org (accessed October 1, 2008).

Edelman, Murray J. 1988. *Constructing the Political Spectacle.* Chicago: University of Chicago Press.

———. 2001. *The Politics of Misinformation.* New York: Cambridge University Press.

Emery, Fred, and Eric Trist. 1965. "The Causal Texture of Organizational Environments." *Human Relations* 18: 21–32.

Friedland, Roger, and Robert Alford. 1991. "Bringing Society Back In: Symbols, Practices and Institutional Contradictions." In *The New Institutionalism in Organizational Analysis,* ed. W.W. Powell and P.J. DiMaggio, 232–67. Chicago: University of Chicago Press.

Friedmann, John. 1979. *The Good Society.* Cambridge, MA: MIT Press.

Gray, Barbara. 1989. *Collaborating.* San Francisco: Jossey-Bass.

Grayling, Anthony C. 2003. *What Is Good? The Search for the Best Way to Live.* London: Weidenfeld & Nicholson.

Hall, Peter D. 2006. "A Historical Overview of Philanthropy, Voluntary Associations, and Nonprofit Organizations in the United States, 1600–2000." In *The Nonprofit Sector: A Research Handbook,* 2d ed., ed. W.W. Powell and R. Steinberg, 32–65. New Haven, CT: Yale University Press.

Hansmann, Henry. 1981. "Reforming Nonprofit Corporation Law." *University of Pennsylvania Law Review* 129: 295–305.

Hennepin County (MN) and City of Minneapolis Commission to End Homelessness. July 2006. *Heading Home Hennepin: The Ten-Year Plan to End Homelessness in Minneapolis and Hennepin County.*

Himmelman, Arthur T. 1996. "On the Theory and Practice of Transformational Collaborations: From Social Service to Social Justice." In *Creating Collaborative Advantage,* ed. C. Huxham, 19–43. Thousand Oaks, CA: Sage.

Hubbard, Elizabeth T. 1995. "Making Sense of Public Service Partnerships: Understanding the Why & How of Interagency Efforts." M.A. thesis, University of Minnesota.

Hudson, Bob; Brian Hardy; Melanie Henwood; and Gerald Wistow. 1999. "In Pursuit of Inter-Agency Collaboration in the Public Sector: What Is the Contribution of Theory and Research?" *Public Management: An International Journal of Research and Theory* 1, no. 2: 235–60.

Human, Sherrie, and Keith Provan. 1997. "An Emergent Theory of Structure and Outcomes in Small-Firm Strategic Manufacturing Networks." *Academy of Management Journal* 40, no. 2: 368–403.

———. 2006. "Legitimacy Building in the Evolution of Small-Firm Multilateral Networks: A Comparative Study of Success and Demise. *Administrative Science Quarterly* 45: 327–65.

Huxham, Chris, ed. 1996. *Creating Collaborative Advantage.* Thousand Oaks, CA: Sage.

Huxham, Chris, and Siv Vangen. 2000. "Leadership in the Shaping and Implementation of Collaboration Agendas: How Things Happen in a (Not Quite) Joined-up World." *Academy of Management Journal* 43, no. 6: 1159–75.

———. 2005. *Managing to Collaborate: The Theory and Practice of Collaborative Advantage.* New York: Routledge.

Keast, Robyn; Myrna Mandell; Kerry Brown; and Geoffrey Woolcock. 2004. "Network Structures: Working Differently and Changing Expectations." *Public Administration Review* 64, no. 3: 363–71.

Krasner, Stephen D. 1983. *Structural Causes and Regime Consequences: Regimes as Intervening Variables.* Ithaca, NY: Cornell University Press.

Light, Paul C. 2002. *Government's Greatest Achievements.* Washington, DC: Brookings Institution Press.

Luke, Jeffrey S. 1998. *Catalytic Leadership: Strategies for an Interconnected World.* San Francisco: Jossey-Bass.

Mattessich, Paul; Marta Murray-Close; and Barbara Monsey. 2001. *Collaboration: What Makes It Work.* St. Paul, MN: Amherst H. Wilder Foundation.

Merrill-Sands, Deborah, and Bridgette Sheridan. 1996. *Developing and Managing Collaborative Alliances: Lessons from a Review of the Literature.* Organizational Change Briefing Note no. 3. Boston: Simmons Institute for Leadership and Change.

Moore, Mark H. 1995. *Creating Public Value.* Cambridge, MA: Harvard University Press.

———. "Managing for Value: Organizational Strategy in For-Profit, Nonprofit, and Governmental Organizations." *Nonprofit and Voluntary Sector Quarterly* 29, no. 1: 183–204.

Oliver, Christine. 1990. "Determinants of Interorganizational Relationships: Integration and Future Direction." *Academy of Management Review* 15, no. 2: 241–65.

Osborne, David, and Peter Plastrik. 1997. *Banishing Bureaucracy: The Five Strategies for Reinventing Government.* Reading, MA: Addison-Wesley.

Osborne, David, and Peter Hutchinson. 2004. *The Price of Government: Getting the Results We Need in an Age of Permanent Fiscal Crisis.* New York: Basic Books.

Ostrower, Francie. 2005. "The Reality Underneath the Buzz of Partnerships: The Potentials and Pitfalls of Partnering." *Stanford Social Innovation Review* (Spring): 34–41.

Pfeffer, Jeffrey, and Gerald Salancik. 1978. *The External Control of Organizations: A Resource Dependence Perspective.* New York: Harper & Row.

Powell, Walter W. 1990. "Neither Market nor Hierarchy: Network Forms of Organization." *Research in Organization Behavior* 12: 295–336.

Putnam, Robert D. 2000. *Bowling Alone: The Collapse and Revival of American Community.* New York: Simon & Schuster.

Rethemeyer, R. Karl. 2005. "Conceptualizing and Measuring Collaborative Networks." *Public Administration Review* 65, no. 1 (January/February): 117–21.

Ring, Peter S., and Andrew Van de Ven. 1994. "Developmental Processes of Cooperative Interorganizational Relationships. *Academy of Management Review* 19, no. 1: 90–118.

Roberts, Nancy C. 2000. "Coping with Wicked Problems: The Case of Afghanistan." *Learning from International Public Management Reform* 11B: 353–75.

Romzek, Barbara S. 1996. "Enhancing Accountability." In *Handbook of Public Administration,* ed. J.L. Perry, 97–114. San Francisco: Jossey-Bass.

Salamon, Lester. 1987. Partners in Public Service: The Scope and Theory of Government-Nonprofit Relationships. In *The Nonprofit Sector: A Research Handbook,* ed. W.W. Powell, 99–117. New Haven, CT: Yale University Press.

———. 1995. *Partners in Public Service: Government-Nonprofit Relations in the Modern Welfare State.* Baltimore: Johns Hopkins University Press.

———. 2002. "The New Governance and the Tools of Public Action: An Introduction." In *The Tools of Government,* ed. L.M. Salamon, 1–47. New York: Oxford University Press.

Sandfort, Jodi, and Melissa M. Stone. 2006. "The State and Local Contexts of Third Party Government: Helping Students Analyze Policy Fields." Paper presented at the annual conference of the National Association of Schools of Public Affairs and Administration, Minneapolis, MN, October 19–21.

Schön, Donald. 1971. *Beyond the Stable State.* New York: Norton.

Schultze, Charles L. 1977. *The Public Use of Private Interest.* Washington, DC: Brookings Institution.

Scott, James C. 1998. *Seeing Like a State: How Certain Schemes to Improve the Human Condition Have Failed.* New Haven, CT: Yale University Press.

Scott, W. Richard, and John W. Meyer. 1991. *The Organization of Societal Sectors: Propositions and Early Evidence.* Chicago: University of Chicago Press.

Senge, Peter M. 1994. *The Fifth Discipline: The Art of Practice of the Learning Organization.* New York: Doubleday.

Sharfman, Mark; Barbara Gray; and Aimin Yin. 1991. "The Context of Interorganizational Collaboration in the Garment Industry: An Institutional Perspective. *Journal of Applied Behavioral Science* 27, no. 20: 181–208.

Smith, Steven Rathgeb, and Michael Lipsky. 1993. *Nonprofits for Hire.* Cambridge, MA: Harvard University Press.

Stone, Deborah A. 2002. *Policy Paradox and Political Reason.* New York: Norton.

Stone, Melissa Middleton, and Jodi Sandfort. 2006. "Constructing Policy Fields to Inform Stone, Melissa Middleton Research in Nonprofit Organizations." Paper presented at the annual conference of the Association for Research on Nonprofit Organizations and Voluntary Action, Chicago, November 16–18.

Suchman, Mark C. 1995. "Managing Legitimacy: Strategic and Institutional Approaches." *Academy of Management Review* 20, no. 3: 571–610.

Thornton, Patricia H., and William Ocasio. 1999. "Institutional Logics and the Historical Contingency of Power in Organizations: Executive Succession in the Higher Education Publishing Industry, 1958–1990." *American Journal of Sociology* 105, no. 3: 801–43.

Waddock, Sandra. 1986. "Public-Private Partnership as Social Product and Process." *Research in Corporate Social Performance and Policy* 8: 273–300.

Weimer, David L., and Aidan R. Vining. 2004. *Policy Analysis: Concepts and Practice.* Englewood Cliffs, NJ: Prentice Hall.

Weisbrod, Burton. 1986. "Toward a Theory of the Voluntary Nonprofit Sector in a Three Sector Economy. In *The Economics of Nonprofit Institutions,* ed. S. Rose Ackerman, 21–44. New York: Oxford University Press.

Wildavsky, Aaron. 1979. *Speaking Truth to Power: The Art and Craft of Policy Analysis.* Boston: Little, Brown.

Williamson, Oliver. 1975. *Markets and Hierarchies: Analysis and Antitrust Implications.* New York: Free Press.

CHAPTER 5

Incentivizing
Collaborative Performance
Aligning Policy Intent, Design, and Impact

PATRICIA WALLACE INGRAHAM AND HEATHER GETHA-TAYLOR

Motivating and rewarding public employees correctly is a topic of significance to elected officials, public managers, the employees themselves, and—of course—to citizens. Specifically, motivation and reward serve as important variables in the performance of critical public functions. As such, connecting appropriate rewards with organizational goals represents a big idea in public management. And this idea has even more currency given the ever-increasing demands for high performance in an environment of shrinking resources. This paradoxical situation has thus contributed to an increased need for collaboration, or working across agency and sector boundaries to accomplish organizational goals. Understanding how to properly motivate and reward such collaborative behavior is a significant research task that has only just begun. Understanding how human resource management reforms such as performance-based pay affect collaborative behavior is a primary goal of this research.

A great deal of the design of incentives for motivation and nature of appropriate reward has been based on several key and relatively simplistic assumptions. All are somewhat controversial; some have been rendered less significant by changes in the environment of public organizations and in changed expectations for members of the public service. The most notable of these is that members of the public service are motivated by exactly the same incentives as their private sector counterparts (but see Perry, Mesch, and Paarlberg 2006). The second follows closely: the most important incentives are financial (Ingraham 1997; Rainey and Ryu 2004). As a result, human resource management reforms have focused almost exclusively on individual performance and financial rewards for it. At the same time, however, the world has changed around policy design activities.

Events of the past decade reflect the tensions thus created. Two examples are significant.

Both have substantial potential impact on public employees and their conditions of work. Sadly, each seems to be proceeding in glorious oblivion of the other. The first emerging condition is an increasing reliance on pay-for-performance, individual performance management, and variable pay (Ingraham 2006; U.S. GAO 2005a). These components are important parts of the management reforms at the Department of Homeland Security, the Department of Defense, and of other reform proposals submitted by members of Congress (Ingraham and Getha-Taylor 2006; Partnership 2006). The arguments underpinning them strongly support the idea that pay linked to individual performance will improve the overall performance and productivity of the organization.

Another set of events, however, shed some doubt on the wisdom of relying so heavily on individual performance and financial incentives. Prominent among these is the increasingly obvious need for collaboration among workers, units of an organization, different organizations, different levels of government, and, indeed, different nations. The war on terror, natural disasters such as Hurricane Katrina, and the complex web of program implementation activities in a federal system of government give little credence to the notion of total reliance on individual effort. This is not to suggest that individual effort does not matter. It does and always will. But increasingly, individual action occurs and makes a difference in the context of a much larger and interdependent web of activity and resources.

This context has serious implications for the ways in which reforms and the incentives they create are considered, designed, and implemented. In this chapter, we explore the fit—or lack thereof—of current reform efforts that emphasize individual performance and financial incentives, with the expanding and very real need for collaboration in public organizations. We ask: Is it possible that current reforms are well behind the curve in identifying the nature of performance critical to public effectiveness, in designing incentives to motivate toward such performance, and in rewarding that performance if it occurs? Is it possible that current reforms, with their learning activities almost solely focused on reforms of the past, focus design and debate on the wrong incentive packages? Are there better solutions?

MOTIVATION AND REWARD IN THE PUBLIC SECTOR WORKPLACE

Incentives in a Bounded Setting

Much of what we know about incentives in the workplace has been derived from experimental settings not located in public sector organizations. Much of the earliest work draws upon the theory of Weber, which assumes that hierarchical settings provide incentives to individuals by utilizing their expertise well, by providing a stable environment, and by clarifying the locations of authority and power within the organization (Weber 1946; also see Rainey 2003, ch. 10). Through the period of "scientific management," the role of organizational context was clearly recognized, but the focus was on the *individual* employee: proper recognition of her skills and talents and appropriate reward for utilizing those skills effectively in a tightly bounded setting. The classification and compensation systems in effect for most of the history of civil service in the United States are examples. Kanter (1983) observes that in what she terms "segmentalist" organizations—organizations characterized by tall hierarchies and "long" chains of command—the presence of thick rule structures inhibits both communication and deviation from rules. Predictable individual action is not only valued, but is cultivated. Rewards are most often tied to individual effort and to "fitting in"—that is, behaving and performing in a way that does not set the employee off from others. Work and research specifically on financial incentives has also focused very strongly on individual effort and reward. Timing of reward, the extent to which the employee values the reward, and the clear ability to link individual reward to specific performance are all frequent foci. Pay-for-performance systems, endemic in all sectors, are based strongly on the linkages summarized by Deci (1985).

At the same time, in the federal government and many other organizations, financial incentives have been viewed as a means of breaking the mold, of encouraging public employees to perform at higher levels and in different ways, and—in theory at least—of rewarding behavior that is different from the norm. This perspective was quickly dashed with the merit pay reforms contained in the Civil Service Reform Act (CSRA) of 1978, but reemerged remarkably fresh in iterations of reform for the Senior Executive Service, in some of the demonstration projects authorized under the CSRA, and certainly in the redesign of major organizations such as the Federal Aviation Administration and the Internal Revenue Service, and in major changes such as the creation of the Department of Homeland Security and the proposed "renovation" of the Department of Defense (Ingraham 1995; Ingraham and Getha-Taylor 2006). The most notable difference from previous reforms is a strong emphasis not on isolated individual performance, but on individual performance clearly linked to objectives outlined by the organizational mission. These linkages are clearly identified by reforms such as the Government Performance and Results Act (Joyce 2001) and by the PART (Program Assessment Rating Tool) efforts undertaken by the Office of Management and Budget.

Incentives in Unbounded Settings

Because incentives have been discussed most often in the context of clearly bounded organizations characterized by a specific and relatively stable set of actors, specific resources, and organization-specific goals and objectives, the theoretical underpinnings of collaboration pose an immediate problem. The porosity of boundaries, the multiorganizational objectives, and the lack of clarity regarding specific actors for specific tasks present both theoretical and practical challenges. Further, the somewhat difficult task of actually defining collaboration and how it looks creates additional murkiness to the incentive design problem. The frequency with which various authors use the terms "partnership," "networks," and "collaboration" interchangeably confounds the problem. Lowndes and Skelcher attempt to resolve the definitional conundrum in the following way: "[P]artnership as an organizational structure is analytically distinct from *network* as a mode of governance—the means by which social coordination is achieved. The creation of a partnership board does not imply that relations between actors are conducted on the basis of mutual benefit, trust, and reciprocity—the characteristics of the network mode of governance . . . partnerships are associated with a variety of forms of social coordination—including network, hierarchy, and market" (1998, 314).

Why are these differences and the difficulties in abilities to distinguish among them relevant to incentive structures and potential rewards? Conditions of trust, ability to clearly understand expectations and rules for achieving them, and a perception that the reward will be valued and worth the effort necessary to achieve it are the foundation of most contemporary incentive schemes. In that sense, familiarity with one organization and one set of actors is more likely to be achieved in a traditional organizational structure; all of the above conditions are uncertain or in flux in a networked, collaborative environment. But the ability to adapt to such an environment—and to perform well within it—is critical to collaborative success. And, as we noted earlier, there is increasing consensus that collaboration is not just a good idea, but a necessity.

FEDERAL HUMAN RESOURCE REFORM—HISTORY AND INCREMENTAL DEVELOPMENT

Policy design is difficult in both practical and theoretical terms. Some analysts have argued that greater precision and clarity in the legislative discussion and approval stages would more clearly link the problem to be addressed, the policy solution, and the expected outcome (Nakamura and Smallwood 1980). Others speak of "wicked" public policy dilemmas and the essential inability to effectively solve them through incremental political steps (Kettl 2005). Still others suggest that deficiencies in both problem analysis and the clarity of potential solutions, in tandem with a lack of political will, inevitably result in policies that are "deformed at birth." This, they argue, is particularly true in the United States (Peters and Hogwood 1985).

In fact, the consistently incremental policy design pattern in much of U.S. federal legislation does reflect a limited analysis of the actual content of the problem being addressed. Political rhetoric and symbolism dilutes the focus even further. In 1978, for example, when Jimmy Carter's administration proposed the first major overhaul of public personnel law in nearly a hundred years, the president identified the problems as "lack of merit in the merit system" and "deadwood in the bureaucracy" (Ingraham and Ban 1984, 17). This is catchy rhetoric, but not a definition of specific problems to be addressed.

The pay-for-performance policies discussed in this chapter have a somewhat similar history. They are intended to address bureaucratic lethargy and lack of productivity, but they make some assumptions about members of the public service that are questionable. Chief among these is that money is the primary—perhaps the only significant—incentive. Similarly, such policies assume that if money matters, enough money to make a difference will be available for public incentive packages. The reforms have spread like wildfire across the world, despite the fact that available evidence suggests both assumptions to be unfounded (Ingraham 1997). Further, an even more basic assumption—that public pay-for-performance programs were modeled after very successful initiatives in the private sector—has also been demonstrated to be untrue except at the very top levels of the organization (Milkovich and Wigdor 1991). In short, there is little or no evidence to link pay-for-performance systems to specific public productivity problems. Add to this the issue of public sector unions and the match between perceived problem and proposed solution becomes very murky indeed.

Despite this record, pay-for-performance became—as we noted earlier—a primary component in the major human resource management (HRM) reforms at the Department of Homeland Security (DHS) and the Department of Defense. There are conflicting reports about how this came to be. It can be argued, for example, that the Research and Demonstration Projects funded under Title VII of the 1978 Civil Service Reform Act provided twenty-five years of experience with pay-for-performance in the public sector and that this information was instrumental in the decision making. Other long-term key actors in federal management reform efforts argue that, over the years, organizations such as the Office of Management and Budget essentially accumulated bits and pieces of reform legislation that was aggregated into one package for the DHS legislation (personal conversation with Jonathan Breul, November 2005). Douglas Brook and colleagues offer a somewhat more chilling account:

> The small White House staff group worked in secret in the Presidential Emergency Operations Center (PEOC). Stung by the failure of an earlier attempt to coordinate a bill on border security throughout the government bureaucracy, the White House decided to draft the homeland security proposal without coordination with the cabinet departments. In fact, most of the members of the Cabinet learned about the proposal, and its impact on their departments, only a day before its public release. As Kay Cole James [director of the Office of Personnel Management] describes, "The phone rang about mid-day, asking that I come over to the White House at 6:00 pm. Then, Mark Everson laid out to me that he and several others had been involved in shaping this thing called the Department of Homeland Security, and it was going to be announced the following morning." No time or opportunity existed for turf wars. (Brook et al. 2006, 90)

To be sure, more specific issues of design and content were hammered out after passage of the legislation, and this process involved leading HRM experts in government as well as members of the public service across the country. It also involved leaders of public sector unions who resisted virtually all of the pay-for-performance and flexibility provisions and have been successful in delaying—and perhaps stopping—many of them in the courts (Pfiffner 2007). Our point here is that design occurred *after* passage of the legislation, and the problem being targeted was the need for greater flexibility in combating the war on terror, not necessarily a more effective public workforce. The more fundamental point, however, is that even to the extent that greater effectiveness was considered, *individual* incentives were created and *team* or *collaborative* incentives were apparently not. This was so in a setting in which the need for collaboration had been dramatically and tragically demonstrated. From all available evidence, policy design proceeded in a way that took all of its signals from past experience and past information (even when erroneous) and may well have created a new policy that places incentives in the wrong places and for the wrong purposes to allow the collaborative endeavors necessary for effective action in the new environment. Do top leaders in public management agree with this assessment, and if so, what are the potential consequences? The following sections of the chapter discuss our research methods and our findings in that regard.

METHODOLOGY AND DATA

This analysis examines three critical questions: First, what are the individual-level incentives that motivate federal civil servants? Second, do they motivate them for collaborative performance and how is that collaborative performance rewarded? Finally, if current reform efforts do *not* support collaboration, which solutions should we consider? To answer these questions, we began by interviewing twenty-three career senior executives via telephone. All but two of these senior executives received the 2005 Presidential Rank Award, the single most prestigious award for career civil servants. The U.S. Office of Personnel Management (OPM) notes that the Presidential Rank Awards are "reserved for executives who have a record of achievement which is recognized throughout the agency and/or is acknowledged on a national or international level," (U.S. OPM 1999). These exceptional leaders were of particular interest for this research, given the fact that the selection criteria for the Presidential Rank Award are based partially on an individual's evidence of successful collaboration. This criterion sample, or sample based on people who are clearly successful, can be used as a first step for comparison studies.

In addition, we interviewed eleven federal human resource management experts in Washington, DC. These individuals were chosen for their expertise in such relevant subjects as organizational learning, leadership development, competency assessment, and performance appraisal. Together, these thirty-four interviewees represent fourteen federal organizations and two nonprofit government-consulting organizations. The interview sample included ten women and twenty-four men. The interviews averaged one hour in length and were semistructured to allow for open-ended responses to questions concerning each interviewee's experiences with collaboration. Interviewees were asked to describe their experience working in/with the federal government, including the relevant incentives for collaborative behavior and rewards for collaborative performance. The data from these interviews are supplemented with findings from the Office of Personnel Management's 2002 and 2004 Federal Human Capital Surveys, scholarly literature, and government reports.

FINDINGS

Motivation to Perform Well

When we consider what employees want from their jobs, lessons from expectancy theory help illuminate the implications of pay-for-performance reform. Expectancy theory demonstrates the relationships among the value of an outcome, the necessary action needed to attain that outcome, and the probability that a particular action will result in the desired outcome. Rainey sums up expectancy theory as follows: "[P]eople will do what they see as most likely to result in the most good and the least bad" (2003, 258).

Lawler (1994) argues that when managers question the productivity (or performance) of employees, they often compare the rewards given to both high and low performers. More often than not, says Lawler, they find no difference. "Thus, the workers' perception of the situation is that the good and the poor performers receive the same treatment, and this view is crucial in determining motivation" (67). A federal executive interviewee echoed Lawler when explaining why performance-based pay is gaining currency as a reform tool: "[W]e treat everyone the same, and this strikes people at an emotional level . . . there is an inequity between borderline and superior performers." And this is the premise that pay-for-performance policy is built upon: Providing differences in performance rewards will improve overall performance by motivating poor performers to improve.

There are two problems with this argument as it relates to the public sector. First, the very nature of public work has evolved. Modern governance requires skills such as creativity, diplomacy, and conflict resolution that are (a) not easily identified, and (b) not easily measured. Differentiating between average and superior performance, therefore, is a significant challenge. Second, money alone is not motivating the public sector workforce. For example, our respondents indicated that nontangible rewards for collaborative action include the opportunity to learn from others and solve problems jointly. "When you get groups together, they will always come up with something that none of us separately could have come up with." There is a general willingness to recognize that there is great value in the group approach to problem solving. "I'm willing to admit that I don't have the answers to everything." Particularly in applications that require an interdisciplinary approach (such as the environmental sciences), collaboration among different government organizations is critical. "We don't work on issues in a vacuum," said one senior executive.

Job Satisfaction and Performance

Equity theory helps to analyze employees' reactions to what they receive—and their resulting satisfaction or dissatisfaction—as well as the broad implications of current policy choices. Satisfaction, according to Adams (1963), is determined by an individual's perception of the input–outcome balance (or equity). Dissatisfaction, then, results when there is inequity between inputs and outcomes. Pay-for-performance speaks to this inequity, and in theory, attempts to correct it. High-performing employees should be rewarded accordingly and the input–outcome equation should be balanced as a result. However, in order to properly reward high performers, it is necessary to (1) determine the valence, or value, of various rewards for individual employees, and (2) consider ways to reinforce nontangible rewards as well as tangible rewards (such as performance-based pay). Simply put, performance-based pay can satisfy employees only if they view it as a valuable—and appropriate—reward for their actions.

Lawler (1994) notes, "satisfaction is determined by the perceived ratio of what a person receives from his job relative to what a person puts into his job" (89). As mentioned above, we must evaluate the full spectrum of rewards as they apply to rewarding collaborative behavior. When we asked respondents about collaboration as a task, most viewed collaboration as something they are *allowed to do,* rather than something they *have to do.* "We are privileged to do what we do." These respondents view collaboration as one more way to serve the public in a manner that contributes to efficiency and effectiveness. Collaboration, from this perspective, is its own reward.

The executives we spoke to actively seek out collaborative opportunities: They see collaboration as an obvious way to accomplish their goals, and it is this goal achievement that provides them with a sense of satisfaction. Based on these interviews, it seems that these civil servants would not be dissatisfied if they were not rewarded for their performance; it is poor performance that would cause their dissatisfaction. As one respondent said, "I get energy from getting things done." Even when the task is daunting, the end result is worth the struggle. One respondent noted that the challenges of public service can be draining: "This is killing me," he said, "but I'm getting a lot from it." Our respondents feel fulfilled when they actively find ways not only to meet their own goals but also to contribute to "the greater good" of public service.

The Changing Nature of Work and Performance

The characteristics of the organizational setting are particularly relevant to the public sector workforce. Scholars have worked to develop a theory of public service motivation (see Brewer, Selden, and Facer 2000; Naff and Crum 1999; Perry 1996, 1997, 2000), which has been defined as "an individual's predisposition to respond to motives grounded primarily or uniquely in public institutions" (Perry and Wise 1990, 368). The public service motivation construct includes two important dimensions that relate directly to the pay-for-performance discussion: commitment to the public interest and self-sacrifice. These two dimensions are integral to the pay-for-performance issue, as it has been noted that public servants are often willing to forgo financial rewards in favor of the rewards they receive from public service (Macy 1971; Perry 1996).

The rewards received from public service include the opportunity to connect with, and contribute to, a public service mission: As one executive said, "We all belong to something bigger." Our interviews revealed that the desire to connect with, and contribute to, the organizational mission was the single most important motivating factor for collaborative behavior among respondents. Despite differing federal mandates among agencies, one respondent summed up the federal calling quite nicely: "Because we all have that interest in meeting the taxpayer's needs as efficiently and effectively as we can, we can develop trust more easily and maintain relationships more easily."

The mission-centered context of public sector work does create a performance evaluation challenge. There is no one simple "bottom line" equivalent for public sector organizations. Implementing pay-for-performance across federal organizations is an awkward proposition when public sector performance evaluation necessarily includes consideration of various stakeholders, balancing competing demands, and justifying both mission relevance and organizational effectiveness. Nonetheless, 83 percent of federal employees indicated in the 2004 Federal Human Capital Survey that they either agree or strongly agree that they are held accountable for achieving results. This proportion held steady from the 2002 survey (82 percent).

Similarly, the proportion of respondents who indicated that their appraisals fairly reflect their performance held steady from 2002 (68 percent) to 2004 (69 percent). Measuring performance in a fair manner—and providing meaningful distinctions in performance—are ongoing questions in public personnel management. These questions are increasingly important when we consider their application to collaborative behaviors. Lawler (1994) notes that evaluation systems do not always measure all the necessary behaviors for performance and the result is that "those behaviors that aren't measured tend to be ignored or performed poorly" (155). Pay-for-performance, and its focus on individual performance, may actually strain interpersonal relationships by valuing competition over cooperation. While relationships may suffer first within work units in a single organization, this effect can diffuse to collaborative relationships that cross organizational boundaries. Respondents noted that they first learned to collaborate through interactions with people in their own organization. A culture that values collaboration is evident when collaboration is valued and modeled by organizational leaders, said one respondent. Further, when asked how they "teach" collaboration, respondents frequently note that starting small is the answer. For instance, executives may allow new employees to shadow them in meetings and collaborative exercises. Rather than focusing on training as the preferred tool to teach people how to collaborate, respondents are more likely to agree with one executive who said, "Informal interactions change behavior."

Incentives for Collaborative Performance

Collaboration, our work indicates, is a two-step process of development: Once employees understand how to work together with people in their own organization, they can begin to work with people in other organizations. Reforms to enhance collaborative performance, then, should focus on measuring and rewarding cooperation both within an organization and collaboration across organizations. Further, it is important to focus on a range of motives. For example, in addition to pay as an external motivator, the influence of social networks (including both leaders and peers) can impact individual performance. In the Reinventing Government movement in the Clinton administration, the creation of idea champions throughout the federal government enhanced trust in the initiative. By involving people at all levels in the reinvention effort, executives believed that "this is a sincere desire to make government more effective and efficient." A skilled idea champion can serve as a strong external motivator to encourage people to engage in new behaviors, including collaboration. "When you respect one another," said one of our respondents, "collaboration comes easily." Collaboration, said another, "is all about relationships."

Not only can interpersonal connections help improve feelings of self-worth and influence in the organization, but for many the opportunity to work with other people is a reward in itself. "I get energy from interaction with other people." Another respondent said the resulting friendships that emerged from collaborative efforts were "an absolute benefit of the whole thing." And building collaborative relationships can have real consequences for organizational performance. In the case of the response to Hurricane Katrina, respondents said that collaborative relationship building ahead of time could have helped build trust among the responding units. Even for federal employees who are not involved in homeland security efforts, the potential negative impact of neglecting relationship building is clear: "If you're smart and you want to get the job done, you're gonna know who you need to collaborate with effectively to get the job done."

The changing nature of governance not only requires that employees build strong relationships across organizations, it also requires that employees are strategic in those relationships. It is impossible for one person or even one organization to have all the skills necessary to solve complex governance problems. Reinvention efforts of the 1990s ushered in reductions in force and appropriation cuts, both of which were accompanied by early retirements and separations in the federal workforce (see Jones 1998). All the while, the remaining federal employees were charged with being more efficient. In light of the changing face of the workforce, junior employees were promoted to senior positions, and serious competency gaps were exposed. Hiring restrictions require today's federal employees to continue trying to fill these competency gaps in any way possible. Collaboration is one way to accomplish this goal. Collaboration is based on the sharing of resources, including knowledge. As one respondent said, in order to be viewed as a credible and integral component of the collaboration, you must bring expertise to the table. The credibility and mutual trust that accompany expertise are core components of successful collaboration and both require time to develop. Performance-based pay systems tend to focus on past and present behavior, and necessarily neglect forecasting or strategic planning. One executive mentioned that under pay-for-performance, employees will likely sacrifice developmental tasks in favor of tasks that demonstrate immediate gains in performance. Collaboration is developmental in the sense that it requires long-term building of relationships of mutual trust. In this respect, individually based performance systems can threaten the very fabric of collaboration.

It is also important to consider incentives for motivation that are linked to cost saving and efficiency. Political initiatives to trim the federal workforce and the federal budget have forced organizations to find innovative ways to meet their obligations. "I can't afford not to collaborate," said one respondent. Resource dependency theory, or the need to obtain critical resources for performance, highlights the motivation that drives collaboration under these conditions. Results from the Federal Human Capital Survey indicate that resource deficiency is a growing problem. In 2002, 48.4 percent of respondents said they agreed or strongly agreed with the following statement: "I have sufficient resources (for example, people, materials, budget, etc.) to get my job done." Two years later, only 39.5 percent of respondents responded similarly. As a result of this trend, civil servants must employ creative ways to get their jobs done. For instance, scientists working for the government often pool their funding in order to purchase or lease expensive equipment. In the example of the University-National Oceanographic Laboratory System, the U.S. Navy leases ships to scientists at a reduced cost, then both benefit from the resulting research. Resource needs are ongoing and nonnegotiable; what is negotiable is how to fulfill them. Collaboration will continue to be a tool of choice for leveraging the necessary resources to accomplish public sector goals. Whether or not performance-based pay can accurately evaluate or reward the kinds of skills necessary for collaborating successfully to leverage such resources is unclear.

Rewards for Collaboration

In 2000, Rainey and Kellough called for "creative developments of incentives besides pay and disciplinary action" (142). With this in mind, we asked our interviewees to provide us with the best options for collaborative rewards. As noted by Cross and Parker (2004), "formal rewards signal whether collaboration or individual achievement is important" (125). The authors continue, "it is counterproductive and little more than rhetoric to advocate the need for collaboration and sharing and then show employees what really matters with reward systems that run counter to sharing or helping colleagues (195)."

Given the emphasis on impending pay-for-performance reform at the Department of Homeland Security, it is interesting to note that across the board, respondents did not emphasize monetary rewards for collaborative behavior. "We're not oblivious to the money thing, but it is not the primary motivator," said one respondent. "I don't know of anyone who does what they do because of money." This broader concept of satisfaction is reflected in findings from the 2002 and 2004 Federal Human Capital Surveys. In 2004, there were increases, albeit slight, in the proportions of people who said that (a) their work gives them a feeling of personal accomplishment (72–73 percent), and (b) they like the kind of work they do (82–83 percent). At the same time, satisfaction with pay also increased in a parallel fashion: 67 percent of respondents indicated they were satisfied or very satisfied with their pay, compared with 66 percent two years earlier.

At the same time, however, there were decreases in other measures of employee satisfaction. First, in the 2002 survey, 58 percent of respondents indicated that they were satisfied with their involvement in decisions that affect their work. Two years later, that figure dropped by two percentage points. Satisfaction with alternative work schedules also decreased: Nearly 62 percent of respondents indicated that they were satisfied in 2002 versus nearly 60 percent in 2004. These dips in satisfaction reflect the core of this manuscript: Satisfaction is multidimensional and extends beyond pay. Policymakers and organizational leaders must consider the value that a particular reward has for different employees before implementing broad-based reforms to enhance multidimensional constructs such as satisfaction and performance. Given these survey results, increased attention should be paid to include performance-based rewards that extend beyond pay alone and include opportunities for job expansion or flexibility.

Rewards for collaborative behavior deserve special attention here given the team-based nature of collaboration. As collaboration typically involves individuals from different organizations, performance-based pay provides another problem. Executives from two separate agencies noted that it is impossible (due to appropriations language) to distribute funds across organizational boundaries. In the event that an organization wanted to reward all members of a collaborative effort, the award could not be pay-based. Interviewees identified several more appropriate, and more affordable, rewards. One of the most valued rewards was recognition, especially the opportunity to be recognized among one's peers or in front of organizational leaders. This, of course, depends on the employee's comfort level with public ceremonies. One executive wanted to formally recognize an employee for her contributions to a collaborative effort, but she was uncomfortable with the idea and requested schedule flexibility instead. The key here is to consider employee preferences when matching an award with performance.

Another interviewee mentioned "meaningful, interesting work," as a reward for collaborative behavior. Convincing employees of their connection to the organization is critical for this reward to hold value. It seems that public organizations are doing their job in this regard. A full 90 percent of Federal Human Capital Survey respondents (in both 2002 and 2004) indicated that they feel that the work they do is important. In addition, we found that praise was an extremely valuable reward for collaborative action. "People want you to think they're doing a good job . . . they're upset if you think they're not." Findings from the Federal Human Capital Survey indicate that satisfaction with such recognition is on the rise. In 2002, 51 percent of respondents indicated that they were satisfied with the recognition they receive for doing a good job. Two years later, that figure rose to 54 percent. According to one respondent, "praise keeps people happy and happy people work hard."

ALIGNING POLICY INITIATIVES WITH COLLABORATIVE BEHAVIOR OUTCOMES

Despite the need for collaboration to achieve public sector goals, not everyone is convinced that policymakers are moving in the right direction to support this means of problem solving, resource leveraging, and learning. "Working with other agencies is a way of life, or is fast becoming one, but it isn't embraced by the government," said one executive. Part of this concern stems from proposed personnel reforms that support performance-based pay. This same executive added, "In order to get our mission accomplished, we have to work together . . . yet, we're considering a performance system that is moving in the opposite direction."

The focus on performance-based pay paralleled the creation of the Department of Homeland Security as part of the 2002 Homeland Security Act. In the wake of the September 11 terrorist attacks, "homeland security" permeated American culture. As evidenced in the months following the attacks, the term "national security" actually "became the maxim that provided the rationale for civil service reform" (Naff and Newman 2004, 195). In addition to creating the Department of Homeland Security in 2002, the Bush administration pushed for coinciding human capital management reforms. And therein lies the policy rub: The performance reforms were advocated for reasons other than successful human resource reform. The reforms were drafted in the absence of input from personnel experts and some would say, in the absence of consideration of merit system principles (Brook et al. 2006; Pfiffner 2007). To be sure, if they work *as hoped,* they will have a positive impact on organizational performance. But that was not their primary purpose, and the ideas that would specifically examine linking employee efforts to the collaborative efforts clearly central to genuine effectiveness were not discussed.

LINKING REFORM NEED TO POLICY TOOLS

The research presented here confirms in many ways what scholars and practitioners have known about the public sector for a very long time. Public sector employees generally value the "public good" contribution their work can make. They value interaction with others and respect for the job they do. Financial incentives play some role, but they are not the only motivator and are most likely not the most significant. So what does the analysis contribute?

First, in light of the very profound need for collaboration in public work, it highlights one more time that motivation in public sector organizations is profoundly complex and multidimensional. It also points to the conclusion that public employees—at least those in our small sample—already know and value the nature and purpose of collaboration. They are far ahead of policymakers in acknowledging its centrality to effectiveness. Second, however, is the very unsettling reality that the set of personnel reforms now being implemented in fits and starts—and with substantial labor opposition—may be another of those American public policies whose time has passed (Peters and Hogwood 1985).

The employees we interviewed and the data we analyzed demonstrate not only that public servants understand the need for collaboration but also that they have a strong sense of how to make it happen. One respondent noted that if collaboration is required or mandated, leaders have to work to communicate why collaboration is important. As that person summarized, you have to give people a reason to care. "Collaboration depends on people wanting to make it happen. The agency may want to make it happen, but if the employees don't [want it], it won't happen." In other words, mandated collaboration is not the answer. "It's gotta be a bottom-up rather than a top-down thing," said one respondent. "The best collaborative efforts are those that aren't sanctioned." All you can mandate, said one respondent, is "going through the motions of collaboration."

The policy mismatch between the need and current reform efforts becomes glaringly evident in light of further comments. First, regardless of the rewards that are created to recognize collaboration, it is important to recognize both the collaborative process and the achievement that was produced via the collaboration. "Collaboration for the sake of collaboration is meaningless," said one executive. In addition, given the finite amount of money each organization will have for performance-based pay, there is no incentive to reward members outside their own organizations, even if the efforts of others helped accomplish a critical objective.

Respondents also argued that connecting the individual with organizational-level outcomes is necessary. In fact, one respondent said that the connection between individual effort and organizational outcomes is government's "secret weapon" to attracting and retaining high performers. "When people own the mission, they tend to reach out in a different way." A 2003 report from the U.S. Government Accountability Office echoed this recommendation and provided steps for improving an organization's "line of sight" or the connection between individual and organizational performance. Unfortunately, evidence from the Federal Human Capital Survey indicates this connection between individual effort and organizational outcomes is slipping. In 2002, 90.7 percent of federal respondents indicated that they agreed or strongly agreed with the following statement: "I know how my work relates to the agency's missions and goals." When the survey was administered two years later, only 84.9 percent of federal respondents answered in the same manner. If pay-for-performance reform is implemented, organizations will have to work even harder to (1) connect individual effort to organizational outcomes, (2) find alternative ways to reward collaborative behavior outside of performance-based pay, and (3) link collaborative behavior to organizational mission.

There are other issues to consider. Today's workforce is a far cry from the largely clerical cadre that existed almost seventy years ago (Ingraham 2005). Even though some reforms in the past twenty-five years—pay banding, for example—have removed some structural obstacles to collaboration, other very important obstacles remain. Today's workforce must be creative, customer-oriented, and collaborative. Measurement of these new skill sets is a daunting task. As one respondent said, "If you don't have good performance measures . . . and if you don't have supervisors who can provide the feedback . . . and make those performance distinctions, then pay-for-performance is going to be a problem." Particularly in instances when 360-degree feedback is not used, there is little basis to validate an employee's self-reports of collaborative behavior. Armstrong and Murlis (1988) remind us that performance-related pay rewards achievement, "not just effort" (211). This is particularly troubling in the context of collaboration, where effort may be the most visible output. It takes time and commitment to build the relationships and structures that facilitate successful collaboration. In fact, our respondents indicated that the most successful collaborative efforts they were ever involved with took more than a year, and often involved a multiyear commitment to see results.

Finally, there is good evidence that at the top levels of the federal government, collaboration is not just a suggestion, it is a requirement. "We'd all love the luxury of playing in our own sandbox, but leaders need to deliver the message that it's not a stove-piped world anymore." The Executive Core Qualifications (ECQs) include competencies that lend themselves to effective collaboration, especially those qualifications that are designed to evaluate an executive's ability to lead people and build coalitions. Promoting individuals who are skilled in collaboration encourages similar behavior by installing role models at the top levels of the organization, according to one respondent. Organizational leaders must demonstrate the organization's cultural values, including collaboration. "My job is to communicate a vision," said one senior executive. Training alone will not result in the type of collaborative behavior that organizations seek today. According to one respondent, "We all have limits on what we can absorb through training." It is the personal relationships that will provide the momentum and encouragement to act collaboratively. "I really think it takes exceptional leadership at the very top who values collaboration . . . and articulates . . . how important that is in an organization." This respondent went on to describe how successful one particular senior executive had been in communicating the value of collaboration to the employees. "His words spoke, but his actions spoke even more loudly."

CONCLUSION

In 1999, twenty-five leading public-sector practitioners joined scholars at the Wye River Plantation to "outline a vision of a system responsive to changes in the labor market and in the delivery of public services" (Ingraham, Selden, and Moynihan 2000, 54). One of the four main points from the conference was a focus on partnerships that include mutual goals and performance objectives. Achieving that end goal should be the focus of personnel management reforms, but pay-for-performance does not seem to fit the bill. With its focus on individual performance, collaboration requires effort above and beyond what would be evaluated. In that respect, if collaboration is necessary for achieving organizational goals but is not accurately captured as part of performance appraisals, leaders have to work even harder to communicate the value of collaboration and reward collaborative action.

This perspective has been reiterated many times: in 2004, the U.S. Government Accountability Office noted, "[M]uch more needs to be done to ensure that agencies' cultures are results oriented, customer focused, and *collaborative in nature*" (U.S. GAO 2004; emphasis added). One respondent was more emphatic: "I can't get anything done as an island." Other executives said that collaboration "is mandatory for success" and "is a very important means to the end." These comments illustrate an even larger trend: indicators from the Federal Human Capital Surveys provide evidence to suggest that collaboration is slowly diffusing throughout the federal government. In 2002, 82 percent of Federal Human Capital Survey (FHCS) respondents strongly agreed or agreed with the following statement: "The people I work with cooperate to get the job done." Two years later, 87 percent of respondents answered similarly. Also in 2002, 55 percent of FHCS respondents agreed or strongly agreed with the following statement: "Managers promote communication among different work units (for example, about projects, goals, needed resources)." In 2004, the proportion of respondents who answered similarly rose—ever so slightly—to 56 percent.

Understanding the incentives that help motivate federal employees to collaborate is not only a big idea in public management—it is also an important task that has only just begun. Identifying the processes and policies that curb collaboration is an equally important task. Further research is needed on this topic in order to design the kind of human resource management systems that will properly evaluate and reward collaborative performance in a manner that is fair and consistent. However, enough is already known to suggest that an early course correction in major reform efforts should be strongly recommended. While previous reform has focused exclusively on individual pay-based incentives, additional options should be considered and implemented. New options must be broader: broader in the sense that the focus shifts beyond individual accomplishment and beyond pay as the only potential reward. This transformation is already taking place in such agencies as the Department of Energy, where annual public recognition ceremonies recognize collaborative efforts. Further, in the interviews for this research, executives mentioned flexible working schedules as another potential reward for collaborative achievements. Just as employee benefits are moving toward cafeteria-style options, so too should employees and managers be able to adopt those rewards have the strongest valence—or impact—for them.

While the proposed human resource reform initiatives at DHS are still in early stages, the importance of these reforms and any subsequent reform cannot be understated. The U.S. GAO (2005b) observes that the proposed changes in DHS are "especially critical" because of their "potential implications for related government wide reform." Yet, we hear only faintly the warning of Rainey and Kellough (2000) which reminds us of the all too easily forgotten lessons of the past: "[P]roblems can arise if such reforms are pursued in isolation from other major considerations and in the absence of a more comprehensive view of reform that considers necessary preconditions and implementation challenges" (135).

We do not argue against rewarding performance. We argue against focusing on pay reform as the only way to incentivize performance and collaborative performance specifically. Rewarding collaboration requires a new set of assumptions, including the acknowledgment that collaboration is not an individual endeavor, that collaboration performance is driven by many factors (the *least* of which may be financial), and that many indispensable collaborative skills cannot be easily measured. For example, both the scholarly literature and interviews conducted for this research indicate that trust is a critical element in collaboration. Yet, trust is a concept that is not easily quantified or measured. Building trust is an activity that takes time, and lots of it. Respondents said that, in many cases, building trust takes years. Given the fact that pay-for-performance focuses on quantifying behavior within the past six to twelve months, long-term efforts that focus on building trust simply do not conform to pay-for-performance assessments, even if such efforts are critical to collaborative success.

In addition, pay-for-performance assessments serve as imperfect means for evaluating collaborative skills, in large part because of confusion about what constitutes collaborative skills. Interviews for this research identified a number of critical skills, most of which are in line with the U.S. Department of Personnel Management's Executive Core Qualifications. These ECQs are divided into five subcomponents (Leading Change, Leading People, Results Drive, Business Acumen, Building Coalitions). In related survey research, Getha-Taylor (2007) found that human resource managers and federal executives differ substantially in what they characterize as "collaborative competencies." While human resource managers align collaborative competencies with the competencies included in Building Coalitions (Partnering, Political Savvy, Influencing/Negotiating), most senior executives identified the competencies included in Leading Change (especially Vision and Strategic Thinking) as the most important collaborative skills. Future research that extends beyond the federal government will help to further develop our shared understanding of what constitutes effective collaborative behavior. This is an important task that has applications across the spectrum of human resource management practice, from selection and training to evaluation and promotion.

Aligning meaningful rewards with important organizational goals, including collaboration, is now and will remain a big idea in public management. This manuscript furthers the development of this idea by examining the relationship between performance-based pay reform and the demand for collaborative governance in the federal government. If there is a clear lesson from this research, it is that public servants are driven by a commitment to mission—and collaboration is a necessary means to achieving a mission. In fact, in the public sector, this mission achievement is the bottom line. In this respect, therefore, motivating and satisfying public employees is very difficult. To be satisfied and motivated, public sector employees need more than money. They need to know that their individual effort is contributing to something larger than themselves. That is what collaboration does and what it can achieve. The policy ideas of incentives and rewards for collaboration must become part of the human resource management reform equation. When that is accomplished, improved performance on all levels will follow.

REFERENCES

Adams, J. Stacy. 1963. "Toward an Understanding of Inequity." *Journal of Abnormal Psychology* 67: 422–36.

Armstrong, Michael, and Helen Murlis. 1988. *Reward Management: A Handbook of Remuneration Strategy and Practice.* 2d ed. London: Kogan Page.

Brewer, Gene A.; Sally C. Selden; and Rex L. Facer II. 2000. "Individual Conceptions of Public Service Motivation." *Public Administration Review* 60, no. 3: 254–64.

Brook, Douglas; Cynthia L. King; David Anderson; and Joshua Bahr. 2006. *Legislating Civil Service Reform: The Homeland Security Act of 2002.* Monterey, CA: Naval Postgraduate School, Center for Defense Management Reform.

Cross, Rob, and Andrew Parker. 2004. *The Hidden Power of Social Networks: Understanding How Work Really Gets Done in Organizations.* Boston: Harvard Business School Press.

Deci, Edward L. 1985. *Intrinsic Motivation and Self-Determination in Human Behavior.* New York: Plenum.

Getha-Taylor, Heather G. 2007. "Specifying and Testing a Model of Collaborative Capacity: Identifying Complementary Competencies, Incentive Structures, and Leadership Lessons for the U.S. Department of Homeland Security." Ph.D. diss. Syracuse University.

Ingraham, Patricia W. 1995. *The Foundation of Merit.* Baltimore: Johns Hopkins University Press.

———. 1997. "Play It Again Sam, It's Still Not Right: Searching for the Right Notes in Administrative Reform. *Public Administration Review* 57, no. 4: 325–31.

———. 2005. "The Federal Public Service: The People and the Challenge." In *The Executive Branch,* ed. J.D. Aberbach and M.A. Peterson, 283–311. New York: Oxford.

———. 2006. "Building Bridges over Troubled Waters: Merit as a Guide." *Public Administration Review* 66, no. 4: 486–95.

Ingraham, Patricia W., and Carolyn Ban. 1984. *Legislating Bureaucratic Change: The Civil Service Reform Act of 1978.* Albany: State University of New York Press.

Ingraham, Patricia W.; Sally C. Selden; and Donald P. Moynihan. 2000. "People and Performance: Challenges for the Future Public Service—The Report from the Wye River Conference." *Public Administration Review* 60, no. 1: 54–60.

Ingraham, Patricia W., and Heather Getha-Taylor. 2006. "Great Expectations but Hazards Ahead: Applying Lessons Learned from Past Demonstration Projects to Emergent Federal HRM Systems." In *Public Personnel Management: Current Concerns, Future* Challenges, 4th ed., ed. Norma Riccucci, 18–35. New York: Longman.

Jones, Vernon D. 1998. *Downsizing the Federal Government: The Management of Public Sector Workforce Reductions.* Armonk, NY: M.E. Sharpe.

Joyce, Philip. 2001. "Beyond the Government Performance and Results Act: Moving Toward Managing for Results." In *Memos to the President: Management Advice from the Nation's Top Public Administrators,* ed. Mark Abramson, 117–24. Lanham, MD: Rowman and Littlefield.

Kanter, Rosabeth M. 1983. *The Change Masters.* New York: Simon & Schuster.

Kettl, Donald F. 2005. "The Worst Is Yet to Come: Lessons from September 11 and Hurricane Katrina." Fels Institute of Government, University of Pennsylvania.

Lawler, Ed E. III. 1994. *Motivation in Work Organizations.* San Francisco: Jossey-Bass.

Lowndes, Vivien, and Chris Skelcher. 1998. "The Dynamics of Multi-organizational Partnerships: An Analysis of Changing Modes of Governance." *Public Administration* 76, no. 2: 313–33.

Macy, John. 1971. *Public Service: The Human Side of Government.* New York: Harper & Row.

Milkovich, George T., and Alexandra K. Wigdor. 1991. *Pay for Performance: Evaluating Performance Appraisal and Merit Pay.* Washington, DC: National Academy Press.

Naff, Katherine C., and John Crum. 1999. "Does Public Service Motivation Make a Difference?" *Review of Public Administration* 19: 5–16.

Naff, Katherine C., and Meredith A. Newman. 2004. "Federal Civil Service Reform: Another Legacy of 9/11?" *Review of Public Personnel Administration* 24, no. 3: 191–201.

Nakamura, Robert T., and Frank Smallwood. 1980. *The Politics of Policy Implementation.* New York: Palgrave Macmillan.

Partnership for Public Service. 2006. "OPM Works Toward Bringing Performance Pay to All Employees." Daily Pipeline. Available at www.ourpublicservice.org (accessed February 7, 2006).

Peters, B. Guy, and Brian W. Hogwood. 1985. "In Search of the Issue Attention Cycle." *Journal of Politics* 47: 238–53.

Perry, James L. 1996. "Measuring Public Service Motivation: An Assessment of Construct Reliability and Validity." *Journal of Public Administration Research and Theory* 6, no. 1: 5–22.

———. 1997. "Antecedents of Public Service Motivation." *Journal of Public Administration Research and Theory* 7, no. 2: 181–97.

———. 2000. "Bringing Society In: Toward a Theory of Public Service Motivation." *Journal of Public Administration Research and Theory* 10, no. 2: 471–88.

Perry, James L., and Lois R. Wise. 1990. "The Motivational Bases of Public Service." *Public Administration Review* (May/June): 367–73.

Perry, James L.; Debra Mesch; and Laurle Paarlberg. 2006. "Motivating Employees in a New Governance Era: The Performance Paradigm Revisited." *Public Administration Review* 66, no. 4: 505–14.

Pfiffner, James P. 2007. "The First MBA President: The Public Administration Legacy of George W. Bush." *Public Administration Review* (January/February): 6–20.

Rainey, Hal G. 2003. *Understanding and Managing Public Organizations.* 3d ed. San Francisco: Jossey-Bass.

Rainey, Hal G., and J. Edward Kellough. 2000. "Civil Service Reform and Incentives in the Public Service." In *The Future of Merit: Twenty Years After the Civil Service Reform Act,* ed. J.P. Phiffner and D.A. Brook, 124–45. Washington, DC: Woodrow Wilson Center Press and Johns Hopkins University Press.

Rainey, Hal G., and Jay E. Ryu. 2004. "Framing High Performance and Innovativeness in Government: A Review and Assessment of Research." In *The Art of Governance: Analyzing Management and Administration,* ed. Patricia W. Ingraham and Laurence E. Lynn, Jr., 20–46. Washington, DC: Georgetown University Press.

U.S. Government Accountability Office (GAO). 2003. "Creating a Clear Linkage between Individual Performance and Organizational Success." GAO-03–488.

———. 2004. "Building on the Current Momentum to Transform the Federal Government." GAO-04–976T.

———. 2005a. "Practices That Can Help Enhance and Sustain Collaboration among Federal Agencies." GAO-06–15.

———. 2005b. "Observations on Final Regulations for DOD's National Security Personnel System." GAO-06–227T.

U.S. Office of Personnel Management (OPM). 1999. "Presidential Rank Awards Evaluation Criteria." Available at www.opm.gov/awards/rank/criteria.htm.

———. 2002. Federal Human Capital Survey.

———. 2004. Federal Human Capital Survey.

Weber, Max. 1946. "Bureaucracy." In *Max Weber: Essays in Sociology,* ed. and trans. H.H. Gerth and C. Wright Mills, 196–244. New York: Oxford University Press.

CHAPTER 6

Linking Collaboration Processes and Outcomes
Foundations for Advancing Empirical Theory

ANN MARIE THOMSON, JAMES L. PERRY, AND
THEODORE K. MILLER

Scholars and practitioners of public and nonprofit management share an interest in understanding the outcomes of the increasingly studied but little understood process called collaboration. That interdependence is the fundamental nature of organizations is nothing new. Resource dependency theory has asserted this reality for a long time (Hudock 2001; Pfeffer 1997; Pfeffer and Salancik 1978). That interdependence characterizes collaboration is also hardly new (Graddy and Chen 2006; Thomson and Perry 2006). Unfortunately, collaboration processes manifest a number of key dimensions that complicate our ability as scholars to examine collaboration outcomes (Thomson and Perry 2006).

To begin to understand collaboration as a process that yields particular outcomes, it is helpful to start with Gray and Wood's (1991) theoretical framework for studying collaboration. To understand collaboration, they argue, scholars need to examine three areas: antecedents to collaboration, the process of collaboration itself, and the outcomes of that process (13). It is noteworthy, however, that these three categories are rarely modeled clearly in collaboration research. Scholars often simultaneously associate antecedents with collaboration processes and outcomes, for example, and fail to distinguish mediating from outcome variables. The literature spanning interorganizational relations (Ring and Van de Ven 1994), policy implementation (O'Toole 1997), cooperation theory (Axelrod 1984), and collaboration research (Huxham 1996) abounds with variables likely to enhance collaborations, but these variables either go unanalyzed or are not systematically modeled. Furthermore, process dimensions of collaboration are frequently presented as outcomes (Wood and Gray 1991).

The purpose of this chapter is to demonstrate how a multidimensional model of collaboration tested on sample data can be used as a means to study collaboration outcomes. The chapter is organized into three parts. We begin by briefly presenting the multidimensional model of collaboration and describe the scale derived from data collected from a large national service program, AmeriCorps State/National.[1] We then turn to the primary focus of the chapter—the relationship between the collaboration process and outcomes. We conclude with a discussion of the results of the outcomes analyses, noting several useful findings.

A MULTIDIMENSIONAL MODEL OF COLLABORATION

Collaboration is an interactive process between organizations that involves negotiation, development and assessment of commitments, and implementation of those commitments. Organizations negotiate, develop, and make assessments about their commitments based on their own interests and on the interests of the collective. This creative tension inherent in the process of collaboration gives collaboration its ambiguous, dynamic, and complex nature.

The theoretical definition of collaboration upon which our model is based derives from a cross-disciplinary review of the literature, a systematic analysis of multiple definitions from a variety of literatures, and case study research conducted between 1995 and 2000. Results from this grounded theory approach yield the following definition:

> Collaboration is a process in which autonomous actors interact through formal and informal negotiation, jointly creating rules and structures governing their relationships and ways to act or decide on the issues that brought them together; it is a process involving shared norms and mutually beneficial interactions. (Thomson and Perry 2006, 23)

Five key dimensions of collaboration are embedded in this definition: governance, administration, mutuality, norms, and organizational autonomy. Each of these dimensions involves process-related activities such as: making joint decisions about rules to govern the collaborative effort (governance); getting things done through an effective operating system that supports clarity of roles and effective communication channels (administration); addressing the implicit tension exhibited in collaborations between organizational self-interests and the collective interests of the group (organizational autonomy); working through differences to arrive at mutually beneficial relationships (mutuality); and finally, developing trust and modes of reciprocity (norms); all of which demand commitment to process over time (Thomson and Perry 2006). The original theoretical model specified in this study included six unobserved factors—collaboration and its five key dimensions—and fifty-six observed indicators (derived from questions on a survey).

Primary data collected through a mail questionnaire sent to 1,382 directors of organizations that participate in the AmeriCorps national service program provide the basis for a higher-order confirmatory factor analysis of the multidimensional model of collaboration (Thomson,

Perry, and Miller 2006).[2] Covariance structure modeling permits empirical testing to assess the extent to which this theoretically derived model of collaboration fits sample data.

The 1,382 organization directors to whom we sent surveys are members of local collaborations that are integral to the AmeriCorps national service program. The local collaborations are typically composed of social and human services organizations that come together to address a community problem (e.g., illiteracy, homelessness) in which they share a common interest. In return for their participation in the collaborative, member organizations become host sites for AmeriCorps members. The local collaborations, which are nested in national and state networks, are at the heart of the AmeriCorps national service program (see Perry et al. [1999] and Lenkowsky and Perry [2000] for more details about the origins and operation of AmeriCorps). Because the local collaborations and participating organizations vary in structure, size, capacity, and goals, the sample provides a rich environment for systematically studying the meaning of collaboration (Thomson 2001).

Overall, the analyses demonstrate empirical support for the theoretical definition of collaboration, but suggest some modifications of the original conceptualization of the five dimensions.[3] Figure 6.1 illustrates this modified higher-order multidimensional model. The six unobserved factors are shown in Figure 6.1 as circles and the seventeen indicators that emerge from this analysis as statistically valid and reliable are shown as squares.

Table 6.1 includes the questionnaire items for the final seventeen-item collaboration scale organized according to the dimension with which they are associated. The governance dimension is manifest in joint decision making through the more informal negotiation mechanisms of brainstorming and appreciation of each other's opinions rather than the formal mechanisms of standard operating procedures and formal agreements. For the administration dimension, the statistically valid indicators are clarity of roles and responsibilities, effective collaboration meetings, goal clarity, and well-coordinated tasks rather than formal mechanisms of reliance on a manager, formal communication channels, and monitoring. The latter indicators differ conceptually from those of governance because the focus is less on institutional supply and more on implementation and management—doing what it takes to achieve a goal.

Indicators of the mutuality dimension that did not withstand statistical scrutiny are questions that attempt to capture the extent of shared interests and interdependence among partners. Collaboration appears to involve forging commonalities from differences rather than finding solidarity through shared interests. Mutuality in collaboration is manifest in partner organizations that combine and use each other's resources so all benefit, share information to strengthen each other's operations and programs, feel respected by each other, achieve their own goals better working with each other than alone, and work through differences to arrive at win-win solutions.

The primary norms dimension indicators that remain statistically significant and valid are trust indicators with surprisingly little support for indicators of reciprocity. Collaboration involves a process characterized by the beliefs that people who represent partner organizations in collaboration are trustworthy, that partner organizations can count on each other to keep their obligations, and that it is more worthwhile to stay in the collaboration than to leave.

Figure 6.1 **Modified Higher-Order Factor Analysis Model of Collaboration**

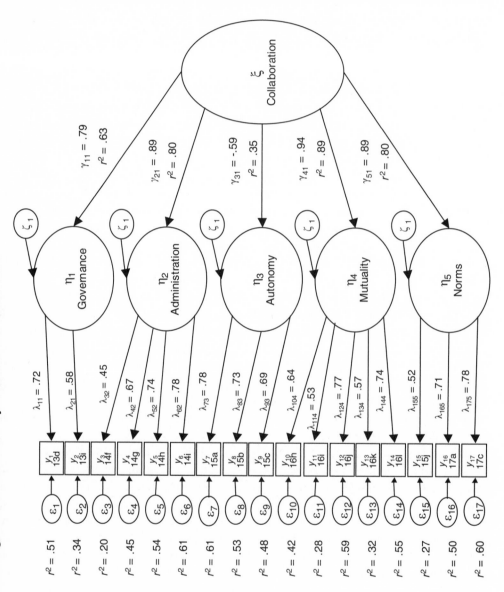

Table 6.1

Five-Dimension, Seventeen-Indicator Collaboration Scale

Dimension	Operationalization
Joint decision making	Partner organizations take your organization's opinions seriously when decisions are made about the collaboration.
	Your organization brainstorms with partner organizations to develop solutions to mission-related problems facing the collaboration.
Administration	You, as a representative of your organization in the collaboration, understand your organization's roles and responsibilities as a member of the collaboration.
	Partner organization meetings accomplish what is necessary for the collaboration to function well.
	Partner organizations (including your organization) agree about the goals of the collaboration.
	Your organization's tasks are well coordinated with those of partner organizations.
Autonomy	The collaboration hinders your organization from meeting its own organizational mission.
	Your organization's independence is affected by having to work with partner organizations on activities related to the collaboration.
	You, as a representative of your organization, feel pulled between trying to meet both your organization's and the collaboration's expectations.
Mutuality	Partner organizations (including your organization) have combined and used each other's resources so all partners benefit from collaborating.
	Your organization shares information with partner organizations that will strengthen their operations and programs.
	You feel that what your organization brings to the collaboration is appreciated and respected by partner organizations.
	Your organization achieves its own goals better working with partner organizations than working alone.
	Partner organizations (including your organization) work through differences to arrive at win-win solutions.
Trust	The people who represent partner organizations in the collaboration are trustworthy (adapted from Cummings and Bromiley 1996).
	My organization can count on each partner organization to meet its obligations to the collaboration (adapted from Cummings and Bromiley 1996).
	Your organization feels it is worthwhile to stay and work with partner organizations rather than leave the collaboration.

Note: For joint decision making, administration, autonomy, and mutuality, responses are recorded on scales ranging from 1 (not at all) to 7 (to a great extent) using the prompt "Circle the number that best indicates how much…." For the trust dimension, responses are recorded on scales ranging from 1 (strongly disagree) to 7 (strongly agree) using the prompt "Circle the number that best indicates how much you disagree or agree with the statements below."

Finally, the analysis suggests that collaboration is a process with both aggregative and integrative elements manifest in the autonomy dimension. This dimension attempts to capture the tension implicit in an individual organization's self-interests and the collective interests of collaborating partners. The statistically significant indicators for this dimension are the extent to which organizations perceive the collaboration hindering them from meeting their own missions, organizations believe their independence is affected by collaborating, and organizations' representatives feel pulled between trying to meet the expectations of their own organizations and those of the collaboration. Findings suggest that for this sample, the greater the tension, the less likely collaboration will occur.

It is interesting to note, however, that collaborations need not exhibit a complete lack of tension. In her evaluation of consensus building, Judith Innes (1999) argues that tension holds within it the potential for creativity. "In totally stable environments," Innes writes, "equilibrium powerfully hinders change [while highly] chaotic environments, on the other hand, produce only random responses, and systems cannot settle into patterns" (644). The key, she writes, rests in finding the intermediate state—on the "edge of chaos" (ibid.)—where participating organizations can find the potential dynamism implicit in this tension between individual and collective interests by maximizing latent synergies among individual differences.

Overall, the model that emerges from this analysis demonstrates a close fit[4] with the empirical data indicating support for the theoretical conceptualization of collaboration, at least in this sample. Furthermore, the seventeen indicators that represent the multidimensional scale of collaboration are theoretically and statistically valid measures for each of the five dimensions. Reliability, which we assess using r-square values in Figure 6.1, is not as high as validity, which underscores an important area for future research.[5] Until the study is replicated in different settings and tested on other independent samples, it is difficult to make generalizations about the "true" nature of collaboration.

EXAMINING COLLABORATION OUTCOMES

The multidimensional model of collaboration, operationalized with a seventeen-indicator scale, takes us a step closer to a firm foundation for studying the relationship between collaboration processes and outcomes. An increasingly important practical question that drives scholars and practitioners is effectiveness. Program directors, donors, partner organizations, upper-level managers, and scholars all seek an answer to this questions: Can collaborations achieve results? How do you know?

It comes as no surprise that a review of the literature suggests the process–outcome relationship is neither straightforward nor easily conceptualized. The outcomes of collaboration vary significantly depending on which theoretical perspective a researcher takes (Gray and Wood 1991). Logsdon (1991), for example, in her study of two social problem-solving collaborative efforts, views solving concrete problems as a successful outcome of the cross-sectoral collaborative efforts. Ostrom (1990), using a different theoretical perspective, views self-governance as the positive outcome of collective action, which emerges only if actors successfully and collectively solve the problems of institutional supply, credible commitment, and monitoring. Huxham (1996) argues that collaboration has both instrumental and ideological outcomes: As organizations interact, concrete goals can be collectively achieved and long-term substantive societal changes may occur.

Results from environmental conflict resolution (ECR) research offer a useful way forward in light of the complexity of process–outcome relationships. Different contexts yield different kinds of outcomes at different stages in collaborative ECR processes. Bingham and her colleagues (2003), for example, suggest that when evaluating the performance of ECR, evaluation criteria tend to fall in "clusters" that are unique to a particular stage of conflict (330). For the early processes of conflict resolution, they identify a cluster of no less than fifteen different possible criteria ranging from information exchange to diversity of views represented. Over the entire ECR process continuum, they identify nearly forty different kinds of criteria for evaluating outcomes. Brogden (2003), in his analysis of a national policy dialogue on State Conservation Agreements, found that the process yielded at least six different outcomes, each with different evaluation criteria relating to different collaborative stakeholders.

To further clarify conceptualization of the process–outcome relationship, Bingham and colleagues (2003) go on to ask a key question—how to assess the relative success or failure of any particular collaborative process. "Consider, for example," they write, "that a collaborative process fails to produce full agreement, but does significantly narrow the range of disagreement and significantly improves relationships among participants. Is the process a success, a failure, neither, or both?" (334). They conclude that when evaluating outcomes, we should avoid labeling them in terms of success or failure unless we are able to identify that the most important indicators consistently point in the same direction over time and across different contexts (334–36).

Bingham and her colleagues' conclusion is relevant for a growing number of scholars who have argued that the value collaboration holds for a postmodern, increasingly networked, society lies in its unique potential to create public value (Bardach 1998; Cropper 1996; Huxham 1996; Sagawa and Segal 2000). In this stream of research, creation of public value is often associated with sustainable collaboration. Cropper (1996) goes so far as to claim that the survival of collaboration depends on the ability of the participants to create and command value (82). He distinguishes between two primary values, consequential and constitutive. Consequential values, on the one hand, include productivity, relative efficiency, security, legitimacy, and adaptability. Constitutive values, on the other hand, define the very identity, place, and mode of conduct that govern interorganizational relationships—the values that organizations negotiate. The more value created through collaboration, the greater the likelihood of its sustainability because "with value comes commitment and with commitment, continued existence" (Cropper 1996, 97).

Bardach (1998), though he does not directly address the issue of sustainability as an outcome, agrees that to be successful, collaboration (what he calls interagency collaborative capacity) must achieve a value-creating purpose. He identifies four criteria for determining value-creation: how much customers of the collaboration value its services; the extent to which process values (fairness, representativeness, inclusiveness, accessibility, openness, and integrity) exist; the extent to which citizens' value what collaboration does; and the extent to which benefits outweigh costs of the collaborative effort (201–6). Bardach's view of public value falls predominantly within Cropper's consequential values category (focusing as it does on costs and benefits and the perceptions of outcomes by clients and citizens), but process values clearly fall within Cropper's constitutive category.

One of these process values is voice or what the procedural justice literature refers to as "process control" (Lind and Tyler 1988). In their extensive analysis of the social psychology of procedural justice, Lind and Tyler demonstrate that voice need not be purely instrumental. Participants in a process like collaboration, for example, may not be as interested in achieving a particular outcome as they are in the relative fairness of procedures that assure that their voice will be heard regarding any particular aspect of the collaboration. Lind and Tyler demonstrate, for example, that as long as participants in a process feel they have had a fair chance to voice their views, they express satisfaction with the process regardless of whether or not an outcome proves to be negative or even whether they feel they are able to exert any control over a particular end result. Satisfaction, as one immediate outcome of collaboration, then, may be independent from any end result that partners may have originally agreed to pursue by collaborating. The complexity of the process–outcome relationship, then, lies not only in the clusters of outcomes that may occur at any given stage in the collaboration process but also in the layers of outcomes nested within each other across the various stages over time.

That the process–outcome relationship is complicated comes as no surprise, but that there remains a strong commitment by scholars and practitioners alike to continue trying to understand the relationship regardless of the methodological and conceptual challenges is heartening. In their chapter on the promise and performance of environmental conflict resolution, Bingham and her colleagues (2003) urge scholars to view evaluation of collaborative ECR "as part of an extended, systematic, learning process" (336) that systematically looks for patterns of outcomes across cases over time. The particular operationalization of the process–outcome relationship presented in this chapter is meant to be one contribution toward this learning process.

For the purposes of our empirical research, we rely primarily on Barbara Gray's (2000) discussion of the issues surrounding evaluation of interorganizational collaboration because the different lenses through which she approaches the assessment of collaboration outcomes seemed particularly appropriate to our study. She identifies five different approaches to the evaluation of collaborative efforts. These are: (1) problem resolution or goal achievement; (2) generation of social capital; (3) creation of shared meaning; (4) changes in network structure; and (5) shifts in power distribution. Each approach derives from a different theoretical perspective that only underscores what we already know—the process–outcome relationship is complex, and it is unlikely we will ever arrive at a single approach to evaluate collaboration outcomes (Gray 2000). Table 6.2 summarizes the survey measures used to operationalize these outcomes in this study.

Table 6.2

Five Collaboration Outcome Variables Operationalized

Outcome	Question						
Perceived effectiveness	Overall, how effective is this collaboration in achieving its expected purpose and outcomes?						
	Not at all effective						Very effective
	1	2	3	4	5	6	7
Perceived increase in quality of working relationships	Overall, how would you rate the quality of working relationships that have developed between your organization and partner organizations as a result of this collaboration?						
	Very low quality						Very high quality
	1	2	3	4	5	6	7
Perceived broadening of views	Overall, to what extent has your organization's view of the issue(s)/problem(s) that brought the collaboration together broadened as a result of listening to partner organizations' views?						
	Not at all						To a great extent
	1	2	3	4	5	6	7
Perceived increase in network density	Overall, to what extent has your organization increased its interaction with partner organizations (like increased referrals and/or service contracts, joint program development) as a result of the collaboration?						
	Not at all						To a great extent
	1	2	3	4	5	6	7
Perceived increase in power relationships	Overall, to what extent has the collaboration helped to make partner organizations' influence on each other more equal?						
	Not at all						To a great extent
	1	2	3	4	5	6	7

RELATIONSHIP BETWEEN COLLABORATION AND ITS OUTCOMES

Using latent variable scores generated from the original data,[6] we specify and estimate five bivariate regression models to explore the relationship between the overall summary construct, collaboration (derived from the hierarchical confirmatory factor model depicted in Figure 6.1), and the five outcome variables to test the proposition,

P1: Collaboration as a process is positively associated with desired outcomes.

In light of the complexity of the process–outcome relationship discussed above, we also specified and estimated five other regression models using the seventeen-indicator multidimensional collaboration scale and the same five outcome variables to test two other propositions about the relationship between the individual process dimensions of collaboration and perceived outcomes.

P2: The greater the degree of joint decision making, administration, mutuality, and trust in collaboration, the more organizations will perceive collaboration as: effective in achieving goals, increasing the quality of partners' working relationships, broadening partners' views, increasing partner interactions, and creating more equitable power relationships among partners.

P3: The greater the degree of organizational autonomy, the less organizations will perceive the collaboration as: effective in achieving goals, increasing the quality of partners' working relationships, broadening partners' views, increasing partner interactions, and creating more equitable power relationships among partners.

Included in our analysis are two control variables—size of the collaboration (in terms of numbers of organizations actively involved in the group) and age (length of time the collaboration has existed). Two views of human organizing inform the propositions—a logic of collective action perspective (Coleman 1990; Olson 1971) and a new institutionalist perspective (March and Olsen 1984, 1989; Ostrom 1990, 1998). A logic of collective action perspective predicts an undersupply of collaboration outcomes due to the "reality" that whenever

> a number of self-interested persons [and organizations] are interested in the same outcome, which can only be brought about by effort that is more costly than the benefits it would provide to any one of them, [there will be] a failure to bring about that outcome. (Coleman 1990, 273)

This perspective would also predict that the more organizations actively engaged in the collaboration, the less likely a collective outcome will emerge (Olson 1971). The autonomy dimension attempts to capture this logic as a measure of tension between self- and collective interests. The greater the tension, the less we would expect organizations to achieve positive collaboration outcomes.

A new institutionalist perspective, on the other hand, argues that norms such as trust, reciprocity, and shared purpose decrease collective action costs making the potential for collaboration outcomes possible (Ostrom 1998). The multidimensional model of collaboration presented here includes dimensions of trust, mutuality, and joint decision making that are hypothesized to enhance the likelihood of positive collaboration outcomes. This perspective would also predict that the longer organizations have had a chance to develop relationships of trust and mutuality, the greater the likelihood of a positive collective outcome (Axelrod 1984, 1997; Ostrom 1998). The administration dimension with its emphasis on clarity of roles and responsibilities, goal agreement, task coordination, and effective partner meetings is also hypothesized to enhance collaboration outcomes.

REGRESSION RESULTS

Table 6.3 summarizes the regression results for the summary construct of collaboration and the five outcomes.

Table 6.3

Regression of Collaboration, Size, and Age on Five Perceived Collaboration Outcomes

Outcomes	Collaboration	Number of organizations actively involved in collaboration	Length of time collaboration has existed (months)	Adjusted R^2
Perceived effectiveness in achieving goals	0.55** (0.04) 13.71	0.00 (0.00) 0.04	0.12** (0.00) 2.88	0.32
Perceived increase in quality of partners' relationships	0.59** (0.04) 15.00	0.03 (0.00) 0.79	0.10** (0.00) 2.56	0.36
Perceived broadening of partners' views	0.41** (0.06) 9.21	0.01 (0.00) 0.24	0.07* (0.00) 1.65	0.17
Perceived increase in partner interactions	0.34** (0.07) 7.41	0.05 (0.00) 1.11	0.12** (0.00) 2.68	0.13
Perceived increase in equitable influence	0.47** (0.07) 10.87	0.03 (0.00) 0.67	0.07 (0.00) 1.61	0.23

$N = 422$; coefficient, (standard error), t-value; *$p < 0.10$; **$p < 0.05$ (critical value for $t = 1.645$); (critical value for $t = 1.960$).

As we expected, the results support the proposition that the collaboration process influences collaboration outcomes. The relationships among the five outcome measures explained by the latent variable scores of collaboration are all positive and highly significant. The results provide further empirical support for the validity of the multidimensional collaboration scale, but they are also useful as empirical support for what we already believed intuitively—that collaboration processes influence collaboration outcomes. Furthermore, in four of the five analyses, length of time the collaboration has existed is significant at the 0.10 level or less while size has no significant effect on outcomes. This suggests support for the new institutionalist perspective that as organizations exhibit trustworthy behavior, over time organizations begin to trust each other and develop reciprocal commitments.

As we have already noted, scholars and practitioners of collaboration acknowledge that the relationship between collaboration processes and outcomes is complex, ambiguous, and dynamic (Gray 2000; Gray and Wood 1991; Huxham and Vangen 2000, 2005; Thomson 2001). Table 6.4 presents additional regression results that examine the relationship between individual collaboration dimensions and the five outcomes (propositions two and three).

As we expected, joint decision making, administration, mutuality, and trust are significant and most of them are positively related to collaboration outcomes, but the significant statistical relationships and the direction of their effects do not extend across all process–outcome relationships. At the 0.10 level of significance or less, for example, joint decision making is only significant and positively related to two outcomes: perceived quality of relationships and the equality of influence organizations have on each other. The administration dimension is significant and positively associated with perceived effectiveness in achieving collaboration goals, as one would expect, but not with the other four outcomes.

Mutuality, which we expected to play an important role in all five outcomes, is significant at the 0.05 level and positively related to three of the five outcomes: perceived broadening of partners' views, increased partner interactions, and the equality of influence among partners. It has no statistically significant impact on perceived effectiveness in achieving goals or perceived increase in the quality of partner relationships. Finally, at the 0.05 level of significance, trust is significant and positively associated with only two of the five outcomes: perceived effectiveness and the quality of partner relationships. Furthermore, length of time that the collaboration has existed is positive and statistically significant for four of the five outcomes, while size has no significant effect on any of the five process–outcome relationships.

Other results, such as the role of the autonomy and mutuality dimensions, also demands a more nuanced explanation than is implied in propositions two and three. Although we predicted negative relationships between autonomy and collaboration outcomes, all but one of the relationships are positive and only one of the five relationships is significant at the 0.05 level. Autonomy is positively associated with perceived increase in partner interactions. As a measure of tension between self- and collective interests, it has no statistically significant effect on any of the other four process–outcome relationships. We examine this further in the discussion below.

Table 6.4

Regression of Joint Decision Making, Administration, Autonomy, Mutuality, and Trust on Five Perceived Collaboration Outcomes

Outcomes	Joint decision making	Administration	Autonomy	Mutuality	Norms (Trust)	Number of organizations actively involved in collaboration	Length of time collaboration has existed (months)	Adjusted R^2
Perceived effectiveness in achieving goals	-0.03 (0.06) -0.54	0.29** (0.09) 3.52	0.02 (0.05) 0.33	0.01 (0.10) 0.13	0.33** (0.09) 4.04	0.01 (0.00) 0.28	0.11** (0.00) 2.81	0.34
Perceived increase in quality of partners' relationships	0.10* (0.06) 1.70	0.04 (0.08) 0.44	-0.01 (0.05) -0.28	0.05 (0.09) 0.54	0.45** (0.08) 5.73	0.04 (0.00) 1.11	0.10** (0.00) 2.54	0.37
Perceived broadening of partners' views	0.05 (0.09) 0.68	0.08 (0.12) 0.90	0.09 (0.07) 1.63	0.25** (0.14) 2.40	0.12 (0.12) 1.26	0.01 (0.00) 0.14	0.07 (0.00) 1.51	0.17
Perceived increase in partner interactions	0.04 (0.10) 0.58	0.12 (0.13) 1.32	0.17** (0.08) 3.13	0.30** (0.15) 2.94	-0.00 (0.13) -0.03	0.04 (0.00) 0.85	0.11** (0.00) 2.49	0.15
Perceived increase in equitable influence	0.23** (0.10) 3.47	-0.12 (0.13) -0.21	0.07 (0.08) 1.41	0.23** (0.15) 2.35	0.13 (0.13) 1.53	0.02 (0.00) 0.46	0.07* (0.00) 1.67	0.24

$N = 422$; coefficient, (standard error), t-value; *$p < 0.10$; (critical value for $t = 1.645$); **$p < 0.05$ (critical value for $t = 1.960$).

DISCUSSION

Overall, the relationships for proposition two are broadly consistent with expectations, but more highly nuanced than expected. Administration and trust, for example, coupled with the control for age of the collaboration, are the only statistically significant variables related to perceived effectiveness in achieving goals. As implementation and collaboration research (Bardach 1998; Cropper 1996) confirm, administrative features such as role clarity, task coordination, goal agreement, and effective meetings are likely prerequisites for effectiveness in achieving goals. Trust, as a means to decrease transaction costs, should also enhance the level of perceived effectiveness in achieving goals in collaborative settings, especially over time as partners continue to develop trusting relationships (Ostrom 1998).

In their work on professional development in business relationships, Shapiro, Sheppard, and Cheraskin (1992) identify different types of trust at work in groups. Deference-based trust, based as it is on the calculation of the benefits of sustaining a relationship relative to the costs of breaking a commitment, is at play in the operationalization of trust used here (see Table 6.1). This kind of trust, write Lewicki and Wiethoff (2000), "tends to occur most frequently in professional, non-intimate, task-oriented relationships"; however, they are quick to point out that when organizations have worked together over time, deference-based trust "can also be the first, early stage in developing intimate personal relationships" (89) that lead to identity-based trust expressed as mutual appreciation of other partners' needs and desires.

Deference-based (also called calculus-based) trust, when combined with the joint decision-making dimension, and the age of a collaboration may help to explain the statistically significant and positive effect of these processes on the perceived increase in quality of partners' relationships. Over time, partners may demonstrate sufficient trustworthy behavior in their brainstorming and willingness to take partners' opinions seriously that calculus-based trust evolves into identity-based trust. The new institutionalist, interorganizational relations, and organizational behavior literature all support these findings (Hellriegel, Slocum, and Woodman 1986; Levine and White 1961; Ostrom 1998; Ring and Van de Ven 1994).

It is interesting to note that in the three cases where mutuality has a statistically significant effect on outcomes, trust does not. This implies either that trust (operationalized in this scale as more calculus-based than identity-based) has no impact on the broadening of partners' view, increased partner interactions, and decreased power imbalances among partners or that the mutuality dimension (with its emphasis on mutual respect, the ability to arrive at win-win solutions, willingness to share information to benefit partners, and the calculation that organizations believe they can better achieve their goals by working with partners than alone) is sufficient regardless of length of time they have worked together or strength of trust among partners (Alter and Hage 1993; Gray 1989, 2000; Huxham 1996).

As noted earlier, the negative effect of autonomy postulated in proposition three is not supported by this analysis. These findings suggest that autonomy plays a different role from that expected by a logic of collective action perspective. Even if autonomy is negatively correlated with collaboration (as demonstrated in Figure 6.1), when it is examined in relation to particular outcomes, outcomes need not be negative.

The positive association between autonomy and collaboration outcomes suggests that Olson's (1971) theory of collective action does not adequately acknowledge the complexity of the negotiation process that characterizes collaboration—a process that involves more than the maximization of self-interest (Thomson and Perry 2006). While the process of negotiation allows for competition and conflict at the margins, Warren (1967) and his colleagues (Warren et al. 1975) argue that organizations tend to advance their own interests only up to a point, which makes possible "a composite result [that] is usually acceptable though never maximal, and perhaps seldom optimal for the community" (Warren 1967, 415).

Both the conflict resolution and the social psychology literatures offer a more complete understanding of this finding. Johnson, Johnson, and Tjosvold (2000), for example, argue that controversy can be constructive depending on the context in which conflicts emerge (70). "Constructive controversy," they write, "tends to promote creative insight by influencing individuals to (1) view problems from new perspectives and (2) re-formulate problems in ways that allow new orientations to a solution to emerge" (73). From this perspective, it is not surprising that the combination of the autonomy and mutuality dimensions would positively influence collaborative outcomes, but the relative degree of tension manifest in the autonomy dimension is statistically significant for only one of the five outcomes: perceived increase in partner interactions. It may be that organizations participating in the collaborations in this sample have found a way over time to reach what Peter Coleman and Morton Deutsch (2000) refer to as "optimal tension" within a cooperative context sufficient to keep them interacting.

Lind and Tyler (1988) provide another way to explain the positive effect of tension on perceived increase in partner interactions. Drawing on a procedural justice model based on self-interest, they suggest that, even in group situations where the modus operandi is to maximize personal gain, social interaction inevitably involves goal trade-offs that lead to the possibility that partners will accept "outcomes and procedures on the basis of their fairness, rather than on the basis of their favorability to one's own interests" (223). Partners in collaborative endeavors may, in the long term, believe they will gain more by cooperating than by working alone. That the autonomy dimension is statistically and positively significant in our model only when it is combined with the mutuality dimension suggests support for Lind and Tyler's (1988) conclusions. That the autonomy dimension is not statistically significant for any of the other four outcomes (though positive in all but one) may suggest that the organizations in this sample have not yet found ways to reap the creative benefits that conflict can produce, such as broadening of partner organizations' views of the problem or improved quality of partners' relationships (Coleman and Deutsch 2000).

The literature on self-efficacy may also help to explain our findings regarding the positive effect of autonomy on perceived increase in partner interactions. Judge and his colleagues (2007) define self-efficacy as "individuals' beliefs about their capabilities to produce designated levels of performance" (107). The autonomy dimension includes an individual-level indicator that focuses on the extent to which individual organizational representatives (people) feel pulled between their organization's and the collaboration's expectations. In their study of self-directed teams in one manufacturing firm, Alper,

Tjosvold, and Law (2000) found that people feel efficacious when they find themselves in "cooperative conflict" experiences where, over time, team members learn to manage conflict constructively. Tension, when combined with the cooperative environment manifest in the mutuality dimension can, over time, result in a willingness to continue to interact with each other.

That the length of time a collaboration has functioned is statistically significant in four of the five outcomes at the 0.10 level of significance or less, while size has no statistical significance suggests that a logic of collective action perspective (Olson 1971) does not adequately explain the process–outcome relationship in collaborative settings. That time plays so critical a role suggests greater support for Axelrod's (1984, 1997) evolutionary approach to cooperation that assumes actors exhibit adaptive behavior, not maximizing behavior. Cooperation emerges as a result of learning about other actors' responses through repeated interactions.

New institutionalism, for example, asserts that institutions accumulate historical experience through learning that enables them to adapt strategies, competencies, and purposes (March and Olsen 1984, 745–46). Ostrom (1998) argues that our evolutionary heritage has "hard-wired us" to learn norms of reciprocity and trust so that over time institutional change is possible (2). Current theories of collective action, she asserts, do not adequately account for the "accretion of institutional capital" and the reality that learning is "an incremental self-transforming process" (Ostrom 1990, 190).

As a measure of tension between self-interest and collective interests, the positive effects of autonomy on increased partner interactions may be best explained by de Tocqueville's (2006) doctrine of "self-interest properly understood." This doctrine asserts a positive correlation between self-interest and the interests of others. It appears that in collaboration, both self-interest and collective interests have the potential to coexist in creative balance such that even though autonomy is negatively related to collaboration, when outcomes are at stake, positive outcomes can be achieved.

In the negotiation process, for example, self-interest may be necessary for joint outcomes to emerge. This is not incompatible with Huxham's (1996) assertion that the first reason to collaborate is self-interest, though this does not mean self-interest at the expense of others (3). Nor is it incompatible with findings from the interorganizational relations literature that assert "because organizations can seldom marshal the necessary resources to attain their goals independently, they must establish exchange relationships with other organizations" to achieve their goals (Van de Ven, Emmett, and Koenig 1975, 22). Tension has the potential to increase interorganizational interaction when partners need resources that other partners have.

Thomson's (2001) view that collaboration involves both aggregative and integrative characteristics provides another way to explain the variation in the individual collaboration dimension–outcome relationships. Aggregative traditions view political institutions as instruments for aggregating private preferences into collective choices (March and Olsen 1989). Integrative traditions, on the other hand, rely on a logic of unity rather than one of exchange (Ibid., 126). Integrative traditions, write March and Olsen, treat conflict of interest as the basis for deliberation and authoritative decision rather than bargaining; [p]resume a process from which emerges mutual understanding, a collective will, trust and sympathy, [and] seek the creation, identification, and implementation of shared preferences. (Ibid.)

From an aggregative perspective, collaboration involves bargaining based on rational self-interested maximizing behavior (the modus operandi of aggregative traditions). Organizations enter collaborative agreements to achieve their own goals, negotiating among competing interests and brokering coalitions among competing value systems, expectations, and self-interested motivations (Hanf and Scharpf 1978; March and Olsen 1989; Ostrom 1990). If collaboration threatens their self-interests, organizations will not hesitate to exit rather than to exercise voice.

A strong case can be made, however, that collaboration also shares much of the logic of integration. Cooperation theory's focus on the increased potential for cooperation through adaptive behavior, repeated interaction, and the development of norms like trust and reciprocity lend support to this view of collaboration (Axelrod 1984, 1997; Ostrom 1990, 1998). In the conclusion to his book, *The Evolution of Cooperation*, Axelrod (1984) writes,

We are used to thinking about competitions in which there is only one winner [but] the world is rarely like that. In a vast range of situations mutual cooperation can be better for *both* sides than mutual defection. The key to doing well lies not in overcoming others but in eliciting their cooperation. (190)

In collaboration processes, then, as partners interact, compete, seek to maximize self-interest (aggregative tendencies) and then decide to satisfice for the sake of the collaborative endeavor (integrative tendencies), different processes will affect different outcomes.

Gray (1989) supports this view of collaboration as a process with aggregative and integrative characteristics, though for her, as partners negotiate, they move beyond mere satisficing to arrive at an unknown but improved outcome. For her, collaboration represents a process "through which parties who see different aspects of a problem can constructively explore their differences and search for solutions that go beyond their own limited vision of what is possible" (Gray 1989, 5). That autonomy is statistically significant in increasing partner interactions in the presence of mutuality and length of time a collaboration continues to exist suggests that Gray's (1989, 11) assertion that collaboration assumes "solutions emerge by dealing constructively with differences" (differences presumably rooted in self-interest) has some merit.

In their study of collective bargaining, Walton and McKersie (1965) propose the possibility of combining distributive bargaining, where one person's gain is another person's loss, with integrative bargaining, where "the nature of a problem permits solutions which benefit both parties, or [solutions where] the gains of one party do not represent equal sacrifices by the other" (5). Distributive and integrative bargaining each assume differences among parties, differences rooted in self-interest. When combined, however, joint gains can occur when the parties use tactics that prevent others from achieving most of the gains in order to guarantee themselves a reasonable share of the gains.

SUMMARY

Overall, the outcomes analysis suggests statistically significant, positive effects of different dimensions on different outcomes with mixed support for propositions two and three. It is important to acknowledge the modest r-square values for each of the five regression models, suggesting that a large portion of the variability in the five outcomes is not explained with the five collaboration dimensions. This is not surprising given the nature of the data used to measure collaboration outcomes. Although the collaboration scale has been subjected to measurement evaluation, the five outcome measures are single indicators and have not been developed through the rigorous analysis that yielded the process measures (Thomson, Perry, and Miller 2006). The measurement error may be significant especially because of the assumption that the single-item questions measure the perceived outcomes of collaboration.

It is also important to acknowledge that our approach is but one of several competing views. It falls within a collective action view of organizations that focuses on networks of symbiotically interdependent, yet semiautonomous organizations that interact to construct or modify their collective environment, working rules, and options (Astley and Van de Ven 1983, 251). We readily admit (as do Astley and Van de Ven) that this view represents only a "partial view of reality" and, as such, our research is meant to be one contribution to an ongoing debate about the meaning of collaboration.

CONCLUSION

An empirically validated theory of collaboration, one that can inform both theory and practice, demands a systematic approach toward understanding the meaning and measurement of collaboration. Without a more systematic approach, inferences about collaboration will depend on which theoretical perspective one takes. This, in turn, makes theory building difficult and evaluation of collaborative arrangements reliant on inconsistent subjective judgments of evaluators.

Scholars of public management agree that the role of theory is to produce knowledge that enhances the ability of managers to manage effectively, though they disagree on what constitutes "knowledge for practice" (Bozeman 1993; Kettl and Milward 1996; Lynn 1996). Lynn's (1996) stance—that knowledge for practice needs to move beyond merely experiential knowledge to analytical knowledge that allows public managers to become trained investigators, "able to examine competing claims [and] to resolve uncertainty in a reasoning way" (114)—is equally relevant for scholars and practitioners of collaboration. We agree with Lynn's assertion that knowledge for practice will suffer without a more explicit focus on rigorous analysis.

Several compelling issues in the collaboration process–outcome relationship call for a more systematic research agenda on collaboration. Wood and Gray (1991), in their excellent discussion of the necessary building blocks for a comprehensive theory on collaboration, identify several overarching issues that are particularly relevant for this study. They urge collaboration scholars to move beyond the individual level of analysis to the aggregate level when studying collaboration processes and outcomes. "A key limitation of existing theory," they write, "is that most perspectives are oriented toward the individual focal organization . . . rather than toward an inter-organizational domain" (140). Bingham and her colleagues (2003) agree. For them, understanding collaborative environmental conflict resolution as a complex system with environmental outcomes demands that measurements of diverse, aggregate-level data need to be collected across ECR participants and at multiple points in time (339).

Our findings also confirm what other researchers in this field have found: When examining the process–outcome relationship in collaborative endeavors, we cannot assume a linear cause–effect relationship (Huxham and Vangen 2005; O'Leary and Bingham 2003). Not only are outcomes layered and occur at different junctures in the collaborative process, different process dimensions yield different outcomes. The important question, then, is: How do scholars and practitioners build on descriptive case studies by examining the collaborative process–outcome relationship as a complex system that changes over time?

Studies such as the one presented here attempt to do just this. By examining patterns of outcomes across a large number of cases, we are able to arrive at system-level hypotheses that can be tested in other contexts and across time. Clearly, the cross-sectional nature of this study, however, limits our ability to move beyond hypotheses to generalized statements. Longitudinal data collection is a must for the field of collaboration research.

Another must, if we are to examine system-level relationships, is to develop measurement models that provide us with ever more valid and reliable indicators and scales for empirical research. The multidimensional scale of collaboration used in this study represents a first attempt to wrestle with the meaning of collaboration and how to measure the process in order to explore empirically relationships such as those between collaboration and its outcomes (Thomson 2001; Thomson, Perry, and Miller 2006). This scale is the first of its kind and is meant to be tested in other contexts and refined. This is especially important when examining the relationship between collaboration and its outcomes. We need to subject our conceptualization of outcomes to evaluation of measurement error just as the process indicators have been evaluated. This is complicated, of course, by the many challenges discussed in this chapter.

Nevertheless, the field of collaboration research suffers from a paucity of large-scale empirical studies, and the refinement of measurement scales is paramount if we are to move from practice to theory. We need more studies like those conducted by Graddy and Chen (2006) and Chen and Graddy (2005) that test the collaboration process–outcome relationship on different samples and in different policy contexts. Comparison of results between multiple studies, like our analysis and Chen and Graddy's (2005), will help to build theory in the field of collaboration research by identifying recurring similarities and differences in the pattern of results. For example, Chen and Graddy (2005) use Thomson's (2001) multidimensional scale of collaboration and her outcome variables (customized in the Chen and Graddy study by referring specifically to the Family Preservation Program) to evaluate interorganizational networks in Los Angeles County's Family Preservation Program. Although they use a different methodology (we use structural equations modeling; Chen and Graddy use fixed-effects modeling), comparing results is informative and illustrates the value of multiple studies in different contexts.

Significant differences in effects of dimensions of collaboration on different outcomes emerge (important differences that warrant further exploration); there are also, however, some interesting similarities. Both analyses identify mutuality (operationalized in Chen and Graddy's study as resource exchange) and trust as the variables with the most predictive power among the five outcomes. The positive though limited role of autonomy in our analysis (only one of the five effects is statistically significant) contrasts with two negative effects (though statistically insignificant) of autonomy in Chen and Graddy's study; both studies, however, found a positive and significant effect of autonomy on increased interactions among partners, and Chen and Graddy also found a positive and highly significant effect of autonomy on increased equality of influence among partners.[7] Comparing the patterns of similarities and differences across multiple studies can only help to further our understanding of the complex and paradoxical nature of collaboration and its effect on outcomes.

The relatively new advances in structural equations modeling have greatly improved the ability of scholars to provide usable knowledge for practice. The ability to estimate latent variables scores is one such advanced technique that holds great promise for theory and practice. Although models of this kind have limitations (Thomson 2001, 63–67; 185–96), they hold the potential to serve as useful heuristics that make complex statistical and theoretical findings meaningful to daily practice. Other methodologies, such as those of Graddy and Chen (2006), are also useful. The refinement of the multidimensional scale of collaboration used in our study is warranted because of the need for more valid and reliable measures of collaboration and should be an important part of any research agenda that seeks to build collaboration theory.

This study on the collaboration process–outcome relationship fits with the broader research agenda posited in the environmental conflict resolution literature by O'Leary and her colleagues (2003). Many of the same methodological and conceptual challenges in this literature are relevant for the field of collaboration research, such as: single, small-n descriptive case studies, practitioner–scholar bias, diversity and uniqueness of cases that make cross-case comparisons and controlling for specific variables difficult (Emerson et al. 2003, 16). We agree that, like the environmental conflict resolutions field, the complexity of the collaboration process–outcome relationship is sufficiently complex to warrant a "continuous learning" perspective that will, over time, allow us to make contingent generalizations about how collaboration processes yield particular outcomes and under which conditions.

NOTES

1. This sample represents the operational level of national service policy implementation characterized by a complex system of nested networks of organizations at the national, state, and local levels. The organizations in this sample demonstrate a wide variety in structure, size, capacity, vision, and goals providing a rich environment for systematically studying the meaning of collaboration. For a detailed description of the sample, see Thomson (2001, ch. 6).

2. Implications for AmeriCorps managers are discussed in an earlier study (Thomson and Miller 2002), where we present the practical uses of the multidimensional model for AmeriCorps respondents.

One example of a practical application is use of the original survey as a self-reflection tool to explore differences in interorganizational perceptions of the collaboration. It is interesting to note that a large number of respondents in the original sample requested a summary of the findings (84 percent) and a copy of the questionnaire to use with their collaboration partners (78 percent). Several organizational directors in the sample, unexpectedly, voluntarily, and independently called to request a second copy of the questionnaire to use with their partners in retreat settings.

3. The theoretical foundations of the five dimensions are discussed in greater detail in Thomson and Perry (2006).

4. For a detailed description of overall fit measures, see Thomson (2001, 131–32) and Thomson, Perry, and Miller (2006).

5. Bollen (1989) suggests that we view the overall theoretical model as a system of linear regression equations composed of a systematic direct effect of the unobserved concept on the observed indicator and an error effect (whatever is not "explained" by the concept). From this perspective, the closer the r-square is to 1, the greater the reliability of the indicator. Of the seventeen indicators in this model, nine have an r-square of 0.50 or greater, three are between 0.42 and 0.48, and the remaining five are between 0.20 and 0.34. As the literature on validity demonstrates, it is possible to have valid but unreliable measures of a particular concept (Bollen 1989; Carmines and Zeller 1983). We view our research as part of a larger research agenda to develop ever more valid and reliable scales. This scale clearly needs cross-validation on other independent samples, but as a first attempt, the empirical findings are promising.

6. Latent variables are variables that cannot actually be measured in the real world but are assumed to influence observed variables that can be measured. In the case of this model, the observed indicators are statistically valid measures of the five key dimensions of collaboration that are, in turn, influenced by the higher-order latent variable, collaboration. The latent variable scores are derived, empirically, from the observed variables—questions on the survey.

7. See discussion in Chen and Graddy (2005, 16–18 and Table 6, 16). Chen and Graddy's model also includes an analysis of the preconditions–outcome relationship, which helps to fill a gap in empirical research on the theoretical antecedent–process–outcome framework often presented in discussions about collaboration (Gray 1989; Gray and Wood 1991).

REFERENCES

Alper, Steve; Dean Tjosvold; and Kenneth S. Law. 2000. "Conflict Management, Efficacy, and Performance in Organizational Teams." *Personnel Psychology* 53: 625–42.

Alter, Catherine, and Jerald Hage. 1993. *Organizations Working Together.* Newberry Park, CA: Sage.

Astley, W. Graham, and Andrew H. Van de Ven. 1983. "Central Perspectives and Debates in Organizational Theory." *Administrative Science Quarterly* 28, no. 2: 245–73.

Axelrod, Robert. 1984. *The Evolution of Cooperation.* Princeton, NJ: Princeton University Press.

———. 1997. *The Complexity of Cooperation: Agent-Based Models of Competition and Collaboration.* Princeton, NJ: Princeton University Press.

Bardach, Eugene. 1998. *Getting Agencies to Work Together: The Practice and Theory of Managerial Craftsmanship.* Washington, DC: Brookings Institution Press.

Bingham, Lisa B.; David Fairman; Daniel J. Fiorino; and Rosemary O'Leary. 2003. "Fulfilling the Promise of Environmental Conflict Resolution." In *The Promise and Performance of Environmental Conflict Resolution,* ed. O'Leary and Bingham, 329–51. Washington, DC: Resources for the Future.

Bollen, Kenneth. A. 1989. *Structural Equations with Latent Variables.* Toronto: Wiley.

Bozeman, Barry. 1993. *Public Management: The State of the Art.* San Francisco: Jossey-Bass.

Brogdon, Mette. 2003. "The Assessment of Environmental Outcomes." In *The Promise and Performance of Environmental Conflict Resolution,* ed. R. O'Leary and L.B. Bingham, 277–300. Washington, DC: Resources for the Future.

Carmines, Edward G., and Richard A. Zeller. 1983. *Reliability and Validity Assessment.* Beverly Hills: Sage.

Chen, Bin, and Elizabeth A. Graddy. 2005. "Inter-Organizational Collaborations for Public Service Delivery: A Framework of Preconditions, Processes, and Perceived Outcomes." Paper presented at the annual meeting of the Association for Research of Nonprofit Organizations and Voluntary Action, Washington, DC, November 17–19.

Coleman, James. S. 1990. *Foundations of Social Theory.* Cambridge, MA: Belknap Press of Harvard University Press.

Coleman, Peter T., and Morton Deutsch. 2000. "Some Guidelines for Developing a Creative Approach to Conflict." In *The Handbook of Conflict Resolution: Theory and Practice,* ed. Deutsch and Coleman, 355–65. San Francisco: Jossey-Bass.

Cropper, Steve. 1996. "Collaborative Working and the Issue of Sustainability." In *Creating Collaborative Advantage,* ed. C. Huxham, 80–100. Thousand Oaks, CA: Sage.

Cummings, L.L., and Philip Bromiley. 1996. "The Organizational Trust Inventory." In *Trust in Organizations,* ed. R.M. Kramer and T.R. Tyler, 302–30. Thousand Oaks, CA: Sage.

de Tocqueville, Alexis. 2006. *Democracy in America,* ed. J.P. Mayer, trans. G. Lawrence. New York: Harper Perennial Modern Classics.

Emerson, Kirk; Tina Nabatchi; Rosemary O'Leary; and John Stephens. 2003. "The Challenges of Environmental Conflict Resolution." In *The Promise and Performance of Environmental Conflict Resolution,* ed. R. O'Leary and L.B. Bingham, 3–26. Washington, DC: Resources for the Future.

Graddy, Elizabeth A., and Bin Chen. 2006. "The Consequences of Partner Selection in Service Delivery Collaborations." Paper presented at Syracuse University's Collaborative Public Management Conference, Washington, DC, September 28–30.

Gray, Barbara. 1989. *Collaborating: Finding Common Ground for Multi-Party Problems.* San Francisco: Jossey-Bass.

———. 2000. "Assessing Inter-Organizational Collaboration: Multiple Conceptions and Multiple Methods." In *Cooperative Strategy: Economic, Business, and Organizational Issues,* ed. D. Faulkner and M. De Rond, 243–60. Oxford: Oxford University Press.

Gray, Barbara, and Donna J.Wood. 1991. "Collaborative Alliances: Moving from Practice to Theory." *Journal of Applied Behavioral Science* 27, no. 2: 3–22.

Hanf, Kenneth, and Fritz W. Scharpf, eds. 1978. *Inter-Organizational Policy Making: Limits to Coordination and Central Control.* Beverly Hills: Sage.

Hellriegel, Don; John W. Slocum; and Richard W. Woodman. 1986. *Organizational Behavior.* 4th ed. New York: West.

Hudock, Ann C. 2001. *NGOs and Civil Society: Democracy by Proxy?* Cambridge, UK: Polity Press.

Huxham, Chris. 1996. "Collaboration and Collaborative Advantage." In *Creating Collaborative Advantage,* ed. Huxham, 1–18. Thousand Oaks, CA: Sage.

Huxham, Chris, and Siv Vangen. 2000. "Ambiguity, Complexity, and Dynamics in the Membership of Collaboration." *Human Relations* 53, no. 6: 771–801.

———. 2005. *Managing to Collaborate: The Theory and Practice of Collaborative Advantage.* New York: Routledge.

Innes, Judith E. 1999. "Evaluating Consensus Building." In *The Consensus Building Handbook: A Comprehensive Guide to Reaching Agreement,* ed. L. Susskind, S. McKearnan, and J. Thomas-Larmer, 631–75. Thousand Oaks, CA: Sage.

Judge, Timothy A.; Christine L. Jackson; John C. Shaw; Brent A. Scott; and Bruce L. Rich. 2007. "Self-Efficacy and Work-Related Performance: The Integral Role of Individual Differences." *Journal of Applied Psychology* 92, no. 1: 107–27.

Johnson, David W.; Roger T. Johnson; and Dean Tjosvold. 2000. "Constructive Controversy: The Value of Intellectual Opposition." In *The Handbook of Conflict Resolution: Theory and Practice,* ed. M. Deutsch and P.T. Coleman, 65–85. San Francisco: Jossey-Bass.

Kettl, Donald F., and H. Brinton Milward, eds. 1996. *The State of Public Management.* Baltimore: Johns Hopkins University Press.

Lenkowsky, Leslie, and James L. Perry. 2000. "Reinventing Government: The Case of National Service." *Public Administration Review* 60, no. 4: 296–307.

Levine, Sol, and Paul E. White. 1961. "Exchange as a Conceptual Framework for the Study of Inter-Organizational Relationships." *Administrative Science Quarterly* 5, no. 4: 581–601.

Lewicki, Roy J., and Carolyn Wiethoff. 2000. "Trust, Trust Development, and Trust Repair." In *The Handbook of Conflict Resolution: Theory and Practice,* ed. M. Deutsch and P.T. Coleman, 86–107. San Francisco: Jossey-Bass.

Lind, E. Allen, and Tom R. Tyler. 1988. *The Social Psychology of Procedural Justice.* New York: Plenum Press.

Logsdon, Jeanne M. 1991. "Interests and Interdependence in the Formation of Problem-Solving Collaborations." *Journal of Applied Behavioral Science* 27, no. 1: 23–37.

Lynn, Laurence E., Jr. 1996. *Public Management as Art, Science, and Profession.* Chatham, NJ: Chatham House.

March, James G., and Johan P. Olsen. 1984. "The New Institutionalism: Organizational Factors in Political Life." *American Political Science Review* 78, no. 3: 734–49.

———. 1989. *Rediscovering Institutions: The Organizational Basis of Politics.* New York: Free Press.

O'Leary, Rosemary, and Lisa B. Bingham, eds. 2003. *The Promise and Performance of Environmental Conflict Resolution.* Washington, DC: Resources for the Future.

Olson, Mancur. 1971. *The Logic of Collective Action: Public Goods and the Theory of Groups.* Cambridge, MA: Harvard University Press.

Ostrom, Elinor. 1990. *Governing the Commons: The Evolution of Institutions for Collective Action.* Cambridge: Cambridge University Press.

———. 1998. "A Behavioral Approach to the Rational Choice Theory of Collective Action: Presidential Address, American Political Science Association, 1997." *American Political Science Review* 92, no. 2: 1–22.

O'Toole, Laurence J., Jr. 1997. "Treating Networks Seriously: Practical and Research-Based Agendas in Public Administration." *Public Administration Review* 57, no. 1: 45–52.

Perry, James L.; Ann Marie Thomson; Mary Tschirhart; Debra Mesch; and Geunjoo Lee. 1999. "Inside a Swiss-Army Knife: An Assessment of AmeriCorps." *Journal of Public Administration Research and Theory* 9, no. 2: 225–50.

Pfeffer, Jeffrey. 1997. *New Directions for Organization Theory: Problems and Prospects.* New York: Oxford University Press.

Pfeffer, Jeffrey, and Gerald R. Salancik. 1978. *The External Control of Organizations: A Resource Dependence Perspective.* New York: Harper and Row.

Ring, Peter S., and Andrew H. Van de Ven. 1994. "Development Processes of Cooperative Inter-Organizational Relationships." *Academy of Management Review* 19, no. 1: 90–118.

Sagawa, Shirley, and Eli Segal. 2000. *Common Interest, Common Good: Creating Value Through Business and Social Service Partnerships.* Boston, MA: Harvard Business School Press.

Shapiro, Debra L.; Blair H. Sheppard; and Lisa Cheraskin. 1992. "Business on a Handshake." *Negotiation Journal* 8, no. 4: 365–77.

Thomson, Ann Marie. 2001. "Collaboration: Meaning and Measurement." Ph.D. diss. Indiana University, Bloomington.

Thomson, Ann Marie, and Theodore K. Miller. 2002. "Knowledge for Practice: The Meaning and Measurement of Collaboration." Paper presented at the annual meeting of the Association for Research of Nonprofit Organizations and Voluntary Action, Montreal, November 14–16.

Thomson, Ann Marie, and James L. Perry. 2006. "Collaboration Processes: Inside the Black Box." *Public Administration Review* 66, no. 6 (Supplement): 20–31.

Thomson, Ann Marie; James L. Perry; and Theodore K. Miller. 2006. "Conceptualizing and Measuring Collaboration." Paper prepared for presentation at the Collaborative Public Management Conference, Maxwell School, Syracuse University, Washington, DC, September 28–30.

Van de Ven, Andrew. H.; Dennis C. Emmett; and Richard Koenig, Jr. 1975. "Theoretical and Conceptual Issues in Inter-Organizational Theory." In *Inter-Organizational Theory,* ed. A.R. Negandhi, 19–38. Kent, OH: Kent State University Press.

Walton, Richard E., and Robert B. McKersie. 1965. *A Behavioral Theory of Labor Negotiation: An Analysis of a Social Interaction System.* New York: McGraw-Hill.

Warren, Roland L. 1967. "The Inter-Organizational Field as a Focus for Investigation." *Administrative Science Quarterly* 12, no. 3: 396–419.

Warren, Roland L.; Ann F. Burgunder; J.Wayne Newton; and Stephen M. Rose. 1975. "The Interaction of Community Decision Organizations: Some Conceptual Considerations and Empirical Findings." In *Inter-Organizational Theory,* ed. A.R. Negandhi, 167–81. Kent, OH: Kent State University Press.

Wood, Donna J., and Barbara Gray. 1991. "Towards a Comprehensive Theory of Collaboration." *Journal of Applied Behavioral Science* 27, no. 2: 139–62.

CHAPTER 7

Legitimacy Building in Organizational Networks

KEITH G. PROVAN, PATRICK KENIS, AND SHERRIE E. HUMAN

Legitimacy is a concept that is central to the evolution of social systems, including organizations. Most insight on the subject has been developed by institutional theorists. They have argued that legitimacy building is the driving force behind decisions regarding organizational strategies and structures (DiMaggio and Powell 1983; Meyer and Rowan 1977; Tolbert and Zucker 1996; Zucker 1987) and that societal acceptance of the organization, and its subsequent survival, is dependent on attaining the support of relevant elements in its environment.

Empirical research on organizational legitimacy in both business and public/nonprofit settings has generally been supportive, concluding, for instance, that legitimacy needs push organizations toward structural conformity with others in their class (D'Aunno, Sutton, and Price 1991; Deephouse 1996; Fligstein 1985), lead young organizations to conform to the expectations of key external constituencies (DiMaggio 1992; Singh, Tucker, and House 1986; Wiewel and Hunter 1985), and are a critical element in the adoption of innovative organizational practices (Westphal, Gulati, and Shortell 1997). More specifically, Delmar and Shane (2004) have demonstrated that organizations responding to legitimacy pressures during the first thirty months after being founded are able to reduce the risk of terminating the business (see also Aldrich and Fiol 1994). In a public sector context, Farmbry and Harper (2005) discussed the importance of building legitimacy for acceptance of land claims court decisions in South Africa following the post-apartheid transition.

Yet, despite considerable evidence for the importance of legitimacy for organizational structures and processes, and even as a rationale for forming interorganizational relations (Oliver 1990), there have been almost no efforts to study the importance of legitimacy for networks. The one major exception to this is a study by Human and Provan (2000), which focused on networks of small manufacturing firms and demonstrated the potential of the legitimacy perspective for better understanding networks. This shortcoming in the literature is somewhat surprising in light of the tremendous interest in and research on organizational networks since the mid-1980s in business (c.f. Brass et al. 2004), public (Agranoff and

McGuire 2003; O'Toole 1997), and nonprofit (Alter and Hage 1993) management. It is also surprising since networks have been touted by many as unique forms (c.f. Powell 1990), and as such, are subject to legitimacy pressures that are not necessarily the same as those of the individual organizations that comprise the network.

This chapter is an attempt to build a broader understanding of network legitimacy over the early stages of network evolution. We argue that legitimacy, or "credibility," is critical for establishing new networks and for network successes and crises as they evolve toward maturity. Economic, resource-dependency, and power perspectives are useful for explaining aspects of network growth and evolution, and scholars have outlined conditions under which networks emerge (Jones, Hesterly, and Borgatti 1997). Networks, however, being essentially cooperative social endeavors, must be legitimate if they are to be sustained. Our ideas on network legitimacy extend the work of Human and Provan (2000) by focusing on networks in general, and on public sector networks in particular.

When discussing the legitimacy of networks, two issues will be addressed. First, what is distinct about network legitimacy and what forms does it take? Second, under what conditions is the need to build network legitimacy most acute? A focus on network legitimacy is especially critical for public managers, many of whom must now manage through collaboration with other organizations, rather than hierarchically. Being a successful collaborative public manager means knowing how to build and maintain an effective network spanning multiple organizations. Learning how to build a network that is credible to both participants and outsiders is an essential part of this process.

LEGITIMACY AND ORGANIZATIONAL NETWORKS

Consistent with Suchman's definition (1995, 574), we define legitimacy as a generalized perception that the actions of a network are desirable, proper, or within some system of norms, values, beliefs, and definitions. These can be held by external groups and/or network member organizations. For organizations as well as networks, legitimacy pressure is produced by others; it is the acquisition of status and acceptability conferred by others based on their perception of the organization's/network's goals, values, actions, structures, processes, and so on. Like Suchman, however, we attempt to take a middle ground between strategic and institutional traditions. Thus, networks, just like organizations, achieve legitimacy through the society and culture in which they are embedded. However, both networks and organizations can and do attempt to manage and manipulate legitimacy and the process by which it is acquired, enabling some networks and organizations within the same social system to become more legitimized than others (Oliver 1990).

We define the term "network" narrowly. Our focus is on networks as groups of three or more legally autonomous organizations that work together collectively and collaboratively to try to achieve not only their own goals but also the collective goal of the network as a whole. This definition is consistent with what Kilduff and Tsai (2003) referred to as a "goal directed," rather than a serendipitous network. When defined in this way, networks can become extremely complex, requiring explanations that go well beyond organization-level thinking or the dyadic approaches that have been traditionally discussed in the organization theory literature.

We also focus here on networks that are primarily voluntary regarding their formation and participation, even if participation is driven by demands from funders. Both voluntary and mandated networks require legitimacy to survive and prosper. But fully mandated networks (required by law) are granted legitimacy, at least externally, from the mandating entity, typically a government agency. Internally, legitimacy can be much more problematic since members may resist cooperating with one another and they may only be weakly committed to network goals. But this is a problem primarily for the agency that mandates the network. We are interested here in networks that are voluntarily formed, and thus, have to work themselves on building legitimacy if they are to move successfully from inception to maturity.

In line with others (cf. O'Toole 1997; Powell 1990), we believe networks to be a genuinely different form of cooperation compared to organizations. That this is true also for legitimacy has been empirically demonstrated by Human and Provan (2000). In their research, legitimacy building was found to be more complex in networks than in organizations, as well as unique, and thus, worthy of study in its own right. Network legitimacy is more complex, since networks experience legitimacy pressures at three distinct levels, and consequently, must eventually build and maintain legitimacy at all three levels.

Based on Human and Provan's findings, legitimacy pressure exists at the level of the network-as-form, the network-as-entity, and the network-as-interaction. First, unlike organizations, the network concept itself often needs to be legitimized. This is what Human and Provan (2000) refer to as the need to legitimize the "network-as-form." While specific organizations, especially new start-up firms, need to be legitimized to attract external resources and support (Stinchcombe 1965), the organizational form itself typically does not (see Kimberly 1979, for an exception). In the public sector, while the formation of a new government agency may raise questions about whether or not it is really necessary, the form itself is seldom questioned. As a means of bringing together people and resources to accomplish task-related goals, formal organizations, regardless of sector, have long assumed the status of "taken-for-grantedness" (Meyer and Rowan 1977) in our society. In contrast, the network is a relatively new form of organizing, and thus, must contend with critical legitimacy challenges that go beyond the liability of newness of any particular member organization. A good example of this is the difficulty associated with getting emergency response agencies or national intelligence agencies to work collaboratively as a network. Although probably less true in the nonprofit sector, where organizations are accustomed to collaboration, the network concept is sufficiently new in some industries and especially, in intersectoral relations involving public and private organizations, that the form itself must be identified and accepted. For instance, scholars and practitioners have sometimes deemed it necessary to distinguish networks from more familiar multiorganizational forms, such as trade associations (Finn 1996; Rosenfeld 1997), intergovernmental relations, or contract-based funding relationships, which either require little or no cooperation and commitment among the member organizations, or they require more of a principal–agent relationship.

Overall, the need to establish the legitimacy of the network form is similar to the challenge of "sector building" that Suchman (1995) described for individual organizations attempting to build their own legitimacy in an industry or sector that has minimal external acceptance. With networks, however, it is the very form of organizing that requires legitimizing. As Human and Provan (2000) note, these legitimacy pressures may come from inside, from member organizations, or from outside. Such internal legitimacy pressures are far more likely in networks than in organizations, where members typically accept the basic form that employs them.

Second, even if the basic form or concept is accepted, networks face legitimacy challenges concerning the specific goals, structure, and governance of the network itself, or what Human and Provan (2000) refer to as the "network-as-entity." While individual organizations may face legitimacy challenges concerning how they are run or what they stand for, they normally have goals and structures that make them readily identifiable, especially to employees. In contrast, networks face significant legitimacy challenges to be seen as viable entities in their own right. Loyalties and rewards are typically tied to the organizations that comprise the network, and not to the network itself (Milward and Provan 2006). Networks must establish a reasonable level of recognition, or identity (Whetten and Godfrey 1998), so that members act as a network, and not just as individual and autonomous entities. Thus, networks face legitimacy challenges that are both more complex and different than those faced by organizations, based on the need to establish the legitimacy of the network as an entity in its own right.

A third reason why network legitimacy is different from that of organizations is that networks must establish the legitimacy of cooperative interactions, or what Human and Provan (2000) refer to as the "network-as-interaction." Trust must first be built, often within a framework of competition (Uzzi 1997), among independent organizations that may have only marginally compatible goals and values. These relationships must be established not just with one or two other organizations, but often with ten, twenty, or more, many of which may be former or potential competitors. Organizations may accept the legitimacy of the network concept, or form, but the concept must then be implemented through actual cooperative interactions among members. Unless these interactions are legitimized, the network will not succeed.

In the remainder of the chapter we develop propositions that address the conditions under which the need to build network legitimacy will be most acute. We focus on how networks build legitimacy as they evolve, by drawing on support from both internal and external stakeholders across each of the three legitimacy dimensions. In general, we propose that the prevalence of legitimacy pressures regarding each dimension, and the extent to which each represents a significant challenge to the existence and effectiveness of a network, depends on the network's stage of development, its governance structure, its composition, and the diffusion of the network form.

DETERMINANTS OF THE NEED TO BUILD NETWORK LEGITIMACY

Network-as-Form

As discussed above, the success of a network depends in part on its acceptance as a legitimate form of organizing. We propose that the critical factor for this dimension of legitimacy is the sector- or area-wide diffusion of networks. In some sectors of the economy, as well as in some countries or regions of countries, networks are a well-established form of doing business. Thus, the form is readily recognized and organizations that operate in that sector are likely to consider being part of a network to be an effective way of conducting operations. For instance, in the United States, the network form appears to be highly diffused in the electronics and biotechnology industries and in health and human services (Barley, Freeman, and Hybels 1992; Luke, Begun, and Pointer 1989; Saxenian 1990; Shan, Walker, and Kogut 1994). It is also a well-established form in most European countries (Axelsson and Easton 1992; Heidenreich 1996; Vanhaverbeke 2001).

Once the basic network form has been legitimized in an economic sector or region, organizations that are not yet involved will view network participation not only as reasonable but as a normal and perhaps critical way of successfully competing. Wide diffusion is likely to encourage network involvement even in the absence of objective, performance-based criteria, as mimetic processes emerge as important. This is precisely what happened in the U.S. health care industry during the 1990s, as local health care organizations continued to try to integrate their activities across the continuum of care, despite the lack of any evidence that such integrated networks had positive benefits (Walston, Kimberly, and Burns 1996). In the public and nonprofit sectors in general, adoption of network forms has gradually become a taken-for-granted assumption, even going so far as to be required by government funders.

In other industries and regions, however, networks are not readily diffused and their legitimacy is likely to be low. For instance, despite increased attention over the past decade (Bosworth and Rosenfeld 1993; Malecki and Tootle 1996), networks are not yet fully accepted among small U.S. firms in general (e.g., Hagedoorn and Schakenraad 1994), and among small manufacturers in non–high-tech fields in particular (Human and Provan 2000; Lichtenstein 1992). When diffusion is low, the network form tends not to be understood or appreciated very well, thus reducing the likelihood that organizations in these industries or regions will consider network involvement as a way of enhancing their effectiveness and competitiveness. Rather than imitating the behavior of those organizations in other industries that have joined networks, organizations in low-diffusion industries will likely view network involvement as an uncertain and risky behavior. Even organizations that do join or form a network are likely to enter into the experience rather cautiously, having little or no evidence available to support the contention that networks work in their industry.

In the public and nonprofit sectors, while networks have become well-accepted institutions, the actual adoption of a network form may be resisted, especially in communities, or across sectoral boundaries, where there is suspicion and a general lack of trust among administrators and their organizations. This is likely to be especially true where network forms have been previously adopted and have failed or have suffered through some difficult experiences and unfulfilled promises (cf. Huxham and Vangen 2005; Teisman and Klijn 2002).

Establishing the legitimacy of the network-as-form will be most critical during the period just prior to formation and during the actual formation of the network. It is at these points that uncertainty about the costs and benefits of network affiliation is greatest. Organizations are likely to be reluctant to become involved in a form that is not well established in their economic sector or region and for which outcomes are unknown or for which past collaborative efforts have been problematic. Once the network has formed and started to move to early growth, issues regarding the network form are likely to decline in importance as factors related to actual network performance and outcomes become more apparent. As the network matures and ultimately moves to sustainment, involved organizations are unlikely to be particularly concerned about the legitimacy of the form. In fact, their success will then be used as a model for other organizations in their region or sector, reinforcing the legitimacy of their own decision to form a network.

Only when faced with a threat to the form, such as through the introduction of antitrust legislation, lack of support by government funders, or strong evidence of poor performance across multiple networks in the same domain, is the legitimacy of the network-as-form likely to resurface. In this case, member organizations, especially those in failed networks, will tend to increase their criticism of the form itself, rather than blame themselves and their implementation of the concept.

Based on these arguments, three propositions can be formulated.

P1: The need to build legitimacy for the network-as-form will be greatest when regional or sector-wide diffusion of networks is low and/or unsuccessful, and will decline in importance as diffusion of networks as a form of organizing in a particular sector or region becomes commonplace.

P2: The need to build legitimacy for the network-as-form will be greatest during preformation and during initial formation of the network and will decline in importance as the network matures.

P3: Once the network reaches relative maturity, the need to reestablish legitimacy of the network-as-form will emerge only during periods of crisis that are severe enough to affect the viability of the network.

Network-as-Entity

For networks to work effectively, the organizations that comprise the network must be able to integrate their activities, or some subset of their activities, in order to act like a single, larger organization, at least regarding key network goals. Especially for outside groups, like clients or funders, the distinct advantage of a network arrangement is that it can "speak with a common voice," collectively representing the skills and resources of all member organizations. This is what Kilduff and Tsai (2003) have referred to as a "goal directed" network. Thus, for instance, networks of small manufacturing firms can work on a project that draws on the assets of its multiple members, allowing it to compete effectively with much larger firms. Alternatively, a network of health care organizations in a small city can provide a full range of services that might otherwise be available only through a large multispecialty clinic in a major metropolitan area. Or a network of public and nonprofit organizations can work together to provide a set of emergency services for hurricane victims that would not otherwise be accessible.

However, customers and clients are not interested in dealing with each network member individually. Rather, clients prefer to work with a single office that will strive to meet their unique needs. Coordinating and managing the network to provide a "seamless" integration of activities and services thus becomes a critical aspect of network governance. When integration occurs, the network acts as if it were a single entity and customers/clients can develop relationships with the network as an entity, rather than as a loose collection of organizations. For instance, Huggins's (2000) case study of four networks in the UK describes portraying the network administrative organization as a business enterprise in its own right as a key marketing strategy. In mental health, the network discussed by Provan, Isett, and Milward (2004) had one common intake point, and clients accessed the full network of services through one of four key providers. In general, a network cannot fully realize its potential unless it achieves legitimacy as an entity in its own right, one that customers/clients, funders, suppliers, and even network members take seriously. How legitimacy for the network-as-entity is established depends largely on its governance structure.

As discussed by Provan and Kenis (2008), networks are typically governed in one of three broad ways. The loosest arrangement is when the organizations involved in the network attempt to govern themselves. This approach can work quite well when the number of participants is small, as in collaborative partnerships or strategic alliances. In these dyadic relationships or in networks having only a small number of organizations, one or more persons in each participating organization may be identified as alliance coordinator who works closely with his/her counterparts in the alliance to ensure that the relationship succeeds. No one network member is considered more or less important than any other, at least regarding network management. This form of governance can also be used in larger networks that need only very weak coordination.

As more organizations become involved and as the need for formal coordination increases, network complexity increases along with the difficulty of managing network activities and interactions. For this reason, multiple organization networks will normally have a single entity do the coordinating and integrating on behalf of the entire network. While the form of governance may differ, this single governing and administrative entity must itself be legitimized.

Some scholars have discussed explicitly the key role of the network broker (Miles and Snow 1986) or negotiator (Ring and Van de Ven 1994), alliance initiator (Larson 1992) or leading firm (Lorenzoni and Ornati 1988). This model is especially common in networks that are dominated by a single major participant, like the primary buyer in a network of supplier firms or a large supplier in a network of smaller buyers. In the public and nonprofit sectors, examples might include health systems dominated by a large hospital (Weiner and Alexander 1998) or a police department as head of a crime reduction network or a community policing collaborative. While the role of this lead organization in a cooperative network must be legitimized by participants for the network to succeed, its legitimacy is often already established, both through its size and control of resources, and through its prior relations with network members.

An alternative governance mechanism is for the network to be coordinated and managed by a separate legal entity set up specifically for that purpose. Such an entity would typically have its own administrative staff, executive director, and governing board. The board is sometimes independent but often consists of all or some members of the network itself. This distinct administrative entity has been referred to as a federation management organization (Provan 1983), or more recently, a network administrative organization or NAO (Human and Provan 2000; Provan and Milward 2001).

The NAO structure is especially common among networks that are not dominated by a powerful lead organization, such as the mental health network discussed by Provan and colleagues (2004), chronic disease prevention and treatment networks (Provan et al. 2003), or the network constructed to battle Exotic Newcastle Disease discussed by Moynihan (2005). Examples are less frequent in business than in the public and nonprofit sectors, but they would include some regional small-firm manufacturing networks (Huggins 2000; Lichtenstein 1992; Malecki and Tootle 1996). While a relatively new phenomenon in the United States, scholars and practitioners have documented the proliferation of such networks in Europe over the past decade (e.g., Borch 1994; Hanssen-Bauer and Snow 1996; Rosenfeld 1997). Many of these networks have involved small firms that seek to gain the advantages of large size without merging, thus retaining their autonomy. It is also a form used to facilitate the formation and governance of organizations that are not used to working together, like the research consortium SEMATECH (Browning, Beyer, and Shetler 1995).

The need for building legitimacy for the network-as-entity depends on which of the above governance mechanisms are used by the network and the role of the governing entity. When the network is self-governed, as is typical of strategic alliances in business, the legitimacy of the network-as-entity is generally not difficult to establish since few organizations are involved, thus minimizing the problem of presenting a common voice to outsiders. In addition, alliance members themselves are typically well established. Finally, there is, by definition, no separate administrative entity that must establish its legitimacy in the eyes of both outsiders and member organizations.

The need for establishing network legitimacy increases when the lead organization model is used. However, as noted above, it is most often the case that the lead organization is already well-established and legitimized by network members. Where this might not be the case is when the lead organization, like U.S. auto manufacturers in the 1980s, has had a long history of opportunistic dealings with its smaller, less powerful suppliers, but then tries to develop more cooperative trust-based relationships in which suppliers are treated more as partners (Mandambi and Helper 1998). In this case, the legitimacy of the lead organization as a key network participant would not be questioned, but its legitimacy as integrator and coordinator of a trust-based collaborative effort would definitely have to be established.

Where establishing the legitimacy of the network-as-entity would be most critical is for NAO-model networks. Legitimacy is a critical issue for the network administrative organization in two respects. For one thing, before the network is formed, the NAO does not exist. Thus, when the NAO is created (typically by a core group of member organizations or by outside groups like funders), it faces start-up pressures not unlike those encountered by any new entity, including the need to legitimize its activities and actions. The NAO faces additional legitimacy hurdles, however, since it is not a form that is widely recognized or understood by outsiders or even by many network members—what Kimberly (1979) referred to as the liability of being both new and different. Despite the importance of its activities for network survival, the NAO is itself new and not well established, often with few successful models to mimic.

Second, despite its role as the primary force behind development and maintenance of the network, the NAO must quickly establish and continually demonstrate its value, both to members and outside stakeholders. Early commitment to the network by these groups is often modest and calculated, and it is the job of the NAO and its leader to generate enthusiasm and support for the network. The successful evolution of a group of autonomous small organizations to a strongly linked and effective network thus depends on the capacity of the NAO to build and establish its own legitimacy. To do this, the NAO must take on what Suchman (1995) described as the second challenge of gaining legitimacy, which is "outreach" to new, allegiant constituencies and to existing entities that can provide support.

The importance of building legitimacy for the network-as-entity is most critical during network formation and early network growth. It is at these stages of evolution that both outsiders (clients, customers, funders, potential new members, etc.) and member organizations feel most uncertain about what the network is and who represents it. During early growth, it is common for the network not to act as a true collective entity at all, but simply as a loose collection of organizations that share some common goals and have a desire to work together. The network concept, or form, may be legitimized by its members but the network as a viable and indentifiable entity is not likely to be well established.

In networks that are not self-governed, the role of the lead organization and NAO at these early stages of evolution is especially critical both for getting the network up and running and for providing a common focal point for network activities. Ultimately, the success of the NAO or lead organization in getting the network, as a unique entity, established and legitimized will also depend on the extent to which the NAO/lead organization itself is seen as a legitimate entity. As noted earlier, this process is most critical for the NAO, which has little or no previous legitimacy to build on. Internally, the NAO leader and his/her staff can work to generate cooperation, good will, and interactions among member organizations while moving quickly to develop outcomes that benefit the members. Externally, NAO leadership can attract new members, develop external sources of funding and other key resources, and enhance the legitimacy and visibility of the network to outsiders.

As the network reaches maturity, the need to establish the legitimacy of the network-as-entity will diminish somewhat, but will still be moderately important. It is the NAO and lead organization that network members will rely on to manage their ongoing interactions. However, at this stage in evolution, network members will already have developed established patterns of interaction and cooperation, thus reducing somewhat the need for strong centralized governance. Some NAO and lead organization networks may eventually evolve to more of a self-governed model, once legitimacy of the network-as-entity has been well established and centralized governance becomes less essential.

Based on these arguments, two propositions can be formulated.

P4: The need to build legitimacy for the network-as-entity will be greatest when the network is governed through a separate and unique network administrative organization and least when the network is self-governed.

P5: The need to build legitimacy for the network-as-entity will be most critical during the early stages of network evolution (formation and early growth) and will decline in importance as the network matures.

Network-as-Interaction

Most studies of networks focus considerable attention on the interactions among member organizations. Such attention is, of course, highly appropriate since networks only exist through interactions. Yet, the legitimacy of the interaction process is seldom discussed explicitly. What is fairly clear (Agranoff and McGuire 2003; D'Aunno and Zuckerman 1987; Doz 1996; Gulati 1995; Ring and Van de Ven 1994), however, is that most cooperative interactions between organizations emerge gradually over time. Organizations typically legitimize cooperative interactions with others by first establishing the basis of trust through low-level, arm's-length ties like traditional market-based and contractual relations, or through simple information sharing, before then moving to the stronger, more collaborative ties that characterize network relationships (Isett and Provan 2005).

For networks to work effectively, cooperative interactions among member organizations must be seen by the members as a legitimate activity. This is not to say that all network organizations must actively cooperate with every other member. Rather, it is the process of cooperative interaction that must be legitimized, leading to enough interactions among members to ensure a sense of "networkness," where members not only recognize and accept their involvement but also work toward accomplishing both their own goals and those of the entire network. Probably the strongest contributor to building the legitimacy of the network-as-interaction is evidence of positive outcomes of the interaction process. If network members see that cooperative interaction works to improve their individual performance, enhance legitimacy, attract resources, develop new ideas, and the like, then they will legitimize cooperative interaction as a viable and valued method of operation, even in mandated networks.

Interaction legitimacy also means that network organizations will be more willing to work and cooperate with other network members with whom they have not previously been linked. Once the legitimacy of cooperative interactions is established within the network, links to new partners within the network are likely to develop more smoothly and quickly than links to most nonmember organizations. Trust will be diffused throughout the network and interactions with new members will be seen as a normal way of conducting operations, particularly when network-level goals are clear and readily accepted. This relates to the concept of legitimacy spillover (Suchman 1995), which in this case, can be especially important for facilitating the building of interactions beyond the network's original members.

Establishing the legitimacy of interactions among network members is most problematic when members have had few prior cooperative relationships with other organizations outside the network and when resistance to form such ties is high. We argue here that these conditions are most likely when network composition is homogeneous. In contrast, having prior ties, even with organizations outside the network, legitimizes the process of cooperative interaction and smoothes the way for new interactions and relationships (Gulati and Gargiulo 1999). In addition, when network members are relatively heterogeneous regarding the mix of products or services they offer, interactions are potentially less competitive and resistance to new ties will be low. In contrast, when network composition is homogeneous, ties will either be seen as unnecessary or potentially competitive, thus increasing the need for legitimacy building regarding the network-as-interaction.

This argument may appear to be counterintuitive, since homogeneous organizations would seem to have much in common, potentially facilitating potential interaction. However, organizations that are doing different, but complementary activities are more likely to be willing to cooperate with one another than organizations that are doing essentially the same thing, and hence, are either actual or potential competitors. Heterogeneous networks may include buyers and suppliers as well as organizations that can provide complementary skills, products, and services. Some of these organizations may even have already established working relationships with one another, based on past contracts or market transactions. Under such circumstances, the legitimacy of developing cooperative interactions may already be relatively well established (Gulati 1995; Isett and Provan 2005). Legitimacy is critical for the formation and maintenance of cooperative network ties, but in heterogeneous networks, either interaction legitimacy tends to have already been established through previous links or the idea of developing ties is considered to be a reasonable way of conducting operations.

In contrast, organizations that provide similar services and compete for the same resources are not natural alliance partners. Thus, an important role of the NAO or lead organization in homogeneous networks is to bring these organizations together, enabling them to find common ground and demonstrating the value of cooperation over competition. Similar organizations that join a network voluntarily will, of course, do so with the expectation of cooperating with each other and increasing competitiveness relative to outsiders. However, the managers of member organizations may have considerable difficulty overcoming their tendency to avoid cooperation with competitors, especially in highly competitive industries. Indeed, Malecki and Tootle describe how the NAO-led U.S. networks they observed served as catalysts for interactions among smaller-firm competitors that "[had] not considered working with . . . other local firms until the network was formed" (1996, 50). NAO-led networks are at a distinct advantage here since the NAO can encourage the development of close working relationships among members while acting as "honest broker" when disputes arise. Once established and legitimized, networks of similar organizations, precisely because of their common interests, may even develop a stronger attachment to their fellow network members than the members of more heterogeneous networks.

In networks having no NAO or lead organization, cooperative interactions must be legitimized by the member organizations themselves, typically through the gradual process of trust building described earlier. Such self-governed networks cannot function at any stage of their development in the absence of direct interaction among the organizations involved in the network. Unlike members of NAO or lead organization networks, the members of self-governed networks have no other organization that they can rely on to develop interactions or to talk with about the importance or benefits of developing interactions. If interactions are not legitimized by the members themselves, then no network will exist. It is for this reason that in self-governed networks, building legitimacy for the network-as-interaction will be most closely related to legitimizing the network-as-entity. Such networks establish their identity through their members' interactions with one another. Thus, of the three forms of governance discussed here, self-governed networks will be most sensitive to the need to legitimize interactions among members and potential members.

In networks governed by or through an NAO or lead organization, building the legitimacy of the interaction process has two aspects—interaction among members and interactions between members and the central administrative entity. In both cases, the NAO or lead organization plays a critical role, especially when cooperative interactions prior to network formation have been limited. In part, it is the success of the NAO or lead organization in building and legitimizing interactions that helps to build its own legitimacy (network-as-entity).

In networks dominated by a powerful entity (hospital, police, large supplier or buyer, etc.) acting as the lead organization, member-to-member interactions may be quite limited, minimizing the importance of this dimension of legitimacy. Such "hub and spoke" arrangements really operate more as an organization set (Aldrich and Whetten 1981), which refers to the network ties of a single organization, rather than as a full-fledged network. In contrast, multilateral networks involve cooperative interactions among many, although not necessarily all, member organizations. The NAO can play a major role in legitimizing interactions among members, first by encouraging their formation and then by working to ensure that they develop in productive ways and are maintained.

The importance of legitimizing the network-as-interaction is likely to be strong even as the network evolves into maturity. This dimension of legitimacy is fragile, however, and susceptible to damage throughout early evolution. This will be especially true in homogeneous networks, until trust is well established and clear evidence of success is apparent. Based on the above arguments, the following three propositions can be formulated:

P6: The need to build legitimacy for the network-as-interaction will be greatest when network composition is relatively homogeneous and competitive, compared to when network composition is relatively heterogeneous and noncompetitive.

P7: The need to build legitimacy for the network-as-interaction will be greatest during the early stages of network evolution (formation and early growth) but will continue to be moderately important into maturity.

P8: The need to build legitimacy for the network-as-interaction regarding member-to-member relationships will be greatest in self-governed networks, weakest in networks dominated by a lead organization, and moderate in NAO-led networks.

OVERLAP AMONG DIMENSIONS

Thus far, we have only explored the importance of each dimension of legitimacy and the conditions under which each is likely to have the greatest impact on network evolution and effectiveness. While each dimension of legitimacy is conceptually unique and important in its own right, networks must attend to all three dimensions if they are to be successful. The point is that legitimacy is a multifaceted concept. Not all dimensions need to be addressed simultaneously, and some types of networks, such as those that are self-governed, may have an easier time than others building legitimacy along some dimensions (i.e., the network-as-entity). Nonetheless, as Human and Provan (2000) found, over time, addressing only one or two dimensions, while ignoring others, is likely to result in legitimacy deficiencies that can ultimately lead to the demise of the network. Consistent with this point, the following hypothesis is proposed:

P9: Network effectiveness will increase relative to the number of dimensions of legitimacy that can be established. Effectiveness will be greatest in networks that are able to build legitimacy for the network-as-form, entity, and interaction.

CONCLUSION

This chapter has focused on the importance of legitimacy building for understanding the success of organizational networks, especially in the early stages of their evolution. While political, economic, and resource acquisition issues are of obvious importance for network growth and survival, our basic argument has been that legitimacy is critical for understanding *why* some networks succeed in attracting resources, improving services, and in general, are sustained, while others flounder or fail.

Networks are unique organizational forms, and thus, have properties and legitimacy pressures not faced by individual organizations. The theory developed here specifies three distinct dimensions of legitimacy that networks must establish as they evolve. Specifically, we have argued that networks must establish the legitimacy of the network-as-form, the network-as-entity, and the network-as-interaction. Not all forms of networks are alike, particularly regarding governance and composition, making the pressures and importance of establishing legitimacy along each dimension somewhat different. Our propositions articulate which of the three dimensions of network legitimacy are most critical and under which key conditions.

The propositions have focused primarily on voluntary networks in the public and non-profit sectors, although we have tried to give examples of how the ideas developed here might apply to business networks, in an effort to make the theory building more generalizable. We have been less explicit about how issues of legitimacy might apply in mandated networks, which are fairly common in public sector settings. In general, we believe that many of the same legitimacy issues would apply, except that the role of the mandating government agency becomes critical in establishing legitimacy, rather than having network members doing it themselves.

The ideas developed here are simple and are designed to stimulate interest and research on an underexplored aspect of organizational networks. One shortcoming is that we have examined only the direct impact of each of the three dimensions of legitimacy on overall network legitimacy. What we did not do was to discuss the relationship among the different dimensions of legitimacy and the relative importance of each. Our propositions did suggest that some dimensions of legitimacy were most critical at certain stages of evolution and that overall effectiveness was most likely for networks that were able to establish legitimacy across all three dimensions. However, the propositions do not address the impact that one dimension of legitimacy might have on another. It is possible, for example, that the strong establishment of legitimacy through one dimension can spill over to another dimension, reducing the amount of time and effort needed to build legitimacy through the second dimension.

For instance, this spillover process might be especially relevant, for instance, for mandated public sector networks, where first establishing legitimacy through the network-as-interaction might be critical for building subsequent legitimacy of the network-as-form and network-as-entity. Alternatively, it may be that when voluntary networks are common in an industry, region, sector, or concerning a particular social problem, thereby legitimizing the network-as-form, the legitimacy of the network-as-interaction may also be enhanced. When network members do not question the value of the network form, they will more readily accept the value of building trust-based interactions with other network members than when few organizations in a community or industry really understand what networks are and how they may benefit members and the community as a whole. All three dimensions of network legitimacy will always need to be addressed, but not necessarily to the same extent.

Potential interactions of this sort are complicated and are beyond the scope of this more general attempt at theorizing. These and other issues will need to be resolved before a truly comprehensive theory of networks and network legitimacy can emerge. Despite some limitations, we have provided an initial systematic attempt to examine the need for legitimacy building in organizational networks. Although the concept of legitimacy has been an integral part of the literature on organizations for many years, especially using an institutional theory perspective, there have been few attempts to extend the concept to the study of organizational networks. We have argued here not only that legitimacy is a critical component of network evolution and sustainment, but that there are important aspects of network legitimacy that make it unique and worthy of study in its own right.

The theory developed here has particular value and relevance to public sector managers. Collaboration among public, nonprofit, and even for-profit sector organizations has become critical as a mechanism for providing public services. Many public services are simply too complex to be carried out by a single organization, as witnessed by the effort to address the aftermath of Hurricane Katrina. If we are to take networks seriously in the public sector, as O'Toole (1997) has argued, we must understand how the collaborative process is established. From a practical perspective, our argument is that building legitimacy, both internally, to network members, and externally, to funders, key stakeholders, and the community at large, is critical for network sustainability and success. If issues of legitimacy are ignored, especially as networks are established, collaboration among organizations is likely to be resisted and the goals of public network managers will be difficult to attain.

ACKNOWLEDGMENT

The authors would like to thank Tina Dacin and Joe Galaskiewicz for their many helpful comments on earlier drafts.

REFERENCES

Agranoff, Robert, and Michael McGuire. 2003. *Collaborative Public Management: New Strategies for Local Governments.* Washington, DC: Georgetown University Press.

Aldrich, Howard, and C. Marlene Fiol. 1994. "Fools Rush In? The Institutional Context of Industry Creation." *Academy of Management Review* 19, no. 4: 645–70.

Aldrich, Howard, and David A. Whetten. 1981. "Organizational Sets, Action Sets and Networks: Making the Most of Simplicity." In *Handbook of Organizational Design,* ed. P.C. Nystrom and W.H. Starbuck, 385–408. London: Oxford University Press.

Alter, Catherine and Jerald Hage. 1993. *Organizations Working Together.* Newbury Park, CA: Sage.

Axelsson, Bjorn, and Geoff Easton. 1992. *Industrial Networks: A New View of Reality.* London: Routledge.

Barley, Stephen R.; John Freeman; and Ralph C. Hybels. 1992. "Strategic Alliances in Commercial Biotechnology." In *Networks and Organizations: Structure, Form, and Action,* ed. N. Nohria and R. Eccles, 311–47. Boston: Harvard Business School Press.

Borch, Odd J. 1994. "The Process of Relational Contracting: Developing Trust-Based Strategic Alliances Among Small Business Enterprises." In *Advances in Strategic Management: A Research Annual,* ed. A. Huff, J. Dutton, and P. Shrivastava, 10B. Greenwich, CT: JAI Press.

Bosworth, Brian, and Stuart Rosenfeld. 1993. *Significant Others: Exploring the Potential of Manufacturing Networks.* Chapel Hill, NC: Regional Technology Strategies.

Brass, Daniel J., Joseph Galaskiewicz, Henrich R. Greve, and Wenpin Tsai. 2004. "Taking Stock of Networks and Organizations: A Multilevel Perspective." *Academy of Management Journal* 47, no. 3: 795–817.

Browning, Larry D.; Janice M. Beyer; and Judy C. Shetler. 1995. "Building Cooperation in a Competitive Industry: SEMATECH and the Semiconductor Industry." *Academy of Management Journal* 38, no. 1: 113–51.

D'Aunno, Thomas A., and Howard S. Zuckerman. 1987. "A Life-cycle Model of Organizational Federations: The Case of Hospitals." *Academy of Management Review* 12, no. 3: 534–45.

D'Aunno, Thomas A.; Robert I. Sutton; and Richard H. Price. 1991. "Isomorphism and External Support in Conflicting Institutional Environments: A Study of Drug Abuse Treatment Units." *Academy of Management Journal* 34, no. 3: 636–61.

Deephouse, David L. 1996. "Does Isomorphism Legitimate?" *Academy of Management Journal* 39, no. 4: 1024–39.

Delmar, Frederic, and Scott Shane. 2004. "Legitimating First: Organizing Activities and the Survival of New Ventures." *Journal of Business Venturing* 19, no. 3: 385–410.

DiMaggio, Paul J. 1992. "Nadel's Paradox Revisited: Relational and Cultural Aspects of Organizational Structure." In *Networks and Organizations: Structure, Form, and Action,* ed. N. Nohria and R. Eccles, 118–42. London: Harvard Business School Press.

DiMaggio, Paul J., and Walter W. Powell. 1983. "The Iron Cage Revisited: Institutional Isomorphism and Collective Rationality in Organizational Fields." *American Sociological Review* 48: 147–67.

Doz, Yves. L. 1996. "The Evolution of Cooperation in Strategic Alliances: Initial Conditions or Learning Processes?" *Strategic Management Journal* 17: 55–83.

Farmbry, Kyle, and Raina Harper. 2005. "Institutional Legitimacy Building in a Context of Transition: The South African Land Claims Court." *Public Administration Review* 65: 678–86.

Finn, Charles B. 1996. "Utilizing Stakeholder Strategies for Positive Collaborative Outcomes." In *Creating Collaborative Advantage,* ed. C. Huxham, 152–64. London: Sage.

Fligstein, Neil. 1985. "The Spread of the Multidivisional Form Among Large Firms, 1919–1979." *American Sociological Review* 50: 377–91.

Gulati, Ranjay. 1995. "Does Familiarity Breed Trust? The Implications of Repeated Ties for Contractual Choice in Alliances." *Academy of Management Journal* 38: 85–112.

Gulati, Ranjay, and Martin Gargiulo. 1999. "Where Do Interorganizational Networks Come from?" *American Journal of Sociology* 104: 1439–93.

Hagedoorn, John, and Jos Schakenraad. 1994. "The Effect of Strategic Technology Alliances on Company Performance." *Strategic Management Journal* 15, no. 4: 291–309.

Hanssen-Bauer, Jon, and Charles Snow. 1996. "Responding to Hypercompetition: The Structure and Processes of a Regional Learning Network Organization." *Organization Science* 7: 413–27.

Heidenreich, Martin. 1996. "Beyond Flexible Specialization: The Rearrangement of Regional Production Orders in Emilia-Romagna and Baden-Wurttemberg." *European Planning Studies* 4: 401–19.

Huggins, Robert. 2000. "The Success and Failure of Policy-implanted Inter-Firm Network Initiatives: Motivations, Processes and Structure." *Entrepreneurship & Regional Development* 12: 111–35.

Human, Sherrie E., and Keith G. Provan. 2000. "Legitimacy Building in the Evolution of Small-Firm Multilateral Networks: A Comparative Study of Success and Demise." *Administrative Science Quarterly* 45: 327–65.

Huxham, Chris, and Siv Vangen. 2005. *Managing to Collaborate.* London: Routledge.

Isett, Kimberley R., and Keith G. Provan. 2005. "The Evolution of Interorganizational Network Relationships over Time: Does Sector Matter?" *Journal of Public Administration Research and Theory* 15: 149–65.

Jones, Candace; William S. Hesterly; and Stephen P. Borgatti. 1997. "A General Theory of Network Governance: Exchange Conditions and Social Mechanisms." *Academy of Management Review* 22: 911–46.

Kilduff, Martin, and Wenpin Tsai. 2003. *Social Networks and Organizations.* London: Sage.

Kimberly, John R. 1979. "Issues in the Creation of Organizations: Initiation, Innovation, and Institutionalization." *Academy of Management Journal* 22: 437–57.

Larson, Andrea. 1992. "Network Dyads in Entrepreneurial Settings: A Study of the Governance of Exchange Relationships." *Administrative Science Quarterly* 37: 76–104.

Lichtenstein, Gregg A. 1992. *A Catalogue of U.S. Manufacturing Networks.* U.S. Dept. of Commerce, Gaithersburg, MD: National Institute of Standards and Technology.

Lorenzoni, Gianni, and Oscar A. Ornati. 1988. "Constellations of Firms and New Ventures." *Journal of Business Venturing* 3: 41–57.

Luke, Roice D.; James W. Begun; and Dennis D. Pointer. 1989. "Quasi Firms: Strategic Interorganizational Forms in the Health Care Industry." *Academy of Management Review* 1989: 9–19.

Malecki, Edward J., and Deborah M. Tootle. 1996. "The Role of Networks in Small Firm Competitiveness." *International Journal of Technology Management* 11, no. 1/2: 43–57.

Mandambi, Ram, and Susan Helper. 1998. "The 'Close but Adversarial' Model of Supplier Relations in the U.S. Auto Industry." *Strategic Management Journal* 19: 775–92.

Meyer, John W., and Brian Rowan. 1977. "Institutionalized Organizations: Formal Structure as Myth and Ceremony." *American Journal of Sociology* 83: 340–63.

Miles, Raymond E., and Charles C. Snow. 1986. "Network Organizations: New Concepts for New Forms." *California Management Review* 28, no. 3: 62–73.

Milward, H. Brinton, and Keith G. Provan. 2006. *A Manager's Guide for Choosing and Using Collaborative Networks.* Washington, DC: IBM Center for the Business of Government.

Moynihan, Donald. 2005. *Leveraging Collaborative Networks in Infrequent Emergency Situations.* Washington, DC: IBM Center for the Business of Government.

Oliver, Christine. 1990. "Determinants of Interorganizational Relationships: Integration and Future Directions." *Academy of Management Review* 15, no. 2: 241–65.

O'Toole, Laurence J. 1997. "Treating Networks Seriously: Practical and Research-Based Agendas in Public Administration." *Public Administration Review* 57, no. 1: 45–52.

Powell, Walter W. 1990. "Neither Market nor Hierarchy: Network Forms of Organization." In *Research in Organizational Behavior,* ed. Barry M. Staw and L.L. Cummings, 295–336. Greenwich, CT: JAI Press.

Provan, Keith G. 1983. "The Federation as an Interorganizational Linkage Network." *Academy of Management Review* 8: 79–89.

Provan, Keith G., and Patrick Kenis. 2008. "Modes of Network Governance: Structure, Management, and Effectiveness." *Journal of Public Administration Research and Theory* 18: in press.

Provan, Keith G., and H. Brinton Milward. 2001. "Do Networks Really Work? A Framework for Evaluating Public-Sector Organizational Networks." *Public Administration Review* 61: 414–23.

Provan, Keith G.; Kimberley R. Isett; and H. Brinton Milward. 2004. "Cooperation and Compromise: A Network Response to Conflicting Institutional Pressures in Community Mental Health." *Nonprofit and Voluntary Sector Quarterly* 33: 489–514.

Provan, Keith G.; Leigh Nakama; Mark A. Veazie; Nicolette I. Teufel-Shone; and Carol Huddleston. 2003. "Building Community Capacity Around Chronic Disease Services Through a Collaborative Interorganizational Network." *Health Education & Behavior* 30: 646–62.

Ring, Peter Smith, and Andrew H. Van de Ven. 1994. "Developmental Processes of Cooperative Interorganizational Relationships." *Academy of Management Review* 19, no. 1: 90-118.

Rosenfeld, Stuart. 1997. "Usenet—With Benefit of Hindsight." *Firm Connections* 5, no. 1: 3–4.

Saxenian, AnnaLee. 1990. "Regional Networks and the Resurgence of Silicon Valley." *California Management Review* 33, no. 1: 89–112.

Shan, Weijan; Gordon Walker; and Bruce Kogut. 1994. "Interfirm Cooperation and Startup Innovation in the Biotechnology Industry." *Strategic Management Journal* 15: 387–94.

Singh, Jitendra V.; David J. Tucker; and Robert J. House. 1986. "Organizational Legitimacy and the Liability of Newness." *Administrative Science Quarterly* 31: 171–93.

Stinchcombe, Arthur L. 1965. "Social Structure and Organizations." In *Handbook of Organizations,* ed. J.G. March, 142–193. Chicago: Rand McNally.

Suchman, Mark C. 1995. "Managing Legitimacy: Strategic and Institutional Approaches." *Academy of Management Review* 20: 571–610.

Teisman, Geert R., and Erik-Hans Klijn. 2002. "Partnership Arrangements: Governmental Rhetoric or Governance Scheme?" *Public Administration Review* 62: 197–205.

Tolbert, Pamela, and Lynne G. Zucker. 1996. "The Institutionalization of Institutional Theory." In *Handbook of Organization Studies,* ed. Stewart R. Clegg, Cynthia Hardy, and Walter R. Nord, 175–90. London: Sage.

Uzzi, Brian. 1997. "Social Structure and Competition in Interfirm Networks: The Paradox of Embeddedness." *Administrative Science Quarterly* 42: 35–67.

Vanhaverbeke, Wim. 2001. "Realizing New Regional Core Competencies: Establishing a Customer-Oriented SME Network." *Entrepreneurship & Regional Development* 13: 97–116.

Walston, Stephen L.; John R. Kimberly; and Lawton R. Burns. 1996. "Owned Vertical Integration and Health Care: Promise and Performance." *Health Care Management Review* 21: 83–92.

Weiner, Bryan J., and Jeffrey A. Alexander. 1998. "The Challenges of Governing Public-Private Community Health Partnerships." *Health Care Management Review* 23, no. 2: 39–55.

Westphal, James D.; Ranjay Gulati; and Stephen M. Shortell. 1997. "Customization or Conformity? An Institutional and Network Perspective on the Content and Consequences of TQM Adoption." *Administrative Science Quarterly* 42: 366–94.

Whetten, David A., and Paul Godfrey, eds. 1998. *Identity in Organizations: Building Theory Through Conversations.* Thousand Oaks, CA: Sage.

Wiewel, Wim, and Albert J. Hunter. 1985. "The Interorganizational Network as a Resource: A Comparative Case Study on Organizational Genesis." *Administrative Science Quarterly* 30: 482–96.

Zucker, Lynne G. 1987. "Institutional Theories of Organization." *Annual Review of Sociology* 13: 443–64.

CHAPTER 8

Managing for Results Across Agencies
Building Collaborative Capacity in the Human Services

STEPHEN PAGE

Public managers collaborating across organizational lines face two fundamental dilemmas. The first is a problem of collective action—catalyzing joint work across different organizational missions, mind-sets, and bases of authority. The second is one of accountability, or ensuring that collaborators work together in ways that accord with the intent of the voters and public officials who authorize their joint efforts.

Because collective action is a threshold condition for interorganizational initiatives—without it, collaboration does not occur—studies of collaborative public management have focused considerable attention on it. Accountability is nevertheless a dilemma for collaborators as well. Collaborators often share authority and wield administrative discretion across organizational lines, creating obstacles to the use of traditional accountability instruments such as hierarchical controls and legal mandates (Radin and Romzek 1996). Without formal controls or mandates, citizens, elected officials, and organizational stakeholders may worry that collaborating staff may play fast and loose with administrative rules, due process regulations, and other compliance requirements that foster democratic accountability. Disregarding those requirements may jeopardize key public values such as democratic participation or individual liberty in order to achieve collaborators' (often equally important) programmatic aims. From a policy analytic standpoint, moreover, collaborators need to demonstrate that the results they produce by working together are worth the time and other organizational resources that collaboration consumes.

Collaborative public managers therefore need to take accountability as seriously in interorganizational pursuits as they do in noncollaborative, intraorganizational undertakings. Fortunately, recent innovations offer principles to enhance the accountability of interorganizational collaboratives (Page 2004). Accountability for results, in particular, has captured the imaginations of elected officials, public managers, and academics. Federal and state laws, such as the U.S. Government Performance and Results Act of 1993, now require public agencies to manage for results (Moynihan and Ingraham 2003; Radin 2000). With the diffusion of the New York

Police Department's Compstat program and kindred initiatives (Behn 2006), managing for results has also become popular among public executives. Compstat shows that managing for results can transform organizational cultures and capabilities, generating notable improvements in outcomes that matter to voters and elected officials (Thompson and Bratton 2001).

Just as managing for results may enable individual organizations to demonstrate their public value to voters and elected officials, it may be useful to interorganizational collaborators. Collaborators who can demonstrate accountability by managing for results can address concerns that their discretion threatens the policy goals of voters and elected officials, or that interorganizational initiatives squander resources. By documenting the public value of their efforts, they may even find ways to sustain their collective endeavors despite the extra time commitments and conflicts among missions, mind-sets, and power bases that collaboration often entails.

Such happy developments are not assured, however: Many attempts to manage for results have limited impacts on organizational performance (Moynihan 2005). Moreover, the techniques that enable individual organizations to manage for results may not apply straightforwardly to interorganizational initiatives. Research suggests that managing for results may be more effective when a manager customizes it to suit her organizational mission and culture than when legislators or funders mandate it from outside (Moynihan and Pandey 2005; Radin 2000). Applying this finding to interorganizational initiatives suggests that collaborators need to develop an interorganizational mission and culture in order to determine how to customize their efforts to manage for results. Developing an interorganizational mission and culture, in turn, requires collaborative capacity (Bardach 1998), but the demands of managing for results may discourage the collective action that generates that capacity: Public managers may be reluctant to hold their organizations accountable for results if the achievement of results depends on voluntary cooperation among multiple organizations, rather than on staff and resources over which they have formal authority.

For all the reasons just discussed, collaborators may benefit from an improved understanding of how to develop and implement interorganizational initiatives to manage for results. In short, policymakers, managers, and scholars need to understand how to build the capacity to manage for results *across*—not just within—organizations.

To identify strategies for building this capacity, this chapter examines nine states' initiatives to encourage local collaboratives of human services agencies to manage for results. The next section reviews the literature to identify the capacities needed to manage for results as well as managerial activities to build collaborative capacity. The following section introduces the nine state initiatives and describes the study's research methods. The chapter then compares how the states have applied the managerial activities for building interorganizational capacity that the literature identifies. The conclusion analyzes the implications of the findings for public managers and poses questions for further research.

RESEARCH ON MANAGING FOR RESULTS AND INTERORGANIZATIONAL CAPACITY

Research on performance management has identified the capacities needed to manage for results in individual agencies (Behn 1991; Moynihan and Ingraham 2003). Studies of networks and interagency collaboration, meanwhile, have recently identified some generic activities useful for building various network and interorganizational capacities (e.g., Agranoff and McGuire 2001; Bardach 1998; McGuire 2002). Knowledge in the field is ripe to connect these two lines of scholarship by identifying activities and strategies to develop the interorganizational capacities necessary to manage for results across agencies.

The public management literature offers several different versions of how to manage for results (e.g., Behn 1991, 2006; Ingraham and Moynihan 2001). Most versions have at their core four managerial capacities:

- Strategic planning around results—consulting with stakeholders to agree on desired results, identifying ways to achieve them, setting goals to measure progress toward them, communicating goals to staff and the public, and linking responsibility for achieving each goal to a particular actor
- Measuring progress—tracking, reporting, and verifying quantifiable data that align with the desired results and limit opportunities for goal displacement and gaming
- Analyzing performance data—comparing progress toward goals against expected benchmarks (e.g., achievements of comparable jurisdictional or organizational units, widely accepted standards, or future projections based on recent trends)
- Using the findings to improve policy and management—modifying goals, strategy, and implementation to correct defects; rewarding actors who achieve their goals.

A number of public organizations have developed these capacities, perhaps the most prominent being the New York City Police Department (Thompson and Bratton 2001) and the City of Baltimore (Behn 2006). Public pressures to achieve policy results that cut across agency lines encourage the extension and application of the capacities to interorganizational initiatives with the resources and expertise to leverage broader policy impacts than those that individual agencies can achieve independently. These pressures increase the urgency for collaborators to develop the capacities to manage for results across agency lines.

Recent studies of networks and collaboration suggest generic activities that managers can use to build various interorganizational capacities. Page (2003) distills entrepreneurial management strategies from the literature on individual organizations that transfer to interorganizational settings: framing mission and goals, embracing accountability, improving production processes, adjusting administrative systems, imposing performance consequences, and building interorganizational culture. Bardach (1998) finds that managers build platforms of interorganizational collaborative capacity by fostering momentum and other developmental dynamics. Agranoff and McGuire (2001) argue that managers in networks activate, frame, mobilize, and synthesize interorganizational capacity—activities that subsume Page's strategies and Bardach's platforms.

For the sake of parsimony and simplicity, this chapter explores the applicability of these latter four activities for building the capacity to manage for results across agencies. *Activating* an interorganizational initiative or network entails recruiting appropriate participants and stakeholders, as well as assembling the skills, expertise, and resources needed to achieve the network's aims. *Framing* articulates and reinforces the shared purposes, rules, values, and norms of the network. *Mobilizing* induces and sustains commitment, support, and motivation to achieve shared purposes. *Synthesizing* interorganizational relationships consists of fostering productive interactions and exchanges among the participants (Agranoff and McGuire 2001; McGuire 2002).

The potential for convergence between these interorganizational management activities and the findings about managing for results is evident in new work by Moynihan and Pandey (2005, 2006). They find that three organizational variables are associated with the development of the capacity to manage for results in individual human services agencies: purposeful management reforms focused on results, support for results management from elected officials, and intraorganizational communication. Each of these variables has clear interorganizational applications and implicates at least one of the generic network management activities discussed above. Purposeful management reforms, for example, require framing goals and purposes as well as activating key players and resources. Support from elected officials results from effective mobilization, and communication can help mobilize and synthesize interorganizational efforts. To explore these applications further, this chapter turns to examine in detail interorganizational efforts to build the capacity to manage for results across agencies.

RESEARCH DESIGN AND METHODS

The capacity to manage for results across agencies, like other interorganizational capacities, consists of a set of platforms (Bardach 1998; Page 2004). To construct these platforms, collaborators can apply the generic network management activities discussed above. To develop a portrait of such applications, this chapter offers an inductive comparison of multiple case studies that differ in the extent to which the capacity to manage for results across agencies has developed. The aim is to generate grounded theory about particular approaches to activating, framing, mobilizing, and synthesizing interorganizational work that contributes to that capacity.

In the late 1980s and early 1990s, a number of states began to promote interagency collaboration to improve the lives of children and families. Some examples include the Family Connection in Georgia, Caring Communities in Missouri, and the Community Partnerships in Maryland and Vermont (Center for the Study of Social Policy 2001). These initiatives engaged a variety of programs and agencies. Some focused on a combination of child welfare, juvenile justice, and children's mental health issues; others, on a mix of public health, family support, child care, and early intervention questions; still others, on employment preparation, training, and support (Kagan et al. 1995; Schorr 1997; Waldfogel 1997). Regardless of their programmatic focus, many of the initiatives evolved similar institutional architectures that combined interorganizational collaboration with accountability for results (Page 2004).

The states authorized collaboration among local public agencies and nongovernmental organizations that administer and deliver human services. Augmented by the participation of civic leaders, neighborhood residents, and recipients of human services, local interagency collaboratives assumed responsibility for designing innovative interventions to assist children and families. They assessed community needs, developed comprehensive plans to address those needs, and implemented their plans using a combination of federal, state, local, and philanthropic funds (Kagan et al. 1995; Waldfogel 1997).

To hold the local collaborators publicly accountable while also giving them the flexibility to serve children and families in new ways, state officials sought to develop the local capacity to manage for results across agencies. A number of states therefore began to track community-level indicators of the well-being of children and families, starting in the early 1990s. Each indicator reflected progress toward a broad social outcome, or "core result," that state policymakers identified as a priority for children and families. Common results included employed parents, children succeeding in school, children safe in their homes, and safe communities (Friedman 1996). In states where data on community-level results were available, local collaborators used them prospectively to inform service design and planning, while state officials used them retrospectively to assess and compare the work of different local collaboratives.

From the pool of states that promoted these arrangements, nine feature in this study: Georgia's Family Connection (begun in 1991), Iowa's Decategorization and Empowerment Initiatives (begun in 1987 and 1998, respectively), Maryland's Community Partnerships (begun in 1989 as "Local Management Boards"), Missouri's Caring Communities (begun in 1993), North Carolina's Smart Start (begun in 1993), Ohio's Families and Children First (begun in 1992), Oregon's Commissions on Children and Families (begun in 1993), Vermont's Community Partnerships (begun in 1990), and Washington's Community Health and Safety Networks (begun in 1994). I selected these states' initiatives because their capacity to manage for results across agencies differs (Page 2004), as do their applications of the four network management activities identified in the literature, as the findings below illustrate. In addition, all the initiatives in the study have persisted for more than a decade, enabling me to compare the evolution of interorganizational management activities in the states over time.

The data below come from reviews of documents and approximately 200 interviews conducted periodically since 1995. The documents I reviewed included strategic plans, process and outcome evaluations, and other reports from the states, their consultants, and the intermediary organizations that supported their initiatives. Among the many sources I consulted, some of the more informative were Bryant and Cohen (2003); Center for the Study of Social Policy (1995, 1996a, 1996b, 1998, 2001); Friedman (1996); Georgia Family Connection (1996); Georgia Policy Council (1994, 1996a, 1996b); Hogan and Murphey (2002); Intergovernmental Administration Working Group (1997); Jewiss and Hasazi (1999); Kimmich et al. (1995); Ohio Family and Children First Cabinet Council (2003); Rozansky (1997a, 1997b); and Swanson-Gribskov (1995). Many states have also published data and reports about their local collaboratives on the World Wide Web. Some of the more helpful state Web sites that informed my research are Georgia's (www. georgiafamilyconnection.org), North Carolina's (www.smartstart-nc.org and www.fpg. unc.edu/~ncnr_assessment/county_map.cfm/), and Washington's (www.fpc.wa.gov/ FPCInfocphsn.html).

My interview informants in each state included:

- the governor's policy adviser on issues related to children and families;
- the commissioners, assistant commissioners, or collaborative liaisons in key state agencies involved in the state's initiative (e.g., social services, education, and public health);
- top staff in the state office or agencies responsible for supporting and overseeing local collaboration to assist children and families; and
- the staff of at least three local collaboratives.

In addition to these informants, I also interviewed a number of independent consultants as well as program directors and researchers in intermediary organizations that supported the states' initiatives. The intermediaries included the Annie E. Casey Foundation, the Center for Child and Family Policy, the Center for the Study of Social Policy, the National Governors' Association, the Finance Project, the Institute for Educational Leadership, the National Civic League's Program for Community Problem Solving, and the National Center for Service Integration.

After conducting the interviews and reviewing the documents, I queried my data regarding how network management activities contributed to the capacity to manage for results across agencies in the states as a group. The queries netted the following italicized applications of the four network management activities in the literature:

- Since activation entails recruiting and assembling network participants and resources (McGuire 2002), I coded each state's initiative according to the *memberships* of the local collaboratives and the annual *funds* they offered their local collaboratives.
- Framing involves articulating the shared purposes (aims, rules, norms) of network members (McGuire 2002). I coded the states' initiatives based on the formal *missions* or overarching goals espoused in their planning documents and in my initial interviews.
- Because mobilization seeks to motivate commitment and support for interorganizational undertakings (McGuire 2002), I examined four tactics in each state:

  1. the *rhetoric* state officials and local collaborators used to advertise the public value of their initiative and mobilize support;
  2. the supporting *coalition* they enlisted;
  3. the *standards* the state required each local collaborative to meet;
  4. the *incentives* the state offered the collaboratives to encourage improvements in results.

- Synthesizing network dynamics is critical to encourage exchange and build relationships among participants (McGuire 2002; see also the discussions of trust, consensus, and cultures of joint problem solving in Bardach 1998). To capture synthesizing efforts, I coded the states' initiatives based on the *governance structures*, *data on results and indicators*, and *communication processes* they used to share information and help local collaborators plan strategically, make joint decisions, and improve results.

Using these categories, I coded the actions of officials in each state based on whether and how they used each application to promote managing for results across agencies—first early in their initiatives (in 1994), and then a decade later (in 2004). By comparing ten institutionally similar initiatives over a decade using the methods described here, the chapter seeks a preliminary understanding of how public managers use the four network management activities to build the capacity to manage for results across agencies.

STATES' USE OF NETWORK MANAGEMENT ACTIVITIES

The data analysis revealed that some states changed their applications of some network management activities over the course of their initiatives. The findings that follow therefore distinguish states' initial applications of each network management activity (circa 1994) from their more recent applications (circa 2004). A sequence of tables summarizes the initial and more recent applications of the four activities, which are italicized in the paragraphs below.

Activating

As the top row of Table 8.1 shows, the states in my sample used membership and funding provisions to activate participation and resources for their local collaboratives.

Membership

To ensure adequate representation and balance in local decision making, many states established membership requirements for their local collaboratives, in addition to encouraging participation by civic leaders, service recipients, and other community members. Iowa, North Carolina, and Ohio required that the boards of their local collaboratives include *representatives from key public agencies* (e.g., human services, education, public health, mental health, or school districts). By contrast, Maryland, Oregon, Washington, and Vermont required that each local collaborative's board include a certain proportion of *lay citizens* with no fiduciary interests in service delivery decisions. Georgia and Missouri adopted an *open-ended* approach, establishing no membership requirements for their local collaboratives. Instead, they encouraged broad representation from community stakeholders, including service recipients, civic leaders, and public agencies and nongovernmental organizations that serve children and families. The open-ended requirements enabled preexisting local collaboratives to join the state initiative without reconfiguring their memberships.

All the states in my sample retained the initial membership provisions (or lack thereof) for their local collaboratives as their initiatives evolved over time. In addition, Iowa created a new initiative in 1998 (the Community Empowerment Initiative) that encouraged local collaboration to assist young children and families, to complement its initial Decategorization Initiative, which sought to improve the stability of troubled families. Because

Table 8.1

Activation Approaches to Promote Managing for Results by Local Collaboratives

	Members required	State and federal funds for:
1994 (states)	1. Public agency reps (*3*—IA, NC, OH) 2. % lay citizens (*4*—MD, OR, VT, WA) 3. Open-ended (*2*—GA, MO)	1. Planning and program (*5*—GA, MO, NC, OH, OR) 2. Share of savings (*2*—IA, MD) 3. Staff (*2*—VT, WA)
2004 (states)		1. Planning and program (*5*—GA, MO, NC, OH, OR) 2. Share of savings + program or staff $$ (*3*—IA, MD, VT) 3. Staff (*1*—WA) +locally generated funds (*all 9*)

the Empowerment Initiative focused on a different population than Decategorization, it required different members on its local boards.

Funding

In the early years of their initiatives, all nine states in my sample offered funding to their local collaboratives. The amounts, sources, and purposes of the funds varied. Georgia, Missouri, North Carolina, Ohio, and Oregon provided funds for *collaborative planning and program delivery* at the local level. Iowa and Maryland offered local collaborators a retrospective *share of savings* they generated by avoiding out-of-home and out-of-state foster placements through the use of intensive family therapy and other supports. Vermont and Washington provided only modest funds to *staff and coordinate* each of their local collaboratives.

By 2004, a decade or more after their initiatives began, five states had sustained the type of funding they initially offered their local collaboratives: Georgia, Missouri, North Carolina, Ohio, and Oregon continued to fund collaborative planning and program delivery at the local level, and Washington continued its modest support for staffing and coordinating its local collaboratives. Four states expanded the types and amounts of funding they initially offered: Iowa, Maryland, and Ohio began to pass funds for additional federal and state programs through to their local collaboratives, and Vermont added a share-in-savings provision similar to Iowa's and Maryland's, while continuing modest support to staff and coordinate its local collaboratives. In addition to their state-supplied funds, by 2004 many *local collaboratives had secured their own funds* to support particular projects from federal, state, local, or philanthropic sources.

Framing

As Table 8.2 indicates, the states in my sample initially framed their initiatives in three different ways. Georgia and Vermont's initiatives sought to *improve results* for children and families. Two variants of this approach appeared in North Carolina, whose initiative

Table 8.2

Framing Approaches to Promote Managing for Results by Local Collaboratives

	Frames
1994 (states)	1. Improve results for children and families (*4*—GA, NC, WA, VT)
	2. Improve services and systems (*2*—OH, OR)
	3. Improve results by changing services (*3*—IA, MD, MO)
2004 (states)	1. Improve results for children and families (*4*—GA, NC, WA, VT)
	2. Improve results by changing services (*5*—IA, MD, MO, OH, OR)

aimed to "improve the lives of young children and families," and Washington, whose initiative sought to "decrease risky behaviors among youth." Ohio's and Oregon's initiatives intended to *improve services and systems* for children and families. The initiatives in Maryland, Missouri, and Iowa combined the other states' frames by aiming to *improve results by changing service delivery*.

As their initiatives developed, most of the states continued to use their initial frames to characterize their initiatives. A few alternative frames came and went (e.g., for several years Oregon billed its initiative as promoting "wellness" among children and families), but the initial frames persisted in most of the states: Ongoing discussions among local collaborators and between state officials and local collaboratives in Georgia and Vermont, for example, focus first on improving results, and only secondarily on services and supports as a means to do so. Comparable discussions in Maryland, Missouri, and Iowa retain a dual focus on results and services. The frames in Ohio and Oregon, however, became more similar to those in Iowa, Maryland, and Missouri: The proponents of Ohio's and Oregon's initiatives increased their attention to results over time, while maintaining an overarching focus on improving services and systems.

MOBILIZING

The top row of Table 8.3 identifies four tactics that the states in my sample used to mobilize support and commitment for their local collaboratives' efforts to manage for results.

Public Value Rhetoric

All the states initially mobilized political support for their initiatives primarily by *invoking the frames* identified above. Each state's frame proved politically salient and effective as a mobilizing tactic. The initial frame of Ohio's initiative—improving services and systems for children and families—proved so popular that the initiative's proponents relied on it alone to capture the public value of their efforts.

Other states, however, used additional rhetoric to enhance the appeal of their initiatives' primary frame. Georgia, Maryland, Iowa, Oregon, Vermont, and Washington reminded

Table 8.3

Mobilization Approaches to Promote Managing for Results by Local Collaboratives

	Rhetoric	Support coalition	Standards	Incentives
1994 (states)	Frame (all 9) plus: 1. Flexible community problem solving (6—GA, IA, MD, OR, VT, WA) 2. Responsible use of state funds (3—IA, MD, WA) 3. Improved *statewide* results (2—MO, NC)	Service providers and recipients (all 9), plus: 1. Governor (5—GA, MO, NC, OH, VT) 2. Legislature (7—IA, MD, NC, OH, OR, VT, WA) 3. Civic leaders and citizens (4—MO, OR, VT, WA) 4. Improve indicators (6—GA, IA, MD, MO, VT, WA)	Needs assessments and strategic plans (all 9), plus: 1. Governance structures (6—IA, MD, NC, OH, OR, WA) 2. Members (7—IA, MD, NC, OH, OR, VT, WA) 3. Program requirements (3—NC, OH, OR)	State reviews of local reports (all 9), plus: 1. State publicity re: changes in local indicators (4—GA, IA, MD, VT) 2. Share in savings (2—IA, MD) 3. Additional responsibility (5—GA, MO, OH, VT, WA)
2004 (states)	Frame (all 9) plus: 1. Flexible community problem solving (7—GA, IA, MD, MO, OR, VT, WA) 2. Responsible use of state funds (4—IA, MD, NC, WA) 3. Improved *local* indicators (5—GA, IA, MD, VT, WA)	Service providers and recipients (all 9), plus: 1. Governor (6—GA, IA, MO, NC, OH, VT) 2. Legislature (8—GA, IA, MD, NC, OH, OR, VT, WA) 3. Civic leaders and citizens (4—MO, OR, VT, WA)	Needs assessments and strategic plans (all 9), plus: 1. Governance structures (7—GA, IA, MD, NC, OH, OR, WA) 2. Members (7—IA, MD, NC, OH, OR, VT, WA) 3. Program requirements (5—IA, MD, NC, OH, OR) 4. Improve indicators (7—GA, IA, MD, MO, OR, VT, WA) 5. Administrative processes (1—NC) 6. Evidence-based programs (4—GA, MO, OH, OR) 7. Logic models (3—IA, OR, WA) 8. Learning (1—WA)	State reviews of local reports (all 9), plus: 1. State publicity re: changes in local indicators (6—GA, IA, MD, NC, OR, VT) 2. Share in savings (3—IA, MD, VT) 3. Additional responsibility (6—GA, MD, MO, OH, VT, WA) 4. Bonus funds (3—MO, NC, WA)

stakeholders that their initiatives fostered *flexible community problem solving* to augment and improve public programs. In a period of general hostility toward government among voters and even some elected officials, this theme held broad appeal, as it resonated with the "devolution revolution" proposed by the Republicans who were ascendant in Congress and in many state governments in the mid-1990s. The proponents of the initiatives in Iowa, Maryland, and Washington added rhetoric with similar political resonance: They argued that their initiatives would *use state funds responsibly* because their local collaboratives understood community problems better than state officials, and could invest in creative solutions that tapped local resources as a complement to federal and state funds. By contrast, initiative proponents in Missouri and North Carolina initially took a different approach to mobilizing political support: Using evidence from statewide evaluations of their initiatives, they argued that the initiatives were producing aggregate *improvements in the well-being of children and families* across the state.

As their initiatives evolved, all of the states continued to rely on their frames to convey their initiatives' public value. The rhetoric of community problem solving and responsible use of state funds also proved durable in the states that used those phrases initially. Ironically—given their frames that focused on improving results—the attempts to win political support by demonstrating aggregate improvements in results for children and families encountered difficulty in both Missouri and North Carolina. Both states' initiatives had strong support in the governor's office and the executive branch of state government, but their initial evaluation results prompted skepticism from some legislators, who questioned the validity of the data. In response, the proponents of both initiatives shifted their rhetoric: Those in Missouri came to stress the virtues of community problem solving, while those in North Carolina took pains to demonstrate that their local collaboratives were using state funds responsibly. The proponents of the initiatives in Georgia, Iowa, Maryland, Vermont, and Washington, meanwhile, began to couple local data with their early rhetoric about community problem solving to demonstrate that their initiatives had *improved specific indicators* in particular communities.

Support Coalition

As Table 8.3 indicates, the coalitions supporting the various states' initiatives were similar in that they all included *service providers and recipients*, who stood to benefit most directly. The core supporters of the states' initiatives differed, however, in other respects— specifically, the extent to which *civic leaders and citizens* in local communities rallied around their local collaboratives, and the support for the statewide initiative from the state *legislature* and the *governor*.

Civic leaders and citizens participated in the local collaboratives in all the states in my sample, but they were especially important early supporters of the initiatives in Missouri, Oregon, Vermont, and Washington. Support among legislators was initially strong in Iowa, Maryland, Oregon, Vermont, and Washington; initial authorizing legislation for local collaboration also passed in North Carolina and Ohio, but the chief early proponent of the initiative in each state was the governor. In addition to those in North Carolina and

Ohio, governors were also strong early supporters of the initiatives in Georgia, Missouri, and Vermont.

As the states' initiatives developed, support from these sources waxed and waned in different measure. Challenges sustaining the original coalitions mobilized to promote managing for results across agencies were nearly universal; at times key supporters lost interest, or threatening opposition developed. In particular, gubernatorial enthusiasm wavered in Georgia, Ohio, and Oregon, and legislators raised hard questions about the initiatives in Maryland, North Carolina, Missouri, and Washington. All the initiatives nevertheless retained at least nominal support from their original coalition. Some even added new coalition members over time: Georgia's legislature eventually authorized its local collaboratives, and a new governor made Iowa's local collaboratives central to his policy agenda.

Standards

As the "Standards" column in Table 8.3 shows, all the states required their collaboratives to *assess the needs* of local children and families and develop *strategic plans* offering comprehensive, family-friendly services to address the most pressing community priorities. In addition, most states in my sample initially required their local collaboratives to develop particular *governance structures* and *memberships*, the exceptions being Georgia, Missouri, and (with specific regard to governance) Vermont. North Carolina, Ohio, and Oregon initially imposed *program requirements* on their collaboratives to ensure adequate staffing and delivery of particular comprehensive services to promote early childhood development and maternal and child health. By contrast, Georgia, Iowa, Maryland, Missouri, Vermont, and Washington required their local collaboratives to *improve indicators* of the well-being of children and families prioritized in each collaborative's strategic plan.

As their initiatives evolved, all the states retained their initial requirements related to governance structures, membership requirements, needs assessments, and strategic plans. In addition, states added a number of new standards over time to supplement the ones with which they started. Oregon started requiring its collaboratives to improve indicators of well-being identified in their local strategic plans. Iowa and Maryland expanded their collaboratives' initial responsibilities from preventing out-of-home foster and institutional placements for children to improving indicators in other program areas as well. Consequently, both states also added program requirements to ensure that the new child care programs that their collaboratives sponsored were adequately staffed. North Carolina, by contrast, slightly narrowed the programmatic scope of its local collaboratives' work, and added new *administrative process* standards to reassure the legislature that the collaboratives were using funds responsibly. Rather than prescribing standards specific to particular programs, Georgia, Missouri, Ohio, and Oregon required their collaboratives' strategic plans to include *evidence-based programs* that research shows can improve local priority indicators. Finally, Iowa, Oregon, and Washington now require each collaborative to articulate the *logic model* or theory of change driving its strategic plan; Washington also asks collaboratives to report on what they have *learned* about improving results for children and families.

Incentives

To encourage the local collaboratives to meet these standards, the states adopted a variety of incentives when their initiatives began. All of them regularly *reviewed reports* from each collaborative that documented which of the required standards it had met. Georgia, Iowa, Maryland, and Vermont all *publicized changes (both positive and negative) in local indicators* that reflected the progress or challenges of individual collaboratives, in order to applaud achievements and create pressure for improvements. Iowa and Maryland supplemented such publicity by awarding their collaboratives a *share in the savings* their services generated (see the "Activation" section above). Georgia, Missouri, Ohio, Vermont, and Washington offered (at least nominal) opportunities to take on *additional responsibilities* for planning and programming to collaboratives whose priority indicators improved.

Over time, several states added new incentives to their initial approaches. Following Georgia, Iowa, Maryland, and Vermont, North Carolina, and Oregon began to publicize changes in local indicators to highlight progress and create pressure for improvements. Vermont emulated Iowa's and Maryland's examples by adding a share-in-savings provision to encourage improvements in indicators related to out-of-home placements of children involved in the child welfare, children's mental health, and juvenile justice systems. Maryland allowed its local collaboratives with proven track records to take on additional responsibility by delegating to them a variety of federal funds for preventive programs. Missouri, North Carolina, and Washington innovated by offering very modest *bonus funds* to those local collaboratives that exceeded key state standards.

Synthesizing

Table 8.4 summarizes the tactics that the states in my sample used to foster exchange and build relationships among local collaborators and between each collaborative and state officials.

Governance Structures

To help collaborators develop the institutional capacity to make joint decisions about community needs and priorities, many of the states issued formal *organizational requirements* when their initiatives began. Iowa, Maryland, Ohio, Oregon, North Carolina, and Washington established their local collaboratives as public authorities, public–private commissions, or legal nonprofits with 501(c)3 status and boards of directors. Georgia, Missouri, and Vermont took an *open-ended approach* to local governance, permitting their collaboratives to decide on their own organizational forms, while encouraging them to adopt formal decision-making structures when they were prepared to do so (e.g., by incorporating as 501(c)3 nonprofits or as public authorities with the capacity to raise and administer funds). Open-ended approaches enabled these states to allow preexisting local

151

Table 8.4

Synthesizing Approaches to Promote Managing for Results by Local Collaboratives

	Governance structures	Data on results and indicators	Communication
1994 (states)	1. Formal organizational requirements (6—IA, MD, NC, OH, OR, WA)	1. Broad results and measurable indicators tracked in communities (4—GA, MO, VT, WA)	1. Information on collaborative strategic planning, decision making, and programming (8—GA, MD, MO, NC, OH, OR, VT, WA)
	2. Open-ended (3—GA, MO, VT)	2. Population-specific indicators tracked in communities (3—IA, MD, NC)	2. Customized assistance to address unmet standards and local challenges (8—GA, MD, MO, NC, OH, OR, VT, WA)
		3. Core results or indicators unidentified or disputed (2—OH, OR)	3. Trend data on changes in local indicators (4—GA, IA, MD, VT)
2004 (states)	1. Formal organizational requirements (6—IA, MD, NC, OH, OR, WA)	1. Broad results and measurable indicators tracked in all communities (7—GA, IA, MD, MO, OH, VT, WA)	1. Information on collaborative strategic planning, decision making, and programming (all 9)
	2. Open-ended (2—MO, VT)	2. Population-specific indicators tracked in all communities (1—NC)	2. Customized assistance to address unmet standards and local challenges (7—GA, IA, MD, NC, OR, VT, WA)
	+ process standards (1—GA)	3. Local priority indicators tracked in individual communities (1—OR)	3. Trend data on changes in: • All core local indicators (6—GA, IA, MD, MO, NC, VT), or • Locally selected priority indicators (2—OR, WA)

collaboratives with diverse organizational auspices to participate in their statewide initiatives without restructuring their institutional forms.

All the states retained these requirements as their initiatives evolved over time. Georgia also added *process standards* to enable state officials to monitor and compare its collaboratives' governance capacities. A self-assessment tool requires local collaborators to document and analyze their capacity to work together and make joint decisions, while ensuring they adhere to "standards for excellence in collaboration and community decision-making" (Family Connection Partnership 2005).

Data

To give collaborators a common base of information about local conditions and how those conditions changed over time as the local collaboratives implemented their strategic plans, most of the states in my sample set out to track data measuring the well-being of children and families. The particular measures they adopted varied, depending on the policy aims of the state's initiative as well as on whether state and local stakeholders could agree on broad results and indicators to track.

Early on in their initiatives, state officials and local collaborators in Georgia, Missouri, Vermont, and Washington committed to tracking and targeting for improvement *broad results and measurable indicators* in communities with local collaboratives.[1] Since the initiatives in Iowa, Maryland, and North Carolina targeted specific populations—children at risk of out-of-home placement in Iowa and Maryland, and young children and families in North Carolina—those states tracked *indicators specific to those populations* in communities with local collaboratives.[2] State officials and local collaborators in Ohio and Oregon, meanwhile, failed to agree on results and indicators to track when their initiatives began. Oregon featured especially contentious discussions about which of the Oregon benchmarks the local collaboratives should be held responsible for improving.

As time went on, the tracking and analysis of indicator data became more detailed and sophisticated in all of the states, enabling the development of the more elaborate standards and incentive provisions detailed above in the "Mobilizing" discussion and in Table 8.3, as well as more communications focused on changes in indicators (discussed immediately below). In addition to deepening their initial approaches to managing and interpreting local indicators, Iowa, Maryland, Ohio, and Oregon adopted other approaches as well. The new approaches in Iowa, Maryland, and Ohio followed the initial examples developed in Georgia, Missouri, Vermont, and Washington. As Iowa's and Maryland's initiatives expanded beyond children at risk of out-of-home placement to encompass improving the lives of all children and families, they built the statewide capacity to track results and indicators reflecting a broader range of outcomes for children and families. State officials and local collaborators in Ohio eventually identified a core set of results and indicators to track and target for improvement. The disputes over the benchmarks in Oregon, meanwhile, were resolved when state officials and local collaborators agreed on a master list of results and indicators from which the collaboratives *prioritize specific indicators* for local improvement and state tracking.

Communication

To build relationships and the will to work together among collaborators, the states in my sample provided three forms of information and assistance to their local collaboratives: generic information about promising practices in the area of interorganizational collaboration to improve results, customized assistance to address local challenges, and data on changes in local indicators. Early in the development of their initiatives, all the states except Iowa offered *information on promising collaborative practices* for data-driven strategic planning, joint decision making, and programming. The same set of states also offered *customized assistance* to ensure that their local collaboratives could meet state standards—either by identifying and troubleshooting local problems directly or by commissioning consultants to do so. The states with adequate systems to track indicators also provided *trend data on changes in local indicators* to their local collaboratives, in order to inform the collaboratives' strategic planning and to create implicit incentives for improvement.

The states' offerings of information and assistance changed in various ways as their initiatives evolved. Iowa began to offer both customized assistance and information on collaborative planning, decision making, and programming after expanding the focus of local collaborative work to improving the general well-being of children and families. (An evaluation of Iowa's early efforts to reduce out-of-home placements had identified a strong need for technical assistance and information among the local collaboratives.) Missouri and Ohio, by contrast, stopped offering customized assistance as their initiatives' state-level staffing and resources diminished over time, though both states continued to offer general information about collaborative planning, decision making, and programming. Finally, Missouri, North Carolina, Oregon, and Washington began providing their local collaboratives with trend data on changes in local indicators once they developed the data systems to do so. While Missouri and North Carolina emulated Georgia's, Iowa's, Maryland's, and Vermont's approach to tracking and communicating trends in all local indicators, Oregon and Washington focused communication on those *indicators that each local collaborative selected as priorities*.

DISCUSSION

These findings suggest five insights and three caveats about the role that states and other superordinate authorities can play in building the capacity to manage for results across agencies.

Insights

First, extending Agranoff and McGuire's (2001) study of the use of four network management activities by local collaborators, my research shows that *superordinate authorities can use the same activities to promote, structure, and assess local collaboration.* At a general level, the states I studied provided resources, guidance, discipline, economies of scale in gathering and analyzing performance data, and cross-site perspective to identify and diffuse promising practices across local collaboratives.

Second, at a more operational level, all nine of my states altered their applications of the four network management activities over time. The states' *changes in their applications cluster into two trajectories*, as the rows in Table 8.5 reveal. (The symbols in Table 8.5 indicate changes between states' early and later applications of the network management activities, summarizing the distinctions between the upper and lower halves of Tables 8.1–8.4.) The first trajectory appears in the many changes and replacements of applications of network management activities that appear in Table 8.5's portraits of the initiatives in Iowa and Maryland, and to a lesser extent those of Missouri, North Carolina, and Oregon. It resembles Bob Behn's concept of "groping along" (1991) in that it entails launching an initiative and adapting it over time in response to challenges and new opportunities. The second trajectory is evident in the comparative dearth of changes of applications in Table 8.5's depictions of the initiatives in Vermont and Georgia. It might be termed "aligned incrementalism" to capture the more straightforward developmental process it entails.

The states with aligned-incremental initiatives secured initial agreements on results and indicators for their collaborators to achieve, developed comprehensive data systems early, and focused their initiatives' frames and rhetoric on community problem solving to improve results. The early alignment of these applications may have enabled consistent growth with fewer changes in network management activities than in the groping states.[3] The states whose initiatives groped along eventually developed and used trend data on relevant local indicators as well, which in turn enabled the development of standards, incentives, rhetoric, and communication, while reinforcing frames that emphasized improving results. Despite their differences, then, both groping along and aligned incrementalism benefit from establishing the capacity to track, analyze, and publicize local data on indicators relevant to local collaborators' aims and accomplishments.

Third, the states' *applications of individual network management activities* reflect both continuity and evolution, as Table 8.5 indicates. The dearth of changes in the membership, framing, coalition, and governance columns of Table 8.5 indicates that the states' approaches to these applications of the network management activities remained fairly consistent. By contrast, the states' approaches to rhetoric, standards, incentives, and communication changed considerably over time. As the number of new applications in the bottom half of the standards column of Table 8.3 documents, the most volatile application was the states' standards for their local collaboratives. The symbols in the "Standards" column of Table 8.5 indicate that all the states except Vermont adopted at least one new standard as their initiatives developed.

At a general level, this proliferation of standards reflects the maturation of government-sponsored collaboration, and likely is a response to the isomorphic and political pressures for accountability that tend to accompany the institutionalization of any government program (Dimaggio and Powell 1983; Wilson 1989). After the North Carolina legislature expressed skepticism about the state's efforts to promote local collaboration to assist children and families, for example, state officials narrowed the types of services for which collaborators could use state funds and added detailed reporting requirements on local activities.

At a more specific level, the proliferation of state standards for local collaboration raises the operational question of why states changed their applications of individual network

Table 8.5

Changes in States' Applications of Network Management Activities, 1994–2004

States	Activating			Mobilizing					Synthesizing	
	Members	Funds	Framing	Rhetoric	Coalition	Standards	Incentives	Governance	Data	Communication
Georgia				+	+	+		+		
Iowa		+		+	+	+, +			new	+, +
Maryland		+		+		+	+		new	
Missouri				new		+	+			–, +
N. Carolina				new		+	+, +			+
Ohio		+	+			+			new	–
Oregon			+			+, +, +	+		new	+
Vermont		+		+			+			
Washington				+		+, +, +	+			+

Notes: + = added an application to supplement initial application(s)

new = replaced one application with another

– = discontinued an application

management activities in the specific ways that they did. Consistent with the pivotal role of performance data in the two trajectories identified above, a substantial majority of the states' changes in standards as well as rhetoric, incentives, and communication derive from improved data. Many states' rhetoric about "community problem solving to improve results," for example, proved convincing to stakeholders only when coupled with the capacity to measure and publicize changes in local indicators that documented and demonstrated collaborators' accountability for results. Once Iowa and Maryland were able to measure additional indicators of the well-being of children and families beyond out-of-home placements, they could allocate resources to provide incentives to their local collaboratives to serve additional populations. Once Oregon secured agreement on a core set of results, state officials could require the local collaboratives to use evidence-based programs and logic models designed to achieve indicators of those results. They could also publicize changes in local indicators and hold the collaboratives accountable for improving priority indicators. The states' uses of outcomes and indicator data to frame and synthesize local collaborators' efforts are consistent with Moynihan and Pandey's (2006) findings about the role of purposeful management reform and robust communication in promoting managing for results in individual agencies: Outcomes and indicators enable state officials to send a clear message about the importance of managing for results, while helping collaborators understand the aims and challenges involved.

Fourth, *noteworthy improvements in relevant local indicators hold catalytic political potential*. When states used local outcomes and indicator data to activate, frame, mobilize, and synthesize collaboration in consistent, mutually reinforcing ways, legislators and other stakeholders developed clear understandings and expectations of local interorganizational efforts. Georgia, Iowa, Maryland, Oregon, Vermont, and Washington, for example, combined mobilizing rhetoric focused on "local decision making" with frames that emphasized "improving results" and synthesizing communications based on improvements in local indicators that collaborators designated as priorities. In doing so, the proponents of collaboration fostered an electoral connection focused on results in local legislative districts: Legislators valued the measurable improvements that collaborators produced (and state officials documented) in their home districts. By contrast, Missouri's and North Carolina's abandonment of their initial attempts to mobilize support by publicizing aggregate, statewide improvements in indicator data suggests that evidence of the public value of collaboration is especially persuasive when grounded in legislative districts. In short, improved performance data can be politically valuable when they have direct links to politicians' electoral prospects.

Fifth, the foregoing paragraphs in combination suggest that *outcomes and indicator data are central to the states' network management attempts to build local collaborative capacities*—both the capacity to manage for results across agencies and the capacity to plan and deliver services jointly across organizational lines. Tracking and publicizing data about changes in local indicators may be a threshold platform that enables other applications of network management activities to promote managing for results across agencies, including standards, incentives, and communication. This finding comes as no surprise, since results and indicators are at the heart of any attempt to manage for results. The potential of results and indicator data to catalyze collaboration as well as stakeholder support for it raises an additional possibility—that using performance data to synthesize interorganizational work may help build collaborative capacity more generally (Page 2003). The interorganizational motivation and communication that good indicator data make possible thus may help collaborators overcome the collective action dilemmas that are a threshold obstacle to interorganizational work.

Caveats

Outcomes and indicator data clearly hold promise as tools state officials can use to build local interorganizational collaborative capacities. The use of data to activate, frame, mobilize, and synthesize collaboration nevertheless raises three caveats.

First, the data measured need to be logically associated with broad policy results that matter to voters and elected officials, yet concrete enough that they hold practical meaning for collaborators. An early requirement in Oregon that the local collaboratives identify ways in which their proposed projects would contribute to the state's official benchmarks, for example, engendered extremely broad and overly optimistic predictions of projects' impacts. Narrow, project-specific performance measures, by contrast, encourage goal distortion by enabling collaborators to accomplish the official measures without necessarily making progress toward the broader policy results that the measures are intended to reflect. Some measures of the quality of local collaboratives' early childhood programs in Iowa and North Carolina, for example, focus on "process" indicators such as staff–child ratios rather than on the developmental progress of the children participating in the programs. Both states therefore supplement these indicators with additional performance measures (such as developmental assessments of children) that better capture the intended outcome of ensuring that young children enter kindergarten ready to learn.

Second, regardless of what indicators are measured, the potential to mobilize and synthesize interorganizational collaboration depends on how collaborators and their overseers use the data. Simply tracking outcomes and associated indicators that reflect local aims as well as voters' and elected officials' hopes may activate and frame collaboration, but the additional catalytic impact is likely to be limited without dedicated efforts to manage for (not just measure) results. The interpretation of local performance data is necessary to understand, improve, and publicize progress toward desired outcomes. In Georgia, for example, state officials conduct comparative statistical analyses of changes in performance data in all 159 counties to identify trends. They then hold annual "community dialogues" with collaborators in each county to review local progress (or lack thereof), and offer suggestions from other counties and insights from their comparative analyses to encourage local innovations and improvements in the future. In Vermont, state officials conduct monthly qualitative analyses of trends in specific indicators to construct "stories behind the numbers" and develop hypotheses about how local collaborators might improve their indicators in the future. The state also publicizes each local collaborative's most promising improvements and most troubling indicator trends broadly at the local and state level, to prompt public approval and inspire further joint efforts. The judicious use of data by state officials to interpret and demonstrate progress thus may help collaborators build public support and understanding for their undertakings, and revise aspects of their work where the data indicate opportunities to improve.

Third, overly aggressive use of performance data to drive interorganizational standards and incentives may hamper network activation by leaving potential collaborators wary of interorganizational work. Such wariness stems from two quite justifiable fears. First, management for results across agencies saddles collaborators with joint responsibility for improving indicators of broad policy results beyond the control of their individual organizations. Second, the dilemmas of collective action inherent in interorganizational work present the risk that some collaborators may shirk or "free ride" from fulfilling their particular responsibilities, leading to underperformance and possible sanctions for the collaborative as a whole. These concerns motivated early disputes over what outcomes and indicators to use to track collaboratives' progress in Oregon, and inspired state officials in Georgia and Vermont to eschew both sanctions and financial rewards for poorly performing collaboratives. These dilemmas suggest that using performance data and associated standards and incentives to build local collaborative capacities is a double-edged sword.

CONCLUSION

Caveats notwithstanding, this study reveals potential benefits of outcomes and indicator data for network management activities dedicated to building interorganizational collaborative capacities. These benefits apply to the dilemmas of both accountability and collective action that public managers confront when they promote or engage in interorganizational collaboration.

To address concerns about the accountability of interorganizational work, local collaborators and state officials can use outcomes and indicator data to drive and align the four network management activities of activating, framing, mobilizing, and synthesizing. Many of the states in my study made prominent use of outcomes and indicators to establish standards, rhetoric, incentives, and communication regarding local collaboration. Such network management activities helped local collaborators in the states build the capacity to manage for results across agencies and, in turn, legitimate their efforts to their stakeholders.

With regard to challenges of collective action, aligning network management activities tightly around outcomes and indicators enabled local collaboration to thrive. In states such as Georgia and Vermont, commitments to achieve broad outcomes and to use indicator data to measure progress toward those outcomes seemed to enhance local collaborators' willingness and ability to work together. In addition to evaluating interorganizational performance and enhancing collaborators' accountability, then, using outcomes and indicator data as network management tools may also catalyze collective action across organizational lines. In short, outcomes and indicators may help make interorganizational collaboration not just more accountable and effective but also more viable.

These possibilities raise important questions regarding the particular sources, or drivers, of the enhancements in accountability and collective action that emerged in my research: Do the enhancements derive from the local collaborators' heightened focus on performance indicators, from the central supports for managing for results (e.g., standards, incentives, data management, communication assistance) that the states in my sample offered, or from both? If the former, how does an increased focus on performance indicators deepen collaborators' commitments to their joint efforts—especially given the possibility of backlash among collaborators in response to proposals to measure performance? If the latter, are some central supports more helpful than others to enable collaborators to demonstrate their accountability to voters and elected officials? Are some supports more important for catalyzing and sustaining collective action among collaborators? Do synergies develop among the various supports, such that different combinations of supports may generate similar levels of accountability and collective action?[4] If both local focus on performance indicators and state supports for managing for results help to enhance local accountability and collective action, which one drives the other—or are they mutually reinforcing?

In light of these questions, future research could focus fruitfully on the roles that states and other superordinate authorities can play in enabling or hindering local collaboration. Two hypotheses, in particular, deserve testing:

1. States (or other superordinate authorities) can use the network management activities of activating, framing, mobilizing, and synthesizing to catalyze local collaboration.
2. The capacity to track and analyze data is essential to establish and align the standards, rhetoric, incentives, and communication approaches needed to mobilize and synthesize local collaborative efforts to manage for results across agencies.

In addition, exploratory studies might examine whether particular network management activities, applications, or strategies are more effective than others in enabling local collaborators to manage for results across agencies successfully.

NOTES

1. For example, Georgia's core results are: healthy children, children ready for school, children succeeding in school, strong families, and self-sufficient families. Several indicators measure progress toward each result. "Self-sufficient families," for example, is measured by reductions in the percentage of children living in poverty, reductions in the percentage of female-headed families living in poverty, increases in the percentage of welfare recipients leaving public assistance because of employment or higher incomes, increases in the rate of growth in employment, reductions in the unemployment rate, and increases in affordable, accessible, quality child care (Georgia Policy Council for Children and Families 1996a, 2).

2. North Carolina, for example, tracked rates of health and developmental screenings, immunizations, and skills at entry into kindergarten among young children (FPG/UNC Evaluation Team 2000).

3. This developmental trajectory in Georgia and Vermont is visible only in hindsight, of course. As they unfolded, especially in their early year, both states' initiatives (especially Georgia's) encountered repeated threats, obstacles, and occasional setbacks due to competing policy priorities, staff turnover, limited funds, and other challenges.

4. This question follows from Bardach's (1998) point that different collaborative capacities are complementary and partially substitutable.

REFERENCES

Agranoff, Robert, and Michael McGuire. 2001. "Big Questions in Public Management Research." *Journal of Public Administration Research and Theory* 11, no. 3: 295–326.

Bardach, Eugene. 1998. *Getting Agencies to Work Together*. Washington, DC: Brookings Institution.

Behn, Robert D. 1991. *Leadership Counts*. Cambridge, MA: Harvard University Press.

———. 2006. "The Varieties of Citistat." *Public Administration Review* 66, no. 3: 332–40.

Bryant, Erika, and Carol Cohen. 2003. *State Networks of Local Comprehensive Community Collaboratives*. Washington, DC: Finance Project.

Center for the Study of Social Policy. 1995. *Trading Outcome Accountability for Fund Flexibility*. Draft. Washington, DC.

———. 1996a. *Systems Change at the Neighborhood Level*. Washington, DC.

———. 1996b. *Toward New Forms of Local Governance: A Progress Report from the Field*. Washington, DC.

———. 1998. *Creating a Community Agenda: How Governance Partnerships Can Improve Results for Children, Youth, and Families*. Washington, DC.

———. 2001. *Building Capacity for Local Decision-making*. Washington, DC.

Dimaggio, Paul, and Walter W. Powell. 1983. "The Iron Cage Revisited: Institutional Isomorphism and Collective Rationality in Organizational Fields." *American Sociological Review* 48, no. 2: 147–60.

Family Connection Partnership. 2005. www.georgiafamilyconnection.org.

FPG/UNC Evaluation Team. 2000. *Smart Start: Services and Successes*. Annual Report.

Friedman, Mark. 1996. *A Strategy Map for Results-Based Budgeting: Moving from Theory to Practice*. Washington, DC: Finance Project.

Georgia Family Connection. 1996. *Aiming for Results: Stronger Families and Healthier Children in Georgia: A Report About the Family Connection*. Atlanta, GA.

Georgia Policy Council. 1994. *A Framework for Improving Results*. Atlanta, GA.

———. 1996a. *Aiming for Results: A Guide to Georgia's Benchmarks for Children and Families*. Atlanta, GA.

———. 1996b. *On Behalf of Our Children*. Atlanta, GA.

Hogan, Cornelius, and David Murphey. 2002. *Outcomes: Reframing Responsibility for Well-being*. Baltimore: Annie E. Casey Foundation.

Ingraham, Patricia, and Donald P. Moynihan. 2001. "Beyond Measurement: Managing for Results in State Government." In *Quicker, Better, Cheaper? Managing Performance in American Government*, ed. D.W. Forsythe, 309–33. Albany, NY: Rockefeller Institute Press.

Intergovernmental Administration Working Group. 1997. "Building the Partnerships: Guidelines for LMBs, Local Government, and the State of Maryland." Interim document, Draft no. 5 (July). Maryland Systems Reform Transition Team.

Jewiss, Jennifer, and Susan Hasazi. 1999. "Advancing Community Well-being: A Developmental Perspective of Two Community Partnerships in Vermont." Available at www.ahs.state.vt.us/pdffiles/9909AdvancingCommunityWellBeing.pdf.

Kagan, Sharon Lynn; Stacie Goffin; Sarit Golub; and Eliza Pritchard. 1995. *Toward Systemic Reform: Service Integration for Young Children and Their Families*. Falls Church, VA: National Center for Service Integration.

Kimmich, Madeline; Mary Coacher; Binnie LeHew; and Mark Robbins. 1995. *Iowa Decategorization and Statewide Child Welfare Reform: A Process Evaluation*. Prepared for the Iowa Department of Human Services.

McGuire, M. 2002. "Managing Networks: Propositions on What Managers Do and Why They Do It." *Public Administration Review* 62, no. 5: 571–81.

Moynihan, Donald P. 2005. "Why and How Do State Governments Adopt and Implement 'Managing for Results' Reforms?" *Journal of Public Administration Research and Theory* 15, no. 2: 219–43.

Moynihan, Donald P., and Patricia Ingraham. 2003. "Look for the Silver Lining: When Performance-Based Accountability Systems Work." *Journal of Public Administration Research and Theory* 13, no. 4: 469–90.

Moynihan, Donald P., and Sanjay Pandey. 2005. "Testing How Management Matters." *Journal of Public Administration Research and Theory* 15, no. 3: 421–39.

———. 2006. "Creating Desirable Organizational Characteristics: How Organizations Create a Focus on Results and Managerial Authority." *Public Management Review* 8, no. 1: 119–40.

Ohio Family and Children First Cabinet Council. 2003. *Partnerships for Success: Progress Report 2002–2003.* Columbus, OH.

Page, Stephen. 2003. "Entrepreneurial Strategies for Managing Interagency Collaboration." *Journal of Public Administration Research and Theory* 13, no. 3: 311–40.

———. 2004. "Measuring Accountability for Results in Interagency Collaboratives." *Public Administration Review* 64, no. 5: 591–606.

Radin, Beryl. 2000. "The Government Performance and Results Act and the Tradition of Federal Management Reform." *Journal of Public Administration Research and Theory* 10, no. 1: 111–35.

Radin, Beryl, and Barbara Romzek. 1996. "Accountability Expectations in an Intergovernmental Arena: The National Rural Development Partnership." *Publius* 26, no. 2: 59–81.

Rozansky, Phyllis. 1997a. *Missourians Working Together: A Progress Report.* St. Louis, MO: Missouri Family Investment Trust.

———. 1997b. *Navigating the River of Change: The Course of Missouri's Community Partnerships.* St. Louis, MO: Missouri Family Investment Trust.

Schorr, Lisbeth. 1997. *Common Purpose.* New York: Anchor/Doubleday.

Swanson-Gribskov, Laurie. 1995. "Policy Implementation and Organizational Response: The Case of Title XX in Oregon—Funding Programs for At Risk Youth and Families." Ph.D. diss. Division of Special Education and Rehabilitation, University of Oregon.

Thompson, Dennis C., and William Bratton. 2001. "Performance Management in New York City: Compstat and the Revolution in Police Management." In *Quicker, Better, Cheaper? Managing Performance in American Government,* ed. D.W. Forsythe, 453–82. Albany, NY: Rockefeller Institute Press.

Waldfogel, Jane. 1997. "The New Wave of Service Integration." *Social Service Review* 71, no. 3: 463–84.

Wilson, James Q. 1989. *Bureaucracy: What Government Agencies Do and Why They Do It.* New York: Basic Books.

CHAPTER 9

Collaboration for Knowledge
Learning from Public Management Networks

ROBERT AGRANOFF

In this era of knowledge-based work, it is well known that collaboration is one key to successful outcomes. For over a decade it has become obvious that, "Virtuoso individuals and commanding CEOs cannot operate effectively without teamwork and production networks. Collaboration has become the name of the game" (Smith 1995, xxi). It is also clear that in addition to adding economic value (Warsh 2006), knowledge workers pose challenges to conventional management wisdom and organizing principles, not only because of their mobility and dispersal, but because less is known about how to supervise, control, and evaluate them. The interdependence and complexity of knowledge work requires workers to collaborate effectively with others in "different functions, physical locations, time zones, and even organizations" (Davenport 2005, 12). In organized settings, where what one knows and what one makes sense out of (Weick 1995) and then applies it to ever-changing challenges, the key is knowledge—"a fluid mix of framed experience, values, contextual information, and expert insight that provides a framework for evaluating and incorporating new experiences and information" (Davenport and Prusak 2000, 5).

The aim of knowledge management is "identifying, extracting, and capturing 'knowledge assets,'" in order to fully exploit them toward accomplishing some goal (Newell et al. 2002, 16). In the public sector one would use knowledge to add some public value (Moore 1995). In this chapter we look in considerable detail at the various collaborative aspects of knowledge management (KM) through the lenses of fourteen public management networks (PMNs), that is, the nature of KM activities that are undertaken and for what purposes they are geared. This look at collaboration in KM should provide some useful insights for public managers, who are now faced with the challenge of getting performance and results as problems become increasingly knowledge-oriented.

Interagency networks like the PMNs are important vehicles of KM. Knowledge itself depends heavily on collaborative action, or what social network analysts call "connectivity."

Problem solving and creative discovery depend heavily on dynamic interaction among people, particularly at strategic points in social networks (Cross and Parker 2004, 8). Shrage (1995, 33) defines collaboration activity as *shared creation,* that is, people working interactively on a process, product, or event. One PMN activist shared that, "Workgroups on various technical issues is the way we learn and grow; integrate new people into our process . . . and while we don't codify process we rely on the institutional knowledge of a lot of people." In regard to information and data systems, they are ever present in the collaborative bodies of public managers, stakeholders, and public representatives studied. "Our most basic knowledge portfolio includes various studies of the conditions within the watershed—two years of biochemical samplings . . . and we put together lots of other studies (conducted by partners), for example hydrologic unit assessments." In this regard, an engineering researcher not connected with this study summarized more than a decade of statistics and found that engineers and scientists were five times more likely to turn to a person for information than to impersonal sources, for example, a database or file cabinet (Allen 1984). Today, of course, one would have to add interpersonal contacts facilitated through e-mail or "blogs" between scientific and technical people. Networks enter this picture in that they use people from different organizations to cross intraorganization information gaps regarding problems and programs. Indeed, it is one of the primary reasons why they are organized, and thus managing such uncertainties becomes a critical network function (Koppenjan and Klijn 2004, 8).

The concern for public sector KM as a focused or formal area of study is emerging but seems to be lagging behind that of the private sector. With few exceptions (e.g., Feldman 1989; Lindblom and Cohen 1979; Milner 2000; Zhang and Dawes 2006), most KM books deal with business practices. Olshfski and Hu (2004) indicate that of 511 articles on KM published since 1996, only one appeared in a public administration journal, whereas 276 were published in business journals, 196 in information technology journals, and 38 in other journals. However, they also point to the more recent emergence of KM programs in a number of Canadian and European governments, as well as thirteen different U.S. federal agencies that now give KM prominence. For example, the Department of the Army employs knowledge portals for authorized user access, and its virtual knowledge center serves as a single information resource to provide classified information to a designated user community. This suggests that the public sector is joining a conversation that the private sector has been engaged in for more than fifteen years.

Although systematic comparative data involving a wide range of public agencies and networks are not available, this study suggests that in terms of KM activities within networks, the practice clearly outstrips academic or research attention. The study finds that the fourteen PMNs are deeply engaged in this emergent aspect of management, but at a more basic, problem-oriented working-level knowledge creation than some of the highly visible extended information technology–oriented KM now associated with lead corporations. Davenport and Prusak (2000, 125), for example, identify expert systems, case-based reasoning, and neural networks that are all based on artificial intelligence as exemplary KM practices. In contrast, the PMNs engage in more "mundane" practices, such as building databases, using communities of practice, and creating knowledge maps. Thus, there is much about public sector KM activity and process that one can learn from the working networks.

The chapter develops these concerns as follows. First, membership of the fourteen PMNs and the study methodology are identified. Second, an overview of KM from the business/ literature is applied to the collaborative aspects of networks. Third, KM techniques are introduced and identified by providing explanatory examples from the study. Fourth, an accounting of some twenty-one KM activities engaged in by the PMNs is presented and analyzed. Fifth, representative outcomes or values added by an exemplary KM project for each PMN are demonstrated. Sixth, the chapter concludes with a general discussion of KM strategies for the public sector, based on the findings of the study.

THE STUDY

The broader research, *Managing Within Networks* (Agranoff 2007), focuses on the internal operations of fourteen PMNs in the central United States. It examines the changing managerial challenges faced by today's public managers as they participate in collaborative undertakings with other governments and the nongovernmental sector. It is a systematic, qualitative grounded-theory study, involving field discussions/studies and inductive case-by-case analysis with over 150 PMN activists, in two waves of data gathering. Public management networks refer to formal and informal structures comprised of representatives from governmental and nongovernmental agencies working interdependently to solve interagency problems and/or jointly formulate and implement policies and programs, usually through their respective organizations. They bring the nonprofit and for-profit sectors together with government in a number of policy arenas, including economic development, health care, disabilities, criminal justice, natural resources, human services, information systems, rural development, biotechnology, transportation, and education. The project is supported, in part, by the IBM Center for the Business of Government (formerly Price Waterhouse Coopers Endowment), Washington, DC, to which a preliminary report was provided (Agranoff 2003).

The fourteen PMNs, their agency composition, their charter/informal status, and their primary composition are summarized in the Appendix on pages 191–192. Since each PMN's shortened identifier will be used, they are also included to allow for ease of subsequent reference. Also, the third column "Type" puts each PMN in one of four categories. Analytical work between the first and second round of field studies revealed that not all of the networks proved to be directly or decisionally engaged in collaborative policy and program adjustments to which the literature constantly referred. Following the norms of grounded theory (Strauss and Corbin 1998), the decision/action–related questions were coded through three levels of analytical treatment until a typology emerged (Agranoff 2007, ch. 3). The typology identified by network is explained in the Appendix on page 190. All fourteen regularly collaborate, but it turns out that some networks (information) basically exchange information, some (developmental) also build partner capacities, others (outreach) perform these functions and blueprint agency or policy strategies but do not formally engage in these activities, *plus* some (action) engage in the foregoing activities and make policy/program adjustments. The typology, as will be demonstrated, proved critical in differentiating many functions, processes, and outputs of networks, particularly the kind of public value that each could add, although in regard to the use of various KM approaches, there appear to be fewer differences by type.

The larger study focuses on the ways that networks are managed as public-serving bodies. It demonstrates how each of the four types of PMNs came together and how they operate. As is the case with regard to this analysis, the larger study takes a cross-case variable-oriented look at various facets of networks. There the analysis focuses on the organized structure, operations, and patterns of influence within the networks, along with the role of PMNs in organizing explicit and tacit knowledge, network performance patterns, and then the positioning of networks vis-à-vis the "boundaries of the state," that is, the extent to which network decisions crowd out government decisions. Thus, the study involves considerably more than the KM focus of this chapter.

ESSENTIAL KNOWLEDGE MANAGEMENT

KM has been identified as dealing with the "knowledge assets" that incorporate data, information, experience, insight, and so on, in order to enhance an outcome such as increased value. According to Davenport and Prusak (2000, 2–6), data refers to a set of discrete, objective facts about events, often in organized efforts such as structured records of transactions. Information is characterized as a message in the form of a document or an audible or visible communication. Information moves about organized bodies through hard networks (wires, satellite dishes, electronic mail boxes) and soft networks (notes, article copy). Knowledge is broader, deeper, and richer than data or information. It is highly mutable and highly contextual but with greater utility, in that it incorporates experience, insight, and contextual information as well. Knowledge is more than facts or data. It is within people, part of the assets of the human capital that are so important in contemporary activities, including all types of management. Indeed, it is intrinsically human. "Knowledge derives from information as information derives from data. If information is to become knowledge, humans must do all the work" (Davenport and Prusak 2000, 6). In effect, knowledge is both a process and an outcome.

It is also clear that knowledge blends what can be documented or formulized with the intuitive sense of knowing how to complete a task. Polanyi (1962, 49) concludes that knowledge is "formulae which have a bearing on experience," in a sense that knowledge is "personal knowing," from map reading to piano playing, to bicycle riding, to scientific work. This requires "skillful action" based on "personal knowing."

KM is thus thought of as having two analytical components, *explicit* and *tacit* knowledge. Explicit knowledge is what can be codified and communicated easily by documenting in words or numbers, charts, or drawings. It is the more familiar form of knowledge. Tacit knowledge is embedded in the senses, individual perceptions, physical experiences, intuition, and rules of thumb. It is rarely documented, but "frequently communicated through conversations with the use of metaphors." It includes know-how, understanding, mental models, insights, and principles inherent to a discipline: All are tacit knowledge (Saint-Onge and Armstrong 2004, 41).

Tacit and explicit knowledge do not, as some are prone to consider, stand in opposition to one another, but are two sides of the same coin. They are separated for analytical purposes only in this chapter. In the real world of network activity, they are joined. All knowing involves *skillful action,* and the knower "necessarily participates in all acts of understanding" (Polanyi and Prosch 1975, 44; italics in original). Explicit knowledge to Tsoukas (2005, 158) is always rendered uncertain without tacit knowledge. "It is vectoral: we know the particulars by relying on our awareness of them for attending to something else." He continues:

> The ineffability of tacit knowledge does not mean that we cannot discuss the skilled performances in which we are involved. We—indeed, should—discuss them, provided we stop insisting on "converting" tacit knowledge and, instead, start recursively drawing our attention to how we draw each other's attention to things. Instructive forms of talk help us reorientate ourselves to how we relate to others and the world around us, thus enabling us to talk and act differently. We can command a clearer view of our tasks at hand if we "remind" ourselves of how we do things, so that distinctions which we had previously not noticed, and features which had previously escaped our attention, may be brought forward. (Ibid.)

Rather than focusing on operationalizing tacit knowledge, greater emphasis needs to be placed on new ways of talking, fresh forms of interacting, and novel ways of distinguishing and connecting. According to Tsoukas (2005, 158–59), tacit knowledge cannot be "captured" "translated" or "converted" but only displayed and manifested as it involves skilled performance, that is, KM praxis is "punctuated through social interaction." As one geographic information system (GIS) expert in Iowa Geographic related, "Knowledge is transmitted through interpersonal contacts and lots of presentations at meetings. We don't write it up. It's just there."

The interaction between the two types of knowledge means that its potential for action is essential. Indeed, Davenport and Prusak (2000, 6) suggest that one of the reasons we find knowledge valuable is its proximity to action in a much more real-world sense than data or information. Knowledge should be evaluated by the decisions or actions to which it leads. Better knowledge can lead to wiser decisions/actions, efficiencies, and results. Moreover, knowledge can move down the value chain, informing information and data. This action potential, conclude Davenport and Prusak (2000, 7–12), is based on the blending of experience, truth, judgment, and rules of thumb. One key member of the Kentuckiana Agency PMN related that, "We try to leave a [formal] trail of what we do, from our intranet, project locations, color coded maps, financing from grants and loans, engineering reports. That is an instant but informal source of knowledge for this agency and for our partners (in the network)."

PMN USE OF KM TOOLS

"It is frustrating that one cannot capture the flavor of the month and bring it right to people . . . but it does not work that way for Indiana Rural Council. It is all about relationship building, finding people, knowledge, skill and linking them . . . and if there is trust there is information sharing among the partners." The various explicit and tacit approaches constitute the ways that KM unfolds within the networks. Many of them will prove to be quite familiar to those involved in public management, although they are rarely billed as such. In fact, most KM approaches have a very familiar ring.

What are the tools of KM? Stewart (2001, 117) indicates that KM activities cover a host of organizational activities: building databases, measuring intellectual capital, establishing corporate libraries, building intranets, sharing best practices, installing groupware, leading training programs, leading cultural change, fostering collaboration, and creating virtual organizations. Olshfski and Hu (2004) identify several additional practices: information portals, informal mentoring, electronic archiving, list serves of discussion groups, knowledge portals, regularly scheduled problem-solving sessions, knowledge maps or organization yellow pages, expert interviews, formal mentoring systems, apprenticeships, and decision support systems. Some organizations, public and private, now appoint a CKO, or chief knowledge officer, incorporating the work of an earlier chief information officer.

The essentials of managing explicit knowledge, as Stewart (2001, 124) maintains, are easy and familiar: assemble, validate, standardize/simplify, update, leverage, ensure that users know about it and how to use it, automate and accelerate retrieval and application, and add to the base. Since tacit knowledge constitutes the "stock of intellectual capital," it is harder to elicit such rules of thumb. But he suggests that it clearly involves processes of internalization, combining (with other knowledge), sharing, and externalization. Techniques such as sharing best practices, fostering collaboration, mentoring groupware, and problem-solving sessions clearly facilitate tacit knowledge acquisition. They are the instruments of handling the essential explicit/tacit–knowledge interface.

Since these business-oriented tools and techniques are reasonably similar to those involved in public management, they will be illustrated rather than defined. Initially, the analysis turns to the PMN study in Table 9.1, which provides a single example of the KM approaches primarily designed toward gathering and transmitting explicit knowledge. For example, the first entry shows how Iowa Communications uses a form of PMN intranet that allows state agencies to interact directly and electronically with its field offices and to employ management information by intranet that can be used in knowledge formation. Each of the other approaches listed there—list serves for discussion groups, databases, network libraries, virtual organizations, information portals, electronic archiving, knowledge maps, decision support systems, and employment of a CKO—are similarly geared to emphasize the explicit dimension of KM.

Tacit knowledge–oriented activities are also quite familiar to most persons involved in public management. Table 9.2 provides an example from the study of those activities found that are more focused on capturing tacit knowledge within the PMN. For example, within Iowa Geographic, best practices are shared through a biannual state GIS conference, held at a university, where approaches and techniques are "tiered," in terms of level of technical sophistication for various users. The other tacit-oriented approaches illustrated—formal and informal mentoring, task forces/work groups, electronic decision work groups, discussion groups, expert interviews, apprenticeships, training programs, cultural change, and

Table 9.1

Explicit-Knowledge Management Activities

Type of activity	PMN	Example/use
Intranet	Iowa Communications	State agency communication system; allows field offices and state headquarters to be in interactive electronic contact and builds selected bodies of management information.
List serves of discussion groups	Indiana Economic Development	Quadriennial plan regional groups; broken down by areas of economic development interest (manufacturing, value-added agriculture, services); first step in plan development.
Databases	Des Moines Metro	Accident frequency and location within the metropolitan area; one input into project/plan development.
Corporate (network) libraries	Indiana Economic Development	Catalogs of independent economic/business listings and how to access them; library provides access by Web links to virtually any business ranking service, related studies, plans.
Virtual organizations	USDA/Nebraska	Value Added Agricultural Partnership, a nonformally organized group of funders/researchers/entrepreneurs that explores data and information and tries to produce new knowledge.
Information portals	Enhanced Data (EDARC)	Access by Internet to various Web uses by nongovernmental organizations and state agencies for planning and decision making, operated by a contract with Access Indiana.
Electronic archiving	Iowa Geographic	Ortho-infrared mapping of the state of Iowa, to the one meter square, a variable for public agency use, for example, in transportation, natural resource, agriculture, other planning/programming.
Knowledge maps	Des Moines Metro	Locational targeting of existing freight terminals, public transport stops, green trails, handicapped access, and so on, for planning purposes.
Decision support systems	Kentuckiana Agency	Travel Demand Forecasting Model; use of current measurable travel habits with projected employment/population estimates for needs-based decisions.
Chief knowledge officer (CKO)	Iowa Communications (ICN)	President of ICN also serves as chief information/knowledge officer for state Department of Administration; uses ICN state agency interactively generated data, information to develop usable knowledge.

Table 9.2

Tacit-Knowledge Management Activities

Type of activity	PMN	Example/use
Sharing best practices	Iowa Geographic	Biannual/state geographic information system (GIS) conference; sharing among three GIS tiers: (1) expert, technically involved, (2) administrator/manager (3) novices, contemplating GIS use.
Informal mentoring	Lower Platte	Field-based watershed coordinator works with landowners, local government officials, others to disseminate degradation and conservation knowledge, including Lower Platte basin studies.
Formal mentoring	Indiana Rural Development	Community visitation teams work with small towns on their community development challenges together to write a formal plan.
Task force/work group	Iowa Enterprise	Special study of the problem of "business succession" in rural small towns, that is, the closing of local businesses when the current entrepreneur retires or otherwise closes the business; for planning and policy purposes.
Electronic decision support group work	317 Group	Using Indiana University electronic Collaborative Work Laboratory to develop proposed program revisions.
Discussion groups	Indiana Rural Development	Organized focus groups to prepare state Rural Economic Development Strategy.
Expert interviews	Iowa Geographic	Presentations/questions of vendor-experts at quarterly meetings to demonstrate latest GIS technology.
Apprenticeships	Darby	A series of plan coordinators at Upper Darby counties are normally university interns or new graduates who primarily find and blend research and plan programs from a variety of federal and state sources.
Training programs	Small Communities (SCEIG)	Operational, conservation, and regulatory compliance workshops for small water company managers and technicians, using SCEIG-developed training materials delivered by Ohio State University Extension.
Cultural change	Partnership for Rural Nebraska	Cooperative development center tries to create natural atmosphere of sharing of informational staff.
Fostering collaboration	317 Group	Rather than petitioner and petitioned, the state FSSA/DDARS division works together with two state-level peak interest groups and a host of nongovernmental organization providers to share information, create program knowledge, and guide the program's future.

fostering collaboration—appear to be designed mainly to foster tacit knowledge within the network.

These approaches are obviously not undertaken with equanimity. Some are very popular among PMNs, whereas others are rare indeed. Tables 9.3 and 9.4 present a comprehensive look at the KM activities—explicit and tacit—along with a brief snapshot of the primary focus of each network's KM objective(s). The first and second columns in both identify the PMN and its type (according to the typology in the Appendix), then the next or third field in each table identifies the major focus of each PMN's KM program. This field is identical for Tables 9.3 and 9.4.

Turning to Table 9.3, the ten columns identify whether, during the study period, they engaged in one of the explicit KM approaches identified in Table 9.1. Let us begin to explain the explicit activities in Table 9.3, where it is clear that, with the exception of Iowa Enterprise and Indiana Rural Council, most of the PMNs engaged in several explicit KM activities, with Iowa Communications, engaging in eight of ten activities, at the high end, and several with six activities. A glance at the totals indicates that intranets, list serves, databases, and network libraries were the most frequently used. The least frequently employed were appointed CKOs, virtual organizations, and electronic archiving.

For example, Iowa Geographic in effect operates a full explicit-knowledge program, including: intranet through the Iowa Communications state communication and full-motion video system for meetings and demonstrations; list serves of discussion groups include categories like ortho-red digital, small local government users, transportation planners, and so on; inventoried GIS databases on their Web-based library; use of the Web site as their library; electronically archived papers from their biannual conferences; use of the ortho-red mapping as a decision support system; and employment of the head of the Iowa State University GIS Laboratory and the state GIS officer in the shared role of CKO. Also of note is Indiana Economic Development's library of state economic development data services, county-by-county vital data, and county/regional plans. Partnership for Rural Nebraska's *Rural News Bits* serves as a vital information portal for the partners as they donate essential grant, loan, workshop, and regulatory information. It also serves as the initial point of entry for exchanging best practices. Finally, the travel usage/demand models employed by the two transportation PMNs, Kentuckiana and Des Moines Metro, are examples of decision support systems.

When it comes to the eleven tacit-knowledge activities described in Table 9.2 and assessed in Table 9.4, a greater range of activities is displayed. Every network had work groups/task forces and almost every network fostered collaboration (of course), shared best practices, engaged training programs, promoted discussion groups, and experienced informal mentoring. At the low end of the scale, of course, was electronic decision making, apprenticeships, and expert interviews at one, two, and three PMNs, respectively. Interestingly, with the exception of Enhanced Data with only three activities, all of the others engaged in at least five or more, with Small Communities the highest at nine of the eleven. There seem to be no real differences among the four types of PMNs, inasmuch as all seek a multifaceted tacit-knowledge program.

No PMN has a more elaborate tacit-knowledge effort than that of the 317 Group,

Table 9.3

PMN Use of Explicit-Knowledge Activities

PMN	Type	Major object/focus of knowledge management for network	Intranets	List serves of discussion groups	Databases	Corporate libraries	Virtual organizations	Information portals	Electronic archives	Knowledge maps	Decision support systems	Chief knowledge officers
Darby	I	Expand knowledge base for watershed partners' assessment activity	X	X	X	X		X		X		
Indiana Economic Development	I	Additions to the state's economic development agenda			X	X		X	X			X
Lower Platte	I	Expanded knowledge base for watershed partners' policy and programs	X	X	X	X		X		X		
Iowa Enterprise	D	Enhance the capabilities of small home business and provide economic development planning	X	X								
Indiana Rural Council	D	Coordinated intergovernmental rural policy/program capabilities	X	X			X					
Partnership for Rural Nebraska	D	Coordinated rural policy/program capabilities for the state	X	X	X			X				
Iowa Geographic	D	Increase capacity of public sector users	X	X	X	X			X		X	X
Small Communities	O	Blueprint funding/program strategies to resolve small-town water problems		X	X	X				X		

(continued)

PMN	Type	Major object/focus of knowledge management for network	Intranets	List serves of discussion groups	Databases	Corporate libraries	Virtual organi-zations	Information portals	Electronic archives	Knowledge maps	Decision sup-port systems	Chief knowl-edge officers
USDA/Nebraska	O	Partner with other funders to blueprint rural development projects	X		X		X	X				
317 Group	O	Support funding and operation of major state—nongovernmental organization programs for developmentally disabled	X	X	X		X				X	
Iowa Communications	A	Support for policies and decisions to operate network services	X		X	X	X	X	X		X	X
Enhanced Data	A	Support rate setting and usage policy decisions for state government Web portal	X	X	X	X		X			X	
Kentuckiana Agency	A	Prepare for transportation improvement and long-range plan decisions/funding	X		X	X		X		X	X	
Des Moines Metro	A	Prepare for transportation improvement and long-range plan decisions/funding		X	X	X			X	X	X	
Total activity use			11	10	12	9	4	8	4	5	6	3

Table 9.4

PMN Use of Tacit-Knowledge Activities

PMN	Type	Major object/focus of knowledge management for network	Sharing best practices	Formal mentor	Informal mentor	Task force work groups	Electronic decision making	Discussion groups	Expert interviews	Apprenticeships	Training programs	Cultural change	Foster collaboration
Darby	I	Expand knowledge base for watershed partners' assessment activity	X	X	X	X		X				X	X
Indiana Economic Development	I	Additions to the state's economic development agenda	X			X		X		X	X		X
Lower Platte	I	Expanded knowledge base for watershed partners' policy and programs	X	X	X	X		X			X	X	X
Iowa Enterprise	D	Enhance the capabilities of small home business and provide economic development planning	X	X	X	X		X			X		
Indiana Rural Council	D	Coordinated intergovernmental rural policy/program capabilities	X	X	X	X		X			X	X	X
Partnership for Rural Nebraska	D	Coordinated rural policy/program capabilities for the state	X	X	X	X		X			X	X	X
Iowa Geographic	D	Increase capacity of public sector users	X	X	X	X		X	X		X	X	X
Small Communities	O	Blueprint funding/program strategies to resolve small-town water problems	X	X	X	X		X		X	X	X	X

(continued)

PMN	Type	Major object/focus of knowledge management for network	Sharing best practices	Formal mentor	Informal mentor	Task force work groups	Electronic decision making	Discussion groups	Expert interviews	Apprenticeships	Training programs	Cultural change	Foster collaboration
USDA/Nebraska	O	Partner with other funders to blueprint rural development projects	X		X	X		X			X		X
317 Group	O	Support funding and operation of major state–nongovernmental organization programs for developmentally disabled	X	X		X	X	X			X		X
Iowa Communications	A	Support for policies and decisions to operate network services			X	X			X		X		X
Enhanced Data	A	Support rate setting and usage policy decisions for state government Web portal				X			X				X
Kentuckiana Agency	A	Prepare for transportation improvement and long-range plan decisions/funding	X		X	X					X		X
Des Moines Metro	A	Prepare for transportation improvement and long-range plan decisions/funding	X			X		X			X		X
Total activity use			10	8	10	14	1	11	3	2	12	5	13

including: regular seminars for sharing best practices on community services, organized by Indiana Association of Rehabilitation Facilities (INARF), a core partner; formal mentoring that is undertaken by both the state agency Developmental Disabilities, Aging and Rehabilitation Services/Family and Social Services Administration (DDARS/FSSA) and the Arc/INARF duo; regular work groups that look at important facets of the program, such as case management, day services, and employment; it is the only PMN that has used electronic decision support through the Indiana University Collaborative Work Laboratory to revise its program strategies; it regularly fosters discussion groups among providers, families, advocates, and so on; the partners regularly train in various aspects of community service, for example, behavior management and school to work transition; and collaboration between the state agencies (Medicaid, DDARS) is fostered through regular reporting, feedback, and all of the other means of tacit-knowledge development. Also of note are Iowa Enterprise's efforts to provide after-hours coaching of small entrepreneurs as both formal and informal mentoring, Indiana Rural Council's community visitation small-town development that not only mentors but provides training, Small Communities' problem-oriented task forces and work groups that serve to promote cultural change, and USDA/Nebraska's propensity to share best practices with a variety of farm organizations, agribusiness, and rural producers organizations, with which they regularly collaborate.

Overall, Tables 9.3 and 9.4 indicate notably high levels of both explicit- and tacit-oriented KM activities, suggesting that, at least in collaborative network activity, many of the same type of activities that are currently popular in the private sector are also occurring in the public sector. The main difference seems to be that public sector managers rarely "package" these activities as KM.

What about the object or public purpose in Tables 9.3 and 9.4 to which each PMN's activities are directed? In this situation there are substantial and meaningful differences by network type, as the third (repeated) column in Tables 9.3 and 9.4 suggests. For the three information networks (Darby, Indiana Economic Development, and Lower Platte), knowledge is managed to expand the base of decision making or policy action that is taken by its partner members and others in their watershed/economic development communities. Development networks (Iowa Enterprise, Indiana Rural Council, Partnership for Rural Nebraska, and Iowa Geographic) are geared to enhance public management capacity. They use KM to make their partners more able GIS users, or rural program managers, or small-business entrepreneurs. Outreach networks (Small Communities, USDA/Nebraska, 317 Group) need knowledge to operate one step removed from policy and program changes, those that they recommend but are made individually by their agencies as partners. Their knowledge provides support and leads to policy adjustments at the next stage of activity. Finally, the action networks (Iowa Communication, Enhanced Data, Kentuckiana, and Des Moines Metro) manage knowledge for direct policy/program decisions. They are able to use the knowledge they manage to develop operations policies, set usage rates, approve funding programs, and establish plans. So to begin to answer the question, knowledge for what? it clearly depends on the type of network under examination.

For all networks, collaboration is nevertheless geared in some way toward processing of knowledge. When it comes to KM, there is considerably more activity to the PMNs than the management literature would suggest. As one network coordinator suggested, "We have lots of knowledge resources, and (PMN) serves to manage them—committee reports, polls, newsletters, Web pages. . . . Informally we have everything, we are small in numbers and interactive." A partner in the same network concluded that "most tacit knowledge is imbedded in [each partners'] systems and we try to dissemble it without taking the [partner threatening] risky step of codifying shared knowledge."

UTILIZATION OF PMN KNOWLEDGE

Knowledge must be managed for a purpose, and in the public sector that clearly means toward adding public value. As Moore (1995, 20) concludes, public managers seek to "discover, define and produce public value," extending discovery of means to focus on ends, becoming "important innovators in changing what public organizations do and how they do it." In this sense, networks are no different from agencies, in that managers working in networks must "look out to the value of what they are producing" and should be considered successful not by the idea of collaboration per se, but only if it produces better performance or lower costs than its alternatives (Bardach 1998, 17). This is the issue or concern for knowledge relevance and utility. Therefore, any program of KM should be geared toward such value seeking. In the larger study (Agranoff 2006, 2007), it has been demonstrated that the PMNs secure many public values for the manager/professional, the home or partner agency, the collaborative process, and the attainment of numerous tangible outputs.

In this chapter, we are most interested in how KM can add to some form of *collaborative* public value. However, to total all of the PMN outcomes identified during the research period would not be possible because they are too numerous to completely document, nor is any sort of counting exercise the aim here. The focus instead is on how KM is part of potential network outputs due to collaboration. This will be analyzed by means of illustration, taking a single KM project from each PMN and demonstrating its connection with specific productive outputs. Table 9.5, which is rather lengthy and involved, summarizes each of fourteen exemplary projects. Reading the table from left to right, after PMN identification and type designation, the project's internal name and description follows, the lead collaborating partners are identified, the primary KM approach (Tables 9.1 and 9.2) is named, the primary explicit- and tacit-knowledge product/process/product is identified, and finally the ultimate use of KM effort is identified.

To illustrate how to read Table 9.5, the second PMN entry, the Broadband Study of Indiana Economic Development is highlighted. Working with a public–private coalition, Indiana Interconnect, this PMN undertook a study that looked at existing and projected dial-up services and needs. The study provided a basic database or knowledge map of broadband within the state, particularly in rural areas. The results were used as the basis of a Broadband conference with Indiana Rural Council support that focused on problems of electronic connection in rural areas. Its ultimate use was indirect, in that rural broadband extension was incorporated as part of the state government's economic development agenda. The other PMN illustrations in the table attempt to demonstrate different KM types and different uses. Darby's Hellbranch Forum indirectly led to a series of collaboratively derived controlled-growth plans. Lower Platte's knowledge maps through its Public Policy Study indirectly led to the mitigation agendas of the three Natural Resource Districts that are its prime partners. Iowa Enterprise's Business Succession Study was more direct, in that this decision support project led to a state-sponsored program funded by the legislature. In the same way, Indiana Rural Council's series of discussion groups led to a development strategy funded by the Indiana General Assembly. Small Communities' Decentralized Cluster Drainage System brought a sharing of best practices through transdisciplinary practice to provide a new permit-friendly and affordable wastewater option for small towns. Finally, Kentuckiana's data and planning mentoring efforts for small towns in its area have directly led to the spreading of expertise and use of a traffic model through the entire two-state planning area.

Several interesting conclusions about the way KM adds collaborative public value emerge from Table 9.5. First, the PMNs follow similar paths to knowledge creation, through: (1) examination of existing data or policy studies, (2) exchange of information and data, (3) collaborative sharing through communities of practice, and (4) for most, some type of public deliberation. An example of this four-stage process is Darby, which spent nearly a decade compiling and aggregating existing agency studies, followed by Ohio EPA–sponsored studies undertaken to fill identified gaps, numerous agency/administrator reporting and digesting sessions, followed by citizen hearings and meetings. If a network needs to convert existing data into usable knowledge, utilizing such communities of practice in this four-step process proves essential. These broad KM process categories characterize virtually all fourteen examples.

Second, while there are many partners within most PMNs, a small number appear to take the lead in each particular project. Generally this is because certain partners possess some combination of need-based interest, resources, and high stakes in the outcome of the KM project. Clearly, any rural development strategy would need the engagement of Indiana Rural Council's major partners, USDA/RD in Indiana and the state Department of Agriculture. The main partners may also have the primary share of knowledge-based human resources and/or technical systems but still have problem-related gaps that need to be filled. Thus, while PMNs usually have many partner organizations, only a few "carry the ball" on particular PM initiatives.

Third, as indicated, while analytically one might separate explicit- and tacit-knowledge approaches (through labeling in the sixth column "Primary KM type"), in practice, each project appears to have both explicit- and tacit-process dimensions and thus some dual product orientation. Iowa Geographic's Color Infrared project required high levels of expertise plus the best in interactive processes to meet the technical expectations and process needs of numerous partners. This blending of explicit/tacit should be no surprise in that the collaboratively derived usable knowledge demonstrated here would involve interorganization processing along with its productive objective of adding public value. Moreover, since networks exist in great measure to exchange and create usable knowledge, the mix becomes more or less natural.

Fourth, as PMNs, the object or use of each in the knowledge arena is some form of short- or long-term policy agenda formulation, public program/policy plan, and/or public policy enactment. Indiana Economic Development is a state strategic plan, Partnership

Table 9.5

KM Project Outputs/Uses

PMN	Type	KM Project	Description/overview	Lead collaborating partners	Primary KM type	Explicit process	Tacit process	Uses
Darby	I	Hellbranch Watershed Forum	Multijurisdiction cooperative agreement to better manage runoff and improve water quality in western Franklin County, a tributary of Big Darby Creek, based on study demonstrating it as an Environmentally Sensitive Development Area (ESDA)	Ohio EPA, Franklin County Engineers, "Metro Parks," The Nature Conservancy	Fostering collaboration	watershed plan based on ESDA Study	Policy and planning work groups	Indirect policy and planning and regulation for ESDA
Indiana Economic Development	I	Broadband Study	Three-step study that: (1) mapped current broadband services, (2) tested of dial-up in 25 communities, (3) survey of business and consumer households	Indiana Interconnect,* IRDC, Indiana Department of Commerce	Database/ knowledge maps	Report to range of communication, higher education, and state agencies	Broadband conference, focusing on rural deficiencies	Indirect means of changing state government economic development agenda
Lower Platte	I	Public Policy Study	Review of the extent and effectiveness of existing federal, state legal regulations and programs geared to protecting and restoring natural resources and reducing flood damage in watershed	U. of Nebraska, Depts. of Regional Planning,* Agricultural Economics,* 3 NRDs in watershed	Knowledge maps	Policy options and model regulations	Basis of 3 NRD Alliance forums and informal mentoring	Indirect basis of Alliance partners' agendas from 2000 to 2005

Iowa Enterprise	D	Business Succession Study	Web-based policy survey on problems of keeping small-town businesses open; supplemented by demographic data	Iowa Rural Development Council; U.S. Small Business Development Centers; Iowa State U.; U.S. Small Business Administration—Iowa Office	Decision support systems	Report to state legislature	Informal discussions with policymakers and legislators	Directly led to state-sponsored business succession program funded by legislature, operated by SBDC at Iowa State U.
Indiana Rural Council	D	Rural Economic Development Strategy	Overview of challenges to rural quality of life in ten areas, including employment, housing, health care, local planning, agriculture, and technology	Indiana Department of Agriculture; USDA/RD–Indiana	Discussion groups/focus groups	Data and conclusions on rural conditions	Collaboration among many partners	Indirect rural agenda for state government; directly led to two small community planning and loan fund grant programs enacted by the General Assembly
Partnership for Rural Nebraska	D	*Rural News Bits*	Monthly electronic newsletter/bulletin board listing events, grant and loan applications, briefs on scientific studies, links to PRN's rural polls, key leaders in rural development, major state and federal rate changes and more	University of Nebraska, Center for Applied Rural Innovation; Nebraska Development Network (merged with PRN in 2004); Nebraska Department of Economic Development; USDA/RD–Nebraska	(corporate) Network libraries	Listings of essential rural policy/programs and management activities in the public sector	Enhances the "virtual" aspect of PRN's umbrella network	Indirect means of "keeping up" for rural policy/program community

(continued)

Table 9.5 (continued)

PMN	Type	KM Project	Description/overview	Lead collaborating partners	Primary KM type	Explicit process	Tacit process	Uses
Iowa Geographic	D	Color Infrared Digital Ortho-photography	Public/private agency cooperative project to base map landscape evaluation efforts to a one-meter resolution	Iowa Sate University, GIS Laboratory; Iowa Department of Natural Resources; Iowa Department of Transportation; U.S. Geological Survey–National Mapping Division	Electronic archiving, decision support	Capacity to plan, program and make policy	Enhanced federal, state, local government–non-governmental organization cooperation	Direct tools for plans and decisions for 8 federal agencies in Iowa, 6 state departments, and numerous local governments
Small Communities	O	Decentralized Cluster Drainage System	Adapted technology for feasible, affordable, permit-friendly peat-biofilter cluster septic collection system for rural areas with cluster housing	Ohio EPA; Ohio Dept of Public Health; Rural Community Action Program; U.S. EPA*	Sharing best practices, cultural change	Less costly alternatives for small towns and rural developments	Trans-disciplinary practice: engineers, lawyers, finance	Direct option for small jurisdictions' wastewater systems
USDA/ Nebraska	O	Nebraska Value-added Partnership	Focused groups that exchange ideas integrate areas involving government agencies, cooperatives, and agribusinesses	Nebraska Rural Cooperatives Council, USDA/ RD; Nebraska Cooperative Bank; Nebraska Cooperative Development Center; University of Nebraska, Community Boards*; Farmers Union*; Farm Bureau*	Virtual organization, discussion groups	Occasional reports	Sharing of applications and new ventures	Direct/indirect impact on state agricultural manufacturing, economic development, and venture capital investment information

317 Group	O	Program Communication	ARC of Indiana-operated multi-electronic system including newsletter, program guide updates, calendar, posted success stories, Web site, weekly "e-memos," legislative updates, fact sheets, photographs, and more	ARC of Indiana; "Governor's Planning Council for Developmental Disabilities; FSSA/DDARS	Intranet	Documented program knowledge	Some sharing of best practices, discussion groups, expert interviews	Direct point of contact between public agencies, provider's peak associations
Iowa Communications	A	Bioterrorism Preparation	ICN works with federal, state, and local agencies to respond to a simulated attack through full-motion video and teleconnections	Iowa Depts. Public Health, Public Safety, Emergency Management; county governments, Federal Emergency Management Agency*; U.S. Dept. of Public Health	Electronic discussion support work group, training programs, fostering collaboration	Expanded caller area for emergencies	Interagency cooperation	Direct means of working with 99 county health and emergency management through ICN full-motion video; increased emergency preparedness
Enhanced Data	A	Portal Manager Reports	Full information on portal access, special projects, marketing efforts, finance reports, trends, project reports	Access Indiana, Indiana Department of Administration; Intelnet Commission*	Information portals/ knowledge maps, databases	Single, EDARC-accessible report	Committee policy discussions	Committee decision making, information for policy and rates

(continued)

Table 9.5 *(continued)*

PMN	Type	KM Project	Description/overview	Lead collaborating partners	Primary KM type	Explicit process	Tacit process	Uses
Kentuckiana Agency	A	Data and Planning Assistance to Area Local Governments	Help local governments' use of travel demand model and other planning tools	KIPDA Transportation and Information Systems Staff; small local governments surrounding Louisville/ Jefferson County in Indiana and Kentucky	Formal and informal mentoring	Data-based local plans, need input data	One-to-one problem related	Allows local government to directly access expertise and models without contacting consultants
Des Moines Metro	A	Roundtables	Specialists and experts in transit freight and urban trails	Iowa Department of Conservation*; Des Moines Area Transit Authority; Des Moines Parks and Recreation*; Iowa Freight Handlers' Association*, Des Moines Chamber of Commerce*	Sharing best practices, discussion groups	Long-range plan impact	Instructions	Direct input into new areas of plan direction by involving nonplanning citizens, business, researchers, local governments

* = Not a regular PMN partner.

for Rural Nebraska is shared resources and heightened awareness, while Iowa Communications is education for improved public service in emergency preparedness. Again, this results focus should not be surprising, inasmuch as the PMNs are constituted of public and nongovernmental organization representatives working on difficult public problems. Their "interactability" means that various forms of knowledge are essential to results.

Fifth, all but one or two of the networks, coincident with the policy or solution process, employ various forms of public engagement in order to enhance "public knowledge" and to test feasibility and acceptance. The watershed networks—Darby and Lower Platte— take their study results to a host of allied landowners associations, conservation groups, environmental activists, and local government officials as next steps. The two transportation metropolitan planning organizations (MPOs) employ a series of roundtables and elected official and citizen boards to digest network-produced knowledge and to suggest courses of action. No water project, including cluster drainage, is approved by Small Communities Environmental Infrastructure Group (SCEIG) partners unless a user survey with detailed cost and quality projections is completed. The 317 Group regularly involves consumers of services, through their family members, in designing program proposals and services adjustments. It is also noteworthy that several of the network boards—Iowa Communications, Enhanced Data, Indiana Economic Development, Indiana Rural Council, 317 Group—have designated citizen members on their official steering committees. Thus, while the primary knowledge-building and utilization activities are undertaken by administrators, citizen involvement in creating and utilizing knowledge also exists as part of the process.

Sixth, and finally, network type does make a clear difference. Most information and developmental networks, such as Darby or Iowa Enterprise, had *indirect* effects on policies, programs, and agendas. Even when their KM effects were direct, it was someone else or the partner agencies that made the real decisions/enactments. In the case of Iowa Enterprise, it was the state legislature. That is not the case with the more strategic or policy/program-oriented outreach or action networks, where more direct KM effects were present in every case. In the case of the outreach PMNs, such as Small Communities, their cluster drainage system directly followed knowledge development, but actual funding and adoption decisions were made by the agencies and small towns. In the action networks, impact is even more direct, as network decisions follow the knowledge developed. For example, the use policies and rates of Enhanced Data follow most portal manager reports. Thus, while all PMNs engage knowledge operations, some have a more direct impact on adding public value than do others.

This snapshot of PMN activity demonstrates the way network outputs are bound up into KM. While none has what can be identified as a formal KM program, few employ a CKO, and few pay formalized attention to the management of tacit knowledge (not to mention writing up process in any way), all are notably engaged in a variety of activities that can be construed as part of KM. One manager's response to the lack of a formal tacit KM process was simply, "we try to structure the process of people educating themselves." In regard to explicit knowledge, one state government program manager said that management means "We have a lot of the pieces . . . the next realm is documentation of the models, better utilization of trends . . . but that will entail overcoming the crossing of boundaries [between organizations] of the next steps in KM that we have not yet crossed."

PUBLIC MANAGEMENT, KNOWLEDGE MANAGEMENT, LEARNING TO LEARN

While the PMNs do accomplish a great deal in the KM area, there is considerably more potential out there. As one Kentuckiana Agency partner representative put it:

> We don't do as well as we could in this (KM) area. The KIPDA staff resist going beyond the data in a PDF format, for example, there are no Excel spreadsheets that are on-line accessible to the partners . . . only to those who work directly with the CMS and the models . . . the construction management system and traffic volume data need to go beyond the current federally required . . . and the agency inputs from the Kentucky Transportation Cabinet, the Air Pollution Control District, the transit district, Metro Parks, and the Waterfront Development Corporation all need to be built into the system so that various work groups and technical committees and subcommittees can do their job.

While these expectations might appear ambitious to those who are engaged in the day-to-day struggle of meeting plans and requirements, perhaps they are not so ambitious when one considers rising expectations for problem resolution, increasingly complex problems and interactions between systems, and the need to combine and apply information into usable knowledge. The challenges and experiences from PMNs can help the public management field learn more about future human capital needs.

1. Collaborative KM Begins with the Partners

From building databases to sharing best practices, knowledge begins within the PMN agencies and the networks' relevant publics. Davenport and Prusak (2000, 165) suggest that a lot of time and money can be expended with complex efforts, such as knowledge mapping, that are transformed into models when many of the data/information sources already exist and are adequate for the "fairly circumscribed knowledge domains of solving particular problems." Lower Platte's Public Policy Study began with an inventory of all of the regulatory impacts that affect the three Natural Resource Districts, based on internal reports by districts and state agencies. This was supplemented by citizen hearings in the three districts. Then they proceeded to meet the information gaps that needed to be filled before creation of their knowledge maps was performed and analyzed. Indiana Economic Development no longer provides county-level economic development data, once their mainstay, but offers electronic links to the numerous existing private-sector inventories and business report cards. In a similar vein, the 317 Group has relied primarily on funding/ service reports compiled by the state agency, as well as assessments by families of clients. Only after these data were analyzed did the group commission an external financing study. Kentuckiana's Travel Demand Forecasting Model relies heavily on data/information supplied by their two state agencies and partner local governments. These data are then analyzed by the various work groups, citizen panels, and roundtables. Often partner data sources will be more data/information rich than can be handled, and can be overwhelming. One key then is to focus on those elements of the data/information stream that can be converted into usable knowledge. As one Lower Platte partner related, "Our research projects are at the core of our KM . . . in the sense that they form the basis of our [problem] discussions and the results are out there as knowledge that can be used."

2. The Problems and the Needs Drive the KM Agenda for Internally Created Knowledge

The parameters for knowledge development begin with formal supports from agencies—in the form of existing information—that account for any policy and legal barriers (Zhang and Dawes 2006). Technical barriers may also be present. As the network proceeds, the "knowledge" created by the PMN tends to follow as next steps as the network approaches its collective challenges. The basic idea, according to organizational psychologists Hodgkinson and Sparrow (2002, 88), is to engage in distributed cognition. As information is propagated around or within networks, it is transformed. "Different interaction strategies (between the human and technological facets of distributed systems) exploit different information structures, and these in turn act as the 'principal' resources for action." In other words, as the actors within the network—administrators, elected officials, citizens—collaboratively interact, they elaborate on needs and problems, blending the search for information with the search for solutions. For example, when Small Communities developed their rural cluster drainage system, knowledge creation involved reiterative interaction between data on the available technology, financing feasibility, and the potential to be permitted by the U.S. Environmental Protection Agency (EPA). Then a willing pilot community had to be consulted. Similarly, when Iowa Geographic built its ortho-infrared mapping by work group, they interactively designed the kind of electronic archiving that would serve maximal user needs, and only when the project was collaboratively designed did they go to an external consultant to do the actual aerial mapping. Iowa Enterprise's business succession study began with input from the major partner stakeholders in rural development and small and home-based business before the data were gathered. PMNs are rather active in various forms of our source-knowledge building, as Table 9.5 illustrates, but they build on partner information, dynamic internal interaction, and collective problem need. One Enhanced Data partner put it this way: "There are multiple sources of explicit knowledge, derived from partner input on agency usage projections, market, potential costs . . . but the holes in this process stimulate the creativity needed to go the next step."

3. Creating a Culture of Mutual Learning and Knowledge Development Is an Essential Dimension of KM

Working on problems within the network usually means working together to create knowledge, a sort of sharing and expanding of human capital. This is particularly important when entities like PMNs move from "first generation" dissemination and imitation to "second generation" education and innovation. "In second generation knowledge management the focus moves from the supply of knowledge to satisfying the organizational demand for knowledge and to creating and maintaining the conditions required for the production of knowledge" (Newell et al. 2002, 189). This is why Iowa Geographic operates in special work groups/committees, holds a GIS Conference biannually, and devotes a good portion of its quarterly meetings to specific problems of public sector agencies. Small Communities' various knowledge-producing projects, such as its cluster sewer and Appalachian Community water projects, normally include adequate agency-committed resources, a broad range of expertise and skills, a reasonable number of boundary-spanning agency officials, a committed project leader/champion, and communities that have canvassed their citizens and have agreed to a buy-in. Iowa Communications' approach when expanding its knowledge base is to always involve technical information staff, program managers, and agency administration in an atmosphere that includes mutual understanding and committed resources along with all of the relevant skills. Collaborative management requires that the network provide the opportunity for partners to create their own knowledge bases tailored to the problems at hand. As a Small Communities partner expressed, "It is the synergistic efforts of people working together on these funding [groundwater] problems . . . the bringing together is how you might say we manage [knowledge]."

4. The Culture of KM Requires That Communities of Practice Within the Network Be a Cornerstone of Any Strategy

The real work of most of the PMNs was done in smaller work groups or special task forces that combined technical expertise, program knowledge, political feasibility, and so on, as the building blocks of collaborative knowledge creation. Communities of practice are self-organizing systems that share the capacity to create and use knowledge through informal learning and mutual engagement. Wenger (2000, 10–14) believes that communities of practice manage knowledge if they are internally supported as social learning systems by promoting the crossing of boundaries, encouraging learning, supporting community infrastructures, and fostering belonging. In effect, the Small Communities become the major form of knowledge communication that connect the other components of knowledge building. Kentuckiana's Technical Coordinating Committee is broken down into work groups of administrators and/or citizen volunteers who focus on various aspects of its plans (pedestrian, bicycles, air quality, interstate access, arterial roads, etc.) with combined teams of citizens, planners, engineers, finance directors, and administrators. Darby's investigating teams are not only geographically broken down, but each includes hydrologists, conservation biologists, aquatic chemists, planners, technical assistance educators, and citizen soil and water conservation board members. USDA/Nebraska's mode of operation in its Value-Added Partnership is to engage multi-interest farming, financing, research, and program specialists in working teams. These communities of practice do the most creative work of the PMNs: Multiple disciplines from multiple agencies and other walks of life explore, learn, and create. As one Iowa Geographic discussant relayed, "The key [to knowledge building] is the interactions, which we try to record as we work and learn from one another."

5. A Knowledge-Seeking Culture and Promotion of Communities of Practice Will Naturally Ease the Explicit/Tacit Distinction

In principle, the PMN partners were not really concerned about some formalized KM strategy involving both types of knowledge but, in practice, most attended to some reasonable number of approaches that served both ends. Tsoukas (2005, 155) reminds us that "tacit knowing is vectoral: we know the particulars by relying on our awareness of them for attending to something else." In a sense, he suggests that explicit knowledge is knowledge awaiting conversion to tacit knowledge. Clearly, that is the way the PMNs approached this interaction, as Tables 9.3 and 9.4 suggest, through the many ways that each activity was undertaken. Lower Platte's KM program demonstrates this connection. Its explicit efforts include: compiling data on flood control, water quality, and flood mitigation; reporting cumulative impacts on the fifty-mile stretch of river; endangerment of the pallid sturgeon; citizen surveys on land use and recreation practices; road location recommendation studies; utilities needs of small cities; and efficiencies in water usage. These results are carried out using a variety of means: Web-based GIS, Web site, intranet contacts, a video, and printed study reports. Its tacit program is fed by these studies: public meetings, collaborative citizen and local elected official discussion groups (on the topics of septic, weed control, sand and gravel), citizen focus groups on specific problems, and one-on-one consultations with local governmental officials and landowners. In the same vein, the 317 Group uses the ARC of Indiana communication arm to distill all of the reports and studies into a multipronged tacit-knowledge approach: a quarterly electronic newsletter, a Medicaid Home and Community Services Waiver Guide, a calendar with 317 success stories, a Web site that updates new regulations and program changes, a weekly "e-memo" to families on the state's waiting list for community services, a legislative "Action-Alert" during assembly sessions, fact sheets for legislators, and a DVD with information and photos on legislators. These missives convert 317 knowledge to an audience of legislators, ARC chapters, providers, advocacy groups, families of persons with developmental disabilities, and other interested individuals. In each PMN, a similar flow of explicit to tacit knowledge flows naturally instead of being formally converted as problems are approached, investigated, and applied. It is through network application or use that tacit normally follows explicit, although several discussants noted the need for considerable improvement in this arena. One Indiana Economic Development partner related that "this area of tapping our (tacit) knowledge is critical . . . we need more expertise because few are very good at it . . . there are lots of people, corporate, government, university whose insights should be tapped . . . we don't use enough of what is out there!"

6. Knowledge Communities Within Networks Are Similar to Those of Today's Open or Conductive Organizations

It is clear that today's human capital-oriented networks seek to build and use knowledge in a fashion similar to that of emergent hierarchical organizations where connectivity is essential. Among the many works on open organizations is Saint-Onge and Armstrong's

The Conductive Organizations. They define a conductive organization as one that "continuously generates and renews capabilities to achieve breakthrough performance by enhancing the quality and flow of knowledge" and calibrating its strategies to the needs of its clientele (2004, 213). Among the keys to building such conductivity is the development of knowledge capital through numerous internal and external partnerships (2004, ch. 3). In many ways, our PMNs are extensions of the many conductive organizations and their boundary spanners that comprise the network structure. Small Communities, for example, is largely comprised of water and wastewater funders—Ohio Water Commission, Ohio Public Works Commission, Ohio Department of Economic Development, Ohio EPA, U.S. EPA, Ohio USDA/RD, U.S. Department of Commerce-EDA—who individually link with a host of local governments and NGOs. Similarly, Iowa Communications is a vehicle or carrier of intranet, Internet, and full-motion video that initially links with state agencies and then hundreds of state and local governments, schools and libraries, universities and colleges, and so on. The conductive organization and the network share similar needs to encourage energizing interactions to develop those intangible assets that are built up through goal-directed human exchange (Cross and Parker 2004, 57). In the process, knowledge that is both internal and external to the public organization partnership and intraorganizational collaboration is provided. As one USDA/Nebraska official suggested, "When we network with others we all put a lot of our internal explicit information on the table, but to get to this point we must trade internally with many in our organizations who develop that knowledge."

7. Public Managers Who Work in Networks and Conductive Organizations Need to Understand and Develop a Sense of Managing Knowledge Programs as a Part of the Collaborative Enterprise

Tapping and sharing collected or collaborated expertise is not enough, but networks and organizations must be organized and operated to guide human capital toward knowledge development. While the arena of managing knowledge workers is relatively new (Davenport 2005, ch. 3), it is clear that, with the exception of those that only apply knowledge (e.g., most direct telephone-call workers), most do not need to be micromanaged, but need to be left alone, allowing for reflection and creative thinking. Productivity needs to be geared toward quality not quantity, not toward hard-to-define "outputs" but toward results. What does not work is top-down job reengineering, scripting, computer-mediated processes, and treating all knowledge workers the same way. If one examines any of the KM projects listed in Table 9.5, process in every case involved high levels of connectivity—the free and creative manifestations of human capital. Each community of practice worked within a collaborative culture where managers/professionals were presented with a problem that required interactively derived expanded knowledge that all were allowed to act upon. Iowa Enterprise's Business Succession Study began with a working group—the Business Development Committee of the Iowa Rural Development Council—and expanded to include more home-based entrepreneurs, business consultants, and federal and state administrators. Their discussions led to the policy survey and analysis of demographic data and ultimately to the action points in a strategy that led to the legislative report, and finally to a program. In the same way, the Small Communities technology transfer cluster-sewer system began with sanitation engineers, regulatory program engineers, and finance specialists who were presented with the problem of how, without utilizing environmentally threatening septics or expensive city sewer systems, to serve the wastewater needs of five to twenty houses that are close together in rural areas. They created a transdisciplinary model, a pilot program, and finally a program without a lot of higher-level intervention or supervision by either their respective agency superiors or by the Small Communities Steering Committee. Managing human capital in knowledge-intensive organizations and in networks like PMNs is probably quite similar, inasmuch as human capital must be oriented by problem challenge or goal and then people need to be creatively enabled. It is hard to go much further at this point. As one Enhanced Data IT program department head put it, "In both this department and in Enhanced Data they must be managed as in an extraordinary distributed environment . . . work is non-standardized . . . it makes resource allocation and economic feasability hard to determine . . . and to manage knowledge in such an environment boils down to the decisions we make about resource allocation. It is hard to get more explicit until government has more experience in this knowledge arena." Finally, KM processes have to operate alongside other key organized functions, such as personnel recruitment, human resource development, compensation management, databases, and information stores. Collaborative tools are not the only means to performance (Cross and Parker 2004, 137).

CONCLUSION

Clearly a great deal more can be said about KM in collaborative networks. One could talk about the differing demands and pressures to reach tangible products in outreach and action networks, as opposed to informational and developmental. The importance of capacity building for development and use of collaborative-based knowledge projects could be highlighted. The need to communicate knowledge through agency feedback and publications could be identified. The importance of trust as a factor in the knowledge process could also be highlighted. Power dynamics within the PMNs, as important agenda setters and resource contributors affect the KM process, could also be identified. These are issues, however, that are part of the overall collaborative management in networks analysis, which are better taken up in vehicles and forums outside of KM.

KM is central to the functioning of networks inasmuch as knowledge-intensive work requires the interaction of human capital. An information/knowledge-oriented environment helps organizational members and network participants begin the process of solving those nettlesome and ambiguous problems they are called upon to undertake (O'Toole 1997). Just as is the case with contemporary open organizations or hierarchical organizations that involve less command and control, collaboration across agencies and organizations is essential to solving problems that have political, legal, financial, and technical dimensions. Knowledge management architectures need to go beyond codification of information to foster learning through *knowledge exchange* or opportunities to share by connecting people, "communities," and expertise (Saint-Onge and Armstrong 2004, 157). This, of course, means interorganization collaborative activity where shared interests broker complimentary knowledge that is otherwise difficult, costly, time consuming, and perishable (Benkler 2004). As one KM manual suggests, "Sharing your knowledge . . . is not a zero-sum game. Unlike conventional assets, knowledge grows when it is shared. The main limitation to infinite knowledge growth is the currency of the information economy-attention" (Groff and Jones 2003, 30).

As demonstrated, KM has become a core function of PMNs. Koppenjan and Klijn suggest that a normal first response to policy uncertainty in public networks is information collection, but research is limited because difficult problems normally carry different opinions with them, and strong opinions can challenge the validity of the research in any event. Moreover, scientific research has its limitations and often raises greater complexities. Problems are often solved by cooperation and learning behavior that can be supported by KM. "Interaction processes are considered to be searches wherein public and private parties from different organizations, [levels of] government and networks jointly learn about the nature of a problem, look at the possibility of doing something about it, and identify the characteristics of the strategic and institutional context within which problem-solving develops" (Koppenjan and Klijn 2004, 10).

The challenge of KM within networks, as Agranoff and McGuire (2003) conclude, is compounded by the constant intergovernmental changes of the past half-century, shifting policies and actions of federal and state governments, and changes in such policy areas as economic development, environmental protection, and developmental disabilities. These forces raise the connectivity quotient, so to speak. As policies, programs, and venues shift, so do the KM demands of governments and collaborative bodies like the PMNs. Nevertheless, whether in networks or in conductive public agencies, the need to engage in KM will increase as the human capital that is compartmentalized in learning, specialized in occupational profession, and divided in organization will be called upon to be transformational in understanding and applications.

APPENDIX: TYPES OF NETWORKS STUDIED

1. *Information Networks:* Partners come together exclusively to exchange agency policies and programs, technologies, and potential solutions. Any actions that might be taken are entirely up to the agencies on a voluntary basis.
2. *Developmental Networks:* Partner information and technical exchange are combined with education and member service that increases member capacity to implement solutions within home agencies or organizations.
3. *Outreach Networks:* Partners come together to exchange information and technologies, sequence programming, exchange resource opportunities, pool client contacts, and enhance access opportunities that lead to new programming avenues. Implementation of designed programs is within an array of public and private agencies themselves.
4. *Action Networks:* Partners come together to make interagency adjustments, formally adopt collaborative courses of action, and/or deliver services along with exchanges of information and technologies.

APPENDIX: NETWORKS UNDER INVESTIGATION

Name of network	Purpose	Type	Enabling authority	Primary agencies
1. Access Indiana/Enhanced Data Access Review Committee (Enhanced Data)	Sets policies for state Web portal, reviews, modifies and approves agency agreements and private use	Action	State government	SA, NGO, Cit, Media
2. Des Moines Area Metropolitan Planning Organization (Des Moines Metro)	Transportation planning for metropolitan area	Action	Intergovernmental agreement	CtyGov, CoGov, SA, FA, R/Met
3. Indiana Economic Development Council (Indiana Economic Development)	Research consultant for state economic development	Informational	Not-for-profit 501C(3)	SA, Priv, NGO, Un
4. Indiana Rural Development Council (Indiana Rural Council)	Forum to address rural issues, establish partnerships, enable partners to take action	Developmental	Intergovernmental agreement/Not-for-profit 501C(3)	FA, SA, CoGov, CtyGov, Legis, NGO
5. Iowa Communications Network (Iowa Communications)	Operates a statewide, state administered, fiber optics network	Action	State government	SA, FA, CtyGov, CoGov, Legis, NGO, Cit
6. Iowa Enterprise Network (Iowa Enterprise)	Supports home-based and micro enterprises	Developmental	Nonformal group	FA, SA, NGO, Priv
7. Iowa Geographic Info. Council (Iowa Geographic)	Clearinghouse for coordinated systems and data sharing	Developmental	State government	Un, FA, SA, R/Met, CoGov CtyGov, NGO, Priv
8. Lower Platte River Corridor Alliance (Lower Platte)	Supports local efforts at water conservation; comprehensive and coordinated land use; promote cooperation among Nebraska organizations	Informational	Intergovernmental agreement	R/Met, SA, FA, Un
9. Partnership for Rural Nebraska (Partnership for Rural Nebraska)	Provide resources and expertise to enhance rural development opportunities	Developmental	Intergovernmental agreement	SA, Un, FA, R/Met
10. Small Communities Environmental Infrastructure Group (Small Communities)	Assist small Ohio governments in their water and wastewater systems	Outreach	Nonformal group	SA, FA, Un, Priv, NGO, R/Met

APPENDIX (*continued*)

Name of network	Purpose	Type	Enabling authority	Primary agencies
11. The Darby Partnership (Darby)	Share information and resources to address central Ohio watershed threats	Informational	Nonformal group	FA, SA, CoGov, CtyGov, R/Met, NGO
12. United States Department of Agriculture/Rural Development Nebraska (USDA/Nebraska)	Outreach and assistance to leverage funds of other programs for public and private development	Outreach	Federal government	FA,NGO, SA, R/Met, Un, CtyGov, Priv
13. Kentuckiana Regional Planning and Development Agency (Kentuckiana Agency)	Transportation planning for two-state Louisville metropolitan area	Action	Intergovernmental agreement	CoGov, CtyGov, FA, SA, R/Met
14. Indiana 317 Taskforce (317 Group)	Strategies for developmentally disabled community services	Outreach	Nonformal	NGO, SA, FA, Un, Cit, Priv

Key

FA	=	Federal government agency at regional or state level
SA	=	State government agency
CoGov	=	County government
CtyGov	=	City government
R/Met	=	Regional or metropolitan agency
Un	=	University, college, and community college
Legis	=	State legislature/congressional staff
NGO	=	Nongovernmental organization/advocacy group
Priv	=	For-profit business organization
Cit	=	Citizen representative

REFERENCES

Agranoff, Robert. 2003. *Leveraging Networks: A Guide for Public Managers Working Across Organizations*. Arlington, VA: IBM Endowment for the Business of Government.

———. 2006. "Public Management Network Performance: A Balance Sheet of Benefits and Costs." Paper presented at the Tenth International Research Symposium on Public Management, Glasgow, Scotland, April 10–12.

———. 2007. *Managing Within Networks: Adding Value to Public Organizations*. Washington, DC: Georgetown University Press.

Agranoff, Robert, and Michael McGuire. 2003. *Collaborative Public Management: New Strategies for Local Governments*. Washington, DC: Georgetown University Press.

Allen, Thomas. 1984. *Managing the Flow of Technology*. Cambridge, MA: MIT Press.

Bardach, Eugene. 1998. *Getting Agencies to Work Together*. Washington, DC: Brookings Institution Press.

Benkler, Yochai. 2004. "Sharing Nicely: On Shareable Goods and the Emergence of Sharing as a Modality in Economic Production." *Yale Law Journal* 114, no. 2: 273–358.

Cross, Rob, and Andrew Parker. 2004. *The Hidden Power of Social Networks*. Boston: Harvard Business School Press.

Davenport, Thomas H. 2005. *Thinking for a Living: How to Get Better Performance and Results from Knowledge Workers*. Boston, MA: Harvard Business School Press.

Davenport, Thomas H., and Laurence Prusak. 2000. *Working Knowledge: How Organizations Manage What They Know*. Boston, MA: Harvard Business Press.

Feldman, Martha S. 1989. *Order without Design: Information Production and Policy-Making*. Stanford, CA: Stanford University Press.

Groff, Theodore R., and Thomas P. Jones. 2003. *Introduction to Knowledge Management*. Amsterdam: Butterworth Heineman.

Hodgkinson, Berard P., and Paul R. Sparrow. 2002. *The Competent Organization*. Buckingham, UK: Open University Press.

Koppenjan, Joop, and Erik Hans Klijn. 2004. *Managing Uncertainties in Networks*. London: Routledge.

Lindblom, Charles E., and David K. Cohen. 1979. *Usable Knowledge*. New Haven, CT: Yale University Press.

Milner, Eileen M. 2000. *Managing Information and Knowledge in the Public Sector*. London: Routledge.

Moore, Mark H. 1995. *Creating Public Value: Strategic Management in Government*. Cambridge, MA: Harvard University Press.

Newell, Sue; Maxine Robertson; Harry Scarbrough; and Jacky Swan. 2002. *Managing Knowledge Work*. Hampshire, UK: Palgrave.

Olshfski, Dorothy, and Lung Teng Hu. 2004. "Seeking Knowledge Management in the U.S." Paper presented at the annual meeting of the American Political Science Association, Chicago, Illinois, September 1-4.

O'Toole, Laurence J. 1997. "Treating Networks Seriously: Practical and Research-Based Agendas in Public Administration." *Public Administration Review* 57, no. 1: 45–52.

Polanyi, Michael. 1962. *Personal Knowledge*. Chicago: University of Chicago Press.

Polanyi, Michael, and Harry Prosch. 1975. *Personal Meaning*. Chicago: University of Chicago Press.

Saint-Onge, Hubert, and Charles Armstrong. 2004. *The Conductive Organization*. Amsterdam: Elsevier.

Shrage, Michael. 1995. *No More Teams! Mastering the Dynamics of Creative Collaboration*. New York: Doubleday.

Smith, Hedrick. 1995. *Rethinking America: Innovative Strategies and Partnerships in Business and Education*. New York: Avon Books.

Stewart, Thomas A. 2001. *The Wealth of Knowledge: Intellectual Capital and the Twenty-First Century Organization.* New York: Doubleday.

Strauss, Anselm, and Juliet Corbin. 1998. *Basics of Qualitative Research: Techniques and Procedures for Developing Grounded Theory.* Thousand Oaks, CA: Sage.

Tsoukas, Haridimos. 2005. *Complex Knowledge.* Oxford: Oxford University Press.

Warsh, David. 2006. *Knowledge and the Wealth of Nations: A Story of Economic Discovery.* New York: Norton.

Weick, Karl E. 1995. *Sensemaking in Organizations.* Thousand Oaks, CA: Sage.

Wenger, Etienne. 2000. "Communities of Practice: The Key to Knowledge Strategy." In *Knowledge and Communities,* ed. Eric L. Lesser, Michael A. Fontaine, and Jason A. Slusher, 3–20. Boston: Butterworth Heinemann.

Zhang, Jing, and Sharon S. Dawes. 2006. "Expectations and Perception of Benefits in Public Sector Knowledge Networks." *Public Performance and Management Review* 29, no. 4: 433–66.

CHAPTER 10

Institutional Collective Action and Local Government Collaboration

RICHARD C. FEIOCK

The delivery of community services in metropolitan areas is often coordinated through networks (Provan and Milward 2001). Collaborative networks for provision of public service are often imposed by statute and are designed and created by a hierarchical coordinating agency. Thus, network managers are responsible for the structure and maintenance of an integrated network among decentralized units.

In this chapter, we instead focus on intergovernmental relationships that are more voluntary and self-organizing in nature, such as voluntary service agreements among local government units to coordinate or jointly provide services. Of particular interest are collaborative institutions in which the agencies or jurisdictions involved are able to enter or exit agreements and craft customized conditions without special review by a single superior coordinating agency.

The development of voluntary coordination mechanisms is particularly salient for metropolitan areas where the problems of fragmentation are frequently most pronounced and the institutional complexity makes the imposition of standardized solutions difficult. U.S. metropolitan areas are characterized by fragmentation of service responsibilities across a multitude of municipal and county governments, specialized agencies, and districts. Decisions of one government or agency impose costs on others. In this context, interlocal agreements and partnerships provide self-organizing governance mechanisms to reduce service costs and increase benefits through collaboration.

Can voluntary collaborations among local governments provide solutions to the regional problems confronting metropolitan areas? Much of the literature in planning and public administration assumes that governmental fragmentation precludes concerted responses to interjurisdictional problems (Downs 1994; Katz 2000). The implication is that local units of government will be incapable of dealing with spillover problems that result when the policy choices in one community impose costs on others (Lowery 2001; Olberding 2002). Practice has proved these assumptions wrong. Cooperation among local governments is common in many service areas (Friesema 1971; Feiock

2007). Local governments share information and jointly respond to emergencies as well as deliver routine services (Agranoff and McGuire 2003). Collaborations through consolidation of functions provide a decentralized regionalism comprised of networks of horizontal interlocal agreements and functionally and geographically defined overlays of nested service units (Feiock and Carr 2001; Parks and Oakerson 1989; Thurmaier and Wood 2002).

What are the strengths, possibilities, and limitations of voluntary exchanges and agreements among independent authorities created to resolve specific sets of externalities and interdependencies? Can we learn better design principles for statutorily imposed coordination institutions by observing the structures that emerge as authorities negotiate customized solutions to their problems? Alternatively, can we uncover policy principles that can be used to increase the likelihood that voluntary solutions will emerge and improve the performance of self-emerging structures? This chapter provides conceptual tools to begin to answer these questions by combining elements of collective action, transaction cost, and social exchange theories within the institutional collective action framework to explain how voluntary arrangements arise and evolve over time to address multijurisdictional or regional problems.

The next section outlines the interests that motivate interlocal collaboration and argues that voluntary agreements emerge from a dynamic political contracting process. Bilateral contracting and multilateral collective action are mechanisms by which two or more governments act collectively to capture the gains from providing or producing services across a larger area. Creation of these institutional mechanisms presents a problem of "institutional collective action" (ICA) for local units (Feiock 2004, 2007). ICA focuses on how local government officials perceive and weigh the various costs and benefits of joint action as they contemplate interlocal service agreements and other forms of intergovernmental collaboration. Although service collaborations can produce substantial benefits, local officials often perceive that the costs of attaining those benefits exceed potential gains. How officials understand these costs will depend on the context of the decision setting, including the characteristics of the good or service being considered, the configurations of political institutions under which they operate, and the networks of existing relationships among local government officials.

We elaborate the ICA framework by identifying how specific community characteristics and formal and informal institutional arrangements reduce transaction costs of information/ coordination, negotiation, enforcement, and agency. After reviewing evidence from ongoing empirical analyses of interlocal collaboration, we discuss the implications of institutional collective action for collaboration and regional governance.

THE BENEFITS AND COSTS OF VOLUNTARY SERVICE COLLABORATION

Mechanisms for voluntary collaboration take many forms, including adaptive or restrictive interlocal agreements, intergovernmental contracts, regional councils, and partnerships.

While voluntary agreements among local governments may need statutory support from higher-level governments, they are not designed or mandated by a single central authority. Instead these mechanisms rely on the voluntary choices of local units to participate. Intergovernmental collaboration can produce both collective and selective benefit for individual government units. Collaborative agreements generate collective benefit by producing efficiencies and economies of scale in the provision and production of services and internalizing spillover problems. They also generate selective benefits if they advance the individual interests of local government officials.

A decentralized system of governments enhances allocative efficiency if it produces a match between community preferences for quantities and qualities of a service and actual service choices and resource allocations, but it can also result in diseconomies of scale in service production and interjurisdictional externalities. Economies of scale result when average cost declines as output increases. Fragmented governments are constrained by their size if there are not enough citizen consumers in a jurisdiction to produce a service at minimum cost. For this reason, economies of scale are often cited as the impetus for interlocal agreements (Bish 2000; Post 2002).

Controlling negative externalities imposed by one jurisdiction on others, such as storm water flooding, incompatible land uses, and crime risks, can produce joint gains. Reducing negative or increasing positive externalities can create strong incentives for local leaders to cooperate.

Selective incentives can also motivate collaboration. Individual career incentives influence the willingness of local leaders to enter into collaborative arrangements. Stein (1990) and McCabe et al. (2008) argue that city managers often act "as if" they were residual claimants who can and do capture a portion of the benefits of local government activity, particularly when those activities produce efficiency gains and economic growth. City managers can use the tangible success represented by service efficiencies to advance their careers, usually by finding better-paying positions in larger and wealthier communities. Recent work argues that the professional standing and employment opportunities of city managers are improved by collaborative service innovations (Carr and LeRoux 2005; Feiock 2004).

Political ambition among elected and nonelected officials operates to both enhance and impede collective action among governments in metropolitan areas (Feiock 2007). Political ambitions to develop electoral constituencies or advance to regional or statewide office can lead local officials to address interlocal problems even in the face of weak citizen demand (Gillette 2000).

Elected officials are primarily responsive to their internal electoral constituencies, but to the extent that interlocal policies influence residential location decisions, they have implications for future constituencies. Bickers (2005) suggests that interlocal cooperation might result from the efforts of local officials seeking to prevent the dilution of the voter groups on whom they rely for electoral support. Collaboration produces political costs as well. Local governments may need to give up some authority to achieve regional coordination. Furthermore, local officials who pursue collaborative solutions that are contrary to their constituents' preferences or prejudices risk being punished at the polls (Gerber and Gibson 2005, 12).

BARRIERS TO INTERLOCAL COLLABORATION

If the structure of the problem situation is positive sum, the Coase (1960) theorem maintains that bargaining can produce welfare-maximizing solutions. In practice, the feasibility of self-organized solutions is greatly limited by the transaction costs of bargaining. The necessary condition for any agreement is an increase in benefits, and the larger that gain, the more likely it will outweigh the transaction costs necessary to achieve it (Libecap 1989; Lubell et al. 2002; Ostrom 1990). Transaction costs from four sources need to be kept low in order for benefits to exceed the costs of collective action (Feiock 2007; Feiock, Steinacker, and Park 2008).

Information Costs

Information on the preferences of all participants over possible outcomes and on their resources should be common knowledge. Information problems include both incomplete information for all participants and differences in information levels across the participants. Incomplete information may prevent organizations from recognizing the potential gains from joint action. The information asymmetry may also impede recognition of desirable joint outcomes, and it can increase concerns about the motivations or trustworthiness of potential partners as each seeks to gain a strategic advantage by concealing information.

The number of governmental units in a metropolitan area, their economic, political, and demographic composition, and their spatial dispersion affect information costs. Economic and demographic homogeneity that indicates potential common interests and service preferences both across and within jurisdictions reduces information costs. Similar interests reduce the range of desired bargaining outcomes, lowering both information and bargaining costs (Libecap 1989; Lubell et al. 2002).

On the other hand, a large number of potential participants to an agreement and greater distance between them make communication more costly. Difficulties in gathering reliable information about preferences and resources increase with the number of governments and the distances between them (Feiock 2007; Post 2002).

When information is imperfect and resources limited, finding partners in a trial-and-error fashion will be inefficient. Thus, information barriers prevent governments from recognizing potential gains from joint action, especially when measurement of outcomes, and thus potential payoffs, are difficult or costly to measure (Williamson 1985).

Agency Costs

Bargaining agents must accurately represent the interests of their constituents. Agency problems complicate the calculus of cooperation because the public officials that negotiate cooperative agreements are themselves agents. Principal–agent problems arise because the preferences of public officials negotiating interlocal agreements may depart from the preferences of citizens they represent (Feiock 2002). Principals and agents may differ in their preferred outcomes, the timing of the outcomes, or their attitudes toward risk. The greater these differences the less likely that a cooperative agreement acceptable to both can be created.

Demographic homogeneity within a city reduces agency problems for officials negotiating interlocal agreements on behalf of citizens. Similarity among constituents provides greater certainty in the principal's desired outcome, making the agent's task easier. The extent to which agency problems are manifest has been linked to the structure and powers of public offices as well as the political security of those who hold them. Strong institutions and long tenure in office increase the value local officials place on cooperative projects (Park and Feiock 2007).

Negotiation/Division Costs

The resource costs associated with the process of negotiating an agreement must be small, and the parties must be able to agree to a division of the bargaining surplus. Even fully informed officials pursuing their constituents' interests will find achieving agreement on the allocation of costs or benefits difficult. Joint gains may exist that would improve the position of all participants, and yet no agreement will be reached if they cannot settle how to divide the gains. Negotiation of an acceptable distribution of benefits will be affected by asymmetries in preferences and political strengths between actors (Heckathorn and Maser 1987). Political opposition to a cooperative solution may result when particpants are heterogeneous and it is clear which party benefits most.

Division problems tend to be less problematic when parties are similar. With large disparities in bargaining power, the stronger partner is more likely to push for the bulk of the gains from cooperation. The weaker partner then has little incentive to participate and may walk away from the agreement. If weaker partners push to receive a fraction of the gains disproportionate to their bargaining strength in the mistaken belief that they are critical to the endeavor, no mutually acceptable split of the joint gains may be possible. With similar agencies or governments, the "fair" division of equally splitting the gains is likely to be a focal point of negotiations, increasing the probability that a deal acceptable to all can be reached.

Enforcement Costs

There can be at most low costs associated with monitoring and enforcing the agreement. Enforcement will be costly unless there are credible commitments by the contracting parties not to defect. Although enforcement problems occur at implementation, the anticipation of enforcement problems adds costs to the process of developing institutions. If jurisdictions are tempted to renege, there is less incentive to reach agreement in the first place. Enforcement costs are reduced when the parties have an ability to make credible commitments to each other over time. For example, close geographic proximity and interactions on a variety of issues over long periods of time can reduce commitment costs.

OVERCOMING COLLECTIVE ACTION PROBLEMS

For bilateral intergovernmental agreements a prisoner's dilemma situation is inexorable for a single interaction (single-shot prisoner's dilemma game). If the same interactions are indefinitely repeated, each player can reward or punish past moves of the other actor. If this endogenous sanctioning is employed in "tit-for-tat" strategies, rewarding cooperation with cooperation and defection with defection, stable cooperation can be achieved in an iterated prisoner's dilemma (Axelrod 1984).

The tit-for-tat solution does not directly apply to multilateral agreements (n-person games) because of the collective action problem (Olson 1965). Free riding is the dominant strategy for each actor, and punishment cannot be easily targeted against the offending player. In an n-player noncooperative game, repeated play is insufficient to resolve the dilemma. Instead, the solution to the first-order problems requires agreement on structures and processes of interaction that permit the adoption and enforcement of collectively binding decisions (Ostrom 1990; Ostrom, Gardner, and Walker 1994).

The examples of interlocal cooperation efforts referenced in this chapter were successful because local governments overcame transaction-cost barriers to cooperation and crafted mutually beneficial accords. What these examples share is a configuration of service types, community contexts, political institutions, and network relationships that reduced the transaction costs described above. The next section more specifically links these four contextual considerations to the transaction costs problems discussed above in order to identify how they impede or facilitate the emergence of voluntary mechanisms for intergovernmental collaboration.

Characteristics of Goods and Service Types

Transaction costs can be great when a relationship involves transaction-specific assets or the qualities of a service are difficult to define and measure. For Williamson (1985), asset specificity—transaction-specific durable investments that cannot easily be redeployed to other uses—is central to choosing among governance structures. When parties make mutual investments of specific assets, it creates mutual dependence. If an agreement requires governments to make investments in specific assets or other long-term commitments, it can alter the options that would be available to them if the agreement broke down in the future (Frieden 1994).

For physical assets that are subject to congestion, such as shared use of a central library or water treatment facility, both the party that provides it and the parties that contract for it are exposed to risk. The party providing the asset must make an investment greater than that necessary to cover its own needs, leaving it vulnerable to excessive costs if other participants later renege on the contract. At the same time, if demand for the service increases, the government providing the good may prefer to terminate the interlocal compact in order to better serve its own citizens. The other participants are then forced to make an unplanned investment to develop their own asset.

Measurement difficulties increase search costs and make coordination of joint action difficult. Effective monitoring requires quantitative measures of outcomes or appropriate level of activity by a service provider, but metering or monitoring the quantity and/or quality of output or benefits of a service can be difficult and costly (Williamson 1985). Services such as sewer, water, or refuse collection have divisible, easily measured outcomes; thus, costs can be allocated based on the benefits received, and beneficiaries' preference is invariant (Steinacker 2004). For services with nontangible outputs or complex production processes, developing cooperative agreements is more difficult.

Characteristics of Communities

Demographic homogeneity among communities reduces the likelihood of political and economic power asymmetries that advantage one of the parties and create problems for negotiating fair divisions of benefits. Neighboring jurisdictions that are similarly situated begin from a position of mutual dependence. Scharpf (1997, 140) argues that mutual dependence can be represented as a battle of the sexes game in which both players have an interest in concluding the deal but have differences in preference for one or the other coordinated outcome. In this situation, both players could achieve their second-best outcome. Since nonagreement would lead to the worst outcomes for each, threats to break off negotiation would not be credible. If instead, power is asymmetrically distributed, the player in an advantaged position can capture all of the benefits or no deal will be struck. Social and economic homogeneity places cities in similar bargaining positions and thus makes an equal sharing of costs a workable solution.

Homogeneity within, not just between, units is important because agency costs for officials negotiating interlocal agreements on behalf of citizens are reduced. Not only are interests likely to be less uniform, it is more difficult to aggregate preferences and hold agents accountable in heterogeneous communities. Thus, we expect that intrajurisdictional homogeneity increases the likelihood of cooperation.

Neighbors can often gain production scale economies from sharing services. Additionally, fixed borders ensure repeat play among neighbors, which creates interdependencies. Governments with common borders are not stuck in a one-shot prisoner's dilemma because the impossibility of exit means that defection from cooperation exposes the defector to future retaliation. The prospect of future play with the same party constrains opportunism by giving each government an incentive to cooperate if there are mutual assurances that each government will contribute to the provision of the collective good (Miller 1992).

Political Institutions

The provisions of state constitutions and enabling legislation vary, but most allow jurisdictions to undertake jointly any activity they can undertake individually (ICMA 1997). Nested within the state institutional framework, local political institutions shape the information available and the structure of incentives faced by government officials. Administrators and elected officials each play a role in forging collaborative alliances with other governments, but they differ in bargaining resources and institutional positions. Political system institutions such as council–manager government and provisions for direct democracy have been demonstrated to constrain risks of opportunistic behavior by both elected and appointed leaders (Feiock 2004).

The city council functions as "veto player" (Tsebelis 2002) in the political system, since council approval typically is necessary to ratify intergovernmental agreements. A council elected at large is more likely to share the preferences of the executive, while councils with district-based representation advocate the interests of the smaller geographic constituencies they represent (Clingermayer and Feiock 2001). Gerber and Gibson (2005) argue that the underlying political dilemma associated with regional governance is that local officials need to give up some authority to achieve regional coordination, but they may then be held accountable for regional policies that are contrary to the preferences of their local constituents. Even if there are regional or citywide benefits from collaboration, district representatives may be unwilling to delegate control of decisions about the scope and location of projects if it has the effect of reducing their ability to direct benefits to district constituencies.

Turnover and short election cycles result in local officials, adopting a myopic perspective that makes cooperation difficult (Clingermayer and Feiock 2001). When political institutions create longer time horizons, short-term defection gains will be outweighed by gains from continued cooperation. Extended tenure in office for elected and administrative officials reduces policy uncertainty and promotes decisions based on longer-term considerations of the collective and selective benefits of collaboration.

Institutional homogeneity, the similarity of political institutions across government units in a region, facilitates exchange because actors tend to cluster with others of similar values, norms, and beliefs characteristics (Carley 1991). Much of the local public administration literature suggests that professional city managers share a common set of training, experience and orientation that leads to common values and an emphasis on efficiency and professionalization that are reinforced by the professional organizations in the field (Frederickson, Johnson, and Wood 2004).

The Structure of Policy Networks

An interlocal agreement between two local government units constitutes a dyadic relationship. If each unit also participates in other agreements with other local governments, together these relations form a macro-level regional governance structure that comprises a set of actors in a social network (see Thurmaier and Wood 2002). Over time, embedded relationships with other local governments accumulate into a regional network that invests the reputation and reciprocity of information in the reliability and competencies of prospective partners (Gulati and Gargiulo 1999).

The existing structure of agreements among local governments reduces transaction problems by increasing information about each other's conduct specified in the agreements and enhancing the credibility of commitments to fulfill their obligations under the agreements. Interlocal agreements provide information about local governments' policies and programs and potential implementation problems. In this way a network of contractual arrangements transforms interlocal relations into repeated games in which a reputation for reciprocity and trustworthiness can mitigate opportunism.

Scholz and Feiock (2007) describe two roles that networks play in reducing the transaction costs of collaboration. First, boundary-spanning or weak-tie networks offer solutions to search/coordination problems. Second, strong-tie or reciprocating structures make trust and credible commitment possible.

Information on opportunities for cooperation and who may be a good partner are necessary for local government units to cooperate. The value of a link between government units is particularly high if it creates a "bridge" to a government with connections to organizations and governments not part of the first unit's network (Berardo and Scholz 2005; Burt 2005; Scholz et al. 2008). Individual actors need to be able to assess the probability that their contributions to a collective good will be efficacious in securing production of that good and be able to coordinate expectations of contributions with others. Information-bridging allows local governments to investigate a broader set of possible gains from other local governments and to reap the advantage of innovation not available within a more highly clustered network. This idea builds on Burt's theory of "structural holes," which argues that ties that bridge structural holes enhance information flow and reduce coordination costs.

Because participants have incentives to free ride or to defect from cooperative agreements, overcoming enforcement problems is a central design issue for cooperative institutions. Strong-tie or reciprocating structures create disincentives for shirking or defection because a strong-tie network reduces the cost of monitoring and enforcing compliance with the terms of agreements. Partners gain information on the efforts, contributions, and behaviors of others that can be used for collective sanctions. Thus, a highly clustered network has the ability to impose constraints on local units that might attempt to shirk or act opportunistically.

Strong-tie intergovernmental relationships have been demonstrated to increase mutual trust and conformance to the provisions of an agreement (Lubell 2007). In a repeated relationship, such as occurs with geographically fixed government units, each actor stands to benefit by acquiring and preserving a positive reputation. In uncertain real world situations, reputation does more than compensate for incomplete information; it is a valuable social capital asset (Dixit 1996).

A history of cooperation among dyads or small groups of local governments builds reciprocity norms that reduce the costs of joint action and build social capital. Repeated small group interactions reduce the effort required to put additional new activities in place as partners develop trust and comfort working together over time (Feiock 2007; Lubell 2007). Reciprocal relationships also provide the opportunity for "side payments" if they link agreements across issue areas. In such relationships, the costs of knowing how counterparts may behave are reduced, since the establishment of a link running in both directions presupposes wider access to information on what type of behavior is expected and the political and social norms regarding the fairness of divisions.

A Research Agenda

Given the transaction costs inherent in crafting collaborative agreements, it is not surprising that much of the literature assumes that centralization of authority and consolidation is necessary for effective action. Certainly there are situations where transaction costs exceed the benefits of cooperation and thus, centralized approaches to regional problems may be necessary. Nevertheless, a long history of empirical work reveals that voluntary regional governance arrangements are quite common (cf. Parks and Oakerson's [1993] studies of service arrangements in the Pittsburgh and St. Louis areas). Consistent with the predictions of ICA, this work reports that collaborative governance arrangements emerge when contexts and institutional configurations reduce the transaction costs of cooperation for local actors.

The Program in Local Governance at Florida State University's Devoe Moore Center supports a research program to systematically test institutional collective action explanations for the emergence of voluntary service collaborations among local governments in metropolitan areas. Ongoing work investigates elements of ICA at several levels of analysis: metropolitan areas or other regional units, cities or other local government units, and individual service agreement ties between government units.

Table 10.1 provides an overview of ongoing research. While several projects are in their initial phases, the first five have produced research products. The evidence accumulated to date provides strong support for ICA explanations of collaboration. The work of Manoj Shrestha (Shrestha 2005; Shrestha and Feiock 2005, 2006) focuses specifically on the propositions regarding the relationships between service types and the structure of collaborations. His first project examines interlocal expenditures for eleven different services that vary in terms of asset specificity and measurement difficulty. This analysis also includes the history of service collaboration for each city. The results reveal that the transaction characteristics of goods influence city choices of whether or not to collaborate—the first stage of the collaborative decision process. This is consistent with the basic transaction cost prediction that actors choose discrete governance mechanisms in a transaction-cost-minimizing way (Williamson 1985).

At the second stage, levels of collaboration, as indicated by the interlocal service expenditure efforts, were not influenced by the type of good. Instead collaboration effort was linked to a history or to reciprocal dyadic relationships. Once cities are engaged in collaboration, their level of effort depends on their past dealings—which shape social trust (Shrestha and Feiock 2006). The importance of service types is confirmed at a more micro level in Shrestha's dissertation research on service agreements in one metropolitan region over time. This evidence indicates that the evolution of collaborative networks is shaped by interactions between service type and network structure.

A second completed project investigates the conditions under which economic development collaborations emerge. A national survey of local development officials provides strong support for several of the propositions advanced here (Feiock, Steinacker, and Park 2008). City attributes that reduced problems with division, agency, and information costs facilitated development collaboration. Interdependencies among neighboring jurisdictions and economic homogeneity created similar bargaining positions and reduced bargaining conflicts. Internal homogeneity in economic development preferences was found to reduce principal–agent conflict for a city's chief executive, enabling her to pursue a wider range of collaborative economic development activities. Finally, the mayor–council form of government increased the likelihood of collaborations for economic development.

Both strong-tie networks of frequent interaction among cities and participation in weak-

Table 10.1

Ongoing Research on Collaboration and Institutional Collective Action

Principal investigators	Collaboration setting sample/population	Units of analysis	Analysis technique
1. Feiock, Steinacker, and Park	Economic development joint ventures	Surveyed cities > 50K population	Probit
2. Shrestha, Feiock, and Zhao	Interlocal service expenditures	Georgia cities	Heckman/HLM
3. Scholz and Berardo	Water projects in Tampa Bay estuary	Network links among stakeholders	SIENA
4. Park and Feiock	Regional economic development partnerships	Metropolitan areas	Probit
5. Andrew*	Various types of public safety ILAs in FL	Cities, agreements	SIENA
6. Ramirez*	Networks among land use actors in Leon County	Building permit applications	OLS
7. Shrestha*	Twenty-five years of ILAs in Pinellas County	Service/agreement	SIENA
8. Feiock, Park, Lee, and Lee	Network survey of collaborations Orlando/Tampa	Collaborative ties among cities	SIENA
9. Kwon*	ILAs among cities within COGs, RPCs, and MPOs	Florida cities	SIENA
10. Berardo, Feiock, and Lubell	Land use regulations in FL	Florida cities and counties	Probit/SIENA
11. Farmer*	Regional special-purpose districts	Counties	Probit
12. Hawkins*	Economic development joint ventures	Cities in twelve metro areas	HLM
13. Scholz and Feiock	Land use, development, and water management	Cities in three metro areas	SIENA
14. Carr, Shrestha, and LaRoux	Intergovernmental service agreements	Cities in Michigan	Heckman/Probit

Note: Additional information on these projects is available at www.fsu.edu/~localgov/research_projects/regional_governance.htm.
*Dissertation research.

tie associational networks increased development collaboration. One implication of these results is that creating occasions for local officials to interact can build the networks and social capital that lead to cooperative solutions. Even membership in a regional association, a weak-tie relationship, was found to enhance the likelihood of partnership activity. This suggests that informal network structures may be effective in generating cooperative benefits in the future.

Follow-up analysis applies exponential random graph models to investigate structural patterns in the communication networks of appointed and elected officials in the Orlando area. Preliminary evidence indicates that local governments prefer to form reciprocal relationships, to contact "popular" governments that others rely on for information, and to contact governments with similar populations and political systems (Feiock et al. 2008).

These analyses confirm that both the attributes of actors and relations among them need to be accounted for in explanations of how and why they decide to collaborate. The empirical results demonstrate that both characteristics of a local government unit and its position in a social network of local actors influence the likelihood of joint ventures. Thus, interlocal policy collaborations provide a realistic alternative for addressing policy externalities. Even in competitive policy arenas such as economic development, voluntary agreements can emerge from a dynamic political contracting process among local government units.

MODELING COLLABORATION

Applications of social network analysis to collaboration have provided interesting insights, but this work has been more descriptive than analytical in its approach. One purpose of the Program in Local Governance is to advance a more analytical approach to the investigation of formal and informal collaborative governance mechanisms. Networks can be statistically modeled. The relevant network analytic techniques include Markov chain Monte Carlo (MCMC) estimation techniques applied to exponential random graphs. These techniques fully control for interdependencies of observations. These interdependencies are common in network data, but violate the assumptions of regression analysis. Several ongoing projects statistically test hypotheses about what contexts lead to the emergence and evolution of collaborative networks using the SIENA (Simulation Investigation for Empirical Network Analysis), a newly developed network analysis software incorporating the latest advances in MCMC models (Snijders et al. 2005). The models of network evolution are based on an actor-oriented model in which local actors evaluate current network configurations and make or terminate agreements to maximize their implicit "utility function" denoted by

$$f_i(x),$$

where f is a parameter vector and x represents a particular configuration of the network of which actor i is a member in the family X of all possible network configurations. When an actor i has the opportunity to create a new link or terminate an existing link, she will do it in such a way that this utility function (1) will be maximized. The network utility function of our actors can include a parameter vector containing both structural properties of the network and the actor attributes defined by the ICA framework. The network and behavioral utility function are estimated using the method of moments implemented as a continuous-time MCMC simulation in three stages. The first of these phases calculates likely starting values for the parameters of all the variables included in the model. Phase two simulates the choice process based on the starting values, compares the resultant simulated network with the observed second-period network, and adjusts values to reduce differences between the observed and the simulated data. The third and last phase uses a number of simulations to determine the frequency distribution of predictions, which then are used to calculate standard errors for the final parameter estimates (Berardo and Scholz 2005, 18). This approach allows us to apply statistical tests for whether any model parameter is significantly different from zero given other parameter values.

CONCLUSION

Institutional collective action explanations focus attention on both service and transaction costs of collaboration. Transaction costs are reduced by formal and informal institutional arrangements that increase the availability of information, reinforce social capital, and reduce the transaction costs of negotiating, monitoring, and enforcing an agreement.

This approach allows us to investigate collaborations among specialized and fragmented governmental units in relation to the network structures in which they are embedded. It also allows predictions to be made based on both the extant structure of network relationships and the characteristics of units simultaneously. We can then test hypotheses about the emergence of ties among members and the evolution of collaboration over time. Our research program has developed unique concepts, measures, and analytic techniques for analyzing relational linkages in longitudinal network data sets. To date, this approach has been applied to public safety and emergency response networks (Andrew 2005, 2007), environmental projects in the Tampa Bay area (Berardo and Scholz 2005), and multiple services in Pinellas County, Florida (Shrestha and Feiock 2006). Instead of examining various components of institutional collective action separately, these projects empirically examine the influence of service types, community characteristics, political institutions, and network structures together.

The institutional collective action framework also directs attention to the dynamics of decentralized systems of governance. One limitation in studies of collective action, transaction costs, and networks alike is their focus on comparative analysis of different institutional structures and relative ignorance of the dynamics by which the institutional structure emerges (Scholz and Feiock 2007). This is particularly problematic for the common situation in which multiple equilibria are possible. The relative likelihood of any given equilibrium can be determined by the process of institutional development.

As collaborations continue to provide benefits to participants, the parties to these exchanges build reputations for being trustworthy, providing in the process a feedback mechanism that enhances future cooperation and collective action. Most governance theories assume fixed preferences in order to emphasize the alteration of outcomes induced for the same preferences by different institutional arrangements. Yet, frequently it is changes in problem definition that induce changes in institutions and in policy outcomes.

Finally, analyzing the development of trust and group formation illustrates another means of understanding the dynamics involved in institutional development. Trust can be viewed as a secondary decision-making preference that can enhance the likelihood of Pareto-superior outcomes. That is, the development of trust is the equivalent of the development of a formal second-order institution to resolve the underlying collective action problem. Analyses of how trust develops therefore provide one approach for understanding the dynamics of institutional development. The study of how these endogenous mechanisms operate deserves greater theoretical and empirical attention.

REFERENCES

Agranoff, Robert, and Michael McGuire. 2003. "Inside the Matrix: Integrating the Paradigms of Intergovernmental and Network Management." *International Journal of Public Administration* 26, 1401–22.

Andrew, Simon A. 2005. "Interlocal Contractual Arrangements in the Provision of Public Safety." Paper presented at Creating Collaborative Communities: Management Networks, Services Cooperation, and Metropolitan Governance, Wayne State University, Detroit MI, October 31.

———. 2007. "Governance by Agreement." Local Governance Working Paper, Florida State University, Tallahassee, September 28.

Axelrod, Robert. 1984. *The Evolution of Cooperation.* New York: Basic Books.

Berardo, Ramiro, and John T. Scholz. 2005. "Micro-incentives and the Dynamics of Policy Networks." Paper presented at the annual meeting of the American Political Science Association, Washington, DC, September 1–4.

Bickers, Kenneth N. 2005. "The Politics of Interlocal Cooperation: A Theory and a Test." Paper presented at Creating Collaborative Communities: Management Networks, Services Cooperation, and Metropolitan Governance, Wayne State University, Detroit MI, October 31.

Bish, Robert L. 2000. "Evolutionary Alternatives for Metropolitan Areas: The Capital Region of British Columbia." *Canadian Journal of Regional Science* 23: 1–19.

Burt, Ronald S. 2005. *Brokerage and Closure: An Introduction to Social Capital.* New York: Oxford University Press.

Carley, Kathleen. 1991. "A Theory of Group Stability." *American Sociological Review* 56: 331–54.

Carr, Jered B., and Kelly LeRoux. 2005. "Which Local Governments Cooperate on Public Safety? Lessons from Michigan." Paper presented at Creating Collaborative Communities: Management Networks, Services Cooperation, and Metropolitan Governance, Wayne State University, Detroit MI, October 31.

Clingermayer, James C., and Richard C. Feiock. 2001. *Institutional Constraints and Policy Choice: An Exploration of Local Governance.* Albany: State University of New York Press.

Coase, Ronald. 1960. "The Problem of Social Cost." *Journal of Law and Economics* 3, no. 1: 1–44.

Dixit, Avinash K. 1996. *The Making of Economic Policy: A Transaction-Cost Politics Perspective.* Cambridge, MA: MIT Press.

Downs, Anthony. 1994. *New Visions for Metropolitan America.* Washington, DC: Brookings Institution.

Feiock, Richard C. 2002. "A Quasi-market Framework for Local Economic Development Competition." *Journal of Urban Affairs* 24: 123–42.

———. 2004. *Metropolitan Governance. Conflict, Competition and Cooperation.* Washington, DC: Georgetown University Press.

———. 2007. "Rational Choice and Regional Governance." *Journal of Urban Affairs* 29, no. 1 (Winter): 49–65.

Feiock, Richard C.; Annette Steinacker; and Hyung Jun Park. 2008. "Institutional Collective Action and Economic Development Joint Ventures." *Public Administration Review* 68, forthcoming.

Feiock, Richard C.; Keon Hyung Lee; Hyung Jun Park; and In-Won Lee. 2008. "ICA and the Structure of Economic Development Policy Networks in the Orlando Metropolitan Area." Paper presented at the annual meeting of the International Social Network Association, St. Pete Beach Florida, January 21.

Feiock, Richard C., and Jered B. Carr. 2001. "Incentives, Entrepreneurs, and Boundary Change." *Urban Affairs Review* 36, no. 3: 382–405.

Frederickson, H. George; Gary A. Johnson; and Curtis H. Wood. 2004. *The Adapted City: Institutional Dynamics and Structural Change.* Armonk, NY: M.E. Sharpe.

Frieden, Jeffry A. 1994. "International Investment and Colonial Control: A New Interpretation." *International Organization* 48, no. 4: 559–93.

Friesema, H. Paul. 1971. *Metropolitan Political Structure: Intergovernmental Relations and Political Integration in the Quad-Cities.* University of Iowa Press, Iowa City.

Gerber, Elisabeth R., and Clark C. Gibson. 2005. "Balancing Competing Interests in American Regional Government." Paper presented at the Program in American Democracy Speaker Series, Notre Dame University, February 1.

Gillette, Clayton P. 2000. "Regionalization and Interlocal Bargains." *NYU Law Review* 76: 190–271.

Gulati, Ranjay, and Martin Gargiulo. 1999. "Where Do Interorganizational Networks Come From?" *American Journal of Sociology* 104, no. 5: 1439–93.

Heckathorn, Douglas, and Steven Maser. 1987. "Bargaining and Constitutional Contracts." *American Journal of Political Science* 31: 42–168.

International City/County Management Association (ICMA). 1997. *Municipal Form of Government, 1996: Trends in Structure, Responsibility, and Composition.* Washington, DC.

Katz, Bruce, ed. 2000. *Reflections on Regionalism.* Washington, DC: Brookings Institution.

Libecap, Gary. 1989. *Contracting for Property Rights.* New York: Cambridge University Press.

Lowery, David. 2001. "Metropolitan Governance Structures from a Neoprogressive Perspective." *Swiss Political Science Review* 7, no. 3: 130–36.

Lubell, Mark. 2007. "Familiarity Breeds Trust: Collective Action in a Policy Domain." *Journal of Politics* 69: 237–50.

Lubell, Mark; Mark. Schneider; John T. Scholz; and Mihriye Mete. 2002. "Watershed Partnerships and the Emergence of Collective Action Institutions." *American Journal of Political Science* 46, no. 1: 148–63.

McCabe, Coyle Barbara; Richard C. Feiock; James C.; Clingermayer and Christopher Stream. 2008. "Turnover Among City Managers. The Role of Political and Economic Change." *Public Administration Review* 68 (2): 380–87.

Miller, Gary J. 1992. *Managerial Dilemmas: The Political Economy of Hierarchy.* Cambridge. Cambridge University Press.

———. 2000. "'Above Politics': Credible Commitment and Efficiency in the Design of Public Agencies." *Journal of Public Administration Research and Theory* 10, no. 2: 298–328.

Olberding, Julie C. 2002. "Does Regionalism Beget Regionalism? The Relationship Between Norms and Regional Partnerships for Economic Development." *Public Administration Review* 62, no. 4: 480–91.

Olson, Mancur. 1965. *The Logic of Collective Action: Public Goods and the Theory of Groups.* Cambridge, MA: Harvard University Press.

Ostrom, Elinor. 1990. *Governing the Commons: The Evolution of Institutions for Collective Action.* New York: Cambridge University Press.

Ostrom, Elinor; Roy Gardner; and James Walker. 1994. *Rules, Games, and Common-pool Resources.* Ann Arbor: University of Michigan Press.

Park, Hyung Jun, and Richard C. Feiock. 2007. "Institutional Collective Action, Social Capital and Regional Development Partnerships." *International Review of Public Administration* 11, no. 2: 57–69.

Parks, Roger B., and Ronald J. Oakerson. 1989. "Metropolitan Organization and Governance: A Local Public Economy Approach." *Urban Affairs Quarterly* 25, no. 1: 18–29.

———. 1993. "Comparative Metropolitan Organization: Service Production and Governance Structures in St. Louis, MO, and Allegheny County, PA." *Publius* 23: 19–39.

Post, Stephanie. 2002. "Local Government Cooperation. The Relationship Between Metropolitan Area Government Geography and Service Provision." Paper presented at the 2002 annual meeting of the American Political Science Association, Boston, MA, August 29–September 1.

Provan, Keith G., and H. Brinton Milward. 2001. "Do Networks Really Work? A Framework for Evaluating Public-Sector Organizational Networks." *Public Administration Review* 61: 414–23.

Scharpf, Fritz W. 1997. *Games Real Actors Play: Actor-centered Institutionalism in Policy Research.* Boulder, CO: Westview Press.

Scholz, John T., and Richard C. Feiock. 2007. "Self-organizing Federalism: Voluntary Coordination in Metropolitan Areas." Paper presented at the Workshop on Networks and Coordination of Fragmented Authority: The Challenge of Institutional Collective Action in Metropolitan Areas, Devoe Moore Center, Florida State University, Tallahassee, February 16–17.

Scholz, John T.; Berardo Ramiro; and Kile Brad. 2008. "Do Networks Solve Collective Action Problems? Credibility, Search and Collaboration." *Journal of Politics*, in press.

Shrestha, Manoj. 2005. "Inter-local Fiscal Cooperation in the Provision of Local Public Services." Paper presented at the annual meeting of the Association for Public Administration, Milwaukee, WI, April 2–5.

Shrestha, Manoj, and Richard C. Feiock. 2005. "The Network Structure of Interlocal Cooperation for Water-Related Services." Paper presented at the Midwest Political Science Association Meeting, Chicago, April 27.

———. 2006. "Do Cities Cooperate in Local Public Goods Supply? A Transaction Cost and Social Exchange Explanation." Paper presented at the Midwest Political Science Association Meeting, Chicago, April 15.

Snijders, Tom A.B.; Christian E.G. Steglichm; and Michael Schweinberger. 2005. "Modeling the co-evolution of networks and behavior." Working paper, University of Groningen, ICS/Department of Sociology.

Stein, Robert M. 1990. *Urban Alternatives: Public and Private Markets in the Provision of Local Services.* Pittsburgh: University of Pittsburgh Press.

Steinacker, Annette. 2004. "Game Theoretic Models of Metropolitan Cooperation." In *Metropolitan Governance. Conflict, Competition and Cooperation,* ed. Richard C. Feiock. Washington, DC: Georgetown University Press.

Thurmaier, Kurt, and Curtis Wood. 2002. "Interlocal Agreements as Social Networks: Picket Fence Regionalism in Metropolitan Kansas City." *Public Administration Review* 62, no. 5: 585–98.

Tsebelis, George. 2002. *Veto Players: How Political Institutions Work.* Princeton, NJ: Princeton University Press.

Williamson, Oliver. 1985. *The Economic Institutions of Capitalism.* New York: Free Press.

CHAPTER 11

Outcomes Achieved Through Citizen-Centered Collaborative Public Management

Terry L. Cooper,
Thomas A. Bryer, and Jack W. Meek

DEMOCRATIZING THE ADMINISTRATIVE STATE

Citizen-centered collaborative public management is one approach to the incongruity between the conditions of the administrative state and the vision of democratic governance. The concept of collaborative public management has been defined as "the process of facilitating and operating in multi-organizational arrangements to solve problems that cannot be solved" (Agranoff and McGuire 2003, 4). Collaborative public management that is citizen-centered extends beyond this definition and focuses on the role of the public in collaborative management arrangements (Cooper, Bryer, and Meek 2006). This chapter introduces an action research program conducted in the city of Los Angeles that has resulted in active relations between public administrators and citizens of the city; we explore the potential for and challenges associated with democratizing city agencies and facilitating the achievement of various collaborative outcomes.

If democratic governance requires ultimate control by the citizenry, an administrative state that tends to dominate the public policy process from initiation through adoption to implementation is antithetical to the ends of democracy (Cooper 2000). It becomes increasingly problematic for the exercise of democratic citizenship. Technical expertise and knowledge, institutional continuity over time, and significant financial and personnel resources—all in the hands of administrative agencies—make it extraordinarily difficult for citizens to exercise any substantial democratic control over the work of these organizations in delivering public services. Elected officials fare only slightly better in attempting to influence and direct these often large and relatively impenetrable agencies.

One result of the inability of citizens to make themselves heard by administrative arms of government is frustration that ultimately festers into distrust and alienation. There is ample evidence of serious levels of generalized distrust of government and alienation from it on the part of the citizenry (King and Stivers 1998; Nye, Zelidow, and King 1997). In the case of Los Angeles, these feelings began taking on active and organized manifestations in the efforts by parts of the city to secede and form their own municipal governments (Box and Musso 2004). One of the main motivating concerns behind these movements was an expressed belief that their communities were not receiving their fair share of public services from city agencies. The San Fernando Valley, with over one million residents, had made several unsuccessful attempts at secession over several decades, but state legislative changes in the 1990s made that process less difficult. The result was that by 1999 three areas of Los Angeles began moving through the legal process of secession: the San Fernando Valley, Hollywood, and the L.A. Harbor areas of San Pedro and Wilmington. The San Fernando Valley and Hollywood qualified for the ballot in a special election but did not receive enough votes to break away (Hogen-Esch 2001; Sonenshein and Hogen-Esch 2006).

A neighborhood council system was advanced during the late 1990s as a way of reducing alienation from the city government of Los Angeles and heading off secession by reconnecting citizens to the governance process. Adopted in the new city charter in 1999, this system of neighborhood councils, each organized by the residents themselves and certified by the new L.A. Board of Neighborhood Commissioners, now includes eighty-eight councils throughout the city.

Our research on neighborhood councils and that of our colleagues in the USC Neighborhood Participation Project indicates that they seem to be achieving some degree of success in providing channels of participation in the formal public policy process (Musso, Weare, and Cooper 2004). Under the new charter the neighborhood councils were entitled to receive early notification about any actions anticipated by the L.A. City Council, however, the councils were provided no clear way to engage the administrative agencies directly. The big city agencies such as the Los Angeles Police Department, the Los Angeles Department of Public Works, and the Los Angeles Department of Transportation, had no direct connection to the neighborhood councils. The Collaborative Learning Project (CLP) was created to explore models for dealing with that problem. The Learning and Design Forum (L&D) process developed by the CLP involved a series of three deliberative sessions to bring together neighborhood council representatives and city department personnel, with homework by each side between sessions. The objective was to see whether a partnership, such as a memorandum of understanding, could be developed and formally adopted about how public services would be delivered differently under the new system.

The research reported in this chapter is a form of action research in which we created arenas for deliberation and collaboration and hired a professional facilitator to run the sessions. We then observed and documented the process, met with the two groups of participants between sessions, surveyed the participants at each stage, and interviewed them at the end. Our intention was to find out whether we could create model processes for helping the neighborhood councils engage effectively with city department personnel to achieve a satisfactory response. We had an end in mind, created conditions we thought might achieve that end and studied the effectiveness of these activities.

During this process we saw how the political environment of the city can affect one's ability to work with administrative agencies. The CLP was begun under a mayor who was enthusiastically supportive of the neighborhood councils and encouraged city departments to actively reach out to them. However, a new mayor was elected in 2005, and, though not actively hostile to the neighborhood councils, he did not seem to see them as central to his agenda. The result was a political environment in which it became more difficult to engage city departments.

COLLABORATIVE LEARNING PROJECT SUMMARY

The central thesis of this chapter is that action research—research designed along with participants with a focus on collaborative learning—provides an opportunity for city agencies, citizens, and researchers to create knowledge about public service that is mutually understood. A collaborative process model we call the Learning and Design Forum focuses on engagement as a central feature of how mutual knowledge is generated.

The action research employed in this work has its theoretical roots in the work of several scholars: John Dewey (1929) and his studies on the educational process and socialization; Daniel Yankelovich (1991) and his work on public judgment; and Chris Argyris (1993) and his studies on learning and actionable knowledge. The value of action research in the study of the interface between citizens and public administration has been demonstrated in the work of Cooper and Kathi (2005), Kathi and Cooper (2005), and Cooper and Musso (1999). Our research extends from these foundations and confirms that there are potential benefits to citizen–administrator collaboration in large metropolitan areas. We also suggest that there are limitations in the extent to which such collaboration can foster sustainable relationships.

The Collaborative Learning Project Design

The findings reported are based on research conducted under the auspices of the Collaborative Learning Project at the School of Policy, Planning and Development (SPPD) at the University of Southern California (USC). Since 2003, the CLP has conducted three differentiated and focused cases of the collaborative process model. Our work has allowed the examination of the effects of citizen–administrator collaboration on administrative officials from three departments in the city of Los Angeles. In each case, citizens and other stakeholders representing newly formed and officially recognized neighborhood councils are joined with a department they have chosen for engagement. Upon agreement to be involved, the department selects administrators for participation in the CLP. The process involves three half-day sessions that are professionally facilitated and carried out over a three- to four-month time span. The culmination of the three sessions is the creation of a service agreement based on mutual understanding that has thus far taken the form of a memorandum of understanding (MOU).

The CLP research process is designed around five procedural steps. The first step, neighborhood council selection, is based on several criteria developed by the research team, including certification by the city of Los Angeles Department of Neighborhood Empowerment, demographic diversity, interest in participating, and history of civic involvement. The second step in each of the three cases involves choosing the city department for participation in the L&D sessions. This selection process is based on a dialogue with neighborhood participants and their interests in working with a particular department based on their unique needs or interests. Following agreement by neighborhood council representatives, the research team contacts the department jointly selected by neighborhood participants to assess feasibility and interest in participation. In all but one case, the department chosen by neighborhood participants agreed to participate in the L&D sessions.[1] After the selection of neighborhood councils and departmental participants, the third procedural step called upon participants to separately conduct a homework assignment prior to the first meeting of all participants that would outline their interpretation and experience of working with each other to this point.

The fourth procedural step of the CLP consists of the three professionally facilitated half-day sessions. A primary goal of these three sessions is to build relationships among participants where each could inform the other about their needs and how these needs can be achieved. The possibility of finalizing formal written agreements among participants is examined in each of the three cases. The fifth step in the CLP process is the implementation of mutually designed agreements established in step four along with department efforts with neighborhood councils to maintain relationships during and beyond implementing agreements. Figure 11.1 graphically summarizes the five steps of the Collaborative Learning Project.

The research design includes three differentiated cases of the collaborative process model administered to address the particular issues of concern to participating neighborhood councils and departments. The differentiated design also allows the researchers to compare results of the L&D sessions and to generate preliminary propositions with regard to what conditions may enhance or detract from collaborative learning outcomes.

The first case includes four contiguous neighborhood councils with units of a large city department; the second case includes one neighborhood council with units of a small city department; and the third case includes four noncontiguous neighborhood councils and units of a large city department. Each of the three cases and the L&D sessions are depicted in Table 11.1 on page 216.

In each case, semistructured interviews were conducted with both neighborhood council and department officials approximately three months following the final L&D session. These were process evaluation interviews that sought to generate knowledge about the value and efficacy of the L&D process, the people involved, and the outcomes achieved. In the first case—the only case with a signed memorandum of understanding—the research team also conducted implementation evaluation interviews with participants. Here we sought to understand how well the agreement was put into practice. These interviews were conducted approximately one year following the signing of the agreement.

OUTCOMES OF COLLABORATION

Innes and Booher (1999) in their research on collaborative planning have offered a useful framework to assess the nature of the new relationships that have been achieved. These

215

Figure 11.1 **Collaborative Learning Project Steps**

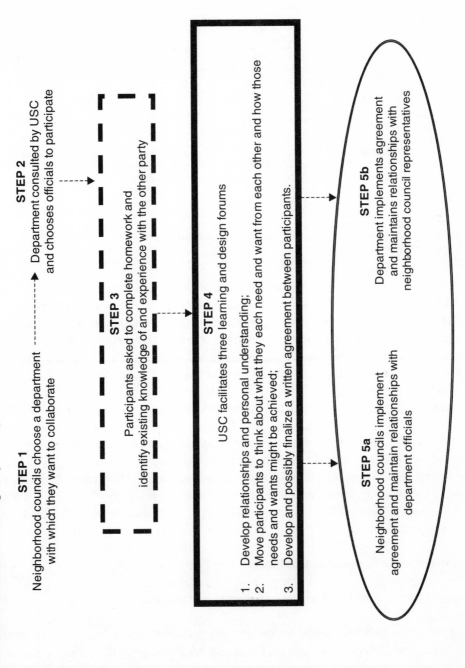

STEP 1
Neighborhood councils choose a department with which they want to collaborate

STEP 2
Department consulted by USC and chooses officials to participate

STEP 3
Participants asked to complete homework and identify existing knowledge of and experience with the other party

STEP 4
USC facilitates three learning and design forums

1. Develop relationships and personal understanding;
2. Move participants to think about what they each need and want from each other and how those needs and wants might be achieved;
3. Develop and possibly finalize a written agreement between participants.

STEP 5a
Neighborhood councils implement agreement and maintain relationships with department officials

STEP 5b
Department implements agreement and maintains relationships with neighborhood council representatives

Table 11.1

Collaborative Learning Project Cases and Learning and Design Forums

	Cases		
	Case 1	Case 2	Case 3
Learning and Design Forums	Four contiguous neighborhood councils and Department 1	One neighborhood council and Department 2	Four noncontiguous neighborhood councils and Department 3
No. of department participants	15	3	5
No. of neighborhood council participants	20	5	18
Total no. of participants	35	8	26
Session One	October 2003	April 2004	October 2005
Session Two	November 2003	May 2004	November 2005
Session Three	January 2004	June 2004	January 2006
Agreement	Signed February 2004	On hold	On hold

Department 1 = Large, extensive service department
Department 2 = Small, narrowly focused service department
Department 3 = Large, extensive service department

levels of achievement consist of first-order outcomes (such as the development of trust and mutual understanding, the ability to come together for agreed ends), second-order outcomes (the development of new partnerships, changes in perception, changes in practice), and third-order outcomes (new collaborations, more coevolution, new institutions). Table 11.2 provides a summary of Innes and Booher's first-, second-, and third-order effects of collaborative planning.

In this chapter, we draw upon this framework of collaborative planning effects to assess findings with regard to the L&D sessions. We begin in this section with a review of findings with regard to first-order effects focusing on challenges related to building social, intellectual, and political capital as well as building high-quality agreements. We then proceed to summarize our observations with regard to second-order effects, namely, lessons drawn from implementing agreements and extending joint learning into the system. Finally, we offer some comment with regard to the challenges related to the possible development of third-order effects.

First-Order Collaborative Challenges

Social Capital: Building Trust and Mutual Understanding

Relationships between public administrators and their stakeholders, when considered in collaborative network terms, coevolve and feed off each other. This is the case with relationships based on responsiveness, communication, and trust (Bryer 2006). Trust in government by citizens has been shown to correlate with citizen participation, thus poten-

Table 11.2

Innes and Booher's (1999) Framework for Effects of Collaboration

First-order effects	• Social capital: trust, relationships
	• Intellectual capital: mutual understanding, shared problem frames, agreed-upon data
	• Political capital: ability to work together for agreed ends
	• High-quality agreements
	• Innovative strategies
Second-order effects	• New partnerships
	• Coordination and joint action
	• Joint learning extends into the community
	• Implementation of agreements
	• Changes in practices
	• Changes in perceptions
Third-order effects	• New collaborations
	• More coevolution, less destructive conflict
	• Results on the ground: adaptation of cities, regions, resources, services
	• New institutions
	• New norms and heuristics
	• New discourses

tially leading to even more trust and more participation. At the same time, trust in citizens by public administrators has been shown to lead to increased willingness to work with citizens (Yang 2005).

The existence and magnitude of trust is difficult to measure; research respondents have varying perceptions of what it means to trust another, particularly in the context of governance relations. Overall, respondents when asked whether they felt trust improved through the collaborative process fell into one of four groupings: (1) trust improved, (2) trust declined, (3) trust is ready to improve, and (4) There is no change in trust.

These groupings are consistent with behavioral patterns associated with two forms of trust: calculus-based and identification-based (Lewicki 2006). Calculus-based trust is based on the perceived risks associated with not acting in an expected manner and thus severing trust bonds and the perceived rewards associated with maintaining and further developing actions that meet expectations, thus preserving and enhancing trust bonds. Once trust bonds become stronger, relations might become more intimate, thus allowing greater mutual understanding and appreciations of wants and desires between multiple actors. This kind of trust is identification-based, as it goes beyond transactions and calculations to embrace a greater degree of personal familiarity, knowledge, and mutual understanding.

In the first case, three out of five department officials and one neighborhood council representative out of four reported a feeling that trust improved through the collaborative process. For instance, a department official reports, "Trust increased. The bureaus learned that the neighborhood councils could be partners, not just critics or consumers.

Neighborhood councils learned that bureaus have restrictions on their resources, but they are professional in their approach to utilizing those resources." Another official sees the actions of neighborhood councils as a manifestation of trust: "People from the neighborhood councils are now acting as spokespeople to other neighborhood groups on behalf of the department . . . that's trust."

Participants in the second and third cases (a small and narrowly defined service department and a large and extensive service department) each report feelings of improved trust, but they focused in their response more on trust with specific individuals, rather than with institutions. One out of two department officials and neighborhood council representatives in the second case report such personal trust. However four out of seven neighborhood council representatives in the third case perceived that trust improved without limiting such trust to individuals. For instance, a participant observes that the trust is based on knowledge of "what the department can and cannot do."

It is only in the first case—the large department with extensive services—that participants report a sense of readiness to improve trust. More time and experience with each other was first necessary. A department official offers that "it takes time to build trust. You need to see results over time for trust to develop." A neighborhood representative observes how the "seeds have been set for improvement, but we're not there yet." Another participant notes, "I am more open to them, but trust has to be built over a period of time." These views are expressed by a minority of participants, but they are suggestive of a possible attitude regarding how trust develops.

The benefits of new knowledge began to sink in for neighborhood council representatives over time in the first case, and thus trust developed as participants hoped it might. "Because these relationships were formed, we got to know each other. The trust is both ways. There are a lot of wacky people attending our meetings, and they probably call [the department] as well. [The department] needs to balance wacky with legitimate, and since we have our relationship, neighborhood councils are known to be legitimate." Another participant offers that "other people's trust is improving because of my communication with others. I am speaking with more authority about the process, not just about problems in the neighborhoods. For instance, I spent an hour speaking with my neighbor about why all potholes are not filled at the same time." Perhaps paradoxically, department officials were less enthusiastic about trust after more time had passed due to the lack of continued interaction on the part of neighborhood councils; the councils were restricted by various bureaucratic hurdles, resource constraints, and board member turnover. As a result, for some department officials, interactions dried up and dampened, the trust that started to develop. This occurrence implicitly deals with a challenge in citizen-centered collaborative public management, which is the issue of sustainability of relationships. Without sustainability, any trust that might develop can be put off track, as seems to have occurred here.

Going into the third case, participants were mixed in the extent to which they reported trust for either neighborhood councils or the department. Officials from the department were optimistic about possibilities for improving trust but realistic in the challenges.[2] Neighborhood council representatives were almost entirely negative in their assessment of trust in the department. Comments centered on the lack of interaction and involvement with neighborhood councils on the part of department officials.

The lack of trust in the department at the start of the process is reflected further by survey findings. At the first session, only three of twelve neighborhood participants indicated that they trusted the department; by the time of the third session, eight of twelve indicated that they trusted the department. At both the first and third sessions, three of five department officials indicated that they trusted neighborhood councils. These findings are consistent with interview responses from both parties as reported in the previous paragraph.

Overall, there is an observed increase in personal familiarity, but trust in the department and in neighborhood councils did not clearly change for all participants across agencies and neighborhood councils. This finding may indicate a limitation of the L&D model in assisting departmental representatives to view citizens differently or for citizens to present themselves in a different light to administrators.

The findings also may be indicative of the dual forms of trust: calculus based and identification based. Some participants were able to move quickly to adopt a representative role, in which, for instance, neighborhood council representatives spoke on behalf of the department to community members. Other participants needed to wait and see how the behaviors of officials on either side continued over time or whether the expectations were met, thus justifying an increase in trust and move toward the stronger bonds of identification-based trust.

Intellectual and Political Capital: Bureaucratic Responsiveness

Bureaucratic responsiveness, particularly in a collaborative setting, is something that is negotiated between the bureaucrats and citizens engaged in collaboration as well as among the bureaucrats, who have obligations to other stakeholders and elected officials. Negotiated responsiveness of bureaucrats is thus subject to change from the time collaboration with citizens commences through when and if collaboration ends (Bryer 2007).

Our findings suggest that responsiveness of bureaucrats to neighborhoods and neighborhood councils did improve, though how and for what reason varied with each case. In the first case, responsiveness improved as neighborhood council representatives developed a greater understanding and appreciation for the work of department employees and as department managers gave neighborhood representatives a more substantive and potentially powerful role in the delivery of services. In the second case, responsiveness did not seem to improve. The lack of participation by department officials in the deliberation process, in comparison to the two other cases, is a possible contributor to the lower levels of trust perceived by neighborhood council participants as reported above. In the third case, we capture more data that allow us to see marked improvement in perceived responsiveness, though the behaviors of department officials were not observed to change at all.

This means collaboration potentially leads to enhanced responsiveness. However, whether or not responsiveness is enhanced will depend on the motivations and objectives of department officials. If they perceive themselves to be politically dependent on neighborhood councils, they might employ a negotiated responsiveness strategy that enhances the extent to which resources are being committed to citizen collaboration and improve perceived responsiveness among citizens (Bryer and Cooper 2007).

In the first case, the department sent officials from all management levels. Top management saw the project as an opportunity to mentor lower-level staff and make them less fearful of working with the public. Such a perspective paid dividends in the recognition they received from neighborhood representatives in the department's attempt to embrace community goals. One neighborhood council member notes that "[The department] is earnestly working towards community goals but is hampered by financial constraints." Another neighborhood council participant notes that "[Neighborhood councils] need to help [the department] spread their message out to citizens and build a supportive environment for them."

The department in the second case paled in comparison to the department in the first case in terms of the resources and people involved in the process. In this case the department was much smaller in scale, mission, and budget. The general manager of the department participated in only the first of three sessions, and in the second two sessions, a lower-ranked official served as the primary representative. Two other department representatives participated, but they contributed less in terms of substance and personality than this one official. As such, neighborhood participants reported stronger relationship development with that one official. There was uncertainty as to whether the department as a whole regarded the neighborhood council in any meaningful way. Responsiveness, thus, was not high and did not seem to improve as the process unfolded.

Department officials in the third case consisted of an assistant general manager, his immediate subordinate, and three senior engineers associated with the different regions of the city represented by the four participating neighborhood councils. The quality of participation by these five department officials was mixed, with the assistant general manager seen to be most open and willing and the others more rigid or reserved.[3]

The finding that emerges in the third case, based upon survey data collected at each collaborative session, is that the department did not change its behavior, but neighborhood representatives changed their perceptions, particularly on the question of whether officials in the department were doing all that they could to meet neighborhood needs. This is consistent with the first L&D case, in which participants expressed greater appreciation for the work and restraints of department officials. Unlike the first case, the behaviors of officials did not change.

High-Quality Agreements

All three sets of L&D sessions resulted in MOU drafts between the participating neighborhood council(s) and city agency. Agency and neighborhood council officials formally signed the MOU in the first case. In the second case, agency officials sought to broaden the scope of the agreement to include more than the one neighborhood council that participated in dialogue and never formally signed a document. In the third case, officials from the agency were prepared to sign the agreement, and three of four neighborhood council boards voted to approve the agreement. However, an instruction from the Office of the Los Angeles Mayor prevented department officials from signing the agreement.

Despite the three different fates of the drafted agreements from each collaborative process, each of the MOU drafts contains indicators of what was accomplished during the collaborative process. Below are the key features across the MOU drafts.

- *Open communication channels:* All three MOU drafts contained provisions for opening communication channels between the parties through a liaison position in each organization and/or a committee structure in the neighborhood council.
- *Education:* All three MOU drafts contained a provision establishing that the department will provide education to neighborhood councils about department services and procedures.
- *Stakeholder participation:* Two of the MOU drafts contained a provision that the neighborhood councils in partnership with the department would lead an effort to ensure that neighborhood stakeholders are involved in decisions related to the department.
- *Service updates and customer satisfaction:* Two of the MOU drafts contained provisions whereby the department would provide service delivery assessment and update reports to the neighborhood councils on a regular basis. One of those MOU drafts required the neighborhood councils to respond with requested changes to the report. The third MOU required that the department provide customer satisfaction surveys to neighborhood councils on a regular basis.

Second-Order Collaborative Effects

Implementation of Agreements

Formal agreements can document the growth in relationships and establish the mechanisms for future growth and enhanced service delivery. If agreements are backed by shared understandings and trust between parties, the commitment can be credible if not legal in nature (Robertson and Tang 1995). The value of the written agreements across the three cases of the CLP is recognized by participants in just this way. However, the limitations on how agreements are viewed by elected officials are clear to participants as well. After the newly elected mayor's office instructed the department in the third case not to sign the MOU—perhaps due to the multiple advances in this area as discussed in the next section—the question of the importance of a signed MOU became apparent. What are its benefits and drawbacks? To explore this question, L&D participants were asked these questions, in addition to a question regarding what barriers might restrict successful implementation of the MOU or the spirit of the MOU. Participants report that the MOU "forces you to focus on the issues that are important." The MOU "codified" what was really needed by both parties and "defined things that we should be doing and how we should be communicating."

Drawbacks to a signed MOU were readily apparent to participants as well, and these relate to the challenges of continuity discussed previously. For instance, one participant observes that "there was no follow-up. While initially our relationship with neighborhood councils was very colorful and interesting, some of those relationships have become prosaic and insipid. There is no continuity." A participant from a department observes that a "signed document makes people nervous," and another participant notes that it "is precedent set-ting. Are we going to end up with lots of MOUs? Managers always look at these things as a creation of work. The cynical view is that the mayor and council are sometimes going to offer promises like offering MOUs with every department, but are elected officials going to increase budget and staff?"

This last statement ties to an often-cited barrier to successful implementation of the MOU or spirit of the MOU: resources. One department official succinctly states, "Budget is the bottom line." Another official more expansively observes that "neighborhood councils learned in the process that if they are disappointed, it is not due to the dedication of city employees, it has to do with budget shortfalls." Yet another official observed that "money is the major hurdle. We can still run the race, but the budget is tight." The resource story is similar on the neighborhood council side: "We're all volunteers; this process is very time consuming."

Can the same outcomes described to this point in the chapter be achieved without an MOU, considering the observed benefits and drawbacks of such an agreement? Participants largely consider the answer to be yes, with a focus on continued development of personal relationships. This is not to suggest that the MOU is meaningless, but if the goal is to de-velop better shared understandings and trust, then open communication may be sufficient. Communication, as a first step, could then lead to coordination and to full collaboration with a sustainable written agreement (Cigler 1999).

For instance, participants offer the importance of "personal relationships, working relationships," "participation in meetings and forums," "personal and group meetings," and "a willingness to get out, face these people and talk to them." There needs to be a "communication channel," such as that provided through liaisons between parties. A neighborhood participant from the third case sums up this sentiment: "Have a picnic, get some face to face. With or without a signature, it doesn't matter unless somebody plans to sue. A marriage license is only important at breakup time. We agreed to stuff that already exists. Now it either is or is not happening."

Joint Learning Extends to the Community

The original call for participation in the L&D sessions was announced at the May 2003 meeting of all neighborhood councils—called the Congress of Neighborhood Councils—held at the Los Angeles Convention Center. Calls for participation in the second and third cases included requests sent to each of the neighborhood councils and included corre-spondence with the Department of Neighborhood Empowerment (DONE). In addition, departmental selection of participation in each of the L&D sessions included approval within the city authority structures. During the tenure of the first two L&D sessions, there was mayoral support for the enhancement of neighborhood councils. Indeed, the signing of the first agreement between four neighborhood councils and the large service department with extensive services was signed in city council chambers. The visibility of the L&D sessions was evident. The collaborative nature as well as the potential benefits to both departments and neighborhood councils of joint public management made L&D sessions an appealing process to emulate. Indeed, a very different variation of the L&D sessions was emerging under city administrative leadership seeking support for actions developed within the Department of Water and Power.

In this case, a large city department (not a participant in the L&D forums) sought rate increases that were found objectionable by neighborhood council leadership. In the first sign of recognition of the emerging power of neighborhood councils in Los Angeles, the city council voted that the department withdraw the rate increase and work with neighborhood councils on an alternative agreement. With one L&D MOU existing, department leadership and neighborhood council activists developed a similar MOU, without the assistance of the CLP, and called upon various groups to support the plan. It should be noted that this MOU is very different from the mutually designed MOU that resulted from the CLP L&D sessions. This department MOU was designed with administrative interests foremost. In an interview with a city administrator, he commented on both how the L&D MOU was adopted for use with the department and the process used to develop support for the department MOU:

> We developed a letter of intent with the [L&D] MOU as the template. We used the same areas as in the [L&D] MOU but fit them to apply specifically [to our department]. We needed the rate increase, but we needed to have support for it as well. We saw the agreement as a way of moving ahead. The best strategy was to develop a long-term relationship. I wanted to turn neighborhood councils into allies and isolate myself from the politics. We developed a process to get information out there and to educate neighborhood councils. We went through the process, formed various workgroups, and negotiated out provisions that we couldn't live with. We kept things that weren't exactly in our interests.
>
> We looked at the L&D forum MOU and saw that we couldn't do exactly what they did. Our department couldn't come out with a neighborhood by neighborhood plan. Our concern is how clean is the water, not how many miles of pipeline run through a neighborhood.

The distinction between the two MOUs, both in terms of process and outcome, are evident. One was mutually designed by citizens and administrators, and the other was used as a tool to enhance neighborhood council power in the administrative environment. One was developed through deliberation and collaboration; the other was the product of adversarial conflict. The learning effects of the mutually designed MOU were muted by the adversarial approach in a hastily adopted format that achieved narrow interests. Interestingly, it very well may be that a mutually designed MOU with the new department would have come to the same solution, but by neglecting the process, both citizens and administrators missed an opportunity to deepen their relationships, as reported by L&D participants.

A second example of adopting the MOU format was in evidence in fall 2005 where a small ad hoc formation committee came together to facilitate yet a different department MOU. Again, this approach started with the adoption of the MOU template and not with the practice of mutual deliberation and learning as outlined in the L&D sessions.

Third-Order Collaborative Effects

Long-term interactions can be understood in two ways: those that are continuous and those that are sustained. The former can be thought of as a pattern of ongoing communication and interaction among partners that are prescribed through specific agreements established in a memorandum. Sustained interaction is not limited by time, nor is it dependent on the actions of specific people. Sustainable relationships rely upon established agreements but move well beyond these requirements into a pattern of innovation and creativity that deepens relationships and becomes a pattern of community interaction that is anticipated, expected, and trusted. This depth of relationship is consistent with Innes and Booher's (1999) third-order effects.

There are considerable, perhaps insurmountable, obstacles to building sustainable relationships among administrative officials and citizens in a dynamic urban environment. First, the culture and leadership of administrative agencies vary in terms of their support for responsiveness toward citizens (Bryer and Cooper 2007), thus making expectations in citizen–administrator interactions inconsistent across agencies. Second, neighborhood councils vary in their capacity to form and maintain active relationships due to turnover of board members, inconsistent committee structures, and the number of active board members. Our findings suggest confirmation of these constraints to continuous and sustainable relationships but also suggest opportunities for the growth of relationships.

In each of the three cases, participants found the experience to be an opportunity to change existing relationships between neighborhood council representatives and department personnel. In the three cases, department participants find the interactions to provide an opportunity for a changed relationship where they could "see people as individuals," "develop friendships," establish a "communication link," and "break down barriers" with neighborhood council participants. One department participant observes that there was a "change on the neighborhood council part," while another reports that he did not "know if there are fruitful changes . . . (but) . . . I want to be more in tune with their needs; I want to do a good job." Neighborhood council participants find that the forums increased departmental "appreciation for us," and that there are better relations, "because I know people, I have attached a name to a face." Other neighborhood council participants report that there are now "better communications," and "we understand better how [the department] operate[s]."

Only the first of the three cases led to a signed memorandum of understanding (MOU) between a department and neighborhood councils. Participants involved in developing the formal agreement were interviewed after implementation of the agreement concerning the nature of the continuous relationship. Four themes emerged from these implementation interviews: (1) meaningful relationships formed during the L&D sessions but dissipated over time, (2) leadership support and neighborhood council capacity are central factors for maintaining relationships over time, (3) some department employees and neighborhood council members were instrumental in MOU implementation, and (4) implementation does not require changes in governance structures or processes to be successful.

The initial relationships formed as a result of the L&D sessions established meaningful links among participants, but these relationships dissipated over time. Upon completion of L&D forums, department officials report a "really good" relationship where "we have a clear idea [of] responsibility for each other." What is also evident is that developing a longer-term relationship is a challenge. Approximately one year after the L&D sessions were completed and MOU agreements needed to be implemented, departmental officials report that "we saw progress [yet] something dies, they changed board members [and] we did not hear from them for a long time." From the department officials' perspective, neighborhood council leadership turnover was an obstacle in developing a stronger relationship. "We saw the neighborhood councils again, but we did not see the same people attending." When department officials provided materials related to the original mutually designed agreements to newly appointed neighborhood council members, the department expected them to report back on neighborhood priorities, "but it never happened." While neighborhood council members report that there is no "downside to the relationship" and "we know each other very well," there is no follow-through with neighborhood council reports on community needs or priorities. As one neighborhood council member reported, "The relationship is still excellent . . . the problem that needs to be overcome is that the neighborhood councils are going through change and learning."

Two factors influence effective implementation: departmental leadership support and neighborhood council capacity. Department participants reported that departmental leadership support and commitment enhanced agreement implementation. Neighborhood council representatives viewed the leadership of department officials and their direct involvement as keys to agreement implementation. On the other hand, the lack of neighborhood council capacity limited departmental ability to follow through with their implementation obligations. As one departmental participant observes, "We got the job done . . . the process was very successful until we put the ball in the neighborhood council court." Another reports, "we provide[d] 87 new neighborhood council assessments [and] nobody gave us a response." Another reports that "the workload of the neighborhood councils, the pressure of current activities and the magnitude of trying to understand and comment on the workload of the department have impeded the implementation of the entire MOU." A neighborhood council respondent feels the councils "had a difficult time getting committees up and going"; another reports that neighborhood councils "lack experience."

In addition to top department leadership support and involvement, department heads and neighborhood council members played central roles in implementing the MOU. Both department and neighborhood council members mentioned individuals that were central to making the relationship work. One neighborhood council representative notes, "I do not want to mention the specific people, everybody is important who has an idea."

Both departmental and neighborhood council representatives reported that changes in department processes or neighborhood council by-laws are not necessary to facilitate implementation. One department respondent indicates that "nothing needs to be changed, we do not have to re-write chapters in the book, maybe re-read some chapters." Another reports, "Everything begins with good communication"; another says, "We need constant educating and communication with each other." Another reports that "neighborhood councils should provide ongoing contact—people who deal with [department] concerns [and who] work with the department and report back to the neighborhood councils." Neighborhood council members report that there is no need for further revision of council by-laws to improve implementation. Instead, a respondent reports the "neighborhood council could probably take more advantage of the MOU than they have . . . it is the general sense of our board that [department personnel] are experts, it is not good for us to interfere."

Overall, in the case noted above, the fluid nature of neighborhood council leadership and the inability of neighborhood councils to organize useful responses to department information are key obstacles in implementing mutual agreements. These factors will limit the ability of participants to develop sustainable relationships in the future.

CONCLUSION

The results of the three cases of the L&D sessions have varied outcomes, including formal agreements, agreements on hold, and citywide spillover effects. Our research indicates several benefits to creating mutual knowledge for action, including exposing unwarranted assumptions, building trust and mutual understanding, and forming actionable agreements.

There are also challenges in employing action research strategies. These challenges include the selection of participants, the significance of communication and facilitation skills during the L&D sessions, the challenge of relationship building and the sustainability of relationships, the creation of capacity, trust, and empowerment, the role of self-learning and reflection in research, the intentional influence of research on practice, and communication of participant interests during action research. Each of these challenges has the potential to influence the outcomes of the action research project. The role of a facilitator, for example, can influence the nature of dialogue among participants, thus shaping the outcome of the participation. These and other examples will be explored in a future study.

In addition to observing various outcomes and assessing challenges in action research that facilitated citizen-centered collaborative public management, this study raises questions for future theoretical and empirical study. These are as follows:

- How can trust bonds that begin to develop in administrator–citizen collaboration be sustained and developed further? This question is based on the finding that trust developed for some participants during the L&D process but seemed to dissipate with the passage of time as regular communication ceased to occur.
- A possible answer to this question might be found in network theory, with a further question: What is the ideal network structure in the design phase of collaboration for developing trust, and what is the ideal network structure in the implementation phase of collaboration for moving toward sustainable identification-based trust?
- A challenge observed in the study is the high rate of turnover among neighborhood council members, which made implementation of the agreement in the first case difficult. Department officials fulfilled their part of the agreement but found that the people with whom they collaborated in the councils were no longer active. How can neighborhood councils or similar community groups incentivize and structure the

creation and maintenance of institutional memory in order to ensure that collaborative relationships are not based on personal relationships alone?

- Last, how can public administrators manage their various stakeholder relationships in order to be fully responsive to citizens with whom they are collaborating? Is there a particular organization structure that needs to be in place for this kind of responsiveness? How should cultural norms be developed to promote responsiveness to citizens without sacrificing responsiveness to other legitimate actors in the governance process?

These questions suggest several challenging issues to confront theoretically, empirically, and practically. We offer some lessons that might begin to answer some of these questions. First, the administrative state can be opened to participation with citizens through the use of action research focused on collaborative learning. Second, we can expect that responses by administrators within an action research program will vary according to the agency culture, agency leadership, and perceived salience of the participating citizens by agency officials (Bryer and Cooper 2007). In order to stand a better chance of opening the administrative state to citizen participation, action research should be sensitive to the particular political, cultural, and technical biases of each participating agency. Finally, the barriers to successful completion or implementation of the MOUs drafted in each case suggest the importance of including other relevant political actors, such as key agency heads, elected city council members, and appointed commission leadership in the project from the beginning. This might ensure that needed resources are made available for the participating agency, and it might ensure that a completed MOU is actually pushed through to implementation. Such assurances can help move collaborative partnerships from the first-order outcomes described by Innes and Booher (1999) to the second- and third-order outcomes that are more difficult to achieve without commitments and resources from relevant political actors.

We have found that democratizing the administrative state with the designed use of smaller units of deliberative administrative–citizen bodies is a bigger challenge than we had thought. While our model has produced some modest effects, the model and experience also informed us of some real weaknesses in this approach even when deemed successful in the signing of an MOU.

We have found that the iterative deliberation process to produce collaboration, in the terms that are set forth in a written MOU, may not go far enough. One of our conclusions is that along with our L&D process there is a need for extended organizational development for both neighborhood councils and city departments. On both sides, this extended organizational development process would focus on capacity building to provide an opportunity where both types of organizations would become more supportive of participation in a sustained fashion. The idea behind this strategy is to move the current relationships from a continuous relationship (or what Innes and Booher [1999] refer to as a first-order effect of collaborative planning) to a sustainable relationship (a third-order effect of collaborative planning).

We have learned from our three cases that this L&D process is useful but not sufficient for fully democratizing the administrative state. Our current thinking is that there is an extended sequence of activities that need to be included if citizens' organizations like neighborhood councils are to be able to realize democratic participation with the administrative state. For instance, targeted organizational development (OD) can provide support to further the capacity of neighborhood councils and city agencies to successfully participate in collaborative activity. The precise nature of the organizational development process (i.e., implementation and design) is likely to be dependent on the unique circumstances of specific groups of neighborhood councils and city agencies. Our preliminary thinking, whatever the OD design, is that such work would have to start on the neighborhood council side to make councils more viable and legitimate actors in the policy arena. Doing so will raise the profile of the councils in the eyes of departmental leadership and elected officials, thus raising the stakes of participation and extending possible outcomes for both city agencies and neighborhood councils. Without this first step, developing the capacity of city agencies to collaborate might not bear fruit due to the lack of overall importance given to neighborhood councils by agency officials.

In summary, we suggest through our analysis that the administrative state can be challenged, as evidenced by findings from our action research, but longer-term and sustained involvement by the academic researchers or other professionals is necessary to generate higher-order outcomes associated with collaboration. We have demonstrated the potential through our limited pilot projects for strengthening the role of citizens within the bureaucracy, but future work will need to examine the mechanisms for further advancing and sustaining the potential that has been realized.

NOTES

The authors are grateful to reviewers of the draft for helpful comments and guidance.

1. A fourth case was planned for the CLP, but the department designated by neighborhood councils was unwilling to commit the necessary staff resources to make the collaborative process possible.

2. "Trust needs to evolve, and we are willing to work at it"; "Neighborhood councils are generally receptive . . . [but there are a] few individuals [who] tend to be rather negative challenging our recommendations and claiming that we did not hear them"; "The more we interact, the more we have trust. However our interaction is sometimes hindered by the vested interests who lobby neighborhood councils to push us for certain measures"; "There are things that [neighborhood councils] want to accomplish, and you have to be concerned: does it deal with the whole neighborhood or just 'my particular street'? But if you're not helping them, then [you hear]: 'I don't want to talk to you anymore.'"

3. A comment from one neighborhood participant captures this dynamic: "I wish the people from [the department] would have made more effort to get to know the neighborhood councils. It was too obvious that they hated being there, and that is just too sad. [There were two department participants who] were the only people from [the department] who opened up and talked and stayed after the session was over. The rest of the [department] I couldn't even catch to say thank you to, that's how fast they ran out the door. The [department] seems to have seen these sessions as more work."

REFERENCES

Agranoff, Robert, and Michael McGuire. 2003. *Collaborative Public Management: New Strategies for Local Governments*. Washington, DC: Georgetown University Press.

Argyris, Chris. 1993. *Knowledge for Action. A Guide To Overcoming Barriers To Organizational Change*. San Francisco: Jossey-Bass.

Box, Richard C., and Juliet A. Musso. 2004. "Experiments with Local Federalism: Secession and the Neighborhood Council Movement in Los Angeles." *American Review of Public Administration* 34: 259–76.

Bryer, Thomas A. 2006. "Stakeholder Approach to Bureaucratic Responsiveness: A Network Based Framework to Analyze Public Administrator Value Preferences." *International Journal of Organization Theory and Behavior* 9, no. 4: 557–77.

———. 2007. "Toward a Relevant Agenda for a Responsive Public Administration." *Journal of Public Administration Research & Theory* 17, no. 3: 479–500.

Bryer, Thomas A., and Terry L. Cooper. 2007. "Challenges in Enhancing Responsiveness in Neighborhood Governance." *Public Performance and Management Review* 31, no. 2: 191-214.

Cigler, Beverly A. 1999. "Pre-Conditions for the Emergence of Multi-Community Collaborative Projects." *Policy Studies Review* 16, no. 1: 86–102.

Cooper, Terry L. 2005. "Civic Engagement in the Twenty-first Century: Toward a Scholarly and Practical Agenda." *Public Administration Review* 65, no. 5: 534–35.

Cooper, Terry L., and Pradeep Chandra Kathi. 2005. "Neighborhood Councils and City Agencies: A Model of Collaborative Co-Production." *National Civic Review* 94, no. 1: 43–53.

Cooper, Terry L., and Juliet A. Musso. 1999. "The Potential for Neighborhood Council Involvement in American Metropolitan Governance." *International Journal of Organization Theory and Behavior* 1, no. 2: 199–232.

Cooper, Terry L.; Thomas A. Bryer; and Jack W. Meek. 2006. "Citizen-Centered Collaborative Public Management." *Public Administration Review* (Special Issue): 76–88.

Dewey, John. 1929. *The Public and Its Problems*. New York: Holt.

Hogen-Esch, Tom. 2001. "Urban Secession and the Politics of Growth: The Case of Los Angeles." *Urban Affairs Review* 36: 783–809.

Innes, Judith, and David Booher. 1999. "Consensus Building and Complex Adaptive Systems: A Framework for Evaluating Collaborative Planning." *Journal of the American Planning Association* 65, no. 4 (Autumn): 412–23.

Kathi, Pradeep C., and Terry L. Cooper. 2005. "Democratizing the Administrative State." *Public Administration Review* 65, no. 5: 559–67.

King, Cheryl S., and Camilla Stivers. 1998. *Government Is Us: Public Administration in an Anti-Government Era*. Thousand Oaks, CA: Sage.

Lewicki, Roy J. 2006. "Trust, Trust Development, and Trust Repair." In *The Handbook of Conflict Resolution: Theory and Practice*, ed. Morton Deutsch, Peter T. Coleman, and Eric C. Marcus, 92–119. San Francisco: Jossey-Bass.

Musso, Juliet A.; Chris Weare; and Terry L. Cooper. 2004. NPP Diversity Report. Los Angeles, CA: Neighborhood Participation Project, University of Southern California.

Nye, Joseph S.; Philip D. Zelidow; and David C. King, eds. 1997. *Why People Don't Trust Government*. Cambridge, MA: Harvard University Press.

Robertson, Peter J., and Shui-Yan Tang. 1995. "The Role of Commitment in Collective Action: Comparing the Organizational Behavior and Rational Choice Perspectives." *Public Administration Review* 55, no. 1: 67–80.

Sonenshein, Raphael J., and Tom Hogen-Esch. 2006. "Bringing the State (Government) Back in: Home Rule and the Politics of Secession in Los Angeles and New York City." *Urban Affairs Review* 41, no. 4: 467–91.

Yang, Kaifeng. 2005. "Public Administrators' Trust in Citizens: A Missing Link in Citizen Involvement Efforts." *Public Administration Review* 65, no. 3: 273-85.

Yankelovich, Daniel. 1991. *Coming to Public Judgment: Making Democracy Work in a Complex World*. Syracuse, NY: Syracuse University Press.

CHAPTER 12

The Space Station and Multinational Collaboration
A Merger of Domestic and Foreign Policy

W. HENRY LAMBRIGHT AND CARLA PIZZARELLA

On January 25, 1984, in his State of the Union address, President Ronald Reagan announced, "Tonight, I am directing NASA to develop a permanently manned space station and to do it within a decade." He said such a station had potential for "research in science, communications, in metals, and in lifesaving medicines which could be manufactured only in space." Then he declared, "We want our friends to help us meet these challenges and share in their benefits. NASA will invite other countries to participate so we can strengthen peace, build prosperity, and expand freedom for all who share our goals" (McCurdy 1990, 190).

Amid the flowery rhetoric was the basic decision that the National Aeronautics and Space Administration (NASA) was to develop a permanently occupied space station in ten years with international partners. How different this decision was from Kennedy's Apollo challenge! Apollo was a pure *national* project; this was intended from the outset to be one NASA would run with allies.

In the year 2008, the space station is still unfinished, while collaboration with allies has continued. However, the most significant change in organization of the project is that a competitor in 1984, Russia, is a collaborator today. Sixteen nations are collaborating on a football-field-sized structure that will weigh close to one million pounds and have a capacity to house at least six astronauts. This facility, for which the United States has spent approximately $40 billion so far, is the most expensive civilian international science and technology project in history (Cookson 2005, 4).[1] More important, the space station represents a breed of collaboration that is bound to become more prevalent in the years ahead—multinational cooperation in very large, long-term, and complex projects involving new technology development and having global political and economic ramifications.

There is no question that existing public problems and those on the horizon demand actions that are international and in some cases global. These problems—energy development, climate change, biodiversity loss, and emergent diseases—transcend state and national borders. Public managers in the United States (and elsewhere) will have to think

230

about domestic and cross-national constituencies at once. The world is getting smaller as issues become vaster. This chapter deals with collaborative public management in the multinational context via a case study that illuminates both possibilities and dilemmas of joint activity.

APPROACH

Our interest is in how multinational projects are put together, sustained, altered, or completed. To get at this matter, we use political and administrative analysis, including leadership and coalition building. The literature on collaborative public management has yet to address this question in depth in terms of large-scale, international science and technology projects. There is valuable work by scholars on infrastructure projects at the regional scale—transportation systems, dams, buildings, and even malls (Agranoff and McGuire 2003). These cases are important, as the recent problems of the "Big Dig" tunnel project in Boston or failures of New Orleans dikes attest. While technological in nature, they have been accomplished before, if on a smaller scale. With projects like the space station, we are dealing with projects new to the world, first of a kind. They entail matters beyond political and economic uncertainty—they may not be technically feasible, at least as their originators envisioned. They are often called "Big Science" to emphasize their "frontier" quality and involvement of scientists and engineers. Nations engage in them because they respond to problems and opportunities that are inherently large and cross-boundary; nations may not have the money to afford them individually; and there may be foreign policy reasons that argue for collaboration.

We extend collaboration research to the international setting and technological projects. Public administration scholars have identified key concepts in collaborative public management through work that is predominantly domestic and oriented to social service delivery. This material is relevant to our work. As others in this volume show, it is extremely difficult to start and maintain collaborative ventures. To succeed, structures of collaboration must have "stability," but they also need to be "adaptive" (Milward and Provan 2000). Many public management scholars stress the leadership dimension of successful and unsuccessful collaboration. Agranoff and McGuire (2003) among many others show how leaders must deal with conflicting forces effecting collaboration. Milward and Provan (2000) indicate that leaders use both directive and consensual approaches. Within this volume, Provan, Kenis, and Human (chapter 7) point to leaders engendering legitimacy for the collaboration in terms of an entity in and of itself. In successful collaborations, partners learn together, develop a "common language," and "shared vision" (Abrahamson, Breul, and Kamensky 2006).

All the above concepts, drawn mainly from the domestic literature, including chapters featured in this book, also apply to multinational projects. The difference is that everything moves to a larger scale in money, actors, and stakes. Moreover, when projects are multinational, the relations within the network become far more complicated owing to sovereignty of the partners. International relations scholars write of "power and interdependence," as the title of a well-known text with this name points out. They discuss such concepts usually in terms of alliances, conflict, and diplomacy (Keohane and Nye 2001). They typically do not look at projects from a management standpoint except in cases of international assistance and development. Multinational projects require penetrating beyond policy formation to the thicket of implementation. Yet, the experiences and outcomes of such projects have direct bearing on international ties and will likely influence how nations approach future collaborative endeavors. They merge domestic politics and foreign policy.

Our analysis emphasizes leadership as the lever on multinational collaboration. It also builds on the work of Doig and Hargrove (1990); Sabatier and Jenkins-Smith (1999); True, Jones, and Baumgartner (1999). Doig and Hargrove (1990) have dealt with leadership; Sabatier and Jenkins-Smith (1999) with coalition-building. True, Jones, and Baumgartner (1999) have contributed studies of "punctuated-equilibrium theory" in accounting for stability and change in policymaking. Leadership makes for change.

We also apply literature on project management from the business administration field. Corporations have increasingly become actors on the global scene as they have gone multinational in scale. This business literature identifies key factors in success of projects that cut across national boundaries. Taken as a whole, this literature shows that projects having certain attributes—such as the need to embrace very diverse cultures, deal with extremely innovative technology, cope with high expense, and maneuver despite economic and political instability—are especially hard to complete (Barnes, Pashby, and Gibbons 2006; Moody and Dodgson 2006; Pownall 1997; Shenhar 1998; Shore and Cross 2005). Issues of trust and commitment loom large. Research in project management and public administration alike find effective leadership to be an important variable in successful collaboration (Bardach 1998; Barnes, Pashby, and Gibbons 2006). Specifically, the existence of a "collaboration champion" through the life of the project is a critical factor (Barnes, Pashby, and Gibbons 2006). More than just a "product champion" whose interest lies in the promotion of the technology, the collaboration champion has a keen interest in sustaining the partnership. The project management literature deals with leadership within the collaborative project team. We extend this concept to the greater political environment. As we see it, the leader becomes a "co-developer," building both a technological system and a coalition of actors to sustain it.[2] At the same time, one system influences and helps shape the other.

As we will indicate, the space station can be conceived as two projects: Space Station Freedom (1984–93) and the International Space Station (ISS) (1993–present). Freedom and the ISS differ because they embody divergent policy interests. The policies are different because the coalitional politics behind them vary. The coalition includes the administrative collaborators—the agencies and others actually implementing the work. It also includes the political actors and others in the project's environment whose support is essential to get the resources to pursue the work. As will be discussed further, the change in the administrative collaborators, namely, the addition of the Russian Space Agency (RSA), enlarged the political support for the initiative.

The policy environment surrounding the space station altered dramatically with the end of the Cold War. The transition from Cold War to post–Cold War was a "punctuation point" in the evolution of space station policy. This enabled NASA as leader (in cooperation with others) to forge and sustain a new partnership with the RSA. Russia's entry into the multinational project changed the leadership strategy of NASA as well as the larger coalitional politics. It created a new equilibrium of interests that has moved the project to the present point. As we will illustrate, collaboration with Europe, Canada, and Japan under Reagan was set forth as a goal but was more of an afterthought than a presidential priority when he made the decision. For Clinton, collaboration with the Russians was much more than a means to an end. It was an end in itself. The space station possessed virtually all the attributes that would seem to destine it for termination, yet it has succeeded in surviving since 1984. The fact that there has been a collaboration champion, a role filled by different actors along the way, helps explain this sustainability in the face of adversity. With projects of this magnitude, leadership requires mobilization of political will, a capacity that resides outside the administrative collaboration structure.

In order to appreciate the significance of the policy change, it is essential to track the historical dynamics of the space station. As we will show, Space Station Freedom represented a Cold War project. The ISS represents a model of post–Cold War science with profound implications for the organization of science and technology in the twenty-first century.

SPACE STATION FREEDOM

There were Cold War rationales, reminiscent of Apollo, when President Reagan made his pro–space station decision in 1984. He wanted to demonstrate U.S. willingness and ability to surpass the Soviet Union in space-station building. The Soviet Union had a modest station in orbit and was building a larger successor. But unlike Apollo, which had an almost unlimited budget, the space station started with an $8 billion estimate. Reagan had higher priorities, mostly in defense, with his Strategic Defense Initiative (Star Wars). The space station was civilian. The reality was that $8 billion would just get the station started. NASA administrator James Beggs emphasized that getting a station was possible for that figure. The question was what kind of station, how big, with what facilities for research and manufacture? The Reagan decision called for scientific and economic uses. Collaborators could make possible a much larger station by their investments. Finally, NASA believed international connections could better assure the project's survival domestically, owing to U.S. obligations abroad. Hence, there were a number of reasons for the United States to collaborate (McCurdy 1990, ch. 2; for interplay of domestic and international politics in foreign policy, see Putman 1988).

Why should other nations—Europe, Japan, Canada, in particular—want to collaborate? Space agencies in allied nations viewed the space station as the flagship for the world in manned spaceflight. To participate meant prestige and also learning, since the station would be a cutting-edge technology project. To participate at that time could mean greater technological autonomy later. Also, participation could indirectly pay economically valuable dividends through technology transfer (Kringe 2006).

And so the project began, eventually with the name "Freedom." It took until 1988 for the United States and its allies to work out their differences and enter into a formal alliance. The single biggest issue was technology transfer (Lambright and Schaefer 2004). NASA wanted to minimize technology sharing, whereas partners wanted to obtain as much technical know-how as possible. The project accommodated different perspectives by becoming *transnational*. NASA was to build the framework of the station, and allies would later add their modules. As Sadeh (2004) has written, the allies provided "augmentations" to a basic structure. This allowed compartmentalizing technology as much as possible. The nations would build their equipment in their own countries, with their own contractors, and this equipment would come together in space. Compartmentalizing enabled the United States to limit technology transfer. The United States was the dominant or managing partner not only in providing the framework but also in integrating components into a system and by enabling assembly. Only the U.S. Space Shuttle could carry the heavy equipment into orbit.

For many reasons, including the Challenger Shuttle accident in 1986, there were delays, redesigns and cost overruns throughout the latter 1980s and into the 1990s. Some of the most significant reasons related to issues in intra-NASA collaboration and congressional pressure. Reagan's interest in the Space Station Freedom was fleeting. Early on, Beggs had to look to Congress for support. Congress oversaw NASA through parochial eyes. This congressional perspective gave the various field centers leverage. Moreover, Congress micromanaged the project. The technical problems were bad enough, but the management and political issues made the space station's situation worse. By 1993, when Bill Clinton became president, Space Station Freedom had cost the United States $10 billion and had little or no hardware developed, nothing in space (Madison and McCurdy 1999).

THE INTERNATIONAL SPACE STATION

Clinton considered cancellation and ordered redesign and scaling back. His NASA administrator, Dan Goldin, had a radical design plan in mind that he believed would save money and get a space station up sooner than other options considered. The international partners, who had invested considerably in parts depending upon the existing design, argued strenuously against radical change. NASA contractors and lawmakers from states with commitments also opposed change. Clinton decided to keep the station but save money through scaling back its size. The overall congressional support for the station had meanwhile declined so much that the House of Representatives in June came within one vote of terminating the project.[3]

Space Station Freedom had been promoted at the outset as a front of the Cold War. The Soviet Union had a space station, and Reagan believed the United States and its allies had to have one, too. It was a matter of competition. Now the Cold War was over. What was its rationale? Goldin and the Russian Space Agency head, Yuri Koptev, decided that the station's rationale should be that of a symbol of post–Cold War cooperation. The Russian and American space station programs could merge. The unpopular Space Station Freedom would "end," and the new International Space Station (ISS) "begin."

What this meant was that the framework for ISS would be a U.S.–Russian station, with the other nations enhancing this structure *after* the U.S.–Russian core was built. This new design would be much more "interdependent" in nature (Sadeh 2004). The United States and Russians would share know-how. The Russians actually had far more experience than the Americans in station building. The technology transfer issues that came up with Freedom were not the dominant ones with ISS. This time there was a different technology transfer issue. Clinton and Gore wanted to have the Russians work with America to prevent their missile and other weapons technology from flowing to U.S. enemies. The space station was thus an instrument of U.S. arms control as well as space policy in the post–Cold War setting. Indeed, for the White House, State Department, and National Security Council, the space station was a vehicle for drawing the Russians into the U.S. camp. The Clinton administration advocated a "strategic" partnership—a concept that raised the space station to a program of higher policy value. Reagan had framed the space station in foreign policy also but had allowed it to become just another space program mired in bureaucratic congressional interest-group bargaining. Clinton made ISS a presidential priority and, primarily through Gore, provided critical backing during the implementation process. Goldin had enlisted the White House in the station coalition, whereas Beggs was more dependent on Congress for support. In 1993, Clinton and congressional leaders agreed to "stabilize" station funding.

The Reagan station goals were thus adapted under Clinton. The ISS was now projected to be fully assembled by 2001 for $17.4 billion beyond what Freedom had already cost. NASA would get $2.1 billion per year for at least the ensuing five-year period and work within that funding envelope. That figure was part of the political understanding for stabilizing the program. The funding was a domestic-political bargain undergirding the foreign policy decision.

Goldin and Koptev developed a close informal relation as they managed the cross-cultural learning and technological development process over the 1990s. This cross-cultural learning was difficult, but taken seriously. U.S. astronauts trained in Russia. Russian cosmonauts trained in the United States. The United States supplied money for technical assistance. Most important in cementing the relationship was "reciprocity." There were quid pro quos that built trust over the 1990s (see Axelrod 1984).

Instead of saving money and speeding the project, as Goldin declared initially, however, Russian involvement cost the United States money and slowed the project down. In going from Freedom's *trans*national to a more intense *inter*national model, the United States had to wait for the Russians to develop certain critical parts before it could launch other segments. The first two sections of the station went up in 1998—one component launched by each nation. Then came a two-year wait for an essential Russian module—arguably the most important single module in the whole project since it provided both propulsion and living quarters. The United States had to start developing contingency technology in case the Russians did not come through, and Goldin gave Koptev an ultimatum. The Russians did launch their critical module in 2000, and subsequently two Russians and an American took up residence in what was the U.S.–Russian core of ISS. Along the way, in 1995, the Republicans had come to congressional power, and some had sought to end the U.S.–Russian collaboration but had failed.

When the Bush administration took power in 2001, it discovered ISS in financial turmoil. It delayed adding international partner components while the United States got its own financial and technological house in order. Then came the Columbia Shuttle accident in 2003, an event that set the project back even further. The number of astronauts in the station was cut from three to two in order to conserve supplies. Russia, which had been criticized, now was praised for providing astronaut transportation via Soyuz rockets to and from the station. In 2000, suspicious that Russia was transferring weapons-relevant technology to Iran, Congress passed legislation preventing U.S. payments to Russia for space station work. With the shuttle down, NASA and the Bush administration pressed Congress to rescind this legislation so it could reimburse Russia for its transportation services. They succeeded in 2005. In spite of challenges and tests throughout the period from 1993, the U.S.–Russian collaboration had held firm, and the larger political coalition with it. Sustaining it had been a significant achievement in administrative leadership for Goldin and his successors.

With the successful test flights of the shuttle in the summer of 2006, there was expectation that at long last assembly of ISS would resume. The international partners who had literally been waiting for years, and invested billions, now had hope they would finally get aboard by the year targeted for completion, 2010.

OUTCOMES

Has the space station been a success or failure so far in terms of its objectives? We have to look at the original 1984 goals of the project and then the reorientation in 1993. We also have to consider unstated goals. The primary technical goal was to build a permanently inhabited station in a decade. The figure $8 billion was used as the cost. Another goal was to construct this station so that it would yield scientific and economic benefits. An additional goal was to build the station collaboratively, as a beacon of the free world vis-à-vis the "evil empire" of the Soviet Union.

Only a beginning in achieving goals took place with the Freedom Station. Agreements for collaboration were consummated, a political coalition undergirding it created, but assembly of a space station was not begun. The International Space Station introduced new goals and targets. The deadline became 2001; the cost was put at $17.4 billion beyond that paid for Freedom. The science and manufacturing goals remained. Collaboration changed, with Russia assuming a more intensive relation than had been the case with other nations.

By 2001, a core space station was in orbit and inhabited, perhaps permanently. Some science had been accomplished, but no manufacturing. The collaboration with Russia had proved essential in getting ISS up and keeping it occupied after Columbia. The cost and deadline goals for a completed station proved to be overly optimistic. Collaboration continues to be a prime means and goal, with additions of other nations' modules to complete the station in 2010. Post–Cold War cooperation with Russia replaced Cold War competition as an objective.

A critical Clinton aim in 1993 was to orient Russia to the West, have Russian technical personnel working on ISS rather than selling missile know-how to enemies. This was accomplished to some degree. Russia did become part of an antiproliferation regime, but some critics believe Russia has violated its pledge. An unstated goal of NASA throughout has been to keep its organization viable through a major manned space program. NASA has been successful on this score. Also, understated until 2004, was the intent to build the space station as a stepping stone to the Moon and Mars. It would be a place from which to learn about long-duration effects on man in space and eventually serve as an assembly point or base camp for exploration missions beyond Earth orbit. That latter objective remains ahead to be realized, but now has a chance for fruition.

Since ISS is still incomplete, a definitive statement about success and failure is impossible. Indeed, there are serious policy questions ahead in 2010 when ISS passes from assembly to utilization, development to operations. The record thus far is mixed. The space station appears to be a technical success and financial failure. But cost and scheduling issues may fade if the scientific and manufacturing objectives are attained. That will take a completed station, one with the full complement of six astronauts possessing the needed skills.

Multinational collaboration as a goal has been tested and so far has stood the test of time. The Russians were slow, but came through with their critical components. They especially showed their mettle as a partner after Columbia. Without question, the Russians caused delays in the building process, but without the Russians, there might not have been a building process after 1993. The fourteen other nations involved in the project have been amazingly patient. If the ISS is finished as planned, it will be a monument to international cooperation and persistence in large-scale science and technology, one from which much can be learned for better and worse. Collaboration may be ISS's most significant legacy. Mike Griffin recently stated, "If we are unable to complete the project that we have before us, the space station, we will have a certain lack of credibility in encouraging others to join us in the exploration of the Moon and Mars. So it's important to finish what we have started" (Morring 2006, 62).

KEY FACTORS

What key factors explained these outcomes? As emphasized, the space station has had two lives—as Freedom (1984–93) and as ISS (1993–present). It is now in the "later-implementation to completion" stage of development. In one life it was a *trans*national project—a U.S. project with foreign enhancements. In the second, it was *inter*national in the sense of having intense interdependency between the United States and Russia. The political coalition surrounding it was more congressionally oriented under Freedom, and more presidentially oriented with ISS. This is not to say that Clinton was personally involved in the oversight of the program, but he gave it a presidential imprimatur that influenced the behavior of others—Gore, the State Department, the Office of Management and Budget, and even Congress.

The space station experience demonstrates that certain elements must converge for the project to be sustained. There are technical, organizational, domestic, and foreign forces that influence the outcomes of a multinational project. Leadership is critical in moving the project toward its goals. Below is a model of leadership's role in managing a multinational project. It builds on numerous studies of leadership and government executives (Doig and Hargrove 1990; Radin 2002; Riccucci 1995; Wilson 1989). The most striking

Figure 12.1   **Model of Multinational Project Management**

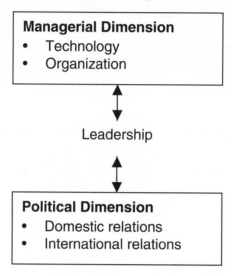

difference between the existing literature and our study of the space station is the inclusion of a foreign connection and its interaction with other elements. The emphases of the model can change over time, with some factors necessitating greater leadership attention than others. At a given point, a leader may concentrate on one factor, but he or she must be cognizant of the totality of interrelationships. As stated earlier, the leader must think in terms of "co-development." He or she is developing a technological system and political coalition at once and in mutual support of each other. The larger the technology, the greater the coalition.

Figure 12.1 presents four factors of multinational project management and the role of leadership in bringing them together. The model may suggest far greater convergence and control than is possible in reality. Below is a discussion of these factors in terms of the space station experience.

Technology

In project management terms, the space station would be classified as a "super-high-tech" project, as it requires development of new technologies or deployment of existing technologies on a scale and in a place wholly novel (Shenhar 1998). Such projects carry high levels of uncertainty and involve extensive testing of alternatives. As with other collaborative R&D projects, the most important technical issues for the space station had to do with design and technology transfer (Moody and Dodgson 2006). Freedom was designed rather straightforwardly in the sense that the United States built a framework and Europe, Canada, and Japan added enhancements. The United States sought to limit the transfer of knowledge to the other countries. Technology transfer was minimized by compartmentalizing the work via "clean interfaces."

In ISS, the United States and Russia merged technical concepts and added a separate phase—called Shuttle-MIR—in which the former adversaries learned about respective technologies, cultural differences, and how to work with one another. These cultural differences were important, and included how each nation dealt with risk. Russians and Americans resolved crises aboard MIR—a fire and collision—that threatened lives. The prime technology transfer issue for the United States had to do with keeping the Russians from selling weapons (chiefly missile) technology to U.S. enemies. The United States (NASA) provided funds for technical assistance, a vehicle also for employing Russian scientists and engineers who might otherwise have looked elsewhere for work. The price Russia paid for joining ISS was signing the Missile Technology Control Regime—a pact critics in Congress believed Russia later violated. While the United States learned about MIR, Russia gained technical knowledge about the space shuttle.

Organization

Systems integration represents a major management problem for a technological project, especially one on the frontier of knowledge (Moody and Dodgson 2006). In this case, we have integration within the agency and between the agency and other space agencies in various countries. The systems created in different countries have to be assembled in space for the first time. In some ways, therefore, the space station represents the ultimate in systems integration.

A project organization was created to administer the effort. The United States was the lead nation and NASA the lead agency. Within NASA, the Freedom model was multicenter and decentralized. To get the field centers aboard as internal collaborators, Beggs used a decentralized management system in which four centers had their own "work packages" and their own contractors. They were coordinated by a separate, new center in Reston, Virginia. These centers brought in their congressional constituents, but the cumbersome organization created a management complexity that exacerbated cost and slippage. This model was abandoned for ISS, and Johnson Space Center (JSC) in Houston was made "lead" center and Boeing prime contractor. The Reston "coordinator" center was eliminated. The NASA administrator and JSC director worked closely on an informal basis, until late in the decade.

When Russia joined the project, it was formally placed under the United States/NASA. But informally, Russia was an equal, at least until the U.S.–Russian core structure was up. Russia's informal power continued when Columbia disintegrated. There was understandable resentment on the part of other collaborating nations that had to wait longer to get their own modules in orbit and were thereby treated (at least informally) as lesser partners.

Domestic Relations

The long-term nature of a super-high-tech project means that it will most likely span multiple presidential administrations, various Congresses, agency head appointments, and other political shifts. A major challenge in propelling large-scale technology projects from design to completion is sustaining political will (Pownall 1997). Freedom started out with support from the president and Congress, but that presidential support waned quickly after 1984. Reagan looked to military space—Star Wars—and that was where he employed his political capital. Without presidential policy priority, OMB and congressional bargaining drove policy. Congressional support for Freedom was focused in the so-called space states— Texas, Florida, Alabama, and California—where large NASA centers were located and ample contracts existed with industry. High-tech jobs were a key factor in congressional support. NASA's links to traditional allies were used by the White House and NASA, at times, to win votes in periodic congressional tests. The Russians as competitors helped some, but support in Congress atrophied in the years of President George H.W. Bush.

As the Cold War ebbed, Congress looked increasingly to reduce the deficit. Congress almost terminated the space station in 1993. At the same time it came within one vote of cancellation in the House, Congress in fact killed the Department of Energy's top Big Science project, the Superconducting Super Collider, a project lacking significant international backing. NASA came up with a new space station rationale—not competition, but collaboration with Russia. With Clinton's strong backing, a number of Democrats with no connection to the "space states," who might have opposed the station as profligate spending, supported it on foreign policy grounds. It was sold as a way to wean Russia toward U.S. interests, a symbol of post–Cold War cooperation. With Clinton and Gore pressing, the White House and Congress struck a deal—ISS would get priority funding, stable funding, within the NASA budget to get it implemented. Implicitly, even if other programs were cut, the ISS would be protected. ISS was not just a NASA priority, but a national priority.

Remarkably, this spending deal lasted through the 1990s and even beyond to the George W. Bush years. In the latter 1990s, even though some conservative Republicans in Congress turned against the Russian connection and put strictures on it, they continued to vote for the space station. Its greatest domestic political test came in 1993, and since passing that hurdle, ISS has been reasonably secure. The coalition did not unravel, although it required continual tending by NASA's leader.

International Relations

Domestic and international politics blended in ISS. NASA had both a domestic and foreign constituency for the space station. The key international political problem for NASA as space station manager was to keep the pressure on Russia to adhere to its technical promises, while also keeping other partners aboard. As NASA lived with domestic political problems, so did Russia and other nations. Russia, in particular, suffered enormous internal disruptions in the mid- and late 1990s. A policy-level commission headed by Gore and his Russian counterpart, Viktor Chernomyrdin, met regularly during the Clinton era to iron out large policy issues between the two nations. These included ISS. The Russian Space Agency delayed in developing components to ISS in part because of a struggle within Russia over whether to keep MIR alive versus putting money into ISS. Nationalists in Russia did not wish to sacrifice autonomy for a merged project. Some in NASA believed that funds it gave RSA for station work may have been diverted to MIR. Then there was the overriding issue of whether Russia was or was not living up to its Missile Technology Control Regime obligations. There were constant strains, but the administration held fast to the idea that the space station was a "strategic" partnership, part of a broad Russian strategy, aimed at shaping the post–Cold War world, building a new equilibrium of interests.

Nothing involving NASA's relations with other partners came near the challenges it faced with Russia. However, there was one point in 1994 when the project might have lost Canada. Canada, like the United States, had experienced a change in government, and the new government was cutting back in a number of budget categories, including space. Canada was scheduled to supply a technological "arm," extremely useful in station assembly. NASA enlisted Clinton in lobbying Canadian political leadership to keep that nation in the project. NASA also negotiated a reduced and less expensive role for Canada than originally intended, as a compromise. Other nations also adjusted their contributions along the way—none, however, did so in such a manner as to threaten the project's survival. Helping secure the collaboration were formal agreements, in some cases treaties, among the partners. More than intangible trust solidified the relationship.

Leadership

Leadership makes the preceding factors move the project forward. While there is a collective leadership, analysis of the space station also reveals the importance of the individual in galvanizing a multinational project (Lambright 2005). Since 1984, NASA has had a sequence of administrative leaders, each of whom has contributed to keeping this project going and some of whom can rightly be called "collaboration champions." The administrative leader has to give attention to both the management and political dynamics—getting the project implemented while simultaneously mobilizing and maintaining external support.

Beggs sold the project to Reagan and developed the first understandings with foreign partners. He got NASA as an organization aboard in the sense of making the station a priority of a number of centers, and also nurtured initial congressional backing. James Fletcher came back to NASA after an earlier stint in the 1970s to help the agency recover after the Challenger shuttle disaster in 1986. He maintained the station as NASA's flagship even while emphasizing the shuttle's return to flight as his immediate priority. Goldin helped save the program when it might have died in 1993, guiding the redesign process, as part of the merger with the Russian station. He reorganized NASA as overall manager of the project, centralizing power under the Johnson Space Center. His most important political move was to help make and then keep the coalition of support president-centered. Russia was not just a collaborator in a technical project, it was the catalyst in obtaining and sustaining presidential and thus congressional support.

Goldin left a legacy of technical achievement and an intact multinational partnership, but with the station in financial turmoil. Sean O'Keefe came in as NASA leader and was moving forward in mitigating ISS's financial problems when fortune frowned and he suffered Columbia. Out of the Columbia tragedy, however, arose a new long-term goal for NASA: exploration of the Moon, Mars, and beyond. What that meant for the station was greater clarity and focus as to purpose—chiefly as a laboratory to learn about human impacts of long-duration stays in space and potentially an assembly point for trips to the Moon and Mars. It was thus explicitly defined as a means to an exploration end.

Mike Griffin, who became NASA's administrator in 2005, has as his task completing the station, or at least moving it decisively in that direction while in office. To do that, he has said he will continue to collaborate with other space agencies and maintain the political coalition he inherited. Succeeding in one cooperative project makes collaboration in future projects, such as lunar bases and manned Mars exploration, more feasible.

Sensing that future projects need collaboration will make an administrator more sensitive to collaboration dynamics in a present project (Axelrod 1984). Leaders of collaborative projects must deal with each of the elements influencing their project—technical, organizational, domestic-political, and international-political. Sometimes they act on their own, sometimes through surrogates. They have to hone skills that embrace technical, administrative, political, and diplomatic considerations at once.

What is said of the NASA administrator may be said of his counterparts in other nations. A succession of space agency heads in the respective partner nations has dealt with different policy contexts. What they have shared is a common interest in a project each has made a top priority of his or her agency. If the multinational project fails, they all fail.

Finally, the most important element in the behavior of our U.S. administrative leaders is their attention to political support. Sustaining a project is a process of framing the project in such a way as to get presidential and congressional attention and backing. That may include jobs and economic development, prestige, international competition, or its opposite, international collaboration. The particular emphasis in packaging depends on the vagaries of historical circumstance and the requirements of politicians, especially the president (Lambright 2006).

CONCLUSION

The space station project reinforces much that is already known about collaboration in general and in R&D projects in particular. It extends our knowledge of collaboration, mostly drawn from domestic policy and social service delivery administration, to the realm of multinational projects, showing how a one-time competitor can become a critical collaborator. Moreover, it shows the interplay of technical, organizational, and domestic/ international political factors in a project that extends over many years. It demonstrates that leaders of projects at the administrative level build coalitions of political support to sustain projects, and collaboration can be both a means and an end. As an end, it matters who is brought into the collaboration to undergird its political coalition and at what point in the life of the project that happens.

At a critical moment (i.e., punctuation point), the space station might have died, but bringing Russia in brought Clinton in. While willing to save the station, his commitment to the project was lukewarm. Russia converted him to a collaboration champion and thus a space station champion in 1993. Clinton enlisted Congress. Large-scale, long-term projects need collaboration champions, and the president is essential for those projects of the largest scale, greatest controversy, and most expense. Political will sustained the space station as much as the hardware. Clinton episodically was a collaboration champion. The NASA administrator had to play this role continuously. Goldin managed the ISS project so that it achieved what Freedom did not—tons of hardware in space. Once a U.S.–Russian core facility was in orbit, there were "sunk costs" of a scale that would propel the project beyond the tenures of Goldin and Clinton. The biggest challenge any long-term, large-scale public technological project faces (aside from its inherent technical feasibility) is political instability. Collaboration as an end and means can mitigate some of that instability, provided the collaboration champion role is played skillfully. If there is one major lesson from the space station experience, it is that the collaboration champion is a co-developer. He or she builds the technological *and* political system. Together, one makes the other possible. Weakness in one means weakness in the other. A major political weakness has been the inability of the project's leadership to get beyond government officials and lawmakers to the general public. The space station does not have civic engagement. It has enough policymaker support to survive and evolve—but not enough public interest to get the resources it needs to move forward more efficiently. At the time of this writing, it is still far from finished.

IMPLICATIONS

What are the station's broader implications? Human spaceflight is not the only area requiring collaboration on a large scale in the future. Society faces a number of challenging policy issues with science and technology components—disease, natural disaster, terrorism. Climate change and, thus, also, global energy loom as the most immediate imperatives (Lane 2005). The space station is driven today by shared visions of opportunity. Climate change and energy are driven by collective visions of threat. With respect to climate change, there is a need for linking various national satellite and surface-based technologies into a global monitoring system. Such a system would monitor the health of the planet as climatic and other global changes take place, thereby providing early warnings of dangers and better guiding mitigating actions. Coping with climate change also requires massive shifts in energy systems. There is an imperative for the world to go through a transition from fossil fuels to alternatives. There are many reasons for this, including resource depletion and geopolitical dynamics of the Middle East and elsewhere. However, the most important reason is climate change.

Scientists increasingly agree that climate change is the number one global environmental problem ahead and it could be unendurable by 2050 unless actions are taken soon to mitigate its impacts. Former vice president Al Gore has a film, *An Inconvenient Truth*, in which he persuasively argues for the importance of the issue. He sees it as a moral problem, in which one generation sentences its successors to a perilous existence through indifference and denial. It may well be a moral problem, but doing something about it requires converting moral exigency into large-scale organized programs and technological projects (Samuelson 2006).[4] The climate change and energy challenge will not be solved by a "Project Independence," which is usually proclaimed on an Apollo or Manhattan Project model. Such a model assumes a crash effort for a decade or less by a single nation. Climate change alters the rules. Nations are too interdependent and this problem too pervasive and chronic for short-term remedies. What happens in China affects the United

States, and vice versa. As the problem is multinational, the solutions must be as well. The upside of ISS is that it shows that long-term, large-scale technological projects are possible on a multinational basis. Nations *can* sustain a project and merge parochial interests into a larger interest. The process is messy, and strategies are not always noble, but at the end of the day a capability exists that can be used, hopefully for good. ISS, for better or worse, is thus a useful reference for climate change and the transition in energy technology in the twenty-first century, because what is needed will take many years, involve many nations, and necessitate collaborative leadership on a global scale.

An energy transition will require not just one project, but many projects. To the extent nations share a common interest in averting the worst of climate change through developing Earth-monitoring systems and sustainable energy technologies, they will cooperate. There is some action under way. For example, the Holy Grail of electrical energy is fusion—a technology that promises unlimited supply with minimum pollution. A somewhat different collaborative model from ISS is presented here with the International Thermonuclear Energy Reactor (ITER). Japan, the United States, the European Union, Russia, China, India, and South Korea have recently agreed to work together to build a $12 billion fusion facility in southern France (Cookson 2005).[5] A Japanese scientist is the director of ITER. What is noteworthy is that the United States is a junior partner in this global project. What this project shows is that different nations can take the lead in various cooperative enterprises. Where a problem is seen as serious, with no one obvious solution, it makes sense to have several nations divide the labor and burdens of collaborative leadership.

It is therefore virtually certain that there will be more multinational cooperative projects in the future, with climate change most likely in the lead, driving development of both a global monitoring system and energy transition. While everyone realizes there are challenges in collaboration, there is little choice but to try to collaborate when the goals are large, attainment is complex, and individual nations are stretched thin in what they can do alone. Multinational, and in some cases global, collaboration, is the wave of the future. If there is a Manhattan or Apollo Project down the road for energy/climate change, it will be "Project Interdependence," multifaceted, global in scale, with the United States, hopefully, a collaboration champion (Rees 2006).[6]

Without question, further research on collaborative multinational projects is needed, with an aim both to improve understanding and management. Students of public administration have long known that administrators have to give simultaneous attention to the internal and external aspects of their jobs. As those jobs increasingly embrace multinational collaboration, these managerial and political dimensions take on far more complexity. International collaboration is a double-edged sword. It adds enormous complexity and difficulty for leaders. But it may also make possible future projects that nations cannot undertake individually. Researchers need to unravel these complexities of twenty-first-century public management. There are also educational implications. Students need to be better prepared for the issues whose solutions will require technological systems and political coalitions across cultural boundaries. They need to think bigger and in terms of co-development. If one-time rivals like the United States and Russia can find common ground in outer space, then other unlikely alliances are possible and desirable in the public interest. We need to enable them.

NOTES

1. Cost figures vary depending on what is or is not included. Some writers cite $100 billion, including all shuttle costs and the phase after development, when utilization occurs. The U.S. cost for development of the station per se, including the former Freedom Space Station project and current International Space Station, is estimated at $40 billion thus far. Other nations compute their costs in varying ways and Russia does not report its costs, even though it has been the major participant in the project other than the United States to date. One estimate for "the world" as of 2005 is $60 billion, but it is not clear how the writer arrived at this figure.

2. The co-developer concept fits an R&D project. Sheila Josanoff has used "co-production" in some of her writing (e.g., Josanoff 2005).

3. For more detail on the events in this summary history, see Lambright's, "Security and Salvation: Bringing Russia Aboard the Space Station" and "Dan Goldin's Catch-22: Building a U.S.-Russian Space Station," in Franke (2005, ch. 12–13). See also Roger Launius (2003) and Karl Leib (2003).

4. Samuelson (2006, A13) takes Gore to task for his moral crusade strategy. Samuelson writes, "The inconvenient truth is that if we don't solve the engineering problem, we're helpless." Gore and Samuelson are both correct—global warming is both a moral dilemma and technical challenge.

5. There was a considerable dispute over where the facility would be located, but the nations ultimately agreed. See Cookson, who regards ITER as "the immediate test of politicians' ability to put short-term national interests and jealousies aside in the long-term interests of humanity" (2005, 4).

6. Martin Rees, president of the UK National Academy of Science, asks political leaders for the vision to consider such an initiative in a recent editorial in *Science* (Rees 2006).

REFERENCES

Abrahamson, Mark; Jonathan D. Breul; and John M. Kamensky. 2006. *Six Trends Transforming Government.* Washington, DC: IBM Center for the Business of Government.

Agranoff, Robert, and Michael McGuire. 2003. *Collaborative Public Management: New Strategies for Local Governments.* Washington, DC: Georgetown University Press.

Axelrod, Robert. 1984. *The Evolution of Cooperation.* New York: Basic Books.

Bardach, Eugene. 1998. *Getting Agencies to Work Together: The Practice and Theory of Managerial Craftsmanship.* Washington, DC: Brookings Institution.

Barnes, Tina A.; Ian R. Pashby; and Anne M. Gibbons. 2006. "Managing Collaborative R&D Projects: Development of a Practical Management Tool." *International Journal of Project Management* 24: 395–404.

Cookson, Clive. 2005. "The Need for Global Collaboration Is Greater Than Ever." *Financial Times,* January 26, 4.

Doig, Jameson, and Erwin Hargrove, eds. 1990. *Leadership and Innovation: Entrepreneurs in Government.* Baltimore: Johns Hopkins University Press.

Franke, Volker, ed. 2005. *Terrorism and Peacekeeping: New Security Challenges.* Westport, CT: Praeger.

Josanoff, Sheila. 2005. *Designs on Nature: Science and Democracy in Europe and the United States.* Princeton, NJ: Princeton University Press.

Keohane, Robert, and Joseph Nye. 2001. *Power and Interdependence.* New York: Longman.

Kringe, John. 2006. "Technology, Foreign Policy, and International Cooperation in Space." In *Critical Issues in the History of Space Flight*, ed. Steven J. Dick and Roger D. Launius, 239–60. Washington, DC: NASA.

Lambright, W. Henry. 2005. "Leadership and Large-Scale Technology: The Case of the International Space Station." *Space Policy* 21: 195–203.

———. 2006. *Executive Response to Changing Fortune.* Washington, DC: IBM Center for the Business of Government.

Lambright, W. Henry, and Agnes G. Schaefer. 2004. "The Political Context of Technology Transfer: NASA and the International Space Station." *Comparative Technology Transfer and Society* 2, no. 1: 1–24.

Lane, Neal. 2005. "Introduction: Energy, the Environment, and Global Change." In *American Association for Advancement of Science, Vision 2033: Linking Science and Policy for Tomorrow's World.* Washington, DC: AAAS.

Launius, Roger. 2003. *Space Stations: Base Camps to the Stars.* Washington, DC: Smithsonian Books.

Leib, Karl. 2003. "Entering the Space Station Era: International Cooperation and the Next Decade in Human Space Flight." In *Space Policy in the Twenty-First Century,* ed. W. Henry Lambright, ch. 4. Baltimore: Johns Hopkins University Press.

Madison, J.J., and Howard McCurdy. 1999. "Spending without Results: Lessons from the Space Station Program." *Space Policy* 15, no. 4: 213–21.

McCurdy, Howard. 1990. *The Space Station Decision.* Baltimore: Johns Hopkins University Press.

Milward, H. Briton, and Keith Provan. 2000. "Governing the Hollow State." *Journal of Public Administration and Research Theory* 10, no. 2: 359–79.

Moody, James B., and Mark Dodgson. 2006. "Managing Complex Collaborative Projects: Lessons from the Development of a New Satellite." *Journal of Technology Transfer* 31: 567–88.

Morring, Frank, Jr. "International Outpost." *Aviation Week and Space Technology* (July): 60–62.

Pownall, Ian. 1997. "Collaborative Development of Hot Fusion Technology Policies: Strategic Issues." *Technology Analysis and Strategic Management* 9, no. 2: 193–212.

Provan, Keith; Patrick Kenis; and Sherrie E. Human. 2008. "Legitimacy Building in Organizational Networks." In *Big Ideas in Collaborative Public Management,* ed. Lisa Blomgren Bingham and Rosemary O'Leary, 121–37. Armonk, NY: M.E. Sharpe.

Putman, Robert. 1988. "Diplomacy and Domestic Games: The Logic of Two-Level Games." *International Organization* 42: 427–60.

Radin, Beryl A. 2002. *The Accountable Juggler: The Art of Leadership in a Federal Agency.* Washington, DC: CQ Press.

Rees, Martin. 2006. "The G8 on Energy: Too Little." *Science* 313 (August): 591.

Riccucci, Norma. 1995. *Unsung Heroes: Federal Execurats Making A Difference.* Washington, DC: Georgetown University Press.

Sabatier, Paul, and Hank Jenkins-Smith. 1999. "The Advocacy Coalition Framework: An Assessment." In *Theories of the Policy Process,* ed. Paul A. Sabatier, 117–66. Boulder, CO: Westview.

Sadeh, Eliger. 2004. "Technical, Organizational, and Political Dynamics of the International Space Station Program." *Space Policy* 20: 171–88.

Samuelson, Robert. 2006. "Global Warming's Real Inconvenient Truth." *Washington Post,* July 5, A13.

Shenhar, Aaron J. 1998. "From Theory to Practice: Towards a Typology of Project-Management Styles." *IEEE Transactions on Engineering Management* 45, no. 1: 33–48.

Shore, Barry, and Benjamin J. Cross. 2005. "Exploring the Role of National Culture in Management of Large-Scale International Science Projects." *International Journal of Project Management* 23: 55–64.

True, James; Bryan Jones; and Frank Baumgartner. 1999. "Punctuated-Equilibrium Theory: Exploring Stability and Change in American Policymaking." In *Theories of the Policy Process,* ed. Paul A. Sabatier, 97–115. Boulder, CO: Westview.

Wilson, James Q. 1989. *Bureaucracy: What Government Agencies Do and Why They Do It.* New York: Basic Books.

CHAPTER 13

Legal Frameworks for Collaboration in Governance and Public Management

LISA BLOMGREN BINGHAM

In *A.L.A. Schechter Poultry Corp. et al. v. United States,* 295 U.S. 495 (1935, affectionately known as "the Sick Chicken case"), the U.S. Supreme Court faced a challenge to the work product of collaborative public management. A New York poultry dealer was convicted of violating regulations adopted pursuant to the National Industrial Recovery Act of 1934 (NIRA, New Deal legislation) for letting customers select individual chickens for kosher slaughter from a coop or lot. The Court observed that the national crisis of the Depression "demanded a broad and intensive cooperative effort by those engaged in trade and industry, and that this necessary cooperation was sought to be fostered by permitting them to initiate the adoption of codes" (295 U.S. at 529). However, the Court noted that this cooperation

> involves the coercive exercise of the law-making power. The codes of fair competition which the statute attempts to authorize are codes of laws. If valid, they place all persons within their reach under the obligation of positive law, binding equally those who assent and those who do not assent. Violations of the provisions of the codes are punishable as crimes.
>
> The Constitution provides that "All legislative powers herein granted shall be vested in a Congress of the United States, which shall consist of a Senate and House of Representatives." Art I, § 1. And the Congress is authorized "To make all laws which shall be necessary and proper for carrying into execution" its general powers. Art. I, § 8, par. 18. The Congress is not permitted to abdicate or to transfer to others the essential legislative functions with which it is thus vested.

***

247

[W]e said that the constant recognition of the necessity and validity of such provisions, and the wide range of administrative authority which has been developed by means of them, cannot be allowed to obscure the limitations of the authority to delegate, if our constitutional system is to be maintained. (Ibid.)

The statute in question expressly purported to "provide for the general welfare by promoting the organization of industry *for the purpose of cooperative action among trade groups*" (ibid. at 531, note 9; emphasis added).

The executive branch argued that the codes will "consist of rules of competition deemed fair for each industry by representative members of that industry—by the persons most vitally concerned and most familiar with its problems" (ibid. at 537). The Court, however, was unimpressed:

But would it be seriously contended that Congress could delegate its legislative authority to trade or industrial associations or groups so as to empower them to enact the laws they deem to be wise and beneficent for the rehabilitation and expansion of their trade or industries? Could trade or industrial associations or groups be constituted legislative bodies for that purpose because such associations or groups are familiar with the problems of their enterprises? And, could an effort of that sort be made valid by such a preface of generalities as to permissible aims as we find in section 1 of title I? The answer is obvious. Such a delegation of legislative power is unknown to our law and is utterly inconsistent with the constitutional prerogatives and duties of Congress. (Ibid.)

The executive branch argued that there are constraints built into the statute that render it a fair process for developing the codes. The president could not approve codes as law unless he first found that the trade or industrial associations or groups were truly representative and did not unfairly restrict membership. The president had also to ensure that the code was not designed to promote monopolies or eliminate, oppress, or discriminate against small competitors. The Court rejected these protections as inadequate to address the delegation problem:

But these restrictions leave virtually untouched the field of policy envisaged by section one, and, in that wide field of legislative possibilities, the proponents of a code, refraining from monopolistic designs, may roam at will and the President may approve or disapprove their proposals as he may see fit. (Ibid. at 538)

The Court concludes that the codes are a legislative undertaking, and that the NIRA is without precedent because it supplies no standards and prescribes no rules of conduct. Instead, it authorizes networks to adopt codes to do this, but sets no standards for the codes (ibid. at 541). The Court concluded: "[T]he code-making authority thus conferred is an unconstitutional delegation of legislative power" (ibid. at 542). Justice Cardozo famously concurs, describing it as "delegation run riot" (ibid. at 553).

The Supreme Court has never overruled *Schechter Poultry*. Most of its rulings on delegation do not return to the question of delegation to a nongovernmental entity or collaborative network of private sector actors, but instead examine the scope of a statute's delegated authority to the executive branch (e.g., *Panama Refining v. Ryan,* 293 U.S. 388 [1935]; *National Broadcasting Co., Inc. v. U.S.,* 319 U.S. 190 [1943]; *National Cable Television v. U.S.,* 415 U.S. 336 [1974]; *Clinton v. U.S.,* 524 U.S. 417 [1998]).

Of course, some seventy years later, the Supreme Court is probably not about to come down on our collective heads to punish collaboration. However, an unfortunately large number of lawyers who represent local, state, and federal government agencies still worry about how to reconcile collaborative public management and collaborative governance with the principle of government within the law. Public administrators have an ethical obligation to know and comply with the Constitution and public law. Robert Agranoff (chapter 9, this volume) finds that legal constraints have an impact on the work of collaborative public management networks; networks with express legislative authorization or charters are more likely to take action rather than simply share information. Whether perceived legal constraints are real or merely feared, we must address them for collaboration to reach its full potential in public management and governance.

This chapter addresses legal constraints on collaboration and sources of authority to involve others in public management and governance. First, it addresses definitions, including collaborative public management, collaborative governance, and legal infrastructure. Second, it discusses the processes for collaboration in governance, specifically, the emergence of new forms of participation by citizens and stakeholders across the policy continuum (legislative, quasi-legislative, quasi-judicial, and judicial). Third, it discusses the scope of existing legal infrastructure as it authorizes collaboration, or provides constraints, obstacles, or barriers. Fourth, it examines selected literature of collaborative public management and examples of the role legal infrastructure plays. Finally, it opens a discussion regarding new legal infrastructure to enable collaborative public management and collaborative governance to strengthen public administration and our democracy.

COLLABORATION IN GOVERNANCE AND MANAGEMENT, AND LEGAL INFRASTRUCTURE

During the final third of the twentieth century, the way that we talk about both government and conflict evolved. Complex problems, from environmental degradation to urban economic development to public health, all challenged the capacity of a single governmental unit operating in hierarchy. Hierarchy's command and control management strategies were less effective in the face of problems that could not be solved or solved easily by an entity acting alone (Agranoff and McGuire 2003). Moreover, while hierarchy is still the dominant and generally successful strategy for public management in a nation-state, it failed entirely as an approach to global and transnational problems, that is, those that cross the jurisdictional boundaries of nation-states. This gave rise to the concept of governance, rather than government (Kettl 2002). Governance suggests steering rather than top-down directing, and in its contemporary usage means a process involving resources and strategic, often collaborative relationships outside a single organization toward achieving a public policy goal. It may involve multiple organizations and stakeholders from public, private, and nonprofit sectors that combine in a network to address a common and shared problem; this is collaborative public management (Agranoff and McGuire 2003; O'Leary, Gerard, and Bingham 2006). It may involve citizens or those governed through institutionalized civic engagement and participatory decision making; this is participatory governance, deliberative democracy, and/or collaborative governance (O'Leary, Gerard, and Bingham 2006).

This chapter uses the following definitions:

- *Collaborative public management* is a concept that describes the process of facilitating and operating in multiorganizational arrangements to solve problems that cannot be solved or easily solved by single organizations. Collaborative means to co-labor to achieve common goals working across boundaries in multisector and multiactor relationships. Collaboration is based on the value of reciprocity.
- *Participatory governance* is the active involvement of citizens in government decision-making. Governance means to steer the process that influences decisions and actions within the private, public, and civic sectors. (O'Leary, Gerard, and Bingham 2006, 8, citing Agranoff and McGuire 2003; and Henton et al. 2005)

A useful definition for collaborative governance has been crafted by the Institute for Local Government, a nonprofit research organization affiliated with the League of California Cities:

- *Collaborative governance* is a term used to describe the integration of reasoned discussions by the citizens and other residents into the decisionmaking of public representatives, especially when these approaches are embedded in the workings of local governance over time. (www.ca-ilg.org)

These definitions refer to collaboration and engagement in any stage of the policy process, including problem identification, identification of preferences, prioritizing among policy preferences, selecting a policy approach, adopting, implementing, and enforcing policy. Collaborative public management and participatory or collaborative governance appear to fall into two categories in the public administration literature: one that focuses on collaboration among organizations, and a second that focuses on civic engagement and ways for citizens to participate in governance. This literature is beginning to look at the processes for collaboration among organizations and with citizens, and authors in this volume make a substantial contribution.

In contrast, from a public law perspective, the relevant statutes largely address only questions of process for participation within a single agency. They are silent on the substantive work of agencies except with regard to judicial review for ultra vires agency action. They are silent on the structure of collaborative networks or other forms of collaborative public management. They may in places require public participation, for example, notice and comment in rulemaking or public hearings, but they are largely silent as to the wide variety of models for collaborative governance in agency policymaking.

The term legal infrastructure has been used to refer to a combined system of constitutional, statutory, decisional, and administrative law, taken together with the available institutional enforcement and support mechanisms. Its most common use is in reference to efforts to develop the rule of law and viable protection of private property and investment in emerging democracies. State and federal legal infrastructure currently addresses two main categories of administrative agency action: quasi-legislative processes for identifying policy problems, identifying possible solutions, and choosing among them in formulating policy; and quasi-judicial processes for implementing and enforcing policy. Statutory approaches that provide legal infrastructure can either help or hinder collaboration. While these statutes authorize individual agencies to use a wide variety of processes to engage citizens and stakeholders in the policy process (Bingham, Nabatchi, and O'Leary 2005), including a broader range of processes with the advent of alternative dispute resolution and negotiated rulemaking, they nevertheless do not explicitly address agencies acting in the context of a collaborative network in partnership with other organizations, citizens, and stakeholders. Legislators drafted the key statutes as legal infrastructure contemplating unilateral and individual agency action.

We need a more holistic view. Collaborative public management is here to stay; collaborative governance is a key way to respond to some criticisms of networked and privatized government action. Public law needs to provide a framework for both that authorizes collaborative management and collaborative governance, facilitates broader and more effective use of collaboration, and preserves accountability to the rule of law and transparency in government.

CITIZEN AND STAKEHOLDER PARTICIPATION ALONG THE POLICY CONTINUUM

While the public sector worked through the evolution from government to governance, a parallel social phenomenon emerged in civil society through two separate communities of practice that advocate for processes to empower citizens and stakeholders in governance: conflict resolution (alternative or appropriate dispute resolution or ADR) and deliberative and participatory democracy.

Conflict Resolution: The ADR Movement

Government institutions and authority were not sufficient to cope with waves of domestic conflict after World War II. Various new institutions evolved outside government to meet this need, including a mature system for collective bargaining. The ADR movement emerged in large part from private justice systems in labor relations. These included negotiation (preferably interest-based and collaborative rather than positional and competitive bargaining [Fisher, Ury, and Patton 1991]), mediation (negotiation with the help of a third party with no decision-making power [Bingham 2003; Moore 2003]), and arbitration (private judging [Bingham 2004]). These processes are not new; they exist informally in every culture through recorded history, for example through the work of village elders and religious leaders. What evolved was the notion of institutionalizing them either outside government or in relation to it as civil society's way of enhancing community, its problem-solving capacity, social capital, and justice. When used in response to an existing conflict involving specific disputants, this movement became known as alternative dispute resolution. It was later renamed "appropriate" dispute resolution in response to criticism that ADR exists independently from the justice system and is thus not "alternative" in all cases.

The ADR movement gave rise to community mediation centers funded in part by the U.S. Department of Justice to address social unrest during the 1960s (www.nafcm.org). During the 1970s and 1980s, the business community adopted ADR to reduce transaction costs in addressing conflict in commercial dealings (www.adr.org; www.cpradr.org). During the 1990s, ADR became institutionalized in many judicial systems, including both state (www.ncsconline.org) and federal in the United States (www.fjc.gov), and increasingly in Europe and other developed economies such as Australia (Alexander 2003). During the past decade, it became institutionalized in U.S. federal agencies (Bingham and Wise 1996; Senger 2003; www.adr.gov).

Civil society contributed to dissemination of these processes in a variety of ways. What follows are a few examples, but by no means a complete account. In the United States, beginning in the 1960s, philanthropic institutions such as the Ford, Carnegie, Rockefeller, and Hewlett Foundations, among others, funded the movement. Hewlett's contribution was central to the development of ADR in the United States (for the history of this program see www.hewlett.org/Publications/confictresolutionbrief.htm; for explanatory monographs on the full spectrum of its work, see Henton et al. [2005]; O'Leary, Kopell, and Amsler [2005]; www.hewlett.org/ECRguide.htm; for a summary of research gaps that Hewlett identified upon completion of its funding program, see Bush and Bingham [2005]).

In Europe and the newly independent states following the end of the Cold War in the 1990s, these same philanthropies, together with the European Union, the American Bar Association and its foundation, the Soros Foundation, the World Bank, and the United States Agency for International Development, among others, funded training and program development to strengthen the rule of law. Similar projects have recently been undertaken in China and other parts of Asia. In addition, there have been numerous independent initiatives and exchanges across national boundaries through institutions of higher education, primarily law schools, for example, regarding the training of judges in South and Central America, and in Eastern Europe, the newly independent states, and Asia.

The following are commonly accepted descriptions of common ADR processes as these terms are generally used for public conflict resolution:

1. Negotiation: Principled or interest-based negotiation (Fisher, Ury, and Patton 1991) is sometimes considered a form of dispute resolution, and these skills are fundamental to all the remaining third-party processes. Disputants negotiate directly and attempt to untangle interpersonal and substantive issues, focus on interests not rights or positions, promote creative problem solving, and use principles rather than power to reach agreement.

2. Conciliation: An agency attempts to negotiate a private settlement generally between two private parties to a dispute subject to the agency's jurisdiction. For example, the Civil Rights Act of 1964 (commonly known as Title VII) mandates

conciliation for disputes regarding discrimination in employment based on race, sex, or other status. This term is also sometimes used to mean mediation.

3. Facilitation: A third party neutral, the facilitator structures group discussions toward a voluntary settlement, asking pointed questions, using collaborative bargaining techniques (Schwarz 2002). This process is more commonly used in multiparty issues or for large groups (Carpenter and Kennedy 1988).

4. Mediation: This is assisted negotiation, in which a third party neutral attempts to help parties reach a mutual agreement (Moore 2003). Sometimes the mediator uses shuttle diplomacy, in which the parties separately and mostly in confidence communicate their interests, goals, and concerns. The mediator identifies a range of possible settlements, but has no power to impose a solution or decide the case. This process is widely used in environmental and public policy conflict resolution (Susskind and Cruikshank 1987).

5. Fact-finding: This is a form of advisory arbitration where a neutral conducts an informal evidentiary hearing to narrow disputed facts.

6. Mini-trials: A form of advisory arbitration where a neutral conducts a more formal but still abbreviated evidentiary hearing, and advises on disputed questions of law.

7. Arbitration: Private adjudication, where a neutral conducts an informal adjudicatory hearing on all disputed issues of fact and law, and renders an award or decision on all issues. Arbitration may be voluntary or mandatory (e.g., *EPA* vs. *Amateur Sports Act*), and may be advisory or binding.

8. Ombuds Program: This is the use of an in-house third-party neutral to assist people in handling conflict. The ombuds can help refer employees or citizens to the appropriate dispute resolution process, can engage in conflict coaching, and can help manage the variety of agency processes.

There is substantial research on these processes in the field of social psychology. One leading theory is that of procedural justice, which suggests that people will judge the outcome of a dispute process to be fair if they judge the process for reaching that outcome to be fair and if they are given opportunities for voice and respectful treatment (Lind and Tyler 1988; for review articles on field studies and evaluation of the uses of various processes in the contexts of employment, education, criminal justice, the environment, family disputes, civil litigation in courts, and community disputes, see Jones 2004.)

Deliberative and Participatory Democracy

The second movement emerged during the past decade, and it is sufficiently new that there is no consensus about what to name it. Terms include participatory democracy, deliberation and dialogue, deliberative democracy, and more broadly, collaborative governance. This movement emerged in response to perceived failings in representative democracy with respect to conflict over public policy. Various manifestations of civil society, through the nonprofit and voluntary sector as well as citizen groups, have pressed for more public participation in the policy process (Forester 1999). This movement seeks more citizen deliberation, dialogue, and shared decision making in governance (Gastil and Levine 2005; Roberts 2003). As is true of ADR, this movement too hopes to address conflict, but at the broader level of public policy. It takes advantage of new technologies for human communication and includes "e-democracy" and "e-government." This movement has also found some support in the institutions of civil society—to some degree from the same foundations that funded work on dispute resolution, such as Hewlett—but usually under different funding programs more concerned with healing the damage of war and ethnic conflict and building democratic institutions.

Central to each of the many evolving forms of participatory governance are notions of dialogue and deliberation (Torres 2003). Dialogue is contrasted with the traditional adversarial processes of governance, which usually entail debate. In dialogue, participants engage in reasoned exchange of viewpoints, in an atmosphere of mutual respect and civility, in a neutral space or forum, with an effort to reach a better mutual understanding and sometimes even consensus. In debate, participants listen in an effort to identify weaknesses in the argument and score points in an effective counterargument. In deliberation and dialogue, participants listen in an effort to better understand the other's viewpoint and identify questions or areas of confusion to probe for a deeper understanding. Deliberation is the thoughtful consideration of information, views, and ideas.

There are more detailed definitions for dialogue and deliberation and a primer of models and techniques on the Web site of the National Coalition for Dialogue and Deliberation (www.thataway.org). That Web site lists the following models and techniques: 21st century town meeting, appreciative inquiry, bohmian dialogue, citizen choicework, citizens juries, compassionate listening, consensus conferences, conversation café, deliberative polling, dynamic facilitation and the wisdom council, future search, Intergroup Dialogue, National Issues Forums, Nonviolent Communication, Online D&D, Open Space Technology, Public Conversations Project, Study Circles, Sustained Dialogue, Wisdom Circles, and World Café (for more description, see also Williamson 2004). It also lists mediation and dispute resolution, processes described above that can be adapted to larger-scale participation.

Governance and the Policy Process

Together, these developments have begun to change the policy process at every jurisdictional level, whether local, regional, state, national, transnational, or global. At its most general, the policy process consists of stages in a continuous and dynamic system. A national court may decide a controversial case that prompts a wave of legislation. The legislature may adopt a law that ends up in court. Because the system is continuous and dynamic, it is arbitrary to begin at any one point, but it is conventional to begin with identifying a policy problem. The following stages assume a division among legislative, executive, and judicial powers. I use the term "power" rather than "branch" because in some nations, multiple powers are combined in a single branch of government. The stages include identifying approaches or tools for solving the policy problem (Salamon 2002), setting priorities among these, selecting from among the priorities, drafting proposed legislation, enacting legislation, identifying policy problems left for the executive to resolve within the boundaries of the legislation, identifying approaches or tools for regulations, setting priorities for these, selecting from among them, drafting proposed regulations, enacting regulations, implementing regulations (through project or program management, or permits), enforcing legislation and regulations through executive power adjudication, and enforcing these through litigation within the jurisdiction of the judicial power.

There is no fixed boundary for each of these stages on the policy continuum. Conflict can and will occur at each of these stages. One helpful metaphor is the flowing stream (Bingham 2006; O'Leary and Bingham 2003). Upstream includes the earliest stages in the policy process up to the point of implementation; these are either legislative or quasi-legislative in nature (Bingham, Nabatchi, and O'Leary 2005; Bingham, O'Leary, and Nabatchi 2005). After legislation is enacted, agencies engage in quasi-legislative action aimed at filling in the details and establishing general standards of behavior for prospective or future application through guidelines or regulations. This upstream agency action entails forms of participatory governance, including deliberative democracy, e-democracy, public conversations, participatory budgeting, citizen juries, study circles, collaborative policymaking, and other forms of deliberation and dialogue among groups of stakeholders or citizens (Booher 2004; Fung and Wright 2003; Torres 2003; Williamson 2004). They also include focus groups, roundtables, deliberative town meeting forums, deliberative polling (Ackerman and Fishkin 2004), choice work dialogues, national issues forums, co-operative management bodies, and other partnership arrangements. The underlying theory is that these processes promote a more civil public discourse and more collaborative and deliberative policymaking among citizens.

Upstream processes for resolving conflict in the policy process vary along several dimensions, including the participants, their authority and power to influence policy decisions, and the process for communication and decision making (Fung 2006). Fung (2006) suggests that categories of participants include the diffuse public sphere, open self-selection, open targeted recruiting, random selection, lay stakeholders, professional stakeholders, elected representatives, and expert administrators. He proposes that types of authority include personal benefits, communicative influence, advise and consult, co-governance, and direct authority. Last, he identifies six modes of communication and decision processes: Participants listen as spectators, express preferences, develop preferences, aggregate and bargain, deliberate and negotiate, and deploy technique and expertise. Using these three dimensions, he creates a "democracy cube," on which he maps different processes.

Others have described different levels of public participation. Arnstein's ladder of participation (1969) ranges from manipulation of the public and therapy at the low end, through levels including informing, consultation, and placation in the middle, to partnership, delegated power, and citizen control on the upper steps of the ladder. The International Association for Public Participation (http://iap2.0rg/displayassociationlinks.cfm) has a Spectrum of Participation in which agencies have the choice to inform, consult, involve, collaborate, or empower the public. Each form of public participation has an implicit promise to the public, ranging from keeping the public informed to implementing what the public decides.

Other commentators have suggested that the quality of these processes depends upon how well they satisfy three criteria: inclusiveness, deliberativeness, and influence (Carson and Hartz-Karp 2005). Inclusiveness is the quality of getting a broadly representative portion of the relevant community to participate. Deliberativeness has to do with the quality of dialogue, information exchanged, and civility of the conversation among participants and decision makers. Influence has to do with the impact of deliberation on policy and decision making.

Using the framework of the U.S. Institute for Environmental Conflict Resolution (www. ecr.gov), midstream stages in the policy process include rulemaking, implementation, and program development. These are both quasi-legislative and quasi-judicial (Bingham, Nabatchi, and O'Leary 2005; Bingham, O'Leary, and Nabatchi 2005). In this part of the continuum, both participatory governance processes and ADR are used to resolve conflict (for numerous case studies, see Susskind, McKearnan, and Thomas-Larmer 1999). An agency may use negotiated rulemaking to draft proposed regulations. The agency may need to craft a permit for a particular land use or development. In this case, implementation through permitting or licensing both sets future standards and also involves defined actors with a specific history of past behaviors (for example, organizations emitting pollutants). The agency might use a policy consensus process or mediation to reach consensus on the permit terms.

There is no strict boundary between upstream and midstream. Somewhere between adopting policy and implementing it, there is a shift in the nature of processes related to governance from more deliberative ones that set priorities to agreement-seeking processes. In agreement-seeking processes, generally a mediator or facilitator works with a group of citizens and stakeholders to build consensus around the elements of a specific plan, permit, or policy proposal (Moore 2003). Typically, that neutral will engage in a conflict assessment process before convening the stakeholder group in order to assess the feasibility of reaching consensus. Mediation is particularly prevalent in environmental governance (O'Leary and Bingham 2003).

The neutral generally uses principles of interest-based bargaining (Fisher, Ury, and Patton 1991). This approach involves a focus on the interests of the parties rather than their adversarial positions. The mediator or facilitator may identify interests by asking problem-solving questions (who, what, where, why, how, why not) to get at the stakeholders' basic human and organizational needs. These will most often fall into one of five categories: needs relating to security, economic well-being, recognition, autonomy, and belonging to a community, organization, or social group (Fisher, Ury, and Patton 1991). Parties engage in brainstorming, a process through which they first generate a list of possible solutions. They next prioritize among these ideas, deliberate on them, and attempt to reach consensus. In the event of impasse, the stakeholders are encouraged to use objective criteria, moral and professional standards, and other sources in a reasoned exchange rather than threaten to use leverage or bargaining power.

In mediation, the neutral can assist the parties with this negotiation process by meeting with subgroups or individual stakeholders in caucus, a private confidential session (Moore 2003). The mediator can also help the parties by using active listening techniques such as paraphrasing, by framing and reframing issues and suggestions, helping them identify their best alternative to a negotiated agreement, and/or reality-testing about what might happen if parties fail to reach an agreement. Facilitators may use many of these techniques, but do not define their task as assisting the parties in reaching an agreement. Instead, they foster an organized discussion; nevertheless, this discussion may produce a consensus.

Downstream in the policy process, appropriate dispute resolution can be used for both executive agency action and disputes within the jurisdiction of the judiciary. Generally, these processes are quasi-judicial or judicial in that they assist specific identified disputants and are retrospective in nature—they examine the facts of past events that gave rise to a dispute. Judicial and quasi-judicial action is aimed at determining rights and responsibilities among a defined set of actors based on past events. Quasi-judicial processes include agency uses of ADR, including mediation, facilitation, early neutral assessment, and arbitration. The processes may either seek a voluntary settlement agreement (mediation) or provide disputants with a decision that ends their conflict more expeditiously than traditional agency or court adjudication (fact-finding, advisory arbitration, or binding arbitration). Generally, ADR, and not deliberative or participatory democracy, is associated with these later stages of the policy process.

The problem with the above account of the policy process is that it is usually understood to refer to a single sovereign actor with legal jurisdiction over certain policy arenas. However, governance entails activity among multiple actors with potentially overlapping jurisdiction. ADR has a well-established history in which agencies have used it to address complex disputes involving multiple actors, sectors, and levels of government. This is less true of deliberative and participatory democracy.

PUBLIC LAW AND NETWORKS: THE LIMITS OF CURRENT LEGAL INFRASTRUCTURE

Administrative law scholars generally occupy themselves with challenges to the legitimacy of the administrative state (Freeman 2000). The absence of any reference to administrative agencies in the Constitution, the combination of legislative, executive, and judicial functions in the agency potentially violating separation of powers, and the absence of direct accountability to the electorate taken together create a simmering brew of concern (Freeman 2000, 545–46). As a result, most scholarship addresses means to constrain agency power and make it accountable, or conversely, to justify it. There is a growing literature on contracting out and privatization of government functions that follows in this tradition. Dannin (2005) explores new conceptions of accountability in privatization, arguing that it is more than just value of services for the public dollar, but should encompass civic values and participatory democracy. Concerns about legitimacy and accountability exist for both federal and state agencies.

Legal Infrastructure in the Federal Executive Branch

In the United States, federal administrative agencies are sometimes thought of as a fourth branch of government in which judicial, legislative, and executive functions from the other three are collapsed (Rosenbloom 2003, 11). They have substantial discretion to choose among different governance processes under the Administrative Procedure Act (5 U.S.C. §§ 551 et seq., hereafter "APA"; Rosenbloom 2003, 6–7), which provides for both quasi-legislative and quasi-judicial agency action. The term quasi-legislative refers to agency action that is synoptic, prospective, and general in application, and that sets standards, guidelines, expectations, or rules and regulations for behavior. Traditional rulemaking can meet these criteria, particularly for substantive or legislative rules (Rosenbloom 2003, 59). The term quasi-judicial usually refers to agency action that is retrospective and fact-based, and that determines the rights or obligations of selected citizens or stakeholders rather than those of the general public. It encompasses formal and informal adjudication.

Within the executive branch, agencies must comply with the Administrative Procedure Act, Freedom of Information Act, Federal Advisory Committee Act, Negotiated Rulemaking Act, and Administrative Dispute Resolution Act. These statutes were not drafted expressly to authorize agencies to collaborate in networks with other actors, nor with a view toward joint agency action. Their unit of analysis, the obligations they impose and processes they authorize all take as their starting place individual agency action.

The Administrative Procedure Act: A Statute for Agencies Acting Alone

The Administrative Procedure Act, enacted in response to the growth of the administrative state during the New Deal, was a substantial breakthrough in the public's right to know about, and participate in, processes of governance in federal administrative agencies. It encompasses formal and informal agency action (Rosenbloom 2003). Formal agency action can take the forms of rulemaking or adjudication. In rulemaking, agencies create general rules of prospective application using published notice and an opportunity for members of the public to comment, although generally not through an oral evidentiary hearing (Cooper 2000, 132; Kerwin 2003; Rosenbloom 2003, 57; Rosenbloom and O'Leary 1997).

In adjudication, an agency determines individual rights through a retrospective examination of evidence and facts. Adjudication procedures range from informal (the kind a school principal engages in when she disciplines a student) to formal adjudication. Formal adjudication under the APA involves an adjudicatory hearing before an administrative law judge with many of the requisites of procedural due process (e.g., notice, the right to present evidence, confrontation and cross-examination of witnesses, oral argument, legal counsel, a written decision stating reasons) enunciated in the landmark Supreme Court decision *Goldberg v. Kelly* (397 U.S. 254 [1970]).

Informal agency action, rulemaking, and adjudication together provide for agency action across the entire policy cycle, from policymaking and implementation to enforcement. The APA fundamentally altered the relation of citizens and stakeholders to the government. It made the work of government more transparent through public notice in rulemaking. It also created an explicit and legitimate voice for citizens through opportunities to comment on proposed rules. Formal and informal adjudication procedures gave citizens and stakeholders a voice and an opportunity to be heard before government substantially interfered with their interests in life, liberty, or property.

However, the APA contemplates action by a single agency, acting alone and not in collaboration with other agencies, whether federal, state, or local. Moreover, it does not have formal provision for collaborative management in networks with other organizations, whether private, nonprofit, or other stakeholders. Neither the word "collaboration," in any form, nor the word "network" appears in its text.

The Freedom of Information Act

The reform movement for more transparency in government gave rise to legal infrastructure creating a right to access to government records, and also, a right to notice regarding the public meetings at which agencies make decisions and take action. These provisions often create issues for agencies using processes for negotiation and collaboration. At what point must the collaborative network disclose documents? What is the public's right to attend meetings? Some commentators have suggested that these laws inhibit the use of consensus-building processes among groups of stakeholders in public policy issues (Boxer-Macomber 2003). Federal dispute resolution laws have provided for confidentiality in certain circumstances (see "Protecting the Confidentiality of Dispute Resolution Proceedings: A Guide for Federal Workplace ADR Program Administrators" April 2006 Guide issued by the Federal Interagency ADR Working Group Steering Committee, www. adr.gov). However, the sunshine laws contemplate traditional action by a single agency, not joint action among several. This can create inefficiencies and barriers.

The Federal Advisory Committees Act

In an effort to make government more responsive, agencies began to create and rely on advisory committees. However, concern arose about their excessive influence and the problem of delegating effective decisional authority to unelected, non-accountable private parties. The committees often met in private, and they were not always balanced among competing points of view. As a result, the Federal Advisory Committees Act (FACA) was adopted to force agencies to give notice of the creation of new advisory committees and to define the scope of their authority. It required that a federal official convene and attend each meeting, that meetings be open to the public, and that there be an element of public participation (Boxer-Macomber 2003, 14). This is an instance of federal legal infrastructure that anticipates a collaborative network, namely, the committee, but again ties it to a single agency to preserve accountability, and requires public records and participation to ensure both transparency and accountability.

The APA and Processes for Collaboration

In the 1980s, some federal agencies engaged in dispute resolution, negotiated rulemaking, and policy consensus processes without explicit authorization. The U.S. Environmental

Protection Agency and the U.S. Army Corps of Engineers among others experimented with ADR for a decade or more (Susskind and Cruikshank 1987). Other agencies declined to use these new techniques, asserting that they were outside their delegated authority. In its original form, the APA had no explicit provision for the processes used in collaboration, for example, alternative dispute resolution (mediation, facilitation, interest-based negotiation, and other processes, or ADR). It had no provision for negotiating or building consensus on regulations with networks of private, nonprofit, or public organizations (negotiated rulemaking or policy consensus processes). In the 1980s, agency lawyers had concerns that their clients had no authority under the APA to use alternative dispute resolution or negotiated rulemaking, and that agencies doing so might be acting ultra vires or outside the scope of their delegation. However, concerns about making government more efficient and responsive to the public led to legislative reform.

Congress passed two separate amendments to the APA in 1990 (made permanent in 1996) to clear up the confusion. These were the Negotiated Rulemaking Act of 1996 (NRA, 5 U.S.C. §§ 561 et seq.) and the Administrative Dispute Resolution Act of 1996 (ADRA, 5 U.S.C. §§ 571 et seq.). These federal laws have no application to state government; they apply only to agencies of the federal government as defined in the APA. These two statutes substantially expanded the forms and opportunities for participation by citizens and stakeholders in federal government decision making. Since Congress passed these statutes, there has been dramatic growth in the use of new governance processes in the federal government (Bingham, Nabatchi, and O'Leary 2005; Bingham and Wise 1996; Senger 2003; see www.adr.gov, the gateway Web site for all information on ADR in the federal government).

The Negotiated Rulemaking Act

The NRA was adopted to allow collaboration among a representative group of organizations and stakeholders to craft draft regulations; it is a top-down, carefully structured statute that contains this form of collaborative public management within express limits. An agency convenes a group of twenty-five or fewer stakeholders to negotiate the text for subsequent public notice and comment (Kerwin 1997). Congress intended to enhance informal rulemaking and encourage innovation. The NRA defines "consensus" as unanimous concurrence among represented interests, unless the committee agrees otherwise. A "negotiated rulemaking committee" is "an advisory committee established by an agency . . . to consider and discuss issues for the purpose of reaching a consensus in the development of a proposed rule." It incorporates APA definitions for agency, party, person, rule, and rulemaking.

A single agency has sole authority to determine the need for a negotiated rulemaking committee. It may seek assistance from a "convener." It must consider the need for a rule, whether there is a limited number of identifiable interests, whether there is a reasonable likelihood of a balanced committee (one that can represent interests affected and is willing to negotiate), the likelihood of consensus within a reasonable time, agency resources, and agency willingness to use consensus for proposed rule. The agency must publish notice so people can apply for membership on the committee. After thirty days, the agency may establish the committee. It may also decide not to go forward with negotiated rulemaking, but instead to use the conventional formal and informal rulemaking process. Membership on the negotiated rulemaking committee is limited to twenty-five persons, unless the agency determines it needs more for balanced representation. The committee must include at least one agency representative. The decision not to have a negotiated rulemaking committee is committed to agency discretion and not subject to judicial review.

Once established, the committee must meet and try to reach consensus and may use an impartial facilitator to assist, chair meetings, and manage record keeping. Records are exempt from disclosure under the Freedom of Information Act. Moreover, the committee itself is exempt from those sections of APA on rulemaking procedures.

The act requires a public report if there is consensus and permits a limited report if there is no consensus, or a consensus on some but not all issues. The committee terminates upon final rule, unless there is some early agency directive or committee agreement on a different termination date. There is judicial review only of a final rule, and then in the same manner and by the same standards as any other rulemaking. The courts do not accord any greater deference to the product of negotiated rulemaking than rules made by the traditional process.

There is an active debate over whether negotiated rulemaking saves agencies time and money. While some claim that negotiated rulemakings are no shorter than traditional ones, others argue that only rules likely to spur litigation and controversy are submitted to negotiated rulemaking, and thus, many administrators view it as an achievement that these rules take *no longer* than traditional rulemaking.

Whatever its effectiveness, from the standpoint of collaborative public management, the statute presents problems. First, it contemplates action within the scope of delegated authority to a single, lead agency. Although it permits that agency to create the working group, it does not contemplate action by multiple agencies. Second, it sets up a tightly prescribed procedure for collaboration. This is a top-down authorization that does not allow for much experimentation.

The Administrative Dispute Resolution Act of 1996

The ADRA contemplates both quasi-legislative and quasi-judicial processes when it authorizes agencies to use alternative dispute resolution (Bingham 1997; Breger, Schatz, and Laufer 2001). Quasi-legislative new governance processes include uses of mediation, facilitation, consensus building, and collaborative policymaking to make, implement, and enforce policy (e.g., environmental policy; see Durant, Fiorino, and O'Leary 2004; O'Leary and Bingham 2003). Under the ADRA, agencies have made quasi-judicial uses of new governance processes (including mediation, facilitation, mini-trials, summary jury trials, fact-finding, and binding and nonbinding arbitration) for disputes arising out of employment, procurement contracts, or civil enforcement of an agency's public law mandate (Bingham 1997; Bingham and Wise 1996).

The ADRA contains four key structural components: authorization to use ADR, a mandate that each agency appoint a dispute resolution specialist, required statements of agency ADR policy for the public, and easing bureaucratic barriers to ADR use. These four elements have combined to spur a dramatic increase in the use of ADR by federal agencies. It is surprising that the ADRA accomplished this without a federal monetary appropriation to support agency efforts to implement programs.

The ADRA authorizes use of "alternative means of dispute resolution" defined as any procedure that is used to resolve issues in controversy, *including but not limited to*, conciliation, facilitation, mediation, fact-finding, mini-trials, arbitration, and use of an ombudsman, or any combination thereof. In other words, the statute creates an inclusive, not an exclusive, list of processes. This allows for continuous innovation. The act does not define the terms for processes, which in turn opens them up for innovation. The express authorization to use ADR eliminated any bar imposed by conservative and risk-averse agency legal counsel.

The ADRA expressly addressed concerns over the delegation of public authority to a private person in the provision for binding arbitration. The U.S. Department of Justice raised concerns about excessive delegation in the first draft of the bill, resulting in a watered-down arbitration clause; the agency had the power to reject the award. However, the 1996 version of the ADRA contains explicit authorization for arbitration that is binding on both parties. It incorporates provisions of the Federal Arbitration Act on enforcing arbitration awards. It gives arbitrators the usual powers to conduct a hearing, administer oaths, subpoena witnesses, and issue awards. It also gives arbitrators the power to interpret and apply "relevant statutory and regulatory requirements, legal precedents, and policy directives." Arbitrators must issue an award within thirty days, unless the parties agree to some other time limit. The act specifies content of an arbitration award, specifically "a brief informal discussion of the factual and legal basis for the award," but does not require that it be formal. Final awards are binding and may be enforced under the Federal Arbitration Act.

Congress addressed the concern about delegation to private decision makers by providing that an arbitration award, unlike an agency adjudications, cannot be used as precedent. Since they are not precedent, unlike agency adjudication, arbitration awards may not be reviewed under the Administrative Procedure Act. Instead, there is judicial review only under the standards of the Federal Arbitration Act. This means that a court will only overturn a binding award upon proof of fraud, collusion, undue influence, exceeding the scope of the submission, or using unlawful procedure. In contrast, the APA standards authorize a reviewing court to overturn an agency's adjudication if it is arbitrary and capricious, affected by an error of law, lacking substantial evidence on the record as a whole, or unconstitutional. It is harder to overturn an arbitration award through judicial review than an agency's adjudication. A federal agency has complete discretion, not subject to judicial review, in deciding whether to use ADR, when the other party agrees to its use.

The ADRA provided new legal infrastructure to ease the bureaucratic barriers to using neutrals. The ADRA authorized agencies to use neutrals from a variety of sources, including the Federal Mediation and Conciliation Service roster, the American Arbitration Association (see www.adr.org) roster, or any individual. It authorized agencies to enter into contracts and establish compensation through agreement with other parties to the dispute.

The statute also provided confidentiality for the parties for dispute resolution communications between a neutral and a party, with certain statutorily enumerated exceptions. All of these had previously been barriers that served agency inertia.

Thus, the ADRA authorizes individual agencies to use the processes of collaboration. Implicity, it authorizes them to participate in multistakeholder dispute resolution processes with other agencies. However, it is not expressly directed at action by a network. The ADRA is increasingly viewed as a success. It may serve as a model for legislation on collaborative public management and collaborative governance, including broader institutionalization of civic engagement and deliberative democracy processes.

Specific Authorizations for Individual Agencies

Congress has enacted specific authorizations to agencies: authorizations for individual agencies to use new governance processes and authorizations for agencies to collaborate in service delivery in specific policy arenas. Individual federal agencies may be authorized, or sometimes required, to use ADR processes for certain kinds of disputes or within certain programs for enforcing public law. Special-purpose authorizations in labor relations have existed for most of the past century. However, in the past two decades, Congress has built such authority into a wide variety of public law programs, including U.S. Department of Agriculture mediation of disputes between the government and farmers over federal agricultural loans; Environmental Protection Agency mediation and arbitration for certain disputes involving the allocation of liability for hazardous waste contamination; mediation of disputes over compliance with the terms of educational grant contracts; and Department of Defense procurement disputes in a variety of forms, including mediation and a form of advisory arbitration known as dispute panels. These are but a few such specific authorizations. By definition, specific authorizations generally run to a single agency; they do not contemplate a network of agencies.

Special Purpose Convening Agencies

Another model for legal infrastructure is to create a special purpose agency with the power to convene stakeholders or mediate. The U.S. Institute for Environmental Conflict Resolution (USIECR) is a relatively young federal agency, established within the Morris Udall Foundation, with the express mission "to assist the Federal Government in implementing section 101 of the National Environmental Policy Act of 1969 (42 U.S.C. 4331) by providing assessment, mediation, and other related services to resolve environmental disputes involving agencies and instrumentalities of the United States" (20 U.S.C. Section 5604). Its mission is to provide a process and mechanism for collaboration across federal, state, local, and Native American sovereign entities for environmental disputes. This work of necessity involves a broader array of nongovernmental stakeholders from both private and nonprofit sectors as well as the broader public through direct citizen participation. By authorizing the USIECR to serve a convening function, the statute indirectly authorizes agencies to participate, and thus to collaborate. Another example is the Federal Mediation and Conciliation Service, which has the power to convene disputing parties in labor and employment and to offer mediation services.

State Legal Infrastructure

Consistent with our federalism, the federal APA and its amendments have no application to state or local agencies. Each state adopts its own framework for state administrative procedure and for public conflict resolution. However, many states look to both the federal government and other states for guidance.

The Model State Administrative Procedures Act

In a model similar to federal law, state administrative procedures acts generally contemplate action by a single agency, not an agency engaged in a collaborative public management network. The United States is blessed with the public service of the National Conference of Commissioners on Uniform State Laws (www.nccusl.org). These scholars and elite practitioners craft model statutes on a wide variety of subjects for states to consider enacting. The Model State Administrative Procedure Act (MSAPA [1981], available on the Web at www.law.upenn.edu/bll/ulc/ulc.htm) is itself silent on alternative dispute resolution and negotiated rulemaking. However, in states that have adopted it, administrators usually have implicit authority to use these processes through their power to enter into contracts. Moreover, most states adopt the MSAPA's general provisions authorizing informal disposition or settlement of cases (§ 1–106), allowing agencies to establish advisory committees (§ 3–101), and requiring agencies to adopt rules for informal procedures available to the public (§ 2–104). All of these provisions provide authority for the kinds of informal, consensus-oriented processes that characterize the new governance.

In the absence of express statutory authorization, binding arbitration, a form of private judging, may raise concerns about unconstitutional delegation of agency regulatory power to private decision makers (Bingham 1997). However, generally none of the other new governance processes pose this problem, because they are all predicated upon agency agreement to the process and to any binding outcome. Moreover, as long as agencies subsequently follow other, more formal procedures for notice and comment to adopt negotiated draft regulations, there is no inherent conflict between traditional rulemaking and negotiated rulemaking, even in the absence of express statutory authority.

However, this legal infrastructure presumes that the final agency action will be taken by one agency acting alone, not as part of a network. The drafters simply did not envision the emergence of networked governance.

State Legal Infrastructure for Negotiation and Dispute Resolution

As is the case in the federal sector, in many states, there is legal infrastructure that authorizes public agencies to use the processes of collaboration, for example, mediation. The

National Conference of Commissioners on Uniform State Laws recently completed work on the new Uniform Mediation Act (available at www.mediate.com/articles/umafinalstyled. cfm). This is another model statute for state legislatures to consider adopting. It provides express authority for government use of mediation in Section 2(6). A number of states have already adopted this uniform act, for example, Illinois.

Many states expressly authorize all state agencies to use new governance processes, either through amendments to their state APAs or executive order (e.g., Massachusetts). As of this writing, there are six comprehensive state offices of dispute resolution, thirty-eight offices focusing on courts, and thirty-four in universities and nonprofits (see www. policyconsensus.org). State legislation on alternative dispute resolution and negotiated rulemaking ranges from the short and broad, to the long and specific. For example, New Mexico simply authorizes agencies to use alternative dispute resolution. In contrast, Texas and Florida have legislation analogous to the federal ADRA and NRA. More common is a general authorization as part of a state administrative procedure act. Indiana authorizes state agencies to use mediation, provided mediators have the same training as mediators for state courts. New Jersey adopted dispute resolution and negotiated rulemaking through the attorney general's power to adopt additional administrative procedures, and these provisions appear in the state administrative code. Again, all of these statutes authorize the processes for collaboration (mediation, facilitation, and negotiation), but they are drafted from the perspective of unitary agency action. A single agency can enter into a process, but the ultimate action is its responsibility, not that of the collaborative.

In addition to these general authorizations, there are myriad specific legislative authorizations for certain state agencies to use particular processes for certain substantive policy work. For example, mediation is a common method for addressing conflicts arising out of special education placements and programs at the state level. State environmental agencies may have the power to use mediation for particular land use disputes, like deciding upon the sites for landfills (Dukes, Piscolish, and Stephens 2000; Institute for Environmental Negotiation 2002; Policy Consensus Initiative 2001).

This legal infrastructure shares the weakness of federal law. It is drafted for a single agency acting alone. It does not expressly address networks or collaborative governance.

COLLABORATIVE PUBLIC MANAGEMENT AND PUBLIC LAW: THE MISSING INDEPENDENT VARIABLE

The study of collaborative public management is an outgrowth of work in intergovernmental relations, privatization, devolution, and nonprofit management. It represents a shift in perspective; instead of viewing relations from the eyes of a single public manager engaged in a linear series of contractual and partnership arrangements, scholars of collaborative public management view the actors from a distance in relation to each other.

When viewed on the policy continuum, collaborative public management is most frequently found midstream, during implementation and project management. Examples include such work as negotiated rulemaking to collaboratively develop rules to implement public law, or collaboration in managing a project, for example, watershed management. In the latter case, a watershed will cross jurisdictional boundaries and implicate the legal authority of federal, state, regional, local, and tribal governments; concerned stakeholders will include various representatives from civil society such as nonprofit environmental organizations, citizen groups representing users of natural resources, and the private sector. Sometimes, a downstream enforcement process, such as a complex piece of multiparty environmental litigation, will be transformed through the mechanism of a negotiated consent decree into an ongoing collaborative public management network for supervising an environmental cleanup, for example.

Law is the invisible independent variable in empirical research on collaborative public management (CPM). A number of authors in this volume note its impact. Agranoff (chapter 9) finds that CPM networks with a legal mandate take action; those without tend to be more informational. There were a number of examples of how law operates as a variable or constraint. Feiok (chapter 10) reports that the state of Florida has enacted a statute authorizing public agencies to collaborate and providing that they can do anything in collaboration that they have power to do apart. Page (chapter 8) explores state mandates for accountability and managing for results in collaboration. Cooper, Bryer, and Meek (chapter 11) discuss how the Los Angeles city charter authorizes and empowers neighborhood councils, which work closely with city agencies on the implementation of policies and programs to deliver public services. Provan, Kenis, and Human (chapter 7) examine legal mandates and legitimacy or effectiveness.

Law is an independent variable that is cropping up, creating incentives, barriers, or obstacles; yet, the nature of these individual statutory provisions is not systematically examined. Law can also be a dependent variable, in that lawmakers decide that an innovation like ADR makes sense and that agencies should make use of it. It is probably safe to say that the majority of legal provisions related to collaborative public management fall into one of two categories: either they were enacted without regard to the emergence of networked structures, or they were enacted after the fact to authorize or mandate collaborative public management once it evolved and was perceived as an effective innovation. This is an area that needs systematic research.

NEW LEGAL INFRASTRUCTURE: ENCOURAGING COLLABORATIVE PUBLIC MANAGEMENT AND COLLABORATIVE GOVERNANCE

While the above statutes pertaining to dispute resolution authorize the processes for collaboration, they were drafted from the perspective of unitary agency decision making. The inherent caution of lawyers may require more explicit language enabling agencies to do this work. There is much experimentation in forms of networked governance; similarly, we are in the "let the thousand flowers bloom" stage of collaborative governance, in which new processes for citizen dialogue and deliberation in the policy process are emerging daily. Legal infrastructure should not inhibit this experimentation. Instead, it should authorize and legitimize it.

There are five key questions that new legal infrastructure must address:

- Delegation: May agencies participate in networks empowered to take action consistent with notions of delegated authority constrained by legislative standards that courts can use in judicial review?
- Authorization to collaborate and Freedom of Information: How do we reconcile collaborative public management and collaborative governance with transparency in government?
- Authorization to involve the public in collaborative governance: How do we foster effective participation in collaborative governance by citizens and stakeholders?
- Authorization to involve the public in collaborative public management: How do we foster broader collaborative governance in public management networks?
- Accountability: What forms and methods of accountability are appropriate in collaboration?

There are a variety of approaches to solving the legal infrastructure problem. One might be a model analogous to a hybrid of the ADRA and NRA. Like the ADRA, it could provide the broad bottom-up authorization for agencies to develop many different collaborative public management and collaborative governance structures through which they are empowered to act collectively, with innovative public participation, and without violating the scope of delegation to any single participant. At the same time, it could provide guidance on what criteria an agency might consider when deciding to use such a collaborative public management structure, much like the NRA criteria to assist an agency in deciding to use negotiated rulemaking. An agency's decision on whether or not to collaborate could, like the decision to use ADR or negotiated rulemaking, be committed to agency discretion. An essential element to foster both transparency and accountability would be, like the case of FACA, to greatly expand public participation and make it effective. Involving the public through collaborative governance would make the work of collaborative public networks more visible and directly accountable in a way that is far more immediate than judicial review. In order to foster continued growth in new processes for dialogue and deliberation, the statute could contain a broad authorization for agencies to use a nonexclusive list of existing models, much like the list in the ADRA of forms of dispute resolution. Similar to the ADRA, it could require that agencies develop capacity in this area by designating a specialist in collaborative governance. The ADRA did not cost money, but an appropriation would have made diffusion of this innovation move more quickly through government.

CONCLUSION

This is only a preliminary attempt to examine the problem of legal infrastructure for collaborative public management and collaborative governance. Agency counsel will be taking much closer looks at the laws pertaining to their specific area of jurisdiction, and there are many, far more precise legal problems they will no doubt articulate. The business of identifying all of these specific issues can be costly for agencies. A more holistic approach to authorizing collaboration, while preserving transparency and accountability, may be in the public interest.

REFERENCES

Ackerman, Bruce, and James Fishkin. 2004. *Deliberation Day.* New Haven, CT: Yale University Press.

Agranoff, Robert, and Michael McGuire. 2003. *Collaborative Public Management: New Strategies for Local Governments.* Washington, DC: Georgetown University Press.

Alexander, Nadja, ed. 2003. *Global Trends in Mediation.* Cologne: Centrale für Mediation.

Arnstein, Sherry. 1969. "A Ladder of Citizen Participation." *Journal of the American Institute of Planners* 35, no. 4: 216–24.

Bingham, Lisa B. 1997. "Alternative Dispute Resolution in Public Administration." In *Handbook of Public Law and Administration,* ed. Phillip J. Cooper and Chester A. Newland, 546–66. San Francisco: Jossey-Bass.

———. 2003. *Mediation at Work: Transforming Workplace Conflict at the United States Postal Service.* Arlington, VA: IBM Center for the Business of Government.

———. 2004. "Control over Dispute System Design and Mandatory Commercial Arbitration." *Law and Contemporary Problems* 67, nos. 1&2: 221–251.

———. 2006. "The New Urban Governance: Processes for Engaging Citizens and Stakeholders." *Review of Policy Research* 23, no. 4: 815–26.

Bingham, Lisa B., and Charles R. Wise. 1996. "The Administrative Dispute Resolution Act of 1990: How Do We Evaluate Its Success?" *Journal of Public Administration, Research and Theory* 6, no. 3: 383–414.

Bingham, Lisa B.; Tina Nabatchi; and Rosemary O'Leary. 2005. "The New Governance: Practices and Processes for Stakeholder and Citizen Participation in the Work of Government." *Public Administration Review* 65, no. 5: 547–58.

Bingham, Lisa B.; Rosemary O'Leary; and Tina Nabatchi. 2005. "New Governance Processes for Stakeholder and Citizen Participation in the Work of Government." *National Civic Review* 94, no. 1: 54–61 (special issue devoted to civic engagement and deliberative democracy).

Booher, David E. 2004. "Collaborative Governance Practices and Democracy." *National Civic Review* 93, no. 4: 32–46.

Boxer-Macomber, Lauri D. 2003. *Too Much Sun? Emerging Challenges Presented by California and Federal Open Meeting Legislation to Public Policy Consensus Building Processes.* Sacramento, CA: Center for Collaborative Policy (www.csus.edu/ccp).

Breger, Marshall J.; Gerald S. Schatz; and Deborah Schick Laufer, eds. 2001. *Federal Administrative Dispute Resolution Deskbook.* Chicago: American Bar Association.

Bush, Robert A. Baruch, and Lisa B. Bingham. 2005. "Knowledge Gaps: The Final Conference of the Hewlett ADR Theory Centers." *Conflict Resolution Quarterly* 23, no. 1: 99–122.

Carpenter, Susan L., and W.J.D. Kennedy. 1988. *Managing Public Disputes: A Practical Guide to Handling Conflict and Reaching Agreements.* San Francisco: Jossey-Bass.

Carson, Lyn, and Janette Hartz-Karp. 2005. "Adapting and Combining Deliberative Designs." In *The Deliberative Democracy Handbook: Strategies for Effective Civic Engagement in the 21st Century,* ed. John Gastil and Peter Levine, 120. San Francisco: Jossey-Bass.

Cooper, Phillip J. 2000. *Public Law and Public Administration.* 3d ed. Itasca, IL: F.E. Peacock.

Dannin, Ellen. 2005. "Red Tape or Accountability: Privatization, Public-ization, and Public Values." *Cornell Journal of Law and Public Policy* 15: 111–63.

Dukes, E. Franklin; Marina A. Piscolish; and John B. Stephens. 2000. *Reaching for Higher Ground in Conflict Resolution: Tools for Powerful Groups and Communities.* San Francisco: Jossey-Bass.

Durant, Robert F.; Daniel J. Fiorino; and Rosemary O'Leary, eds. 2004. *Environmental Governance Reconsidered: Challenges, Choices, and Opportunities.* Cambridge, MA: MIT Press.

Fisher, Roger; William Ury; and Bruce Patton. 1991. *Getting to Yes.* 2d ed. New York: Penguin.

Forester, John. 1999. *The Deliberative Practitioner: Encouraging Participatory Planning Processes.* Cambridge, MA: MIT Press.

Freeman, Jody. 2000. "The Private Role in Public Governance." *New York University Law Review* 75: 543–675.

Fung, Archon. 2006. "Varieties of Participation in Complex Governance." *Public Administration Review* 66, no. 1: 66–75.

Fung, Archon, and Erik Olin Wright, eds. 2003. *Deepening Democracy: Institutional Innovations in Empowered Participatory Governance.* London: Verso.

Gastil, John, and Peter Levine. 2005. *The Deliberative Democracy Handbook: Strategies for Effective Civic Engagement in the 21st Century.* San Francisco: Jossey-Bass.

Henton, Doug; John Melville; Terry Amsler; and Malka Kopell. 2005. *Collaborative Governance: A Guide for Grantmakers.* Menlo Park, CA: William and Flora Hewlett Foundation.

Institute for Environmental Negotiation. 2002. *A Stream Corridor Protection Strategy for Local Government.* Charlottesville: University of Virginia.

Jones, Tricia S., ed. 2004. "Conflict Resolution in the Field: Special Symposium." *Conflict Resolution Quarterly* 22, no. 1–2: 1–320.

Kerwin, Cornelius M. 1997. "Negotiated Rulemaking." In *The Handbook of Public Law and Public Administration,* ed. Phillip J. Cooper and Chester A. Newland, 225–36. San Francisco: Jossey-Bass.

———. 2003. *Rulemaking: How Government Agencies Write Law and Make Policy.* 3rd ed. Washington, DC: CQ Press.

Kettl, Donald F. 2002. *The Transformation of Governance: Public Administration for Twenty-First Century America.* Baltimore: Johns Hopkins University Press.

Lind, E. Allan, and Thomas R. Tyler. 1988. *The Social Psychology of Procedural Justice.* New York: Plenum Press.

Moore, Christopher W. 2003. *The Mediation Process: Practical Strategies for Resolving Conflict.* 3d ed. San Francisco: Jossey-Bass.

O'Leary, Rosemary, and Lisa B. Bingham, eds. 2003. *The Promise and Performance of Environmental Conflict Resolution.* Washington, DC: Resources for the Future.

O'Leary, Rosemary; Catherine Gerard; and Lisa B. Bingham, eds. 2006. "Symposium: Collaborative Public Management: Introduction." *Public Administration Review* 66, no. 1: 6–9.

O'Leary, Rosemary; Malka Kopell; and Terry Amsler. 2005. *Environmental Conflict Resolution: A Guide for Grantmakers.* Menlo Park, CA: William and Flora Hewlett Foundation.

Policy Consensus Initiative. 2001. *States Mediating Change: Improving Governance Through Collaboration.* Santa Fe, NM and Bismarck, ND: Policy Consensus Initiative.

Roberts, Nancy. 2003. "Public Deliberation in an Age of Direct Citizen Participation." *American Review of Public Administration* 33, no. 1: 1–39.

Rosenbloom, David H. 2003. *Administrative Law for Public Managers.* Boulder, CO: Westview Press.

Rosenbloom, David H., and Rosemary O'Leary. 1997. *Public Administration and Law.* 2d ed. New York: Marcel Dekker.

Salamon, Lester, ed. 2002. *The Tools of Government: A Guide to the New Governance.* New York: Oxford University Press.

Schwarz, Roger. 2002. *The Skilled Facilitator: A Comprehensive Resource for Consultants, Facilitators, Managers, Trainers, and Coaches.* San Francisco: Jossey-Bass.

Senger, Jeffrey M. 2003. *Federal Dispute Resolution: Using ADR with the United States Government.* San Francisco: Jossey-Bass.

Susskind, Lawrence, and Jeffrey Cruikshank. 1987. *Breaking the Impasse: Consensual Approaches to Resolving Public Disputes.* New York: Basic Books.

Susskind, Lawrence; Sarah McKearnan; and Jennifer Thomas-Larmer. 1999. *The Consensus-Building Handbook: A Comprehensive Guide to Reaching Agreement.* Thousand Oaks, CA: Sage.

Torres, Lars Hasselblad. 2003. *Deliberative Democracy: A Survey of the Field, A Report Prepared for the William and Flora Hewlett Foundation.* Washington, DC: AmericaSpeaks.

Williamson, Abigail. 2004. *Mapping Public Deliberation.* Cambridge, MA: John F. Kennedy School of Government.

CHAPTER 14

Learning to Do and Doing to Learn
Teaching Managers to Collaborate in Networks

LISA BLOMGREN BINGHAM, JODI SANDFORT, AND
ROSEMARY O'LEARY

How do we cultivate the practice of collaborative public management? George Frederickson early observed (1999, 702) that public administration is moving "toward theories of cooperation, networking, governance, and institution building and maintenance" in response to the "declining relationship between jurisdiction and public management" in a "fragmented and disarticulated state." Frederickson emphasized institutionalism, public sector network theory, and governance theory as relevant to the future of public administration research. He defined institutionalism as pertaining to "social constructs of rules, roles, norms, and the expectations that constrain individual and group choice and behavior" (703), public sector network theory as pertaining to "structures of interdependence" that have "formal and informal linkages that include exchange or reciprocal relations, common interests, and bonds of shared beliefs and professional perspectives" (704–5), and governance theory as occurring at institutional, organizational or managerial, and technical or work levels, including formal and informal rules, hierarchies, and procedures, and influenced by administrative law, principal–agent theory, transaction cost analysis, leadership theory, and others (705–6).

Bryson and Crosby (chapter 4, this volume) theorize that collaboration across sectors emerges after the failure of a single sector to address a public policy problem; they define sectors as markets and business, nonprofit organizations, community and the public, the media, and government. Lester Salamon (2005, 16) recently observed, "Unlike both traditional public administration and the new public management, the new governance shifts the emphasis from management skills and the control of large bureaucratic organizations to enablement skills, the skills required to engage partners arrayed horizontally in networks, to bring multiple stakeholders together for a common end in a situation of interdependence." McGuire (forthcoming 2008, 2) observes, "A 'profession' emerges as an occupational grouping matures and there is an identifiable body of technical knowledge—perhaps what we need to do in public management is reconfigure the professional identity to match the new third-party governance world."

How does public administration as a field begin to reconfigure managers' professional identity? This is a new landscape (Posner forthcoming 2008). In a recent article, Feldman and colleagues (2006, 93) provide a compelling vision of this new professional identity: "The public manager as inclusive manager facilitates the practice of democracy by creating opportunities for people with different ways of knowing public problems to work together in a collective space to solve problems." Public managers and administrators need to combine many different disciplines; they need a synthesis of what we are learning not only in public affairs but also in political science, social psychology, organizational behavior, and communications (Bingham and O'Leary 2006). They need to combine management skills with network theory, negotiation theory, and institutional theory to inform practice. They need to practice public policy dispute resolution, stakeholder processes, and civic engagement. They need to operate within public law's frameworks for collaboration. They need to understand collaborative governance at the local, regional, state, national, and transnational levels.

Agranoff (chapter 9, this volume) observes that in collaborative public management, knowledge is the key. However, knowledge is not a disembodied platonic idea; Agranoff describes it as a combination of experience, value, context, and insight, because it is knowledge as applied to make sense of new experiences and information. Drawing upon scholars of the philosophy of science, he distinguishes between explicit knowledge and tacit knowledge. When we consider the various new knowledge and practices required now of public managers, these concepts become helpful as analytical categories to inform teaching techniques.

However, this is not a question of simply using book learning for explicit knowledge about analytical tools or theory, on the one hand, and workshops on practical skills for developing tacit knowledge, on the other. For us, this approach misses a critical opportunity. Rather than seeing explicit knowledge and tacit knowledge as a dichotomy, we must strive to create learning opportunities that embrace both as a single phenomenon. As new social theories illustrate, in reality, both are two sides of the same coin, both are equally important to the accomplishment of effective collaborative management (Giddens 1984; Nicolini, Yanow, and Gherardi 2003; Sewell 1992). It certainly may be easier to develop explicit knowledge by bringing in other people to fill in gaps, read articles, or attend seminars. However, it may be more difficult to develop the implicit, tacit knowledge of how to work with diverse people, analyze situations in real time, or seize the moment in collaboration to achieve consensus by reading articles or attending seminars. Agranoff observes that "[k]nowledge is broader, deeper, and richer than data or information"; knowledge is how humans combine information with experience and insight to do work: It is "both a process and an outcome" (Agranoff, chapter 9, this volume).

Public managers need to learn to do and do to learn how to inhabit this new role. Its practice includes many capabilities, such as designing a network with the necessary players at the table, structuring governance for the collaborative group, participating in the varieties and structures of networks effectively using collaborative practices, negotiating ethically to best leverage agency resources, facilitating meetings of the network, managing conflict among network members, effectively engaging the public, including designing and sequencing civic engagement to make effective use of public knowledge, designing useful systems for evaluating the outcomes of collaboration, and operating within the legal constraints on collaborative public agency action. In order for public managers to engage in artful practice of these various areas of competence, our teaching methods must adapt. In this concluding chapter, we hope to map out an approach to cultivating artful and effective practice of collaborative public management.

THE COLLABORATIVE PUBLIC MANAGER: GOVERNANCE IN A NETWORK

A number of scholars note the disconnect between the institutional reality and dominant concepts of public management education. Lester Salamon (2005, 7–8) recently noted, "We need to move from training public servants or policy analysts toward training what I call professional citizens." Traditionally, public servants and policy analysts are taught to function in an expertise-driven decisional process. We train public administrators to function within a hierarchical bureaucracy, which is essentially a deductive process. Managers start with a theory of the policy problem, collect information and evidence regarding different approaches, evaluate reliability, and make a considered judgment about how to advance the public good within the scope of their delegated authority. This is a paternalistic model in which those governed are asked to accept arguments from authority based on claims of superior technical expertise. The model depends upon a linear, top-down authority structure and the notion of a chain of command (as in "the buck stops here").

Networks differ fundamentally from a single agency in the essence of their organization (Powell 1990). Instead of a single member of a chain of command making an executive decision, multiple managers and stakeholders negotiate the decision. Moreover, they are not simply negotiating the final outcome; they are negotiating every intermediate issue, including but not limited to the process through which decisions are made, relevant information, nature and form of intermediate and final outcomes, decision rules, role of the public, and steps for implementation. Everything is on the table; there is no assumption that traditionally authoritative expertise such as that of trained policy analysts will determine the outcomes. The very terms of knowing are open for negotiation; multiple types of substantive expertise are needed for addressing the policy problem and multiple sources are often consulted.

Network participants may each come from an independent chain of command, or they may come from an organization with a nonhierarchical structure. Some of the network participants may not have the power to commit their organization to a binding outcome, but instead only the power to recommend its approval, perhaps even ratification, through a vote of the membership or a nonprofit's board of directors.

A network's decision process also differs from the traditional conception of expert administration. The outcome is not rationally dictated through a deductive process; it may be knowledge or wisdom developed inductively by incorporating the different frames of reference, backgrounds, values, and experiences of the participants.

A naive student might ask how this differs from a committee, team, or working group within a traditional bureaucracy, but the difference goes to the heart of the work. Within a traditional bureaucracy, the team, committee, or group always reports to someone up the food chain who has the power to impose a decision in the event of an impasse. The question of what happens if the members of the network reach an impasse is itself subject to negotiation and agreement. Moreover, most networks start from the position of consensus as a decision norm; in other words, there is no majority vote—there must instead be unanimity. One participant can veto an agreement on any of the issues under negotiation. Public administrators need fully to understand the importance of this form of public management and the absolute necessity of mastering the skill sets for collaboration, negotiation, conflict management, and facilitation to function in a network.

Connelly, Zhang, and Faerman (chapter 2, this volume) explain how collaboration presents many new paradoxes for the public manager. They find that as managers work both within their own organizations and within networks, they are challenged in very different ways. Collaborative managers must work both with autonomy (within their own organizations) and interdependence (as members of a network). Collaborative managers and their networks have both common and diverse goals. Collaborative managers must work both with a fewer number (because organizations are blended into a network) and a greater variety of groups that are increasingly more diverse. Collaborative managers need to be both participative and authoritative. Collaborative managers need to see the forest and the trees. Collaborative managers need to balance advocacy and inquiry.

As our contributors to this volume document and illustrate, there has been dramatic growth in both theoretical and empirical literature describing the nature and breadth of collaboration across the varieties of collaborative networks. Networks vary in the nature of their membership, governance, structure, and the nature of ties. There is a growing body of theoretical work on varieties of network structure and function, descriptions of how networks vary from local, regional, state, and national to transnational governance issues, and selected empirical case studies of specific networks.

To be an effective manager in a networked world, these challenges demand different skill sets. This is a new type of leadership: they must inspire; they cannot dictate. In their case study of the International Space Station, Lambright and Pizzarella (chapter 12, this volume) illustrate the critical role of the collaboration champion, the manager who keeps the project and partnership going. There is not only differentiation of roles; managers need the skills to tolerate the paradoxes and the corresponding ambiguity. This practice requires artistry and tacit knowledge in the context of limited authority; managers need to inspire rather than impose. Connelly, Zhang, and Faerman (chapter 2, this volume) also point out the basic paradox of collaboration—that both parties can "win" (cf. Fisher, Ury, and Patton, 1991). Together, the participants in the network can search for solutions that fundamentally transcend the position of any single participant. Connelly, Zhang, and Faerman discuss four factors: (1) initial dispositions to collaborate, (2) issues and incentives, (3) number and variety of groups, and (4) leadership. These factors map very closely to the issues that Huxham and Vangan (2005) discuss in their synthesis of many years of study of collaborative practice. In various settings, they find that continued and focused attention must be paid to the process of collaboration itself in order for network structures to maintain their form and achieve the desired outcomes. In *Educating the Reflective Practitioner*, Donald Schön (1987) proposed an active learning model in which people are (1) doing, (2) reflecting, (3) modifying practice, and (4) doing again. Reflective practice cultivates integrative thinking. This results in "skilled social action" (Fligstein 2001). Sharon Parks (2005) has written a book about how Ron Heifetz teaches leadership at the Kennedy School of Harvard University. The pedagogy she documents embodies this approach. These paradoxes capture the artfulness of collaborative practice.

McGuire (forthcoming 2008) conducts an empirical study of county-level emergency management agencies. Emergency management is an interesting case because the professional institutional boundaries are being formed at a time when the work is dependent upon abilities of staff to collaborate. McGuire examines how exposure to different flavors of professional development training contributes to collaborative management practice. While education overall is a significant predictor, the results also suggest that mid-career professional development courses matter—the specialized training in two cases is a significant predictor of collaborative activity (even when it is not stressing collaborative practices, in and of itself). For the high-performing counties, in fact, this professional development is a more important predictor. McGuire discusses the causal mechanisms for this effect and how it can be true when collaboration is not a focus in the training. He suggests that knowledge transfer among participants teaches that collaboration is the way to get things done. Thus, it is increasingly clear that to engage in networked governance, students must both do to learn and learn to do collaborative public management.

ARTFUL AND EFFECTIVE PRACTICE: COLLABORATIVE CAPABILITIES

New network realities necessitate a different type of practice and new capacities. We use the word "capability" advisedly, in the sense of being able to do, not simply being passively competent. The collaborative public manager needs capabilities in:

- Designing a network with the necessary players at the table;
- Structuring governance for the collaborative group;
- Negotiating ethically to best leverage agency resources;
- Facilitating meetings of the network;
- Managing conflict among network members;
- Effectively engaging the public, including designing and sequencing civic engagement to make effective use of public knowledge;
- Designing useful systems for evaluating the outcomes of collaboration; and
- Operating within the legal constraints on collaborative public agency action.

There is a already a substantial body of research and curricula upon which the field of public administration can draw to develop these capabilities in public managers; it exists in the fields of negotiation, conflict resolution, conflict management, and participatory democracy.

Designing the Network: Knowing When to Collaborate and with Whom

McGuire's study (forthcoming 2008) suggests that the field of public administration needs to redesign both degree programs and mid-career professional development to more closely map to what people are grappling with in the field: how analytically to determine when and how to collaborate. Collaboration as a process is itself the subject of a growing body of literature. This literature is both theoretical and empirical, and examines the conditions precedent to successful collaboration, how to measure collaboration, and collaboration as both a process and a skill set of best practices. Collaboration is pervasive, but not always necessary. Managers first need to recognize whether they need to collaborate with partners (other agencies, nonprofit organizations, the private sector, other elements of the public or civil society) in order to accomplish a policy goal or objective. Next, they need to know when to collaborate (is the problem sufficiently identified and developed or ripe for collaboration?). Finally, collaboration starts with the right players. In order for collaboration to be effective, public managers may need the skills to analyze relevant stakeholders and convene a representative group.

Provan, Kenis, and Human (chapter 7, this volume) identify three dimensions of legitimacy that networks must establish: network-as-form, network-as-entity, and network-as-interaction. In other words, they must establish that the network form of governance is necessary and appropriate, that the network's structure, goals, and governance are legitimate, and that cooperative interactions are legitimate. These findings speak directly to the issue of network design. There is a literature on convening stakeholder groups from the discipline of environmental and public policy conflict resolution that is instructive (Moore 2003; Susskind, McKearnan, and Thomas-Larmer 1999). For example, it can help managers identify which players have the ability to veto a deal or prevent its implementation. It can help managers identify which players have authority and jurisdiction over an issue. Managers need to learn to inhabit the role of convener. They need to see their roles as related to broad framing of public problems to inspire participation.

There are substantive areas of knowledge that can help managers understand how one might motivate the necessary players to collaborate. For example, managers can benefit from organizational theory, including contingency theory (alignment/lack of alignment), multiple frames, and performance measurement. Managers can use organizational behavior (motivation, group dynamics such as formation stages of development, decision making) and differences in taking in and processing information (e.g., Myers-Briggs tests). Ingraham and Getha-Taylor (chapter 5, this volume) discuss the current disconnect between institutional design in the redesigned federal human resources system and the espoused goals of the public sector workforce, for example, more working across boundaries and problem solving. Managers are motivated to collaborate because people want rewarding work and to feel like they are making a difference working on significant problems. To achieve this, they rarely fit within the boundaries of one organization. Moreover, incentives for collaboration may include cost savings and efficiency. Design of the network should identify and take advantage of these potential incentives, and structure rewards for collaborative behavior not only at the individual level but also at the program level if individual rewards are not feasible.

Structuring Governance for the Collaborative Network

Like any other organization, members of a collaborative public network need to reach an understanding of how they will govern themselves to accomplish their task. This includes skills like identifying goals, framing the mission, and setting an agenda of work. It includes identifying ground rules, agreeing upon conflict management processes, and selecting decision norms (majority vote or consensus, for example). Members should address how they will communicate their ongoing work to their respective organizations, agencies, or constituencies. Governance may also include decisions about transparency or communication with the public, civic engagement and the public voice, and accountability to each other and to the public. Research on multiparty negotiation suggests that reaching agreement on these preliminary issues can help build trust for the balance of the negotiation (Moore 2003). Research on facilitated collaborative management of watersheds suggests that the work of reaching agreement on these issues can help build social capital among the stakeholders that carries over to other collaborative work over time (Leach and Sabatier 2003).

Negotiating in a Network

Every leading scholar writing on collaborative public management emphasizes that negotiation skills are essential to effective participation. It is the fundamental skill set for collaborative problem solving. It helps managers recognize and use different types of knowledge and find ways of processing and reconciling differences. They need to learn negotiation analysis, which entails recognizing their best alternative to a negotiated agreement, their own interests, and reservation prices or the outer bound of the bargaining set. The relevant skills entail interest-based, principled, or integrative bargaining (Fisher, Ury, and Patton 1991; Lax and Sebenius 1986; Schneider and Honeyman 2006). These forms of bargaining help managers learn how to identify interests or basic needs such as security, economic well-being, belonging, recognition, and autonomy, determine which ones are shared, reconcilable, and conflicting, and craft agreements to maximize joint gains to the greatest possible extent. Negotiators must also learn the difference between interest-based and competitive bargaining, between creating value and claiming it in a negotiation, and how to recognize bad faith or hard bargaining tactics.

This family of skills also includes active listening and communication. Active listening includes learning to paraphrase, ask open-ended questions (who, what, where, why, how, why not?), and to make statements in the first person (I or we statements) rather than second person (you statements are often heard as accusations). Mastery of negotiation skills gives managers the ability to suspend judgment and consider alternatives, which is an essential quality of creativity. Creativity helps managers to recognize cultural differences and symbols; this in turn enables them to cross boundaries and surmount barriers to agreement. Through extensive use of simulations involving multiparty negotiation, students and managers can become comfortable with the notion of negotiating as a stakeholder in a group. By learning these skills, they will be more effective at leveraging agency resources to accomplish shared goals and at the same time knowing when the agency can function most effectively without collaboration.

Facilitating Meetings of the Group

Unless the group hires an outside facilitator, members will need to have someone run the meetings. There is an art and science to good facilitation skills, that is, skills that allow each participant in a meeting to contribute their knowledge constructively and feel that they have been heard (Schwarz 1994, 19–41). These skills include active listening (paraphrasing, mirroring, problem-solving questions), knowing when to suggest that the group break down into small group meetings or committees, and knowing when stakeholders need to caucus or meet privately with one or more other participants to address some issue. Facilitators can help group members engage in brainstorming to generate ideas for solving a shared problem. There are a variety of techniques for brainstorming, visioning, and story-boarding, which are all procedures for encouraging group members to "think outside the box." The facilitator acts as a recorder, keeps stakeholders from criticizing any idea prematurely, helps the group members set priorities for the ideas they want to discuss, and helps them to combine these ideas in ways that yield a workable agreement. Group members develop social capital and learn how to resolve conflict. Role-plays and interactive simulations can permit students and managers to become comfortable in the facilitator role. Empirical research on facilitation in networks can deepen students' understanding of this dynamic (Leach and Sabatier 2003).

Managing Conflict in a Network

Milward and Provan (2006) find that one of the most important tasks for network managers is to try to minimize the occurrence of conflict and try to resolve it successfully if and when it does occur. Although network organizations generally commit to achieving network-level goals, conflict among network participants is inevitable. Networks, by their very nature, are composed of multiple members with different organization-level goals, methods of operation and service, and cultures.

Networks are interorganizational and interpersonal. There are multiple forums for decision making. There are multiple parties and multiple issues. Often there is technical complexity. There are often unequal power and resources. Conflicts in networks often are public and sometimes political. All of these characteristics make managing conflicts in networks extraordinarily challenging.

Conflict resolution is effectively group problem solving (Deutsch and Coleman 2000). There are many guiding principles from the conflict resolution literature that can assist in managing conflicts in networks. These include reframing (redefining) conflicts as mutual problems to be solved together (Moore 2003); educating each other in order to better understand the problem; developing a conflict management plan that addresses procedures, substance, and relationships; involving the members of the network in designing the process and developing a solution; balanced representation; insisting that network members participate directly, fully, and in good faith; maintaining transparency; timeliness; and implementability of agreements.

Effectively Engaging the Public

Boyte (2005) reenvisions public administration education as training to be a "citizen professional." Perhaps the citizen professional relates to communities organically, as a member of the community rather than a servant or provider of services to be consumed. All public managers have ethical and legal obligations to involve the public in decision making. When policy issues concern the public, conflict may emerge (Dukes 1996). Similarly, when a collaborative public network does the public's work, appropriate civic engagement is important both to address the potential conflicts and to foster participation in democracy. Collaborative public management networks have been criticized for their lack of transparency and lack of accountability to the public. The appropriate use of civic engagement, with the public as an essential partner in governance, can provide a mechanism through which to make the decision process and content transparent, and can enhance managers' accountability by providing them with an independent source of information on public preferences and values.

New forms of civic engagement allow managers to work in partnership with the public, within the scope of their delegated authority and the constraints of representative democracy. Cooper, Bryer, and Meek (chapter 11, this volume) provide a rich description of citizen-centered collaborative public management through the use of neighborhood councils in Los Angeles. In these councils, neighborhoods negotiate directly with city agencies regarding public services and community needs, creating new memoranda of understanding and lines of communication.

There are a wide variety of tools and approaches inherent in collaborative governance, "a term used to describe the integration of reasoned discussions by the citizens and other residents into the decision-making of public representatives, especially when these approaches are embedded in the workings of local governance over time" (www.ca-ilg.org, an excellent resource for information on local government uses). Collaborative governance includes deliberative democracy, a form of participatory democracy in which citizens engage in civil, small group discussions, exchanging viewpoints, and sharing their informed judgment and values with public managers and elected officials to influence decision making. This alternative to adversarial democracy envisions citizens engaging in face-to-face discussion in an effort to reach consensus rather than in acrimonious debate (Mansbridge 1980). Through deliberative practice, public officials "work and learn with others" (Forester 1999, 2).

There is a growing literature on new forms of dialogue, deliberation, deliberative democracy, and collaborative governance (Gastil and Levine 2005; Innes and Booher 2004). These include deliberative polling, choicework dialogues, 21st Century Town Meetings, study circles, public solutions dialogues, citizen juries, national issues forums, and a variety of other models (Bingham, Nabatchi, and O'Leary 2005). Managers need to know how to design a sequence of processes for meaningful civic engagement by a network. For example, in determining how to allocate limited vaccine supplies during a possible future flu pandemic, the Centers for Disease Control and a number of network partners have designed a series of dialogues to engage the public in setting priorities and weighing important values (www.everyday-democracy.org). Collaborative public managers need to develop both the substantive, explicit knowledge of these new forms and the facility to work within them and use them for networks to become both transparent and accountable to the public.

Evaluating Collaborative Public Management: Accountability and Staying the Course

Another essential response to the criticism that collaborative public management networks are not sufficiently accountable for accomplishing the public's work is to conduct a rigorous, responsible, well-designed, and useful evaluation. Evaluation should be a piece of the network's initial design and construction. Evaluation can help the network learn continuously. Public administrators should be introduced to principles from public program evaluation as they apply to the collaborative context. Page (chapter 8, this volume) draws upon the Agranoff and McGuire (2003) typology of skills: activating, framing, motivating, synthesizing. They developed this typology over a period of time in their study of networks for economic development. Page's study illustrates how literature on the explicit knowledge of performance measurement can be an important tool for maintaining and directing collaborative efforts in practice.

Thomson, Perry, and Miller (chapter 6, this volume) provide the tools, model, and framework for evaluating the quality of collaboration in the network to its outcomes. They propose a multidimensional model with governance, administration, mutuality, norms, and autonomy as factors related to the quality of collaboration. They describe how this in turn provides a foundation for examining the relation between collaboration processes and outcomes.

There is a substantial literature on evaluating collaboration in environmental conflict resolution and policy consensus processes that has a direct bearing on collaborative public management and collaborative governance (Bingham et al. 2003; Bingham and O'Leary 2006). Environmental conflict resolution entails the creation of a collaborative network of governmental stakeholders from federal, state, and local government, tribal sovereign governments, nongovernmental organizations, citizen groups, and the private sector. It incorporates elements of civic engagement. The upstream/midstream/downstream frame for the policy process has proved useful in that context (O'Leary and Bingham 2003). Upstream includes the formation of policy, midstream its implementation, and downstream its enforcement. For assessing success upstream in the policy process, indicators include incorporating public values, improving decision quality, resolving conflict, building trust, educating the public, socioeconomic representativeness, consultation and/or outreach with the wider public, diversity of participants and views represented, integration of concerns, information exchange, mutual learning, effectiveness, efficiency and equity, cost avoidance, project/decision acceptability as legitimate, mutual respect, social capital, increased overall knowledge, increased individual stakeholder knowledge, identifying threats, goals, and management actions, adequacy of plan to achieve goals, and certainty of agreement on implementation.

For midstream uses, indicators include positive net benefits, measurable objectives, cost-effective implementation, financial feasibility, fair distribution of costs among parties, flexibility, incentive compatibility, improved problem-solving capacity, enhanced social capital, clear documentation protocols, reduction in conflict and hostility, improved relations, cognitive and affective shift, ability to resolve subsequent disputes, durable agreements, comprehensive or complete agreements, improved party capacity, and improved government decision making. For downstream uses, researchers have looked to participant procedural justice, comparative satisfaction of different categories of disputants, reducing or narrowing issues, referrals, and voluntary use rates.

Many of these criteria, developed to assess collaboration in one context, have a direct bearing on evaluating the success of collaboration in the new governance. Public managers need a framework for thinking about how to measure results in collaboration.

Operating Within Legal Constraints on Collaborative Agency Action

Public administrators have an obligation to know and comply with the Constitution and public law. Robert Agranoff (2007) finds that legal constraints have an impact on the work of collaborative public management networks; networks with express legislative authorization or charters are more likely to take action rather than simply to share information. Feiock (chapter 10, this volume) illustrates how legal authority to collaborate facilitates local government collective action. Whether perceived legal constraints are real or merely feared, managers must address them for collaboration to reach its full potential in public management and governance. Existing legal infrastructure in state and federal administrative law provides that a public agency may use certain processes in governance across the policy continuum (legislative, quasi-legislative, quasi-judicial, and judicial; see Bingham, Nabatchi, and O'Leary et al. 2005). These statutes do not expressly refer to collaborative public management networks (Bingham chapter 13, this volume). However, they have been used to authorize collaboration in the fields of environmental and public policy conflict resolution. Understanding the scope of existing legal infrastructure as it provides authority and incentives, or presents constraints, obstacles, and barriers, is an important form of explicit knowledge that can shape practice.

TEACHING COLLABORATIVE PUBLIC MANAGEMENT

Conditions within the field require those of us involved in training the next and current generations of public managers to deeply consider *what* we teach, *why* we teach, and *how* we bring these new topics into the classroom. This is a tall charge. Most of us involved in teaching were, ourselves, trained during an era that emphasized the control and mastery of facts rather than application. We were socialized into academic disciplines that focused on the development and refinement of abstract knowledge rather than that gleaned through practice experience. In short, many of us feel more comfortable teaching topics that draw upon explicit knowledge—concrete information, facts, predictable relationships—rather than situations requiring the development and refinement of tacit knowledge. Some professional education creates a dichotomy between these two types of learning; law schools, for example, have doctrinal classes where students master explicit knowledge and clinics where they develop tacit knowledge through practice. Yet, the potential in public affairs is to bridge these two traditions, recognizing that the new public management practice requires professionals who are skilled as analytic and social actors. We must strive to create learning opportunities that embrace both as a single phenomenon. As McGuire (forthcoming 2008) points out, a professional emerges through the training of people in particular knowledge and skills. In public management, we must align our pedagogy with the realities that public management occurs in networks of many different actors.

In this chapter, we have described a new body of skills that need to be taught if people are to be equipped to function effectively as professionals. They must understand the optimal design and functioning of networks as well as possess the interpersonal skills to navigate the distinct worldviews of network actors. They must understand the processes of negotiation, facilitation, and techniques of conflict management. They must see models of deep public engagement and relevant program evaluation, as well as learn how to improvise to adapt good ideas from these models to particular circumstances. They must understand the legal parameters of public institutions and how to work effectively with them. One response would be merely to add such topics to the conventional curriculum and push even more content into already dense courses or develop content modules for mid-career training programs.

However, more fundamental questions also demand attention: Why do we teach what we teach? How do we teach it? Unfortunately, few of us take the time to ask such questions about the work we do in the classroom. Yet, they lie at the heart of what must be addressed if we are to help new professionals learn to do the work of collaborative management and comprehend that professionalism is an ongoing process of learning. More than twenty years ago, Donald Schön (1987) challenged instructors in professional schools to grapple with these fundamental questions. His thesis was simple and rings even more true today: the claim professions make as the keeper of extraordinary knowledge is in question, as the most important areas of professional practice are beyond conventional boundaries. While research is supposed to provide professional schools with explicit knowledge to teach, the very form and function of research assures that less and less of this knowledge is useful in practice. Instead, competent practice lies in artistry that involves problem framing, implementation, and improvisation, all of which draw upon and move beyond explicit knowledge coming from science. In this concept, students cannot be taught what they need to know. Instead, they can be coached, through practicing what they need to do, much as what is done in architectural studios and music conservatories. Through these experiences, they are initiated into the traditions of the practice that is their professional work (Davenport and Prusak 2000).

For Schön and for others who use such an approach (Heifetz 1998; Parks 2005), the classroom becomes a setting where students engage in active learning. They act, reflect, modify their practice, and act again. Through such processes, they develop experience that integrates the explicit knowledge of their profession with the tacit knowledge of skilled social action (Fligstein 2001). This approach allows them to grapple with paradox and the challenge of responding to the unexpected. It gives them experience in thinking from outside their own perspectives, managing their time, and performing under pressure. Such experiences prepare them for managing the diverse interests and worldviews inherent in the practice of public management. For Schön (1987), such a reflective practicum should be at the center of professional school curricula, embodied in courses such as the capstone workshops now conventionally found in most public policy and management schools, and woven through all other courses.

This conception, though, begs the question of how instructors are to bring such an approach into the classroom. Case studies (written, video, or audio) bring some of the complexity of practice into the classroom. However, for case teaching to be useful in the cultivating of reflective practice, the case studies must be used as triggers for experience rather than examples exemplifying particular principles. Rather than focusing case analysis on trying to determine the causal element of the situation, cases can be more appropriately used to provide contextual details for analysis. For example, an initial exercise might include a collaboration assessment in which students learn how to determine whether collaboration is appropriate and likely to succeed.

Case studies also can be used to provide the backdrop of simulations or role plays, providing critical details about who, what, why, and where. For a unit on network governance, for example, students might be put into groups and asked to reach agreement on governance for a particular network. Multistakeholder negotiation exercises can help emphasize the importance of communicating in ways that accommodate different worldviews. Thoroughly debriefing such experiences, though, is critical to deep learning. Through reflection in discussion or writing, students can begin to glean more insight about how explicit and tacit knowledge work together in effective practice.

The purposive use of teams for ongoing simulations or class projects also can be a potent source of professional experience and reflection. Such teams can provide the setting for learning about group formation, and students can model facilitation for each other by taking turns in the facilitator's seat. They can experience conflict management in the realities of working together or in team role plays where they resolve hypothetical disputes based on their actual knowledge of the personalities and temperaments of their team members. They also can work in the group to address the challenge of evaluation in networks, grappling with how to identify goals, define measures, and establish indicators of success when there are divergent opinions. Instructors can teach lessons from the research literature while students work together and reflect upon their lived experiences.

Alternatively, if a course is not focused on such substantive topics, group work can still be accompanied by structured reflection. This reflection can occur in small group discussions, written responses to particular questions, or regularly submitted reflection journals; it is important to align the format with the overall objective of the course to make it consistent with the type of reflective practice most germane to other course material.

Finally, capstone workshops can provide the centerpiece for public affairs curricula focused on cultivating reflective practice. In these courses, student teams typically work on a policy or public management issue for a community client. They must develop relationships with the client, conduct research to understand the nature of the problem, craft team processes to carry out the investigation, and develop a professional product. These settings can provide a rich laboratory if they are purposively structured. Students' activities must be supported with training in project management, client management, research design, and analysis. Instructors must possess enough content knowledge about the clients and projects to offer relevant and timely coaching about problems encountered. Opportunities must be created for reflection, either in the moment or after the fact. Integration experiences can be developed to share learning across teams or connect lived experience with other seminar materials. Although they are not a panacea, such workshops offer the possibility of deep, reflective learning if they are crafted appropriately.

Public administration also needs to distinguish the training of public managers from regular "strategic management" as it is taught business schools. This stream of training often sees the individual as supreme. In teaching collaborative management, public administration needs to help people to see both their own agency and the constraints put upon them by the systems and structures within which they work.

In the end, collaborative public management requires neither simply a body of substantive knowledge nor a set of practice skills. It requires that professionals use both in action. To support this practice, we must alter what we teach in the public affairs classroom, explore why we teach, and consider new methods for assisting students in the transformation to public management professionals. It may require that public administration scholars learn to do and do to learn how to teach these new competencies.

CONCLUSION

The public administration curriculum needs to adapt to the new realities of administrative practice in a world of networked governance. As a field, we need to reconfigure managers' professional identity. We need to cultivate capacities including convening a network with the right members, structuring governance processes, engaging in collaborative practice using the skills of negotiation, facilitation, and conflict management, designing processes for public engagement, evaluating progress toward outcomes, and ensuring that the network operates in a transparent and accountable fashion within public law. We argue that these can only best be cultivated through active and experiential learning. These capacities are the enactment of both explicit and tacit knowledge in context. In other words, public managers must learn to do collaborative practice, and only through doing can they learn to be effective in this new landscape.

REFERENCES

Agranoff, Robert. 2007. *Managing Within Networks: Adding Value to Public Organizations.* Washington, DC: Georgetown University Press.

Agranoff, Robert, and Michael McGuire. 2003. *Collaborative Public Management: New Strategies for Local Governments.* Washington, DC: Georgetown University Press.

Bingham, Lisa B., and Rosemary O'Leary. 2006. "Conclusion: Parallel Play, Not Collaboration: Missing Questions, Missing Connections." *Public Administration Review* 66, no. S1: 161–67.

Bingham, Lisa B.; Tina Nabatchi; and Rosemary O'Leary. 2005. "The New Governance: Practices and Processes for Stakeholder and Citizen Participation in the Work of Government." *Public Administration Review* 65, no. 5: 547–48.

Bingham, Lisa B.; David Fairman; Dan Fiorino; and Rosemary O'Leary. 2003. "Fulfilling the Promise of Environmental Conflict Resolution." In *The Promise and Performance of Environmental Conflict Resolution,* ed. O'Leary and Bingham, 329–52. Washington, DC: Resources for the Future Press.

Boyte, Harry. 2005. "Reframing Democracy: Governance, Civic Agency and Politics." *Public Administration Review* 65, no. 5: 536–46.

Davenport, Thomas H., and Laurence Prusak. 2000. *Working Knowledge: How Organizations Manage What They Know.* Boston, MA: Harvard Business School Press.

Deutsch, Morton, and Peter T. Coleman, eds. 2000. *The Handbook of Conflict Resolution: Theory and Practice.* San Francisco: Jossey-Bass.

Dukes, E. Franklin. 1996. *Resolving Public Conflict: Transforming Community and Governance.* Manchester and New York: Manchester University Press.

Feldman, Martha S.; Anne M. Khademian; Helen Ingram; and Anne S. Schneider. 2006. "Ways of Knowing and Inclusive Management Practices." *Public Administration Review* 66, no. S1: 89–99.

Fisher, Roger; William Ury; and Bruce Patton. 1991. *Getting to Yes.* New York: Penguin.

Fligstein, Neil. 2001. "Social Skill and the Theory of Fields." *Sociological Theory* 19, no. 2: 105–25.

Forester, John. 1999. *The Deliberative Practitioner.* Cambridge, MA: MIT Press.

Frederickson, George. 1999. "The Repositioning of American Public Administration." *PS: Political Science and Politics* 32, no. 4: 701–11.

Gastil, John, and Peter Levine, eds. 2005. *The Deliberative Democracy Handbook: Strategies for Effective Civic Engagement in the Twenty-First Century.* San Francisco: Jossey-Bass.

Giddens, Anthony. 1984. *The Constitution of Society: Outline of a Theory of Structuration.* Berkeley: University of California Press.

Heifetz, Ronald A. 1998. *Leadership without Easy Answers.* Cambridge, MA: Belknap Press.

Huxham, Chris, and Siv Vangen. 2005. *Managing to Collaborate: The Theory and Practice of Collaborative Advantage.* New York: Routledge.

Innes, Judith, and David Booher. 2004. "Reframing Public Participation: Strategies for the 21st Century." *Planning Theory and Practice* 5, no. 4: 419–36.

Lax, David A., and James K. Sebenius. 1986. *The Manager as Negotiator: Bargaining for Cooperation and Competitive Gain.* New York: Free Press.

Leach, William, and Paul Sabatier. 2003. "Facilitators, Coordinators, and Outcomes." In *The Promise and Performance of Environmental Conflict Resolution*, ed. Rosemary O'Leary and Lisa B. Bingham, 148–171. Washington, DC: Resources for the Future Press.

Mansbridge, Jane J. 1980. *Beyond Adversarial Democracy.* New York: Basic Books.

McGuire, Michael. Forthcoming 2008. "The New Professionalism and Collaborative Activity in Local Emergency Management." In *The Collaborative Public Manager,* ed. Rosemary O'Leary and Lisa Blomgren Bingham. Washington, DC: Georgetown University Press.

Milward, Brint, and Keith Provan. 2006. *A Manager's Guide to Choosing and Using Collaborative Networks.* Washington DC: IBM Center for the Business of Government.

Moore, Christopher. 2003. *The Mediation Process.* 2d ed. San Francisco: Jossey-Bass.

Nicolini, Davide; Dvora Yanow; and Silvia Gherardi, eds. 2003. *Knowing in Organizations: A Practice-Based Approach.* Armonk, NY: M.E. Sharpe.

O'Leary, Rosemary, and Bingham, Lisa B., eds. 2003. *The Promise and Performance of Environmental Conflict Resolution.* Washington, DC: Resources for the Future Press.

Parks, Sharon. 2005. *Leadership Can Be Taught: A Bold Approach for a Complex World.* Cambridge, MA: Harvard Business School Press.

Posner, Paul. Forthcoming 2008. "Public Administration Education for Third Party Governance Era: Reclaiming Leadership in the Field." In *The Collaborative Public Manager,* ed. Rosemary O'Leary and Lisa Blomgren Bingham. Washington, DC: Georgetown University Press.

Powell, W.W. 1990. "Neither Market Nor Hierarchy: Network Forms of Organization." *Research in Organizational Behavior* 12: 295–336.

Salamon, Lester M. 2005. "Training Professional Citizens: Getting Beyond the Right Answer to the Wrong Question in Public Affairs Education." *Journal of Public Affairs Education* 11, no. 1: 7–19.

Schneider, Andrea Kupfer, and Christopher Honeyman, eds. 2006. *The Negotiator's Fieldbook: The Desk Reference for the Experienced Negotiator.* Washington, DC: American Bar Association.

Schön, Donald A. 1987. *Educating the Reflective Practitioner: Toward a New Design for Teaching and Learning in the Professions.* San Francisco: Jossey-Bass.

Schwarz, Roger M. 1994. *The Skilled Facilitator.* San Francisco: Jossey-Bass.

Sewell, W. 1992. "A Theory of Structure: Duality, Agency, and Transformation." *American Journal of Sociology* 98, no. 1: 1–29.

Susskind, Lawrence; Sarah McKearnan; and Jennifer Thomas-Larmer. 1999. *The Consensus Building Handbook: A Comprehensive Guide to Reaching Agreement.* Thousand Oaks, CA: Sage.

About the Editors and Contributors

Robert Agranoff is professor emeritus in the School of Public and Environmental Affairs, Indiana University-Bloomington, and since 1990 he has been affiliated with the Instituto Universitario Ortega y Gasset in Madrid. In addition, he has taught at Complutense University of Madrid, Universitat Autonoma of Barcelona, and the University of the Basque Country in Bilbao, all in Spain. He is the 2000 recipient of the Donald Stone Intergovernmental Management Award from the American Society for Public Administration, the 2003 Louis Brownlow Book Award from the National Academy of Public Administration for his co-authored *Collaborative Public Management,* and the 2005 Daniel Elazar Distinguished Scholar Award in Federalism and Intergovernmental Relations from the American Political Science Association. His latest book is *Managing Within Networks* (Washington, DC: Georgetown University Press); and he is completing a book on the status of local governments in intergovernmental relations in federal Spain (Montreal: McGill-Queen's University Press). He is a fellow of the National Academy of Public Administration.

Lisa Blomgren Bingham is Keller-Runden Professor of Public Service at Indiana University's School of Public and Environmental Affairs, Bloomington. A graduate of Smith College and the University of Connecticut School of Law, she received the Association for Conflict Resolution's Abner Award in 2002 for excellence in research. In 2006, she received the Rubin Theory-to-Practice Award from the International Association for Conflict Management and the Harvard Project on Negotiation recognizing research that makes a significant impact on practice. She is a fellow of the National Academy of Public Administration. Her research interests include collaboration in governance and dispute system design.

Thomas A. Bryer is an assistant professor in the Department of Public Administration, University of Central Florida. His research interests include bureaucratic responsiveness, civic engagement, and citizen-centered collaborative public management. He has published in the *American Review of Public Administration, Journal of Public Administration Research and Theory, Public Administration Review,* and *Public Performance and Management Review.* He holds a PhD in Public Administration from the University of Southern California.

John M. Bryson is McKnight Presidential Professor of Planning and Public Affairs and associate dean for research and centers at the Hubert H. Humphrey Institute of Public Affairs at the University of Minnesota. His research focuses on leadership, strategic management, and the design of participation processes. He is a fellow of the National Academy of Public Administration.

Christine Carlson is executive director of the Policy Consensus Initiative (PCI) a national, nonprofit, bipartisan organization. PCI works with states and state leaders throughout the country to establish and strengthen the use of collaborative approaches to governance in states. She has been a leader in the field of public policy dispute resolution for more than twenty years, serving as mediator, facilitator, trainer, and consultant. She was the founding executive director of the Ohio Commission on Dispute Resolution. Prior to that, she was program and legal officer at the Kettering Foundation. She is a contributing author to the *Consensus Building Handbook*. She has a J.D. from the University of Dayton and a B.S. from Case University.

David R. Connelly holds a PhD (2005) from the University at Albany and currently teaches public administration courses in the Political Science Department at Western Illinois University. His research interests include leadership in collaborative environments, information technology issues in the public sector, and public sector management reform.

Terry L. Cooper, PhD, is the Maria B. Crutcher Professor in Citizenship and Democratic Values (Social Ethics, University of Southern California). His research centers on citizen participation and public ethics. Currently he is one of the co-principal investigators in the USC Neighborhood Participation Project (NPP) conducting research on the role of neighborhood organizations in governance in the City of Los Angeles through the system of neighborhood councils established in 1999. Also, he is the director of the USC Civic Engagement Initiative, which is expanding the work of the NPP beyond neighborhood councils and beyond L.A. He is author of *The Responsible Administrator: An Approach to Ethics for the Administrative Role* (5th ed., Jossey-Bass, 2006) and *An Ethic of Citizenship for Public Administration* (Prentice Hall, 1991). He is the co-editor of *Exemplary Public Administrators: Character and Leadership in Government* (Jossey-Bass, 1992) and the editor of *Handbook of Administrative Ethics* (2d ed., Marcel Dekker, 2001). He is a fellow of the National Academy of Public Administration.

Barbara C. Crosby is associate professor at the Hubert H. Humphrey Institute of Public Affairs, and a member of the Institute's Public and Nonprofit Leadership Center at the University of Minnesota. During 2002–3, she was a visiting fellow at the University of Strathclyde, Glasgow, Scotland. She has taught and written extensively about leadership and public policy, women in leadership, media and public policy, and strategic planning. She is the author of *Leadership for Global Citizenship* (1999) and co-author with John M. Bryson of *Leadership for the Common Good: Tackling Public Problems in a Shared-Power World* (2d ed., 2005). She is an associate editor of *Leadership Quarterly*. University and an MA degree in journalism and mass communication from the University of Wisconsin-Madison. She has a PhD in leadership studies from the Union Institute.

Sue Faerman is vice provost for undergraduate education and professor in the Department of Public Administration and Policy at the University at Albany-SUNY. Her teaching and research interests are in managerial leadership, organizational change and development, and conflict and organizational collaboration, particularly under conditions where organizations are, by definition, in an adversarial or competitive position. A central theme running through all of her research interests is the paradoxical nature of organizational life.

Richard C. Feiock is the Augustus B. Turnbull Professor of Public Administration and Affiliate Professor of Political Science at Florida State University. He directs the DeVoe Moore Center Program in Local Governance. He was the 2005 recipient of the APSA Herbert Kaufman Award. His recent books include *Institutional Constraints and Local Government* (SUNY Press, 2001), *City-County Consolidation and Its Alternatives* (M.E. Sharpe, 2004) and *Metropolitan Governance: Conflict, Competition and Cooperation,* (Georgetown University Press, 2004).

Beth Gazley is assistant professor of public and environmental affairs at Indiana University-Bloomington, where she teaches nonprofit and public management. She conducts research and publishes on government–nonprofit relations and interorganizational collaboration, including the role of nonprofits in local government emergency planning, service delivery networks, and also on New Governance and volunteerism. Before entering academia, she served in public interest politics and the nonprofit sector as a fundraiser, volunteer, board member, and management consultant.

Heather Getha-Taylor is an assistant professor in the Department of Political Science at the University of South Carolina. She received her PhD from the Maxwell School of Syracuse University and her MPA from the University of Georgia. Her research focuses on the intersection between human resource management and organizational capacity for performance.

Sherrie E. Human, associate professor in management and entrepreneurship in the Williams College of Business at Xavier University, teaches undergraduate and MBA courses in managerial behavior, new venture planning, and entrepreneurship. She was appointed as Xavier's first Castellini Chair in Entrepreneurial Studies and received recognition from McGraw-Hill and the Academy of Management Entrepreneurship Division for excellence in redesigning the Xavier entrepreneurship academic program (ranked in the top fifteen entrepreneurial campuses by *Princeton Review*). She also earned first place in the 2006 3E Learning Award competition, sponsored by Delta Epsilon Chi, George Washington University Center for Entrepreneurial Excellence and Kauffman Foundation.

Patricia Wallace Ingraham is founding dean of Binghamton University's College of Community and Public Affairs. Ingraham, formerly Distinguished Professor of Public Administration at Syracuse University's Maxwell School, was the founding director of the Alan K. Campbell Public Affairs Institute. She has received the John Gaus Award for distinguished career contributions from the American Political Science Association and the Dwight Waldo, Donald Stone, and Paul Van Riper Awards for distinguished research and service from the American Society for Public Administration. She has written extensively in the areas of public sector leadership, organizational change, and performance. She is a fellow of the National Academy of Public Administration.

Patrick Kenis is a professor at the Faculty of Social and Behavioural Sciences at Tilburg University, the Netherlands, where he is head of the Department of Organisation Studies. He is also a fellow of TiasNimbas (the Business School of Tilburg University). He has worked at the Free University, Amsterdam, the University of Konstanz, Germany, the European Centre for Social Welfare Policy and Research, Vienna, and the European University Institute, Florence. He received his PhD in Social and Political Sciences from the European University Institute in Florence, Italy. His research interest focuses on organizational and network responses in different areas.

W. Henry (Harry) Lambright is professor of political science and public administration at the Maxwell School of Syracuse University. His research interests include federal decision making on space technology, environmental policy, transboundary issues, national security, the integration of science with policy, ecosystem management, biotechnology, technology transfer, and leadership issues. He has written scores of articles and has written or edited seven books, including *Powering Apollo: James E. Webb of NASA* (Johns Hopkins University Press, 1995). His most recent book, which he edited, is *Space Policy in the 21st Century* (Johns Hopkins University Press, 2003). He earned his PhD from Columbia University in 1966.

Jack W. Meek, PhD, is professor of public administration at the College of Business and Public Management at the University of La Verne, and since 2003, visiting scholar at the School of Policy Planning and Development at the University of Southern California, working with the Civic Engagement Initiative led by Terry L. Cooper. His research focuses on civic engagement, metropolitan governance, regional collaboration, cross-jurisdictional administrative relationships, and policy networks. He has published articles in various encyclopedias, books, and academic journals, including the *International Journal of Public Administration, Public Administration Quarterly, Journal of Public Administration Education, Administrative Theory and Practice, Public Productivity and Management Review,* and the *Public Administration Review.* He serves on the editorial board of *International Journal of Organizational Theory and Behavior.*

Theodore K. Miller is professor emeritus of public and environmental affairs at Indiana University Bloomington. His academic interests are in applied statistical analysis and statistics education. He received his PhD from the University of Iowa in 1970. He previously served as co-director of the Interdisciplinary Consortium for Statistical Applications at Indiana University and as associate dean of faculties.

Rosemary O'Leary is Distinguished Professor and Maxwell School Advisory Board Endowed Chair at Syracuse University: Her areas of expertise include collaborative public management, collaborative governance, collaborative decision-making, and conflict resolution. She has won ten national research awards and eight teaching awards. She is the only person to win three National Association of Schools of Public Affairs and Administration awards for Best Dissertation (1989), Excellence in Teaching (1996) and Distinguished Research (2004). She is a fellow of the National Academy of Public Administration.

Stephen Page is associate professor at the Daniel J. Evans School of Public Affairs at the University of Washington. He holds a PhD and a masters degree in political science from MIT, has worked in state government, and has consulted to state and local governments and nonprofit organizations. His research examines reforms to improve the performance of large bureaucracies such as school districts, housing authorities, human services agencies, and health care systems. He teaches courses at the Evans School on various aspects of management, ethics, and community engagement.

James L. Perry is Chancellor's Professor in the School of Public and Environmental Affairs (SPEA) at Indiana University. He also holds adjunct appointments on the faculties of philanthropy and political science. He has served on the faculties of the University of California, Irvine, Chinese University of Hong Kong, University of Wisconsin, Madison, Katholieke Universiteit Leuven, and Yonsei University, Seoul. His research focuses on service motivation, national and community service, and government reform. He is author and editor of many scholarly articles and books. His most recent books are *Civic Service: What Difference Does It Make?* (Armonk, NY: M.E. Sharpe, 2004) and *Quick Hits for Educating Citizens* (Bloomington: Indiana University Press, 2006). He has held senior staff positions with the U.S. Department of Health and Human Services and Corporation for National and Community Service. He is recipient of the Yoder-Heneman Award for innovative personnel research from the Society for Human Resource Management, the Charles H. Levine Award for Excellence in Public Administration, the NASPAA/ASPA Distinguished Research Award, ASPA's Paul P. Van Riper Award for Excellence and Service and Dwight Waldo Award, and two Fulbright awards. He is a fellow of the National Academy of Public Administration.

Carla Pizzarella earned her MPA and Master of Urban Planning from the University of Kansas in 1997. She has held various positions within and relating to state and local government.

Keith G. Provan is McClelland Professor, Eller College of Management, University of Arizona. He holds joint appointments in the School of Public Administration and Policy and the Management and Organizations Department. He is also a Visiting Senior Scholar at Tilburg University in the Netherlands. His research interests have focused on interorganizational and network relationships, including network structure, evolution, governance, and effectiveness. He has published over fifty journal articles and scholarly book chapters and is one of only thirty-three members of the Academy of Management's "Journals Hall of Fame." He received his PhD from the State University of New York, Buffalo.

Jodi Sandfort is an associate professor at the Humphrey Institute of Public Affairs at the University of Minnesota. Her research, teaching, and practice focus on improving the implementation of social policy, particularly those policies designed to support low-income children and their families. At the Institute, she teaches courses in public and nonprofit management, government–nonprofit relationships, and organizational change. She is also a senior fellow at the Minnesota Council of Nonprofits where she develops and implements a statewide leadership development program.

Ann Marie Thomson is an adjunct assistant professor at the School of Public and Environmental Affairs, Indiana University, Bloomington. She received a BA in International Relations from North Park University in 1978, an Associate Degree in Nursing, with registered nurse licensure in 1982, a Masters in Public Affairs in 1992, and a PhD in Public Policy in 2001. She co-founded an education nongovernmental organization to provide education opportunities for young people in the Democratic Republic of Congo. She has received several awards such as an Outstanding Teaching Award, Indiana University, School of Public and Environmental Affairs (2006), the 2002 NASPAA Annual Dissertation Award, and the Nonprofit Division, Academy of Management Award for Best Book Published, 2002–4, which she received with her co-author, James L. Perry. Her research interests include the comparative study of interorganizational collaboration as a community development strategy and the role of higher education in fostering civic engagement through service-centered education across widely different cultures and contexts.

Jing Zhang is an assistant professor at the Graduate School of Management of Clark University. Her research focuses on knowledge sharing and knowledge networking, and on the organizational impact of information technology and innovations in E-Government initiatives. She received her PhD in Information Science from the University at Albany, State University of New York.

Index